I Wish I Had An Orange

Written by
K. V. Loucks

Dedication

To the Lord who gives us our strength, the men and women,
the technicians, programmers, and linemen who dedicate their
lives to keep our electrical grids functional so we can live.

Prologue

His given name was Gene. He'd been tagged with the nickname of "Shaky." This came from the palsy he'd acquired as a result of a sledding accident at age eleven. He'd hit a truck and the collision knocked him out, giving him a concussion.

In those early days, medical care was as much a guess as science. The other lasting condition in addition to the palsy was the dreams. Sometimes he couldn't sort reality from "dream life." He'd be confused occasionally as to whether he went to college or dreamed it. Gene took to writing in a journal documenting his real life and when the confusion came, he could refer to the journal. If not written in the book, it wasn't real. Then he would know which was "real life" for sure.

He'd attained a better than average education with the letters to follow. That seemed like a dream, but he had the sheep skin on his office wall to show for the effort. Then he would have experiences like he'd lived in the Old West or some parallel universe. Those experiences seemed every bit as real in his mind, but they weren't in his journal. Jessie, his wife, kept reminding him she was the real "real" and not an imaginary person or in an imaginary time.

With several dimensions active in his mind, he had to keep a reign on his comments, otherwise people looked at him funny. Always he treated people the best he knew how in dream or in reality. If his hand weren't twitching, they might believe "Shaky" was a handle that implied something less than sanity. It might be said he had been blessed with several complete life experiences and the problems accompanying them all. Yet only the real one was documented in his journal.

He'd been taught to respect older folks because they were wise with years. Gene now showed some age and the middle-age spread so many in their mid-sixties carried. The problem was, Gene was still enthusiastic and still felt young, younger than those wise old folks. Now that he was getting longer in the fang, he was able to understand how wisdom gained from experience, when applied, could win over youthful enthusiasm and energy.

Now, having grown older, it occurred to him he hadn't done anything with his life that accounted for something he considered of value. Thus, over the last few years he'd been wanting to make a mark with his life efforts. He was proud he had raised a fine family. He was pleased with the training he had given to his three kids and to other young people in the community. He had lived decently through the years, but still that naggin' feeling of *my life hasn't amounted to much that will be lastin* bothered him. When gone, he too would be forgotten after a time like those who'd gone on before. He wondered if he were experiencing a "mid-life crisis" some thirty-five years late. It dawned on Gene that the important point of life was what came after death. He was a Christian but had spent most of his time focusing on making a living and enjoying the company of family and friends. Now after long and deep thought, Gene was convinced he needed to spend more time offering people everlasting security.

Many young men have a change of attitude and opinion at about age thirty as to who they are and what their lives are about. Well, Gene didn't recall this had ever been the case with him until lately. When it would have been a convenient thing to occur, he didn't have the time to deal with it. He was always in the throes of a crisis with his job or one of those alternate lives, or some or another circumstance. There was more than enough to focus on rather than questioning "ifin' he was livin' a life of productivity that would be satisfactory."

Gene considered this and many other things that seemed to push their way into his thoughts as of late. At his age, it was time for a normal man to retire and live off what he'd paid the government to set aside for his twilight years. But he hadn't spent much time looking' forward to retirement. He'd been too busy living' enough for two or three. He seldom had worked for someone else in a wage kind of job. He'd always been taught "we are the rugged individualists" and somehow the idea had kept him doin' his own thing. Now that he considered it, his siblings were the same. None of them fit the stereotype nine-to-five kind of people and all of them were distinctly individual in their attitudes, vocations, avocations, and hobbies.

Over his lifetime, he had collected barns and buildings full of miscellaneous stuff, sometimes duplicates, and all his treasures. He was a pack rat. The saying, "Two is one and one is none" made perfect since to him. If one should fail, a person would be done. If there were two, he'd have a backup or at least parts to fix the first.

His kids called it junk.

"Ah, Dad, you need to get rid of some of this treasure," they would encourage not so jokingly. "It's going to take a year to go through all your stuff when you're gone if we do nothin' but throw it away. It'll take two if we sort the stuff. Why don't you start sortin' some of this out now?"

"Well," he'd reply, "I might need some of it sometime and if you've watched the price of washers at the hardware store, a rusty one on the street is worth thirty cents and who would pass up a penny on the parking lot?"

He guessed the kids thought that a dumb statement but, so what? They did, but he darn sure didn't. "I think you kids drop pennies just to see if us old geezers can get down and back up with a penny captured after spotting it on the parking lot pavement. Besides, I use a lot of this stuff every now and again. Sometimes I think I haven't collected enough because I still have to go the hardware store for a screw, a bolt, or a washer the right size. It just kills me to have to do that."

"I have a few old tools which I've come by just in case," Gene continued. "Most of them are hardly ever used by anybody anymore because they're obsolete. But there might be a time when they come in handy if the power goes out. That seems to be happening in the East and Mid-west more and more these days for days on end. People get to depending and forget how to do. Well, if I need to do, I got stuff I can do with."

He had seemingly entered into one of his alter-worlds or had locked into another of his dreams. At least he hoped it to be a dream, a vision, or nightmare. Most likely, a combination, and it shook him to the tips of his toes. This dream was so real and lasted so long he thought he had died and gone to Hell in a nightmare.

He heard over a period of years about this thing called electro-magnetic pulse. From what he understood, if there were to be a solar flare directed toward the earth from the sun or a specifically placed atomic blast some thirty miles above the good old USA, the pulse sent out from either would fry every electric circuit within its reach. The damage would include all computers, electric grid systems, auto computers, and power systems not shielded. Most systems in this day and age had not been built with shielding.

He'd read the Book of Revelations, Jeremiah, Zachariah, and Isiah, about what he believed was the foretelling of the demise of the United States. As a viable nation and world power, the USA wouldn't exist. Contemplating such events disturbed him. All he held dear other than the Lord Himself and his family was his beloved United States and what it represented in way of the pioneer spirit, self-determination, and the right to make one's own errors. At least it used to be that way before government intervention on most levels would make unwanted decisions for people. Like thousands these days, Gene resented that.

Chapter 1

The Event Remembered

Journal entry:

“This is my last will and testament, although I really have my doubts as to whether any person will ever read this. How long has it been, maybe two weeks, since I've seen another person and three since I've seen another living soul?”

Before finishing the entry, Gene's mind wandered as he viewed the valley below with its fresh spring green and the hills on the far side with their spring green budding trees. He marveled every year at the splendor the Maker had created. This year seemed no different in any respect, except he set on the high outcropping scanning the valley below for some form of life and saw no evidence of a man, woman, or child. Gene hadn't even seen a dog or a large wild animal for a while, all having been eaten by a decimated starving population less able to recuperate these days than to perish.

He could hear explosions somewhere in the valleys some twenty miles in the distance. With his prior experience in the populated areas, Gene wished to avoid those at nearly every cost. He wandered if he would find his family in the chaos from which those heavy sounds of explosion filtered upland.

Gene knew the seven-hundred-mile roundtrip to find his son had been risky at best, but he had to know if Seth was okay. There hadn't been any word and the boy had been living in Metropolis, the city where times now had gone beyond tough. The riots and civil unrest had taken its toll. Thieves and gangs moved at will without the slightest effort to conceal themselves. Gene had discovered that the hard way. The uncontrolled chaos everywhere on the east side of the Continental Divide left society in shambles. Food was scarce or nonexistent and civility was nearly as scarce. Roving gangs ruled and martial law been ineffective. Every poor soul was on his or her own or had grouped up with others in a herd mentality.

After many months of arduous, cold, and dangerous travel, the outcome of this trip had poor ascertainable results. Gene reluctantly gave up the search and made the trek homeward to where the rest of his family would be waiting. Now upon his return, everybody at home seemed to have disappeared. Gene had received news from a man named Thor, an acquaintance of his daughter, Bonnie. The news was of her unorthodox activities, but no recent word of where she could be located. The family was not in the usual places to be found upon his return. The home he and Jessie loved on the mountain now was in shambles and burned to the foundation. Now his search for Jessie, their daughter, and Jake his cousin and his wife Meg seemed fruitless. He continued searching for several days without a sign either in the valley below at Jake and Meg's ranch or where he and Jessie used to live.

"Lord, what has happened to the world I used to live in?" he muttered under his breath.

Was it time to wake up or was it time to make another diary entry? He hadn't completed the last.

The two long trips to retrieve family members and the events from those trips had taken their toll on him and changed his physical condition and his confidence. He had his faith in God above but now was some fifty pounds lighter in weight. His mindset was that his time on this wretched pitiful earth was getting short and it neared time to go home. The scripture plainly said he was but just a sojourner in this worldly place, the earth, that earth isn't his real home. Heaven was. He now wondered if he had missed the rapture and was in the tribulation. Times had been and were so hard now, but God had and continued sustaining him.

"Lord, if I missed it, I pray Jessie and the family were caught up and out of this world of hard times. Maybe that's why I can't seem to find them." He knew he had a strong faith in God and Christ as savior. He couldn't imagine the others being raptured for anything less than the faith he believed.

The rare news which filtered through the national grapevine had been the Middle East was in full war but the good old USA was now so crippled by events one year prior, it had been left out of the action and was no longer a viable credible power.

So here was about to be his last will and testament.

Continued journal entry:

"In the year of my Lord 2018, I, Gene Tucker, known as 'Shaky,' bequeath all my possessions, what's left of them, which I now carry, to Jessie my wife and then to my kids after her. Most of all, I bequeath any excess portion of my faith in God, Jesus and the Holy Spirit above to the one who finds this last will and testament. As for the memories of what the world was like before this total catastrophe came upon our land, I leave to the public so they can understand and hopefully learn from mankind's mistakes. My hole-riddled moccasins and my hide coat are to be used to. . ."

Gene drifted back in his memories and remembered when the changes started, not subtle changes, but changes as sudden as a train wreck.

As he thought about the past long year and about when there was the noise of automobiles and electricity, abundant electricity, electricity to run lights and stoves and tools and cell phones and computers and televisions and games. . . Oh, how simple. . . And how easy life had been when they had electricity. How the people had taken it for granted, like one does a wife who always was there with the meals, the reminders to remove the garbage, and the immeasurable steadiness required to make a house the home.

After it happened, without electricity, the gas pumps wouldn't pump gas out of underground storage tanks. Many non-operating car gas tanks had been siphoned for their remaining fuel. Even those cars that would run wouldn't when the fuel ran out. Fried, that's what they were, the electric grids, and any electronics connected to them were fried. Many cars wouldn't run because they weren't protected

13

by a full metal body. The ones with fiberglass or part plastic bodies just stopped running. Stored food spoiled. Any that wasn't canned and then much of that which was canned froze and the containers broke during the following winter's freeze.

Then there was the problem of water, the lack of potable water or that of untreated drinking water. Water treatment plants couldn't get electricity. Most water sources became fouled by indiscriminate letting of human waste. The lack of electricity to deliver and treat sewage waste caused conditions to deteriorate further to beyond terrible. Sicknesses, cholera, and typhoid became rampant and Lord knows what other plagues befell household after household.

As Gene thought more about those times, the worst memory was how many were utterly unprepared for any catastrophic emergency. Most had little or no potable water reserves and little or no food stores. People had no alternate heat source or hand tools with which to carry on everyday life. When power as society knew and depended on disappeared, life for many ceased.

When it hit, there was a flash. He had a strange foreboding feeling, as if his heart were skipping and everything around him stopped. The office lights momentary burned bright then went out, leaving only the afternoon sunlight seeping in through a blinded window. The ever-present and many surrounding noises of the building, streets, and equipment just slumped to a quiet. He could hear a fly buzz nearby and some voices outside his office but no whir of computer fans or heating elements inside snapping and cracking as they heated up or cooled down.

The quiet wasn't unlike the quiet of the woods he would sometimes experience while setting on a hunting blind except. . . a few scattered voices and an occasional sound of a still running automobile on the street drifted in. Sounds of car doors closing as several cars came to a rolling stop and many of their occupants stepped out to ascertain what the malfunction might be. In the distance, there was a crash and the breaking of glass when someone's car struck something.

What in Heaven's name was going on, Gene wondered.

Gene's office door burst open. "Please, Shaky, may we use your phone to call 911? Mr. Jolsin is havng some sort of difficulty with his heart," exclaimed Julia the receptionist from the dental office next door.

She was frantic and wanted to use the phone; theirs wasn't working. Mr. Jolsin was a middle-aged man whose pacemaker seemed to be malfunctioning and his heart fluttered badly. Gene's phones and all the cell phones had no signal.

Gene's mind raced to make sense of all that now wasn't happening. He recalled lectures he'd heard about an event called electromagnetic pulse, or "EMP" for short. The theory was if a thermonuclear blast was set off in the sky above or a direct hit from a solar flare occurred, the electric surge from the explosion would cauterize most power grids, telephone lines and any electronic devices attached. Surely this wasn't one of those events. In theory the event would be possible, but the general passive belief was it wouldn't happen here. Besides, hardly any of the general public understood, was aware of, or knew anything about EMP. At best, the knowledge was only a blip in the public mind.

"My, oh my, oh my, oh my, what to do now?" He exclaimed under his breath. In his mind, he had fears and misgivings about what he believed would become the inevitable.

Returning from the office next door where he was of absolutely no help, he grabbed his coat, locked his office, went to his car, and tried to start it. He was going home, just seven miles' distance up the mountain. The car wouldn't even consider starting.

I am a fat old man, Gene thought. *I pray these legs keep going at least 'till I get home.* Three quarters of a mile out of Pinedale, he passed a dozen or so people walking down the highway toward the town and looking nearly as weary as he knew he looked. One gentleman hailed him to ask if there were any vehicles running at all. He declared he had left his wife in their car parked when it had quit running.

"She can't walk too good you know," he explained.

"Well, mister," Gene said, "I haven't seen many."

"Well, she's kinda cold and I need to find help." The man appeared worried.

"How far up the road is she?" Gene asked.

15

"Our car is around the corner about a quarter mile. We've been out drivin', looking at the new spring foliage, ya know. Kate likes to look for indication of new spring leaves when they come out. It gives a body hope ta see the new leaves in the start of spring."

"Mister," Gene said "my home is up past there, so I'm going that direction. I'll check on her for you and see what I can do for her. You say her name is Kate?"

"Yes," the man said. "I'm very tired, but I'll be along shortly."

"What's your name?" Gene inquired further.

"Oh, it's Henry," the man replied. "Henry Carver. My wife up there is Katherine. Everybody calls her Kate. Well, thank you, mister. Thank you and bless you for helping us." Henry Carver looked totally spent from his walk toward town.

After walking two miles then turning the corner, then three quarters of a mile to the side of the road, a newer late model car, one of the fiberglass body kind, was parked just half off the pavement. In the passenger seat sat a large lady, not tall, and maybe eighty years of age. Henry lagged some quarter mile back. He tried to call out to Kate, but his voice was so weak, she couldn't hear him. When Kate saw Gene, she scrunched down in the seat as far as she could so as not to be seen. Scrunching didn't make much of a difference as she only shortened by maybe an inch or two after doing so.

When Gene came near the car, she hadn't seen nor heard Henry, so she demanded of Gene, "Go away. Don't you come any closer now, do ya hear?"

Gene greeted, "Katherine?"

She didn't answer.

"Katherine," repeated Gene, "Henry and I came to get you, Katherine. He is back down the road a bit."

She blustered with the fury of a very angry woman frustrated with the apparent lack of control over her situation. "I told him not to go anywhere; someone would be along. That old fool shouldn't have taken off down the road like that leavin' me here alone. You stay back now. I got a stick. I can hurt you!"

"Katherine, I'm not here to harm you," assured Gene. "Henry is OK. He's coming along. Is there anything you need?"

By this time Katherine was blubbering and regurgitating unintelligible words. Gene could see she was cold and offered his jacket. She told him to stay away, she had a stick. That much he understood.

Oh Lord, he thought. *Show her I mean no harm.*

"Katherine, I know you are cold," Gene said. "I only have a mile or so to my home, but I'll take you and Henry there if you want. Here, have my coat so you can stay warm."

She hesitantly opened her car door and he slipped his coat off and held it out to her. She drew the coat over her shoulders and reminded him she had a stick and it was sharp if he thought about trying anything.

"Katherine, are you starting to warm a little?" Gene asked after a time.

"I can feel it a little."

"Great! You should be OK now. Katherine, can you walk any distance?"

Kate was so insecure and distrustful she refused to respond. She finally said she couldn't walk very far. It was her hips that hurt so bad. Henry had rested enough and came to Gene's aid. When Kate saw Henry, she showed relief.

"Henry, why didn't you tell me you were here?" she demanded.

Henry just shook his head and said nothing. When they all settled, Gene thought of a used wheelchair he had in his storage barn. Gene told them he thought he might have a solution to Katherine's immobility. He explained about the wheelchair and said he would fetch it for them. Kate was not so excited. She didn't want to be seen as an invalid. Gene left them in the relative comfort of their car while he trucked up the hill to his own home. Gene had become nearly exhausted now. Locating the chair, he procured it, dusted it off, and returned down the hill to the Carver location some two hours later. He had ridden the chair down the paved road until his hands became sore from breaking the speed.

Wishing the Carvers farewell, Gene started his return hike up the hill toward home. Winded and foot sore from walking over seven miles and climbing the fifteen hundred feet elevation, Gene moved much slower now. Late in the afternoon now, he had covered all those miles on foot, five times any distance he'd walked in the last fifteen years.

Dog tired this late in the day, the higher up the mountain he got, the colder he got, and he wished he now had his jacket. Mrs. Carver had kept it. These mountain breezes could be quite cold at sundown if one doesn't have enough cover. He reached his driveway and saw his house with the chimney flowing with smoke. Gene and his wife hadn't built a fire in the fireplace in over five years. His wife had found the necessity for heat he reckoned. He walked up the drive to the backdoor. In this part of the world, most country folks enter their homes by way of the backdoor. He opened it and stepped in.

"Hi there, I'm home," he greeted her.

Jessie his wife had been quilting in a rocker by the fire. Gathering her quilting, she set it aside in a laundry basket on the floor.

"The electricity is off," she said. "It's been off all afternoon and was getting cool in here. I saw a flash just before the lights went out. Do you know why it's off? I didn't hear you drive in. Where's your car? I tried to call, but my cellphone won't work. There was a heavy rumble after the flash." Gene listened to Jessie's end to end comments and questions. The heat was off and because of the lack of power. The water had shut off too.

If the power didn't come back on soon, the freezers would start thawing. He'd seen that happen at a number of disasters where he had worked as a restoration contractor and insurance claim manager when the electricity had been out for an extended period of time. What stored water they had would need to be used wisely until "the 'lectricity" restored. Water service wouldn't happen until power was on. Gene was now dog-tired and his dogs hurt. He wanted to soak them. He leaned back in his recliner, pulled a hand-quilted blanket over his lap and shoulders, and closed his eyelids for a short rest.

As he pondered the events of the day, for a moment he realized if an EMP bomb had gone off, life as they had known it would change and not for the better. His gut knotted and he had to focus on turning near panic over to the Higher Power. In his exhaustion, he contemplated the ramifications of the day's events. He'd considered before what possible events like these could mean. He had felt like many others did that an outage from an EMP wasn't very likely.

Now unexpectedly, it may have just happened. If so, this part of the world's greatest economic, financial, and military power had in just moments been reduced to less than a third world country by a nuclear explosion some thirty miles in the sky. Less than a third world nation because only a few people in this society would have a small idea how to survive the next month, the next six months, or even where to start.

He thought back to the Y2K days when many had spent substantial sums on survival just to be ridiculed when Y2K turned out to be nothing. *People are not prepared, just not prepared*, Gene thought to himself.

General knowledge was there was less than three days' food supply in Metropolis grocery stores. People would starve in a week. They would eat their neighbor's horses, cows, goats, and dogs. They would harvest every deer, rabbit, elk, pheasant, pigeon, and sparrow in the state. Then they would eat their cats and compete for the mice simply to keep from starving. Hundreds of thousands, maybe millions, could starve and perish over the next year.

"Please, God, have mercy on us all," Gene exclaimed aloud.

"Gene, are you okay?" Jessie asked. "Are you in this world or another of your fantasies? What are you thinking about?"

Jessie called Gene's alter-worlds "fantasies."

"Jessie, we are in serious trouble. I don't mean just you and me. I mean our whole world, our friends, our kids, our neighbors—everybody."

"Oh, you're just tired," said Jessie. "Rest a bit and I'll get some wiener dogs out of the fridge. We can roast them in the fireplace. I have some bread in the cupboard, and you can peel an orange to start with."

Gene liked oranges. He liked fruit, but he especially liked oranges and apples.

Dogs, ha. Now I am already eating dogs and this crisis is just eight hours old, thought Gene.

"Jessie," Gene repeated, "we are in serious trouble here. The juice isn't coming back on. The terrorists have set off a thermo nuclear blast somewhere up there." He pointed to the ceiling. "They have fried every electronic circuit from the Eastern Seaboard through the Midwest and the Western US.

"Oh sure, it will," she said. "It may be a couple days or weeks, but they'll get it back on".

"Jessie," Gene said, "I don't think you understand the gravity of this, how utterly serious this situation may become. Think about it: What is going to happen if the 'lectricity doesn't come back on? What if auto and trucking transportation as we know it just stops running due to lack of fuel? What then? There won't be any more trucking because trucks don't run without fuel. There won't be any fuel to run the engines because refineries are shut down. What fuel there is will deteriorate in a few short months. How are people going to survive?"

"Gene, it will work out," encouraged Jessie. "Everything will be OK, you'll see."

Gene turned directly toward Jessie and with urgency in his voice insisted, "No, Jess, I'm not kidding, things could get real, real bad. We need to do some planning. First, the food, let's take inventory. There won't be any edible wildlife or cows left in existence before winter. Without trucking and shipping, the stores will be empty. There will be some people who die over this before it's done. Second, Jessie, I'm going to Riverton to get the kids and bring them home if they will come out of the city. They can last a few days there, but things could get thin for them."

"Well. . ." Gene continued.

Jessie cut him off in mid-sentence. "You are not going to go without me!"

"Jessie, you will be better off here at home," said Gene. "You have your pantry and firewood for the rest of the month. If I get delayed, you can move to the basement where the temperature stays constant. I believe we should can and jerk the freezer meat if the electricity stays out and I believe it will. If you aren't here it will just spoil. We will prepare tomorrow, Thursday, and Friday. I will leave on Saturday."

Jessie pointedly stated, "You say the cars won't be running. How on earth do you think you're going to get there? You are completely worn out just coming home today from town. And you are not going to leave me here alone, do you understand? How do you think we are going to get there, fly? We can't drive."

"If the boy's bicycles in the shed are working, I will ride one of them." Gene ignored her "we" part of the comment. "As out of shape as I am, it probably will take several days for me to get there."

Jessie protested, "I don't want you going by yourself. . . Not to burst your bubble, but you're not as young as you used to be, ya know."

"No, but I am some smarter," he replied. "Let's get some rest."

Chapter 2

The First of Two

Before the sun turned to twilight, they both awoke. They lay still just listening to the quiet before daybreak. Usually by this time, Jessie would arise stirring about preparing for the day. She would set under a lamp studying her Bible and pouring over her morning devotions. When completed, she would spend time meditating upon what she read, petitioning God for the needs of others, and thanking Him for their blessings. As a prayer warrior, she wasn't always sure of her effectiveness, but Gene could see the results time after time. Jessie had a wonderful gift in her own quiet, unassuming way and applied it like a superhero on the way to vanquish the villain.

"Of course," she would always say, "it is the Lord's power which is applied. I only ask for His guidance and knowledge as to where it should be applied; then, I ask it be applied there. I have my preferences, but if it is the Lord's will when he allows my prayer requests to be filled."

With a mother's prayer strength, she focused daily on praying for the kids and friends. Then she requested the Lord's blessing upon the day as it lay before Gene and her. Jessie would complete a short physical training routine, stretching to keep her muscle tone, then head off into her day of jobs and tasks. However, this day was different. There would be no artificial light with which to get a jump on the day. The shorter winter days gradually were getting longer, but they still were short, which left some early morning time before daybreak to think and contemplate.

Gene, as a rule, was not so industrious in the morning. He would start with reading his Bible and meditation. This usually started after Jessie had started her morning tasks. He had awakened this morning earlier than usual with the recent events on his mind. Both Gene and Jessie were still cozily in their quilts when Jessie inquired quietly, "You awake?"

Gene said, "Naw, but I am now. . . Good morning. I've been tryin' to work out in my mind what to expect from this situation. I'm not sure what to expect."

Jessie said, "You're worryin'. Stop worryin'! You know worryin's not of God. It's a sin."

"I'm not worryin', I'm just tryn' to think ahead and through," he replied. "You're sure not up and around so early as usual."

Jessie simply stated, "There's no light, so I been doin' my prayin' right here."

Gene mused, "Today's not a day ta overlook that, wouldn't ya think?"

The house is cold, time to kindle a fire, Gene thought as he slipped out into the cool morning air.

Generally, they kept their quiet time separately with a joint prayer before they started the day. This morning they started the day with a joint prayer before getting out of bed. When daylight broke, they would need to get right to the tasks at hand. Today would be a little different. Gene would carry a bucket the distance down to the creek for water. The domestic pipeline had gone dry for now. When he dipped the bucket, he'd already thought about where a fish might be hiding under the outcropping or near a rock. Just a mental note for future reference and a quick meal if need be. Walking back up to the house some two hundred feet he could feel the crisp morning breeze on his cheek and ear. He pulled his collar up to a standing position to cut the bite a little. This early morning was a bit nippy in the early light and he was glad to close the door behind him.

"Well, dear, you brought part of the creek bottom with you," said Jessie.

"I see," said Gene. "Did I get a fish in the dip too?"

"No, just a strange bug of some kind. It won't drink much," she replied. "I think I will make some pancakes and a couple eggs before they go bad. We'll have to cook 'em on your new barbeque 'cause the stove is cold. No 'lectricity ya know."

"No kiddin'," Gene retorted.

While trying to spark the propane burner alive with fire, Gene realized the spark igniter was another electrical mechanism not likely to work, but it did work. He could have retrieved the long fireplace matches and ignited the burner that way, but igniter sparked as designed. They cooked pancakes and eggs, heated the water for coffee and Jessie's tea, then they ate. Before shutting off the propane, he placed a large pan of water on to heat to be used for a G.I. bath and dishwater.

Some realities brought to mind in the last thirty minutes were: the propane wouldn't last forever, the matches would be worth their weight in gold, and cold baths loomed like a monster dragon from the Middle Ages. They would have to carefully think through this situation for the future so they would know what they would need in the foreseeable months to exist.

As Gene brought out a pencil and pad, he and Jessie sat and compiled a list of basic requirements. These they would need to stay alive.

List:

Fire

#1 Matches

The matches would last for a while, but if this outage lasted, matches tended to deteriorate with age and climate conditions.

#2 Flint, striker, magnesium stick, tinder

Flint could be found almost anywhere in these hills. The striker could be just about any piece of metal. With American society being so wasteful, old nails, bolts, re-bar, survey stakes and old car parts could be found nearly everywhere.

The magnesium stick would be one out of Gene's survival and hunting supply. These weren't so easy to come by. The hunting knife and the pocket tool would do to strike a spark if needed. In this part of the country, tinder could be made from cedar bark but it was better to have fine steel wool, cotton balls soaked in Vaseline and coated with wax, or charred cotton patches to strike into. Jute cord soaked in wax worked well and was another of Gene's favorites.

#3 Warm Clothing

Water-resistant and wicking outerwear, hats, poly-fill coats, woolen pants, wool socks, shoes, waterproof rain gear or ponchos, thermo blankets, insulated underwear, heavy trash bags, bandanas, pillowcases.

#4 Medical Supplies
Medications – or substitutes, pain tablets.

#5 First Aid Supplies
Band-aids, gauze, container of coal oil

#6 Hygiene Supplies
Toothbrush, comb, soap, sunscreen

#7 Food

Jerked current freezer meat, canned goods stored below ground – eliminate freezing jars and cans, dehydrated fruits and stored nuts – kept in the dark; Inventory list of edible berries, plants, and herbs

Wildlife
Deer, elk, bear, lion, whistle pig, porcupine, bugs (not bunny), squirrel, rabbit, skunk—well could be et if need be.

Domestic
Bovine, sheep, goats, chickens, pigs, llamas, dogs, rabbits

#8 Hunting gear and traps
Guns and ammo, crossbow, slingshot, bow and arrows, knives
Nets and traps snares, including guitar and piano strings
Fishing poles, lines and leader, hooks, flies, and sinkers

#9 Transportation
Horseback, buggy, and wagon
Bicycles
Walking
Sleigh, skies, and sled dogs

#10 Shelter
House and basement
Underground and with cooking and water nearby
Tents, rain flies, caves

This was the start of a basic list. They would need these items or close alternatives as basic requirements to get along. Many of these items were already in Gene's possession but were woefully unorganized. Well, the activity this day would be dedicated to gathering the inventory of needed items.

During the day, the discussion between Gene and Jessie ranged from the welfare of their adult children to whether Gene would be going to collect them by himself.

"What am I to do in the meantime?" was Jessie's concern.

Intense as the discussions became several times, Gene realized Jessie wouldn't be left at home while he traipsed across the sixty-some miles of desert to Riverton where their daughter was going to college and where their younger son and his family made their home.

Bonnie their daughter was an attractive young lady, but not one of the movie star beauties who often were so admired by the many roving young suitors. She was one of inner-character beauty and beauty of the soul. She was a competitor at anything that required competition and chiefly a superior marksman, or markswoman, in trap and skeet competition. She had won several awards. Her championships were enough to finance part of her college expenses and tuition. She had been one who achieved unrecognized Eagle Scout status while her older brother Seth had acquired his. He received the official recognition. Bonnie did not.

Self-assured as Bonnie was, Gene worried about the conditions in a city where chaos would be rampant without the general ease of life provided by electricity. Gene became determined to assess the conditions and situation surrounding their daughter firsthand. Jessie, on the other hand, remained reluctant, even deadset against Gene going alone into the unknown of a possible primeval civilization.

Samuel, their younger son, lived in Riverton with his happy young family. The family lived with all the conditions of sibling love and squabbles. Samuel and family were deeply committed to mission work and evangelism throughout the city. They spent many hours in recreation bicycling and partaking of the many hiking trails and public parks just meeting people to minister to.

After much heated discussion, Gene decided to present Jessie with an alternative solution he knew she wouldn't like, but one that resolved the issue of her staying at the mountain home in solitude. They would pack their packs and traverse some dozen miles to a cousin's home where Jessie could stay and collectively help to strengthen the clan with her presence. Jake and his wife Meg were some six or seven years older than Gene and, in their early seventies, would do well to have additional hands for the chores.

Jessie, on the other hand, strenuously continued to object to Gene's planned solo trek to Riverton without the aid of a partner. Gene knew secretly her objections held validity, but he wasn't about to admit he that. The dangers were very real. He could fall, breaking a bone, succumb to illness, or suffer from hypothermia or the lack of proper nourishment. He might become prey to marauders and despots needing anything of value he carried to sustain themselves. The Lord only knew the many other perils might befall him as a lone traveler.

On the other hand, Gene possessed a lifetime of experience as an outdoorsman, woodsman, rancher, and sportsman and had years of experience dealing with and on behalf of people of all kinds of personalities and persuasions. Gene could now hear in his mind the kids saying, "Dad, you're getting too old for such a trip." He knew

Jessie was trying to tell him the same thing and in the back of his mind he knew it may well be very true.

If experience didn't prove enough, Gene could, he knew, depend upon the Lord for direction and assistance, if not an outright miracle when needed. Many people would say a person of faith would leave the fate of Bonnie and their son so far away in Riverton in the Lord's hands. Gene was a man of faith and so Gene depending in part on that faith would go with God's assistance to Riverton after the kids just as Abraham went to retrieve Lot in Hobah.

Chapter 3

The Trek

After three days of preparation and storing newly canned goods in the basement storage and the fourth night's stay at the mountain home, Gene and Jessie started their dozen-mile trek down the mountain to Cousin Jake's ranch. The coolness in the early morning helped keep the early walk comfortable. By midday, they had crossed the first ridge and rested while overlooking the next valley below.

They could see the Smith Ranch about a half a mile distance's to the southeast, and far down the valley to the south was the location of Jake's ranch. As Gene watched, he saw a movement that disturbed him. Retrieving his binoculars from his pack, he looked at the Smith Ranch yard to see one of the Smith daughters in a physical altercation with a man. As he watched, he saw one of the three sisters lying seemingly collapsed near the barn. The front door of the house stood open; Gene and Jessie heard a faint distant scream coming from the farm. Gene left his pack and as fast as he could covered the distance down the hill and through the brush to the home. The younger Smith girl struggled with of all people, one of the Gilder brothers. She wasn't enjoying the conflict. Gene picked up a three-inch cottonwood branch and thumped the younger Gilder across the back with a crack that broke the branch. Josh Gilder collapsed as much from the surprise of being caught in such a compromising situation as from the impact of the blow. Gene breathlessly demanded to know where Toby the older Gilder brother was. Sally Smith pointed to the house, saying "Toby dragged Laurie, kicking and screaming into the house."

Gene drew his .357 and entered. The noise coming from the nearest bedroom was that of Laurie Smith pleading for Toby to stop.

Gene entered the doorway and exclaimed, "Now, isn't that a fine place to find a Gilder boy, makin' a girl beg fer her virginity?"

Gene struck Toby hard on the side of the head with his pistol butt before Toby knew what was coming. Toby, with his pants down, fell hard against the wall and then started to rise as Gene kicked him in the ribs hard enough to crack a couple of them. Gilder doubled over and Gene, having regained some of his own wind, kicked the boy in the bare thigh. Jamming the barrel of the pistol hard against Gilder's forehead. Gene ordered the young man out of the house. Limping from the thigh bruise, doubled over from the broken ribs, and bleeding from the cut on the side of his head, Gilder tried to pull his pants up with the hand not holding his ribs. As he stumbled out the door, Gene booted him hard further ejecting him out the door. Toby Gilder stumbled off the porch and then fell flat facedown into the yard dirt.

Josh Gilder stood against the side of the house with his hands covering his head. Sally and Jessie were about to lay another series of blows about his head, neck, and shoulders with clubs.

"Josh," Gene shouted.

"Josh," Gene commanded, "go help Toby. Get him outta here before we decide to string him up or remove what's left of his manly pride! If I ever hear of you two coming back here uninvited again, I will shoot you on sight myself."

Gene pointed his pistol at Josh's forehead.

"Needless to say if I see your dad, I will enlighten him on your activities here. I don't believe he will be so pleased. If any one of these girls sees you anywhere around here again, they will shoot you on sight, do you understand? You know they can shoot. I trained them!" stated Gene with emphasis.

Josh, bruised on the forehead, went to Toby and assisted him to his feet. Toby still bleeding, breathing roughly, and pale in color from the whipping, was assisted by Josh to his feet. He heard all of

Gene's comments to Josh and they departed, Toby limping down the driveway.

Laurie, still crying, found her way to the side of the middle sister Sonja, who now started stirring. She had been knocked senseless when Toby slugged her. Jessie gathered and wet a dishtowel and applied it to Sonja's forehead. Sonja appeared to have a concussion from the blow. After a time, Sonja was half carried by Sally, Jessie, and Laurie to the house. The late morning sunshine was getting hot and it was no place for a stricken girl to be lying in.

Laurie had been a classmate of Bonnie's. She, like Bonnie, became one of the better marksmen in the youth trap and skeet club. Unlike Bonnie, Laurie did not have a desire to attend college. She preferred to stay home at the ranch with her dad and sisters. She loved the way of life and imagined she would grow old there. Unlike Bonnie, Laurie was one of those movie-star-beautiful country girls the boys jump through hoops for and fantasize about their whole lives. Laurie was intelligent and talented in music, and her voice was pristine. She had no ambition other than to live the life of a ranch owner. She could ride, rope, train animals, hunt, and work as efficiently as the best of cowboys in their country.

Sally and Sonja were equally as capable as Laurie. They, on the other hand, like most youths in the small Pinedale community, dreamed of going away to a distant university or big city bright lights some other place.

All the girls were fit physically and mentally.

Gene and Jessie asked the girls what happened to cause the recent events. Sonja explained they had some unwanted advances from Toby this last year and Josh had been hanging around. The situation had quit being a problem when their dad talked with Mr. Gilder. Mr. Gilder assured Mr. Smith the boys would learn some manners. Since the lights went out all bets were off. First, Toby started hanging around. Sonja had set the dog on him twice to run him off. The third time, Toby shot and killed the dog.

This morning Toby and Josh showed up before any of the girls knew they were there. Sonja was doing chores when Toby caught her coming out of the barn. Sally had been feeding the chickens when Josh grabbed her. She screamed and Laurie came on the run.

Toby had already hit Sonja, then surprised Laurie as she came out the door and scuffled with her before dragging her back into the house. Just about the time Sally and Josh started struggling was the time Gene saw the activity from the hill above.

Gene inquired as to the Mr. Smith's whereabouts.

Laurie having now collected herself said, "Papa is in the hospital in Riverton. He went there to have some tests and a biopsy. I think Toby and Josh knew he was gone and wouldn't be back for a couple days. He was supposed to come home yesterday. He insisted we stay together here to take care of the place. He said he would be alright. I think he was still in Riverton when the electricity went off. We're still waiting for it to come back on."

Gene explained his theory about the EMP. Laurie and Sonja listened and were thoughtful. Sally, on the other hand, looked as if she would go screaming through the trees at any moment. Gene knew the girls had ample canned food for a couple years. Gene suggested they jerk and can the freezer meat and dehydrate the frozen vegetables they couldn't preserve by canning. They could use the window screens not made of metal to dry the food on. The metal screens could poison the food. They could cool their milk products with a wet burlap bag over a frame about the milk, cheese, and butter. They would need to keep the gunnysack wet to make the cooling work. Still, they would have plenty of cheese curds available.

Gene explained he and Jessie were going to Jake's and if the girls needed anything, they could go there. Gene explained he was on his way from Jake's to Riverton and he would try to locate Mr. Smith if he could.

"You girls need to arm yourselves and stay alert," Gene instructed. "If you need to, shoot to kill. It won't be pleasant, but you have a choice: kill or be raped and maybe killed yourself. Try not to be caught alone if possible. Be sure to keep each other appraised of where you plan to go and be. Don't vary from what you say without good reason. Don't get caught out after dark. One of you be on lookout all the time. Stay together whenever you can! You will need to plan for winter now. Cut firewood and store your canned goods in the root cellar. Grow a large garden if you have seeds. I can assure you, there is no, nada, help in town. You're so much better off out here than in all the cities anywhere in the Western United States. When I get back from Riverton, I will try to check in on you. Please don't shoot me."

Gene and Jessie worked their way back up to the crest of the hill where their packs had been dropped, gathered them, and returned to the house. The girls offered their dad's bedroom to them for the night. Gene and Jessie both felt they should stay at least the night in case Toby and Josh returned. The night, however, was as restful as a strange bed can be.

Morning came with ham, eggs served with hot coffee, and apple butter on the biscuits pasted with fresh homemade butter. Sonja's face had a bad bruise where Toby had hit her. Her eyes had started turning black. They kept a cool wet rag on her face and head to help reduce the swelling.

Gene and Jessie started the journey south toward Jake's. Gene had become very tired. He was old, fat, and out of shape. The pack he carried was heavy. In fact, it was a bit too heavy. Progress slowed with many stops to rest and to recuperate. They crossed a couple county roads and worked their way down country to the upper edge of Jake's ranch. Dusk had set in and they were still a full mile from the ranch house. Gene contemplated the reception he and Jessie would receive from Jake in the dark if unannounced, Jake not knowing who was about. Jake's dogs would announce their arrival before he and Jessie could get close enough to yell their identities. Jake might unchain one or two of the dogs and that was an event Gene didn't want to experience.

They talked about the possibilities and decided to make camp and announce their arrival in the morning after sun up. That decided, they located a campsite to place their sleeping bags. Having dropped some two thousand feet in elevation, the climate had warmed some thirty degrees. A fire would not be necessary this night. Besides, at this elevation, a campfire's heat would attract scorpions and rattlesnakes, which would crawl into anything warm like a shed coat or a boot. Over the years Gene developed the habit in the desert of always shaking the contents out of his boots every morning before putting them on when camping.

There were several other important things one had to do if one wanted to stay healthy in the out of doors. Never go to bed in wet sweaty clothing, stay well hydrated by drinking water as often as one can. Pay attention to the color and smell of one's urine. If it were to start smelling strong, one was likely not drinking enough water. Certain plants like asparagus will leave urine with a definite odor. Avoid soft drinks and alcohol. *Well, commercial soft drinks will soon be a ghost of the past,* Gene mused. *On the other hand, alcohol will be available until the end of time.*

Walking across the north pasture two hundred yards above the house, Gene saw Jake emerge from the machine shed. Gene waved with the full length of his arm. Jake did not reciprocate. He fired one shot into the air and yelled, "turn around and get out the way you came!"

Gene hollered, "Jake, it's me, Shaky. Jake, it's us, Shaky and Jessie."

Jake replied with a question, "Who'd you say?"

"Jake, it's us, Shaky and Jessie," Gene yelled again.

"Why didn't you say so? You was fixin' ta be shot," said Jake.

When they closed the distance Jake said, "Whatcha doin' down in this part of the world walkin' around like ya was lost?"

Gene explained the situation and that he felt there wasn't anyone else Jessie would be safer with.

Gene inquired after Jake's wife and kids, "How're Meg, Mike and Cindy?"

"Mike and Cindy are good, considerin' the circumstances," Jake replied. "Like everybody else, they're havin' to cope with this new old lifestyle. They're haven' to use creek water and that old wood stove Mike has on the porch to cook with. That 'lectric heat is out as well as their 'lectric hot-water heater. Meg's in the house yonder. Go on in."

Jake said Mike and Cindy had four hundred chickens they had been raising for the meat market. Now they were running out of feed and had no way to get more. Mike had ridden nine miles horseback to the settlements and found the mill not operating without power. He returned home puzzled as to what the next step would be to take.

34

The feed they had was enough for another week and then it would be depleted.

"We've been trappn' and shootin' every fox, coyote, and coon we see and huntin' fer more. We figured we will have to turn all them birds out to forage for themselves. Can't figure what else to do. Any ideas?" Jake asked.

"Are the birds ready for the market?"

"Not quite," said Jake flatly. "They need another four weeks yet to finish. When Mike went to town, he discovered people were hungry but had no money. He's afraid if we start taking chickens to town, people will follow him back and raid the farm, maybe harm his family. We can't take enough at one time to satisfy the need. Money has little value now. We would have to barter and there really isn't anything we need other than medications. The problem is, there are no supplies. So. . . We decided we would let them all out and let them be free range and forage for their own food. We'll harvest them as needed. That's why the war on the predators."

"Well, you might consider turning part of them out now and keeping enough to finish growing with the remainder of the feed you have," suggested Gene.

"I'm ridin' there early tomorrow to see them. We'll talk about that. I should be back before you city folks get breakfast," said Jake with a slight smirk. "You and Jessie are welcome as long as you need to stay. We're not bad off and we have plenty to get by on. We're glad to have the company."

Gene and Jessie settled into an east-facing bedroom. The windows and patio door opened out onto a deck overlooking the creek and pond below. This was a pleasant serene setting. Gene felt Jessie would be as content here as any place considering the circumstances.

Early the next morning Gene prepared to depart for Riverton. He enjoyed the smell of fresh-brewed coffee when Jake returned from Mike and Cindy's.

"Mornin', Jake," greeted Gene.

"Mornin', Shaky," Jake replied. "Are you about ready to go?"

"Yes, just about."

"Shaky," said Jake, "you be real careful—I mean real careful. I rode to Mike's about daybreak. There are some bad characters out there. A bunch jumped Cindy's cousins, you know them, Toby and Josh Gilder, and beat the livin' daylights out of 'em."

Gene nearly swallowed his cup.

"Is that so?" exclaimed Gene. "Jake, let me tell you a little story. Those boys were tromped by one man, a lady, and a girl. That one man was me, the lady was Jessie, and the girl was Sally Smith. Sally was being accosted by Josh when I hit him with a tree limb. Jessie and Sally kept him down with some different limbs. When I got to Toby in the house, he was fixin' to make a mama out of Laurie Smith. She wasn't havin' any part of it, but he had her down and was about to start. I clipped him hard on the side of the head with my pistol butt and before he could get up I kicked him in the ribs. I thought I heard bones crack. Just to ensure he didn't get up too fast, I kicked his thigh as hard as I humanely could. I shoulda' shot him in the leg. Let him explain the hole in the leg and no hole in the pant leg. I took him out, gave him to Josh, and told them I was going to talk to their pa.

Toby had hit Sonja Smith so hard she was out cold. She had a bruise on her cheek and both eyes will be black for a couple months. Jake, you can ask Jessie about what happened to the Smith girls. Those two boys just got caught, that's all. They made up the story to hide their evil activities. Jake, I told those boys before they left if they even looked crossways at the Smith girls I would personally hunt them down. Jake, you know me as being a tolerant man, but there are some things that aren't tolerable. I'd appreciate this not gettin' around too much, but I thought you should know the truth."

Jake leaned back in his chair and paused a moment before saying a word. He then said, "Shaky, you're a little guy. Who'd ever believe you tore them up as bad as they said they had been? Mmm mm."

Gene paused a moment before commenting, "Jake, you know the old adage, 'If you pick a fight with a man who is too old to fight, he won't fight, he'll just kill ya.' Kinda' applies in this situation. Those boys can thank their lucky stars they are still alive."

Chapter 4

Trek To Riverton

G ene was now learning there wasn't much in the way of comfort for the spirit when one sees the abject misery of a once prosperous people after a calamity. The standard of living had dropped to such a level that was unimaginable in weeks past. It had been a short two weeks since the event that had now reduced humanity to a low standard of hunger and starvation. All those people became cold pathetic beggars and wretches. They became worse off than any people of any third world nation ever had been. The individuals among this society just hadn't known or understood how to cope with such lack of resources and starvation.

Abject poverty had become their newfound situation. True, there would be many who might survive because there are always survivors. Some would survive because they were thieves and because they had little compassion for their fellow man. There would be many multiple times as many who would die of malnutrition, succumb to disease and plague like cholera, typhus, and West Nile Fever due to lack of adequate preparation and ample medical supplies. Many would be terrorized by thugs and bands of the lawless who had little mercy as they pillage and plunder. This was the state of how Gene viewed humanity at the time.

He considered these things along his journey while he walked from Jake's toward and then past the settlements on his way to the city of Homington, a bedroom community of Riverton. Homington was where his younger son Samuel and family lived. Riverton was where his daughter Bonnie was going to college. Because of his observations, he became wary of any group or gathering and avoided them at great length. There were a number of automobiles stranded along the four-laner leading to Homington. Gene saw only a couple mobile autos. Both were older.

From experience, having worked in many disaster locations, including Katrina and Sandy, he'd observed as long as people have hope and a smattering of resources, a few will rise to the top taking charge. He saw some who shut down, curled into a ball, and died. In the short run, people did well to encourage one another and bear each other's burdens. But when all became bleak for a long periods of time survival mode set in for most.

Even with official organization or martial law, there seemed to always be thugs and bullies prowling around like ravenous wolves looking for the weak and disadvantaged to prey upon. They mostly stole and plundered, but now and again they would rape and the level of cruelty seemed to escalate as time advanced.

Literal packs of canines would form as the dogs had been turned out to fend for themselves because their masters couldn't or wouldn't supply the food necessary to sustain them. These packs became a real danger because a pack could hunt a man down faster than a gang of thugs, and domestic dogs gone wild rarely have natural fear of humans. Gene had known a man who died with his pets in the house. They consumed him before it was discovered he had passed on.

Being older now, it seemed Gene had lost a lot of his youthful strength. To walk a most direct route to the Riverton area and Homington would mean going cross-country through the desert. Not being a real desert, the semi-arid wasteland could be a challenge to live in. The sixty-mile trip would likely take a young person two or three days. It would take Gene a week or longer if he had no delays.

When started, walking did seem to take longer this time. Sleeping conditions had not been quite as comfortable as when coming home to a warm bed after a long day of hunting. It seemed the aches and pains caused by the physical exertions and the strain of uncertainty lasted longer with extended recovery time. Gene was mindful of his Ibuprofen, at least until he could replenish the supply. The walk home on that first day made his feet sore. The trek with Jessie to Jake's house further exhausted him as well. He'd always found it took him a week to physically adjust to new adventures before he became comfortable with the daily rigors. As of late, it seemed recovery from physical exertion took even longer yet although acclamation to the new physical conditions always seemed to progress.

Another phenomenon was becoming accustomed to his physical surroundings, being aware of his surroundings like wild animals are. Gene had always experienced this during extended outings of fishing, hunting, and hiking treks. When on horseback, he would watch the horse's movements, the cocked ears, the responses to its surroundings, and awareness of the big and little events going on around it.

Gene's physical awareness would re-calibrate the longer he stayed out. His hearing would sharpen and he would start hearing minute sounds he wouldn't ordinarily hear among civilization. His sense of smell, too, would re-calibrate and smells normally not detected in the civilized world would now be sensed. The slightest motion not in his direct line of sight would be picked up instantly as well. Varied shades of the same color would be more distinct as if the contrast were black and white. Now that the mechanized world had nearly halted, Gene would be able to detect vibrations in the earth before the sound reached his ears. These vibrations might come from a horse walking (as few as they were), a deer bounding, or a bear turning a log over for grubs. And so, with each passing day, his senses sharpened, becoming more acute than he had ever thought possible.

On the other hand his tolerance for the extremes of the outdoor elements during the first few days caused him great misery and he thought at times he wouldn't be able to endure the conditions. As the days progressed, he found the cold at night didn't bother him as much and the hardness of the ground at night was not as bothersome either.

He had to remember in heat and cold he needed to stay hydrated. In this location, staying hydrated wasn't difficult. There existed many small streams coming off the mountain separated every mile or two. If he stayed high enough on the desert plateaus before the streams soaked into the gully floors, he could get water that was arguably the best on earth. If he dropped to the alkali adobe foothills and flats below where he could see sojourners moving about in the distance, he would find only brackish water at best. Most of those travelers weren't conscious of contamination and took little care of the watershed. They tended to foul what water was present, good or bad.

While staying high on the terrain, he wasn't likely to run into the marauders he suspected had been praying on the hapless travelers as they moved along the highway. Gene knew it wasn't hard to remain out of sight if one stayed to the cover of the junipers and scrub oaks. A major danger he had to remember was that the telltale signs of smoke from even a small fire would give a camper away. Gene had already skirted around a couple camps where there were telltale signs of an encampment from the campfire smoke filtering through the air. He could just about guess the distance and direction from the strength of the odor. He could tell what was being cooked for the meal from the aroma.

The first few days he had the aroma of beef, goat, chicken, turkey and then later he wasn't sure what dinner may consist of. It wasn't rabbit, he knew. It could possibly be dog or, being near the river, maybe muskrat.

Just as smoke gives away the encampment locations and the menus, smoke would tell what fuel was being charred, like trash, cans, and plastic. That would likely change as people started running out of supplies. Gene could even ascertain whether people were lazy in gathering fuel for their fires. Many were starting to burn old painted lumber and furniture rather than gathering proper fire fuel. Gene would himself have to be ever so careful not to telegraph his existence or location with an indiscriminate smoke signal.

Journal entry:

"Five days only brings me thirty-five miles closer to Riverton and I am worn and tired. I stoned one rabbit to eat and twisted another out of a hole with a length of barbwire like we did when I was a kid. I remember that being a real game. Dad would show us how and then challenge us to do it. After a few tries, it would work and I perfected the process. I didn't dream I would need it in the future to survive.

I've been reluctant to shoot a deer, as I can't eat that much and I don't want to waste the meat, especially in these times. In my mind, wasting food would be akin to defiling a neighbor's daughter."

Gene had spent many days and hours as a child and youth roaming about similar hills some miles from his present location. There were many adobe ridges sparsely covered with juniper and pine foliage. As a boy, Gene played cowboys and Indians with neighbor kids, hunted rabbits, and tracked deer, elk, and cats, and just explored from daylight to dusk. They'd saddle a horse and ride the day in the mountains or just ride to see the country at hand. Sometimes they would spend summers at the mountain cow camp, the Alkali as it was called, while livestock grazed the high-country range.

Exploring remote places was one of Gene's most beloved pastimes. Nearly everyplace had been explored in the past from every angle, but it was fun to see if anything had changed since the last exploration. In the days before the Californians and Texans started movin' in, Gene and his compadres would go just about anywhere without a complaint from the property owner. There existed one set of rules: If you found a gate open, ya left it open. If you found it closed, ya closed it behind ya after ya went through. If ya found a sick critter, ya reported it to the owner. Ya knew who the owner was from the stock brand, earmarks, or rare ear tags. That was a good life growin' up in these mountains.

He had a lot of practice in these hills and on the mountains above. Many a time he stood or set a spot and watched deer, elk, and a couple times a bear or a lion walk by never knowing he was there until they would get a scent of him on the breeze. More often than not, whatever it was still wouldn't know just where he stood as long as he didn't move.

Sometimes, as an observer one couldn't even blink an eyelash. He had grown to be a relatively capable tree or rock when he needed to be. On the other hand he had learned to slip up on creatures with some training from an old relative. He was fair at doing that, only not so good as him, the old timer. That man was one of the last of the old-timers who had fought in the Spanish American War in the Philippines.

On more than one occasion after leaving Jessie in the safety of Jake's, Gene would be working his way toward Riverton and there'd be some tenderfoot out foraging for anything they could eat. Gene would stay still and watch them as they passed never knowing Gene was within a mile. He even watched a guy turn over a rotten log like a bear, then eat the insects he found there. Gene prayed he wouldn't get that hungry. The man completed his feeding and went on. Gene hadn't twitched a muscle or blinked an eyelash.

Gene carried his stainless .357 pistol and pocket tool on his belt and a smaller 9mm handgun concealed in his armpit under his vest and used a crossbow for quiet work. A gunshot could bring unwanted company and he preferred to be solitary. To expend a cartridge would be like spending gold, so those he had he would use sparingly and they would be carefully counted. He only had six bolts for the bow and preferred to save those as well. His backpack contained a lightweight tent, a ground cloth doubling as a poncho, and the remains of what food he hadn't given away to an old man in a wheelchair and his wife. Included in his pack were two boxes of ammo, piano wire for snares, two butane lighters, a sewing kit, fishhooks and line, a quality mountaineering coat, rain chaps together with cotton and wool socks, a change of clothes, a poly-fill sleeping bag, a knife, matches, fire tinder, a small mountaineer camp stove, a small bottle of white gas, a small aluminum bottle of coal oil, a canteen, medical supplies, a small Gideon Bible, and his journal.

I'm getting too old to carry a lot of weight, he thought. The gas would be conserved jealously and used only in extreme need. When it ran out, the mountaineering stove would be deposited some place safe and out of his pack.

On the seventh day, Gene approached the outskirts of Homington where his son and family lived. From time to time, he started seeing more people foraging for food. Many hunted roots and rose hips that had survived the winter. New rose hips hadn't formed yet. Up higher, some gathered acorns and various roots. He noticed the closer to town he came, the more scarce game seemed to be. Livestock seemed to be fit enough and so too were the guards with hunting rifles guarding them. He skirted these places and people in groups. A couple times he stayed stationary as a person would walk past not having a clue Gene was in the country, let alone within fifty or a hundred feet and just watching 'em pass. Gene didn't understand how a passerby couldn't smell him. Boy, how he needed a bath. Gene was convinced robbery had become commonplace. He was ever so cautious about contact with anyone, especially an unknown passerby.

Gene heard an occasional vehicle on the highway below and had seen a truck with armed men making its way along the winding route. He assumed these must be people with authority as few others had means for fuel. The people with authority weren't necessarily officials, however, but were ones with might. Gene had seen an occasional light and heard the sound of generators when the cataclysm first occurred. Now he saw fewer of these and heard fewer combustion engines.

As he worked his way out of the high country and hills down toward the highway river bridge near Homington, he began to realize, from that point forward could have great exposure to adverse encounters. That's when Gene committed an error in judgment.

He'd watched his intended path carefully for a period, then advanced a distance and then did the same again. He could see the bridge and some form of complex in the distance, an enclosure with a tall wire fence where people moved about performing daily activities. At the second from the last planned observation stop before he reached the bridge, a man's voice from behind and to his right warned him not to move or turn. "What you doin' spyin' on us?"

Gene replied, "I'm just being cautious before crossing the bridge and nothing else." He added, "Just bein' careful."

The man ordered Gene to put his crossbow and pistol on the ground and not to turn around. Gene couldn't see if the man was armed. Gene had to assume he was because everyone possesses guns in this part of the world. The EMP had not disabled any of those weapons as near as Gene knew. Gene followed orders very carefully so as not to draw unwanted action from the man. When Gene had done as ordered the man instructed Gene to move forward a distance, and then called to someone hidden in the brush to collect

Gene's equipment. Gene had been caught with his guard down and now capture had been the consequence.

While being directed off the hillside and across the bridge, Gene tried to reason out his circumstances. If they'd wanted to kill him, his spirit would have already been risen "up through the sky above as some believe." Gene possessed little of value if they intended to rob him except his weapons and backpack. Those might be enough. They could have ambushed him and been done with it. It was not likely they were going to kill him. Over and over in his mind he reasoned. They had both his crossbow and his .357 but had not bothered to search his person or take his pack. If they had, they'd have found his concealed 9mm auto. They hadn't robbed him as much as captured him. Gene considered using his hide-a-way but reasoned if the man and his companion intended to kill and rob him, they would have done so then made off with the spoils. There must be something more. Gene continued to follow instructions.

Trying to ease the tension some, Gene introduced himself. "They call me Shaky."

Gene's captor just said, "Ya, keep movin'."

Gene kept probing. "I wasn't intending any harm. Jes tryin' to be careful. One needs to be careful these days, don't you think?"

"Ya, keep movin'," said the man.

A person can learn a lot when people talk and a person can learn a lot when they don't. Gene wasn't quite sure what "keep movin'" meant except they seemed to have a destination in mind and it wasn't likely Gene would be dispatched in or near the town. That idea could be faulty, however, and Gene decided if he got a chance he should get away if he could. The problem was, as he thought, *I'm not fast. I'm not agile. I'm getting old in my mid-sixties and I am out of shape.* On the other hand they already had a chance to dispose of his body and unless they were really bad they wouldn't do so in a settlement. People hadn't had enough time to degenerate into really bad folks in a couple weeks.

These dudes weren't professional or they would have found his 9mm. They hadn't even taken his pocket tool or hunting knife, which was in plain sight on his belt. Not being professional meant

Gene needed to be very careful not to trigger an ignorant adverse unexpected response from one of them.

"Who do I have the pleasure of being captured by?" Gene inquired.

Gene couldn't buy an answer.

The big man just simply said, "Jes keep movin'" and no more.

The response told Gene he expressed little if any emotions and that could be good and bad. If he wasn't friendly, he was equally not unfriendly. The total expression of neutrality from the non-professional indicated to Gene no malice or animosity. Gene thought he'd try one more question so he asked, "Where we headed?"

"Down the road," the big guy responded. Although they were already going up the road as they had crossed the bridge over the big river and were ascending up the other side. The statement could indicate some distance left before they would reach their destination.

Reading sign when dealing with people is not unlike reading sign when tracking an animal. Their responses often relay a thought or action pattern where they have been and some about where they will go. They may not know themselves, but like a tick in a poker game, the opponent often will reveal their direction or thought without knowing they are doing so.

In this unlawful world, some men who are uninhibited live beyond the law and become overbearing, taking advantage of and bully others. Their negative actions happen in small amounts at first, but as they are unchecked and find weak boundaries, they encroach more and more on others. In current conditions without rule of enforceable law, these natural bullies emerge.

Some bullies find a steady direct stare will intimidate the target. When the target responds weakly and passively, the bully tends to be encouraged and progresses if unchecked. If the target acts with a firm self-assured response, one of two results may occur. If the bully is a coward, they will back off or throw a fit of temper. A temper fit is nothing more than a control ploy. Gene understood a temper fit thrown by a person who is not well acquainted with the target is simply an act to control the response of the target.

Most often, the result is the temper thrower gets his or her way. A temper thrower knows the fit works to achieve a desired result, but he or she most often has no clue as to why it works. On the other hand, the one who knows how to use a temper fit is a manipulator by design and becomes proficient in using this technique time after time. It works simply on people who don't know or understand the activity. They simply want to avoid conflict.

If the bully is looking for a challenge and/or confrontation, the bully will respond to a return challenge. The old axiom of "he who blinks first loses" is ever so true. The initial or subsequent challenges sometimes will manifest in form of an intended physical challenge, a bump, or loud vocal abuse, and sometimes in combinations.

Gene had experienced all these as a kid growing up on the school playground. He had observed many recipients of the activity being humiliated. Those who hadn't learned signs of a bully became prey as a consequence. If a kid was fast and mean and showed no weakness, he would generally not be bothered further. Gene was neither fast nor mean, so he learned to be observant and to respond with unexpected responses. Often this would throw off the intended result of the bully, neutralizing a negative situation.

Gene's captor seemed not to be a bully, although he was considerably bigger in stature than himself. He had big raw bones and had the appearance of having physically worked hard a lot. The other, by Gene's guess, was a youth in his mid-teens with a medium build, was attentive to their task. He made no offer to do anything he wasn't directed to do. He was very serious and direct in his purpose.

Captors and captive proceeded up the road where there were people scattered here and there in small groups near the bridge. They'd been fishin' with little luck. The river contained a few trout, some catfish, and suckers, a kind of carp not heretofore regarded as a palatable food by most people. Gene's family clan called them red-horse suckers. Most people cast the suckers upon the bank in normal times as a trash fish. As he glanced around, he concluded suckers had now attained the status of prize. None went to waste.

During Gene's childhood years, Gene would go with the clan the old timers to the river with a gill net and catch the pickup truck full of suckers. They had to let the trout go because it was illegal to net a trout. The pickup beds at that time were not as large as current day trucks, but the old trucks held a real nice mess of trash fish. Gene thought now and again about how tasty the fish patties made from canned sucker had been. Better than canned tuna or salmon and not near so fishy tasting.

Ya see, when you pressure cook a jar full of sucker meat, all those little bones that make them uneatable dissolve and the fish meat becomes most edible. Gene wanted to tell somebody.

Gene thought, *Good fishin' ta those folks.*

Chapter 5

Compound J

"OK, hold up," said the big man.
They arrived at the fenced area with a six-foot chain-link fence and barrier wire at the top.

Gene was instructed to turn at a gated entry. When the gate-keeper saw the big man, he summoned a man named Hoover. A robust red-haired man in his late forties or early fifties approached the closed gate from the other side and motioned the big man to the fence, where they conferred a bit. Hoover instructed the gatekeeper to open the gate and motioned Gene through the hole. Several others had collected within and encircled Gene as he stepped through. The gate closed and Gene now was outnumbered eight to one. The big man and the youth conferred with Hoover again, then returned back the way from which they had come.

"Well stranger, who are you and why are you spying on our compound?" inquired Hoover.

Gene explained he wasn't spying on the compound. He was only being careful before approaching the bridge to cross the river. He introduced himself as Shaky by name. He felt the name unusual enough that should the kids hear it, they would know of his presence.

Hoover's measured gaze seemed to be sizing Gene up. "Armed a little heavy for a casual traveler, aren't you?"

Gene explained he was traveling from Pinedale on a quest to locate his son and family who live in Homington and his daughter who attended college in Riverton. Gene explained the arms were for protection from marauding thugs and for acquiring food.

Hoover seemed to accept the explanations without comment. He then gestured and uttered, "come" as he walked away.

Gene followed, flanked by two dudes, one tattooed from finger-nail to earlobe and another who looked like a contestant for the local Atlas contest.

When Hoover stopped, he turned and said, "We don't have a lot here, but a guest eats one time. Then all work for their next meal. If you don't work, you don't eat."

"Well, that's very Biblical. I don't intend on staying or being a burden," Gene stated. "I will be on my way to locate my kids. If you would be so kind as to return my pack and my weapons, I will be on my way ASAP."

Hoover turned and replied, "You don't seem to understand the gravity of social conditions hereabouts. There is social unrest, mayhem, murder, robbery, rape, slavery, and God knows what else is going on. You are safe as long as you are in our compound and not safe outside of it. We have other compounds in the area as well. We travel between them in armed details and all follow strict guide-lines for orderly living. If we determine you are not a spy, you will be welcome to stay as a contributing member. If you go, you will be treated as an advisory henceforth. Your arms will remain under compound control for the foreseeable future. We will assist you with information and intelligence about your family if we can obtain it. Mr. Shaky, we have powerful enemies in the community, ones who would control everyone and every facet of this new society. They are a fascist bunch and allow no expression of opinion or self-de-termination such as we do. They function under the guise of martial law at a local government level. We refer to them as Martial Law Services, or 'MLS' in short. As near as we can determine, they have no legal authority to exist. They would wipe us out to the man and assimilate our survivors, our stores, and our compounds and they would rule by anarchy. They have confiscated all fuel supplies and siphoned the fuel tanks of any vehicles they found unattended or otherwise. Do you understand me?"

"Now, if we determine you are a spy for this MLS," continued Hoover, "you will simply vanish. We will find out if what you say is true and if not then, there will be consequences. Now, will you partake in our meager fare?"

Grace was offered before the meal. This made Gene feel a little more confident, although the question in the back of his mind remained how they would confirm his identity.

Gene did eat, more like *slurped*, the meal and was able to chew the last two mouths full from the bottom of the bowl. He found the supplies there less than basic. These folks were in need. After the meal, he was escorted to the men's sleeping area and offered wash facilities and a spot to sleep on.

Gene thought about his situation. *This is a problem. The guards had neglected to search me. I still have the 9mm under my shirt covered by a loose fitting vest. If I disrobed to wash, my weapon will be exposed.*

Pondering the situation, he contemplated his options: First, try to bed down without the benefit of the sailor's bath. This might bring questions as to why with these comforts available, he didn't avail himself of the convenient facilities.

His second option would be to excuse himself for a latrine call, try to hide his weapon and holster in the privacy of the toilet, then return. He would go to the latrine the first time to reconnoiter. He would excuse himself the second time with the excuse of the two-step from irregular food to discard and hide his weapon before bathing. He later would return a third time after the bath to retrieve the pistol.

A third option was a bit unsettling. He would simply go to Hoover and reveal the gun with no malice and turn it over to Hoover in good faith. That action would take faith on Gene's part and huge trust, hopefully not a misguided trust, in a mere stranger. Gene disliked deeply the idea of giving up control of his last physical equalizer. That action would take a lot of trust and faith in Hoover and the Lord Himself.

The fourth option, well, there wasn't one, as near as he could think.

The third option was very risky but might prove to be the most productive. It was most encouraging that the compound had graced the meal, as scanty as it was. That indicated to Gene these folks were more than they said. The gracing of the meal was most encouraging and he felt them to be genuine. On the other hand, if he were discovered with a hideaway, it might tarnish their opinion of him. Even so, if these people were genuine, he would be secure and if they had resources, they would be a welcome and more direct information avenue to the kids.

OK then, the decision has been made, Gene thought.

Gene called the watchman and requested he be taken to see Hoover. The watchman objected with a shake of the head. Gene insisted and informed the watchman he had information Hoover needed to be apprised of.

"It's important," Gene insisted.

"Very well." The watchman relented and walked off in another direction from where Hoover had taken Gene upon their first encounter. After a few minutes, Hoover appeared out of the dark with a scowl on his face and anger in his eyes.

"What in tarnation is so almighty important that it can't wait until morning?" he demanded.

"Mr. Hoover, as near as I can tell, you have been straightforward with me and I want to be the same with you. I requested your presence to make sure we understand each other clearly."

"Get to the point!" Hoover spouted.

"Yes, sir. I'm trusting in your integrity and want you to trust in mine as well."

Hoover listened, not knowing where this conversation was leading

"Mr. Hoover," Gene continued, "your security here is lousy. If you will allow me, I will surrender one last weapon your security didn't detect. I fully expect to get it returned with my other weapons upon my departure."

Gene slowly lifted his arms to the side and said, "If you will check my left armpit, you will find my 9mm auto under my shirt."

Hoover motioned one of the nearby onlookers to check. He removed the pistol and handed it to Hoover.

Hoover said, "I appreciate you being forthcoming about this. I will have to think about this."

"Mr. Hoover, if I intended harm to any of you, I would not have surrendered my weapon. Please keep that in mind as you consider," Gene said quietly.

Hoover turned on his heel and, without a word, disappeared into the dark from whence he came. Gene settled down to sleep after bathing and slept reasonably well for a bed in strange surroundings.

Activities came early, earlier than even Gene was used to. Men started stirring well before daybreak and were out of the sleeping quarters first thing. These people were no slouches. Gene emerged and observed all were busy with various tasks about the compound. He looked for a project or task where he could be useful. He first saw men packing water from the river. The water was dirty with mud and sure to be fouled with feces of riverbank dwellers. Gene's first thought was cholera—that is, the disease of filth and dysentery found in so many unkempt camps. Gene hadn't seen evidence of such illness in this compound. Now he understood why. He pitched in to carry water from the river to the pots where the water was sterilized by the boiling. When the particulates settled then roughly filtered to clear as possible, it was boiled and the hotpots were set aside to cool.

Gene noticed armed guards stationed between the river and the compound. When straining and sterilization had been completed, filling of assorted sizes of water bottles commenced.

Gene was occupied with the chore at hand when Hoover spoke to him saying, "Shaky, you do well. Generally, we assign daily tasks so all gets done. We rotate these between work crews. This morning you were able to help with our water purification process. Water is one commodity we can trade for goods with which we can eat, clothe, and medicate. It takes many gallons of water to acquire a small bottle of propane. Propane is the one commodity we require to run our refrigerator to keep certain medications cool. Cooling meds will soon end if we are not able acquire propane. The biggest general cost is camp fuel used for boiling and cooking. That is a challenge. So we conserve fuel. The raw water is free as long as we have hands to obtain and process. The containers we protect jealously. We don't let any go. We trade purified water not only for goods but in an attempt to keep the general population from getting cholera. It also encourages them to be active and productive to get clean water. We try to keep the barter price low."

Gene wondered why Hoover would be telling him these details. Hoover must have some confidence in Gene as a result of Gene's straightforwardness.

"Shaky, do you have any special training like medical or logistics analysis?" inquired Hoover.

Gene indicated he had worked in disaster areas as a vocation, both with the Red Cross and as a private contractor for restoration.

"Very well, you will be assigned to one of the work crews to carry out daily chores. We work until the task is complete and when finished we look to see where else we can be useful. I want to meet with you this afternoon. We must get additional information from you about your family."

Gene continued his present job and wondered what he would be doing next. He also considered just how much information he should give about the kids. Would he be putting them in danger? At any rate, he would do what he could to speed the process.

The midday sun had passed the high noon spot and Gene thought the time to be a quarter to one or a little later. There were a few windup watches, non-electronic, but those were of little use except for synchronization and circumstances where close timing was important. Telling time by the sun was what was left without the use of digital gadgets. Telling time by the sun wasn't a new thing to Gene. He had used the sun to indicate the time of day all his life from early boyhood. It was a learned skill like so many others from years past and before the EMP. One thing he did miss was illumination before daybreak and after dusk to read the Scripture and other books by. Coal oil was much too valuable these days to be spent on such extravagance. Coal oil was needed entirely for emergencies and no other purpose.

The time came to see Hoover. Gene decided to give just enough information to get the ball started. He would stick to Shaky as his name. It would be the one most recognized by the kids and significantly would mean little else to anyone else.

One of the watchmen summoned Shaky to come. Following, Gene was led to a construction office-type trailer where Hoover, seated inside, was poring over documents. When Gene knocked, Hoover looked up and said, "Shaky, come in. By the way, what's your real name?"

Gene replied, "It's always been Shaky due to this tremor caused by a sledding accident when I was a kid. No one would recognize my given name if they heard it. I'm known as Shaky. I don't even need a last name in my community. Shaky gets the job done. It will here too for my purposes. My given name is Gene, but I suspect for your background check on me here, Shaky will work very well. Most importantly, my kids will recognize it as it is a bit unusual, wouldn't you agree?" commented Gene.

Gene hadn't considered that he would need to carry his ID for this situation. He didn't need to drive, so left his license at home. His passport was safely tucked away in the safe at the mountain home. Those were the only photo IDs he possessed.

Hoover pondered these comments and said, "I see. . . I find this highly irregular; a person doesn't have identification and wants to keep his real name so private. You make things difficult for us to confirm or disprove you as a spy. What will you tell me that I can verify?"

Gene said, "I will give you the name of my kids, as I hope to locate them with your assistance. You should be able to verify I am who I say I am and not a spy from that information. If you have connections with Pinedale, you will find that's where I'm from. I'l give you my kid's addresses here and I would appreciate any information I could use to locate them. I don't expect you to care for or retrieve them. I will do that. I do expect to regain my equipment, all of it, when I leave."

"Shaky, or Gene, or whatever your name is, you could be using that name as a spy and cover. We will need a personal ID witness to prove who you are, who you say you are. We have resources here and we will find out. As for your equipment, we will see. Now you can return to your assigned work crew. We will notify you when we find out further information. Now, write down the information and anything you can that will help us locate your children."

Gene did so and returned to his assigned chores.

At dinner time, the noon meal in Gene's world came as a repeat of last evening's fare. He ate better on his own with an occasional rabbit or whistle pig. This thin soup was barely sustaining. Nobody was fat here, although some had been heavier not long ago. Sleep came easy as the day had drained his energy. Without good food, energy was a scarce commodity.

Morning came early again. The routine remained the same, except Gene's assigned task crew repaired and patched one of the shelters. Materials were plentiful, but all the work was done by hand without the use of power tools. Sawing, nailing, and screwing by Armstrong as the old joke went. How the world had taken for granted the convenience of power. Many people who could cut a square cut with power tools couldn't cut a square cut with a hand saw now if their life depended on it. Most couldn't keep a saw sharp or set the teeth to the proper set. They didn't have the training. There were few who could and they had become the experts. The problem now was most who possessed the knowledge were very old and had a very difficult time surviving. Everybody was on the threshold of running out of medications with little chance of renewing them. Shipping had stopped. The pharmacies, the ones that hadn't been ransacked and plundered, were low on supplies. In Gene's opinion, conditions would get much worse before getting better.

It seemed this compound had some supplies of medicine and medical equipment. There had been an accident with one of the workers on the fix and repair crew the day before and bandages were readily at hand.

Everybody became more careful as they completed their tasks after that. Injury was not an option these days. One good thing, a person couldn't nail his fingers together with an automatic nailer like in the days before EMP. One sure wouldn't lose a finger to a power saw now. He might sever a toe with an axe if not careful, but it wouldn't be with a chainsaw.

Gene started thinking about radial saws and lathes powered by bows and belts. The activity had been pure mechanical before, but it was more effective for sawing than sawing by hand. During his lunch break, he located paper and a pencil and sketched the idea for future reference. He folded the sketch and pocketed it.

Hoover summoned him after lunch to the office trailer. "Shaky, we've located a party who says they know you by sight. That person is at Compound J. You are to be escorted under guard to J for identification. If you are identified as the real Shaky, that will go a long way toward confirming your story. We haven't located your children yet but are working on more information. The information vine takes some time. We will need to find them to confirm the rest of your identity and what you are doing here. You are still not cleared of being a possible spy for the local Gestapo."

"Mr. Hoover, on another subject, since I've been here, I made a sketch of a mechanical power saw and belt-driven apparatus that could help save time and labor for the repair and construction crews. You might be able to adapt it to metalwork as well. When you ask if I had experience in the medical field, I hadn't considered I am a trained machinist. Some of the old timers did mill work, that is, metalwork without electricity. The same principals apply to woodworking equipment. Here is a rough sketch depicting a general system that would benefit your community if you choose to utilize it."

"Ah. . . Interesting. Shaky, could you put this together if you had the materials?" asked Hoover.

Gene's reply was measured and curious. "Most likely, but with your indulgence, I have more pressing matters. When I locate my kids, then I have another over and across the mountains I intend to locate. Otherwise, I would be pleased to assist you here for a bit. You ask as if I were a welcome candidate for your society here. May I inquire as to what you know that would change my status from possible spy to welcome member?"

Hoover studied Gene a moment, contemplating what he'd say next. "Shaky, we have word your son and his family are in the Salvation Army camp. It seems they're working there to minister to the refugees who have no other place to go. I must say conditions are bleak there. The Salvation Army is under great pressure, as we have been, from this Martial Law group to come under their jurisdiction. If that happens, the Martial Law Services will drain off what resources the Salvation Army possesses. They, unlike us, are unarmed and have no defense other than prayer. Even if they were armed, it isn't very likely they would use those arms for defense.

"We will try to get more information for you, but as usual, information is hard to come by. You ask why, well, simply, this information helps to corroborate your story. You still will go to Compound J to confirm your identity."

"How long will that take?" asked Gene. "I need to get going.".

Hoover was direct in his comment and, while civil, gave no sign of reconciliation. "If you're planning on going to the Salvation Army camp, Compound J is on the way. Not only will your trip to Compound J be safer with our escort, but you will be considerably closer after you arrive. If your ID checks out, I will recommend you be released. If it doesn't, you will be detained. To answer the question you undoubtedly have in mind. . . Yes, if we release you, it will be as you came, with all your equipment. It's all intact and in secure keeping. You will be leaving for Compound J in the morning."

Gene simply replied, "OK."

Gene went back to the work crew and resumed his project. *Well, he thought, maybe progress is being made.* The progress wasn't nearly as rapid as he wished. Hoover was right about the escort making his transfer to Compound J safer. In and of itself that would be some progress. As Gene thought back, his being captured and brought there must have been the hand of God in action. Whether from Jessie's prayers, his own, or a combination of both, he viewed his capture as a blessing in disguise.

The work gave Gene time to think and consider the alternatives if alternatives were needed. He wasn't long on ideas. He was in unfamiliar territory and with who knows what adversaries at every turn. Now that he had arrived on the outskirts of Homington, a suburb of Riverton, news of Samuel's location had changed Gene's destination. The Salvation Army headquarters was located in the middle of Riverton. Bonnie was in Riverton too as near as Gene knew. The main goal now had changed. The next step, get to Riverton and then go find Bonnie wherever she was.

Supper, the evening meal, was liquid again. It was welcome. Actually this time, it had an acceptable flavor. As before, the last two bites were chewable. Or if you preferred, the first two bites were chewable and the rest drinkable. This meal was a little thicker and contained some sort of unidentifiable green particles. Gene guessed the green might be the weed called purslane. It satisfied, and the times for cleaning, reading, meditation, and then sleep had arrived in turn. One didn't get a lot of time for meditation here and as one of the workers said, "The scriptures tell us we are to be in prayer at all times." Gene agreed with and was pleased to hear it from another.

Tired as he was, Gene slept restless with anticipation of the morrow's travel and the unknowns ahead of him. Even though Hoover had news of Samuel, he had no information about Gene's daughter Bonnie. That concerned Gene, but there was nothing to do now without some thread to follow. The uncertainty of who might identify him by sight in Compound J lay on his mind. He was more curious than concerned. Over the last forty-five years he had known scores of folks and interacted with maybe thousands of others.

Gene awoke before the others in camp had awoken. He got up, bathed, and dressed before most the others had stirred. One of the watchmen greeted him as he exited the barracks and commented, "Shaky, you must be eager to get to work early."

Obviously no one, or very few, knew of his transport to Compound J. He had the feeling "the goings-on were not common camp knowledge."

Another man called him and said Mr. Hoover was requesting his presence. Gene responded. As soon as he approached the construction trailer, Hoover descended the entry stair and inquired as to Gene's welfare.

"Shaky, inside are the men who are going to Compound J. You know two of them. They are your friends, but don't underestimate their resolve to carry out their assignment, which is precisely to deliver you to Compound J with my letters of instruction. According to my instruction, all I told you will be carried out. The other two you don't know and they don't know you. If you have any doubts, let me assure you they will not hesitate to complete the task assigned, you understand?"

Gene nodded.

"Good," Hoover continued. "Now if you wouldn't mind, we have goods that need to go to Compound J. They are of some value, and rather than burden one of your guards and protectors, we would like you to share in the burden. You think that would be OK?"

Gene nodded his consent and Hoover rapped the side of the trailer. The four men emerged. The first carried a backpack of some weight, a 30-30 Winchester, and wore a combat belt with pistol. The second and third were armed with AK47s, pistols and combat belts. The fourth, Mike, carried Gene's backpack with gear, crossbow, and bolts. He had Gene's .357 and his 9mm on a belt, which he handed Hoover.

Hoover quickly stepped to Gene, handed Gene his arms and said, "Make no mistake. These are not loaded but for the sake of appearances, you can appear armed while in route. You will carry this pack and Mike there will retain your ammo until you reach Compound J."

Mike reached back into the office door and retrieved a .12 gauge riot gun.

Hoover addressed to all, "God be with you and be alert."

The detail, with Gene in the midst, exited the compound gate and turned north. At about a mile distant, they turned west. Just before the turn, people, creatures just existing started following at a distance at first, then within a half mile started closing. John, one of the escorts whom Gene didn't know, turned and loudly called warnings with no question as to what would occur if the pursuit continued. The ragtag bunch held back some. They apparently were aware of the warning had teeth. John commented, "That should hold them for a while." He had once before been involved in an attempted rout from the same group and it hadn't turned out well for them.

A couple miles down the road a man with three others stepped onto the road as if to block their way. Mike said, "Be on your toes. There are some in the brush on the left and I saw a hat in the ditch on the right. Shaky, if I were you, I would get your guns out. That may be enough show to change the balance of strength in their minds"

The guard in the lead raised his riot gun and commanded, "Clear the way!"

With no response from the blockers, he fired one round from the shotgun over their heads. They hesitated for a moment and then stepped aside. Mike reminded the others they should be conscious of the sides and rear. "If they were more than bluff, they would have started shooting with no warning. Keep your eyes open, though."

Gene was just about to crawl out of his skin. This wasn't his idea of an efficient way to get from one point to the other. He would have rather moved by stealth, not in the open. Maybe this show of firepower was best in this urban setting. Gene didn't have experience with in-town combat. Many who had returned from the recent Middle East conflicts had been well-schooled in urban setting conflicts and combat.

A couple more miles went without further event. Near the rail yards the detail turned south to the river edge and proceeded to what turned out to be Compound J. Upon approach, the gatekeeper signaled others inside and they collected to greet the detail. Upon the squad's entry, a stout man shorter in stature emerged from one side of the welcoming crowd and proceeded to command Gene to set down the pack. After a quick glance toward Mike for confirmation, Gene set the pack on the ground.

"Thank you. You must be the one they call Shaky," he stated. "Mike, you know where to go. Please show our guest to his quarters. Thank you, gentlemen, we will convene at the office at 1500 hours." He turned with the pack and disappeared among the gathered people.

"Mike," Gene asked, "so what's next?"

"We'll refresh ourselves, eat a bit, and go to convene at three," Mike stated. "Here, this is where you'll stay for the time being. I'll come and get you. By the way, you need to relinquish your side arms now."

As Gene unbelted and handed the pistols to Mike, he was uneasy. Having had control of his possessions only briefly had given his spirits a lift. Now the lift started fading.

The fare at Compound J wasn't much different than the food at their previous location. The setting was closer to the river. When the meal came, Gene recognized lamb's quarter in the salad. The other parts he wasn't sure about, except it appeared to be forms of wild plants and there was boiled beet top in the gruel. The meat was purplish red. All of a sudden, Gene realized this soup was a crude beet-top soup. *Oh well. With seasoning, the soup isn't bad for a noon meal.*

Gene watched the activity for a while and saw an opportunity where he could lend a hand. What he could do wasn't much, but as the Scripture says, "Many hands make work lite." Gene did as much as possible before Mike tapped him on the shoulder and said, "It's time."

Chapter 6

Identification

G ene was led to a central location where people waited for something. The stocky leader stood from behind a table. He turned to address the gathering. "People, this proceeding is of the greatest importance. If any of you know this man, please step forward."

Out of the group to the right emerged an older lady. "I think I know him," she quietly said. "His name is Shaky. I knew him in Pinedale when we lived there."

"Mrs. Huddleston, how have you been? I haven't seen you for thirty years," Gene said quickly, thinking a quick recognition would solidify his identification.

The lady said, "Shaky, my name isn't Huddleston."

Gene's heart double beat for a second. He wondered if he had just shot himself in the foot, or worse yet, just made it more likely they'd think he was a spy. He knew her as Mrs. Huddleston, but she was quite a lot older and maybe in her late eighties or mid-nineties. Gene worked with her husband Tom liquidating some construction equipment.

The lady continued, "Shaky, my name is Jones now. Tom died twenty years ago and I remarried, to Seth Jones. Oh, I know that doesn't matter. When they ask if anyone knows the name of Shaky, I spoke right up. They said I should identify you if able. I pray that is a good thing. It is, isn't it?"

"Mrs. Huddle. . . Ah. . . Mrs. Jones, that is, it's a very good thing," Gene assured. He was greatly relieved but now anxiously awaited the results.

The man in charge dismissed the group and motioned to Gene and Mike to come to the headquarters. When they entered, the leader suggested Gene have a seat.

"Shaky, I appreciate that you indulged our precautions. Hoover apprised me through these memos as to your situation. Also, should you prove to be who you said and not a spy for the MLS, then we are to give you any assistance we can within reason. With Mrs. Jones giving us a positive identification on you, it clears the way for you to go on from here."

He continued, "It is reported you are a fair hand and will work, so you are welcome to stay if you want. We have a little more information on your children. Your son and family are faring well at the Salvation Army facilities. If the MLS takes over, that could change. Your daughter Bonnie, as near as we can find out, was located somewhere near the campus. It seems she's vanished after the raids and maybe moved to a new location. We'll give you as much information as we have. I'm afraid we know little of her wellbeing. According to Hoover's instruction, you will be released when you choose to go on your way with all your belongings. We will not escort you. We just don't have the extra man power. You will be on your own. On the other hand, you are welcome to stay here as long as you carry your own weight."

He offered more information. "Each compound is independent from the others. We self-govern based upon the same 'Articles of Government.' We have alliances with each other against common enemies who may wish to overtake any one of our compounds. The worst of these is the MLS. They continue to infiltrate with spies who communicate logistical information. To that end, they mean no good purpose. They have the advantage, as they have confiscated all available fuel supplies and use them for transporting equipment and personnel. They also confiscate food goods from the outlying countryside in the name of Martial Law and use them to barter for labor, coerced labor, and general cooperation from the public.

"The Salvation Army where your son is located is a neutral origination. They are receiving great pressure from the MLS to submit to the MLS authority. They're being told the MLS could provide greater resources for their work. Frankly, I don't see them buckling because the Major is a strong faithful man with a very strong will. He is smart and sees through the MLS intentions. On the other hand, if he is removed by whatever method, the SA might fold like paper in a brisk wind."

"Thank you, sir," said Gene. "How am I to address you?"

"Shaky. . . . I like nicknames, but 'Shaky' is a strange one and not so politically correct. I guess that doesn't matter much these days. The camp calls me Joe. Joe is good enough for me."

"Joe," said Gene, "I'll leave in the morning and if your outside guys would give me some directions and urban survival pointers, it would be appreciated."

"Very well, the earlier you go the better," said Joe. "Many of the ne'er-do-wells don't get up until long after sunrise. On the other hand, they stay out long after dark. You would be wise to find a defensible hold-up considerably before dark and try not to expose its location after midday."

The evening meal was a repeat of the noon meal. It was filling because more water had been added. Satisfying because of the nutrients it contained and these days everybody learned satisfaction with less than a Super Big Bacon Hamburger. Gene caught himself now and again wanting, no, *craving* a good greasy hamburger. He supposed even if he could find one, it would make him sick after the meager fare of the last few weeks.

Gene talked with Mike and John about the city layout. There were landmarks and danger spots for ambush. Gene was to avoid some of no-man's lands at all costs. John helped Gene rig a hideaway knife for emergency. The 9mm and .357 would be returned when he left. The crossbow was given to him then and the bolts would be returned with the pistol cartridges.

John sat a while and then said, "Shaky, I'm instructed to offer you some survival information. You see I served in the Special Forces in Afghanistan. Afghanistan was not unlike what we are now. The one difference is they have lived with their laws and traditions for thousands of years. The Afghanis lived under impoverished conditions a very long time and the dust has had time to settle there during those eons. We, on the other hand, have just about three weeks' experience with such things and there is no rule, no tradition, and no customs established yet to guide peoples' activities. So, you must move carefully and draw on every willpower you have not to act impulsively. Every action must be thought out. You must be sure of the results before you act. Remember, there are twenty three ways to kill a human but also remember the human body is extremely resilient and can recover from the most incredible trauma. Make your decisions in advance and know what you are going to do without hesitation if a particular situation arises. Above all, remember your actions are guided by your predetermined decisions. Avoid whenever possible confrontation. The next guy will likely have better training than you. The day you forget that may be your last.

"Weapons exist all around you when needed: a rock, a pencil, sand in the eyes, scalding water, and so on. Know you can use a weapon effectively before you choose it. If you run short of bolts for that crossbow, you can use anything from rosebush canes or any hardwood shaft. Weight of the shaft is critical. It needs to be sturdy, not light like an arrow. Be sure to wrap the string end tight with floss or rawhide to keep the bolt from shattering on launch. You can fire harden the tips of wood shafts for penetration. An expended cartridge will work well for a stun tip to kill small game and birds. Remember there is a lot of food value in ants and grasshoppers. Raw fish aren't bad either when you're hungry."

Gene had already known much of this information from prior survival training but was grateful for the reminders and for the additional knowledge.

John added, "Back to the city—it isn't unlike the country. Watch the animals for indications of unusual circumstances and things out of place. Dogs bark, birds fly, horses watch, cats watch, and squirrels chatter. Read the signs. Humans tend to be creatures of habit. Observe comings and goings. Watch the water sources. Animals need to drink often. They can go without food for a long time but need water often. That also applies to you too, so plan your drink ahead.

"Choose who you trust with the slightest confidences. They can come back to condemn you."

Sleep time came to Gene with relief and confidence he would be whole with possessions intact. He slept better than any time in the past week.

Early morning came quickly. Gene arose before most of the others in the compound. A guard half hidden by a porch post waited for Gene to step out from the barracks.

After Gene passed, the guard said, "Mornin'."

Gene was somewhat startled. The guard was just being cordial. Gene, on the other hand, felt irritated with himself for not having been aware of the guard's presence.

"Mornin'," Gene replied in a low tone. "It smells like we could have some rain today."

"Yes, I think you're right. There's been a moon dog all night and the birds seem to be gathern'," the guard replied. "I understand you're lookin' fur your kids. Are you headin' out today? Well, not to get nosy, but the Salvation Army won't let you in with your hardware. I jes tell you so you can plan ahead before you get there. They are fine folks and all, but all that trusting God and no precautions is beyond my understandin'."

Gene thought for a second and said, "I understand it. I believe they do take a great physical risk. Now, if you're wondering how those at the SA will get by without a gun or spear. They have faith in God. The way they look at it is, whatever happens will be God's will. God is in control. If they have to follow Him unto death, then they will be in Heaven five minutes before the devil knows they're gone. That's better than all the reward here on earth. In the meantime, they do what they can to feed the starving, tend the sick, and save the lost. They do it all with a cheerful heart.

"I believe God provided additional ways of self-protection. Weapons work as a deterrent as much as for destruction. Peter carried a sword while with Jesus. It may have been for self-assurance; the Lord knows protection wasn't needed. In Bible days, even King David had his arms and armies, as did Joshua. Because they were righteous men, God guided them, backed them, and many times fought their battles for them. When they ceased to obey, then trouble befell them. Just because God fought their battles unto victory doesn't mean they went unarmed. No, they were armed with the latest and best.

"God prefers we show love and one way is non-violence toward others. But God is no stranger to warfare. Because King David was a man of war rather than one of peace, God denied him the honor of building His Temple. The honor went to his son, King Solomon.

"Now, with a person has a faith as strong as those folks at the Salvation Army, there is no fear of death. Therefore, they serve the best they can in the situation God has placed them in. I agree with the idea, but on the other hand one can choose to serve in other ways as well."

"Say, what is your thought on God and all that stuff?" Gene asked.

The guard replied, "Well, I don't rightly know. I've always tried to do good and not harm other people. In the end, I can't say I see much results other than momentary happiness for them or for me. I think a good man ought to go to Heaven if he's been good enough."

"How do you know if you've been good enough? Do you know if you're going to Heaven for sure?" Gene asked.

"Well, no, not for sure. I jus' think a fella ought to be rewarded for the things he does good," replied the guard.

"The Bible says in John chapter 3 verse 16, 'For God so loved the world that he gave his one and only Son, that whoever should believe in him shall not perish but have eternal life.' That means Heaven," said Gene.

Gene continued, "The Bible doesn't say if we do good things we will go to heaven. What it says is, if a person believes in the Son, he will go to Heaven.

"In Galatians chapter 2 verse 16 the Bible says, 'A person is not saved to Heaven by works, but by faith in Jesus Christ.' The Bible goes on to say, 'If a man depends upon his good works he is cursed.' How would you like the rewards for the bad you've done?

"You see, we who are real Christians do the good works as a response to wanting to please God and not so we can get to Heaven.

"Fella, if you are serious about getting to Heaven, the only way is to put your faith in God, Jesus the Christ, and the Holy Spirit. That way you can be assured a spot in Heaven. If you're a good man, you will be a better man and you will be being a good man for the right reason,"

Gene continued, "The first of the three steps saves you to Heaven, the second identifies you with Christ Himself for remission of your sins, and the third is the gift of the Holy Spirit allowing you to function in communion and identification with God. All that is not so complicated, but simple salvation to Heaven is to admit your sins and ask Jesus to be Lord of your life."

Opportunities to introduce people to Christ come at the strangest times. This was one of those. Gene explained the simple ABC steps of salvation and the short process of prayer.

A – Admit you are a sinner. Romans 3:23 says, "For all have sinned and fall short of the glory of God." Admit you are a sinner not by choice even but by nature.

B – Believe in Jesus as the savior from spiritual consequences of those sins. Romans 10:13 says, "Everyone who calls on the name of the Lord will be saved."

C – Acknowledge Jesus as Lord of your life. John 1:12 says, "To all who receive him, to those who believed in his name, he gave the right to become children of God."

Gene led the guard through the prayer of salvation.

"Dear God,

I know I am a sinner and I wish to be forgiven of those sins. I ask you to forgive them and come into my life as Lord and Savior.

Amen."

The camp was starting to stir and the guard was ready to end his shift. Gene prayed the guard would have further opportunity to consider his decision. Often times a newly confessed Christian will have hours of near euphoria with a feeling God is in their presence. Gene wished he had an extra Bible handy to give him, then remembered the Gideon Bible in his pack. Gene took the Gideon from his pack and gave it to the guard.

"When you get the chance to read the book of John, the first book in the New Testament, it tells you more there about your newly made decision. Look for others who are Christians and ask many questions. If you can find a study group, it will help you hold on to your newly found treasure. I look forward to meeting you again," said Gene.

Gene was never again to see this man on this side of Heaven after that day, but he had a great feeling and knew thousands of angels were rejoicing in Heaven at the guard's prayer of salvation, as they do for all who accept Christ as Savior.

The morning fare was again a porridge type of barley soup with some green in it. Gene thought he detected lamb's quarter, purslane, and another grain of some kind in the mixture. It was warm and had a vegetarian kind of flavor.

After the meal, Gene went to the headquarters to gather his goods. Mike and John the prior escorts met him there. They had his equipment and walked with Gene to the gate. Handing Gene his guns, Mike wished Shaky farewell. John also had Gene's bolts and the knife for which he had helped Gene rig the concealed sheath.

"Well, Shaky," said John, "keep your eyes and ears open. You won't likely get a second chance. Be careful now, you hear. I hope you find your children." He turned and walked back toward the headquarters.

Remembering the directions Mike had given him earlier, Gene left Compound J just after the break of day. The Salvation Army refugee facilities were some three miles to the west and near the middle of the city. Gene walked toward the site for about two hours and now it was just in front of him. He remembered the warning about no weapons being allowed within. He decided to go to the entry and ask for Samuel his son by name. The man at the door invited Gene in, but Gene declined. The man asked, "Who's asking for Samuel?"

Gene said, "My name is Shaky. Samuel is my son."

Moments later, Samuel and his wife came to the entry. "Dad, what are you doing here? How is Mom? Where is Mom? Have you seen Bonnie and have you heard from Seth?" Samuel fired questions like shooting rounds out of an AK 47. "How did you get here?"

Gene couldn't get an answer out before the next question spit out. This seemed to be a family trait gained from Jessie. Gene smiled inwardly when he thought of this characteristic.

"I walked," said Gene. "It's taken a while and yes, as near as I know, your mom is okay. I left her with Jake and Meg. This trip hasn't been without incident, but things are okay considering. I assume you haven't seen Bonnie. I came to get her and you guys if you want to go home."

Samuel looked at his wife and back to Gene. Gene knew they were doing what they were being led by God to do. They had hearts of servants and they were in their element here at the Army's Camp.

"Dad, won't you come in?" Samuel asked. "We have some food and a safe place where you can sleep. You will have to shed your gun and bow. Your covered stuff too, Dad."

You know me well, my son, Gene thought.

Samuel did know his dad's characteristics well. Samuel's wife, on the other hand, had little approval of Gene's self-defense beliefs.

"No, son, I'd rather not. If you're okay, I'll try to locate Bonnie. If I can find her, I will bring her back by here on our way home. If you want to join me, we'll all go home together. If you want to remain, I will understand. The greatest thing I have found this month is you, Janna and the kids okay. Now, tell me about the last place you talked to Bonnie and if there's anything you can remember about her plans."

Samuel thought a moment and said, "Bonnie had made some new friends at that new church near 24th and Olive. They had planned a party during the time the lights went out. I tried to find her for a week and left messages for her everywhere but had no leads. I needed to get my own family to safety. Things started to get rough out there. I am so amazed at the extreme levels of kindness and sacrifice, and yet the extreme level of thoughtless cruelty on the other end. We finally got so overwhelmed here taking care of refuges, I had less and less opportunity to make forays to find her. To be honest, I thought she would show up here."

Gene said, "Tell me about every place you looked and what you saw."

Samuel enumerated the places he'd been and where he had left messages. The bulletin boards had hundreds of messages and were filling up, but there was no message from Bonnie on any of them. The clearing centers where a person could leave a contact and welfare message had none from Bonnie. Samuel said some of these were well organized and some were inefficient. He indicated he had checked the campus clearing center and bulletin board as well. That's where he expected to find word from Bonnie. Some of the centers were running message couriers between themselves in an effort to facilitate greater effectiveness.

Samuel again offered his dad a place to sleep, but Gene declined. Samuel gathered up a package of food and sent it with Gene as he left to find the most logical place he thought Bonnie might be.

Chapter 7

The Search

Bonnie's apartment was located on the opposite side of the campus across town from the Salvation Army location. To walk there would take three or four hours. Walking time would put Gene in the middle of the fully-awake populace. Gene remembered John's advice about finding a holdup early. Gene watched people foraging for food and he saw a couple watching him with what seemed to be more than casual interest. Gene took care to keep track of their movements as he passed. His greatest concern was any hidden observers he couldn't see or track. He decided on a plan of varied direction and unpredictable course of travel. As he walked, he varied his speed and changed the distance before he made a change in direction. While he moved, Gene scoped out possible night holdups in several locations.

As he traveled, he saddened at the thought that Samuel and Janna would stay in Riverton rather than returning home with him. Gene wasn't sure where to start looking for Bonnie and hoped she wouldn't decide to stay in the city. But first, he had to find her, wherever she may be. Gene stopped at the first bullion center he came to to go over the possible messages and to leave a short one which said, "Shaky trying to locate Bonnie. Will check in at SA where Samuel is. April 23rd, 2017."

With that complete, Gene went on to another nearby bulletin board. It took him nearly half an hour to sort through all the bulletins. He found none from Bonnie but left one the same as at the bullion center.

Daylight burned and he needed to find a place secure enough to hold up. He had noticed an office building with the windows boarded up on one side. He would bet there existed an entry some place in an obscure location. Gene walked down the alley and didn't find an opening, but, better yet, he found a brick enclave or U-shaped parking space for a trash receptacle. With the trash bin partly in place, a spot remained just behind the trash bin large enough to rest for the night. Just in case he might be discovered by thugs, Gene would sleep with pistol in hand. There wasn't much danger of a dumpster diver finding him, as the dumpsters had all since been raided for anything of value they might yield. Gene wouldn't sleep in the dumpster. There was too much a chance of being trapped inside by assailants. He would, however, use it and the three brick walls behind it as a cover to hide behind and he would feel fairly secure for the night.

He studied the surroundings before circling the potential nest. There seemed to be no one watching and after he watched and waited from a concealed location, he slipped into the newly found lodging.

Journal entry:

"My journal has been impounded for a while, so now I have the opportunity to update. I met some folks who provided me with direction and sustenance. I was able to introduce one of the camp guards to Jesus. I left my Gideon Bible with him. I need to locate another. I've been fortunate to meet some folks who gathered information on Samuel and family. Samuel seems well and determined to continue ministering at the SA center. It's difficult to express the pride a man has for a son with such strong commitment to serve. There seems to be no sign of Bonnie as of yet. Funny, in partaking of the fare served by the camp, as liquid as it was, I had a sudden craving for banana bread. I am not particularly fond of banana bread and am quite sure I may never see a banana again. They don't grow so well here. I miss oranges. I wish I had an orange."

A little after dark, Gene heard a stirring near the front of the dumpster. Then someone opened the lid gently and climbed in, letting the lid down quietly. The sound of rustling came from inside, then all became quiet. Gene was glad he hadn't chosen the bin to sleep in.

Chapter 8

Smith

Morning revealed Gene's location to be just blocks from the regional hospital. Remembering his promise to the Smith girls, Gene directed his attention to the hospital. He may find word of Bonnie there. He hoped not. His next challenge was what to do with his gear. He found a grove of trees in a nearby residential neighborhood not far from the hospital entrance and found secure hiding spots for his bow and .357. These locations were separate but could be reached within seconds of one another. He watched for an inordinate amount of time to see if he was being observed and, satisfied he wasn't, hid his crossbow among some limbs and leaves on top of a backyard storage building. His .357 he placed under an old abandoned piece of tin in a stack of refuse. Satisfied, Gene worked his way to the hospital entrance.

The hospital resembled the disorder of an overused third-world country medical facility. There was little organization and people in varied conditions scattered throughout the hallways. Gene inquired for information and was directed toward the end of a hallway where a bright-looking older woman possessed a clipboard with pages of names and locations. Gene inquired about Bonnie. "I'm looking for my daughter. Her name is Bonnie. Do you have any Bonnies on your list?"

"Do you have a last name?" she queried.

"Tucker."

"I'm sorry. I have no current record of a Bonnie Tucker. Would she be using a different name?" the attendant inquired.

"I have an old record of a Bonnie Towner, but it shows she was released two days ago. She doesn't have the same last name you gave me. Can I help you further?" she asked. So she hadn't been there. That was a mixed relief.

Gene said, "Yes, I am also looking for Zachery Smith from Pinedale. Do you have information about Zack?"

"Yes, here he is. He's on the fourth floor. You'll have to take the stairs. We have no working elevators you know," she replied.

Gene thanked her, then found the nearest stairwell. He proceeded to climb the stairs. Life certainly was different when all one had to do was push a button. When Gene located him, Zack was in an isolated location. Zack recognized Gene when he walked in.

Zack had contracted one of those hard-to-control infections, a staph sort. Authorities had been trying to detour further compromise of the facilities to infections.

Zack Smith was none too good from the experience. Just as the surgeons were taking the biopsy sample was when the electricity went out. It seemed the facility generator had been shielded from the EMP, but the hospital wiring and switch equipment attached hadn't been. The wiring now in place was for emergency use only and fuel was in short supply. These conditions complicated things a great deal as a result and Zack had contracted a raging infection. The doctors were doing all they knew how, but Zack was a very sick puppy. The strong antibiotics Zack needed were in short supply as was everything. So were Zack's feel-good days.

"Shaky, have you been to Pinedale sense this outage?" he asked.

Gene replied he had and he had talked with Zack's daughters. They requested Shaky look him up if he would.

"The girls are alright," Gene said. "What about you? How are you doing?"

Zack said, "Not so good. I contracted a staph infection and they don't have the drugs to kill it. There's a good chance I won't leave here. Are you going back to Pinedale?"

Gene nodded the affirmative.

"Shaky, would you mind taking a letter to my girls when you go?" asked Zack.

"I wouldn't mind at all, Zack," Gene replied. "It may take a while. Society is treacherous just now and so is travel. I would be pleased to carry it to them for you. I was going to check in on them anyway."

Zack gathered a paper and pencil from a nurse and began to write:

"My darling daughters,

Circumstances find me stuck in this hospital for a time without the benefit of proper medical care. Shaky has agreed to fill you in about the details of my stay here.

I wanted to express my love for you as only a dad can for his daughters and remind you about what's most important, … I love you each very much. What is most important is your faith in Jesus. Above all else, do not give your faith up for anything. These times have become perilous and each of you needs to be vigilant in all you do. This goes for your thoughts, physical actions, attitude about others, and your work.

Uphold each other and minister to those who are less fortunate than you when you can. You will be blessed for it. Be careful not to value anything more than your relationship with God. Spend time reading the Book and discuss its meanings and ideas with each other.

I am doing my best to recover and will return as soon as God allows. As for the ranch, Laurie knows the place nearly as good as I do. She can run the ranch and trust her to make important decisions. Laurie, you need to get an opinion from Sonja and Sally where it may concern them or their welfare.

I am making this my official Power of Attorney given to Laurie Smith on all things having to do with my affairs financial and otherwise until I return home. If Laurie is unable to act on my behalf, then Sonja will have the authority, and after that, Sally.

Signed,
Zachery Ingle Smith
May 5, 2017
Remember, I will always love you,

Dad"

Gene witnessed Zack's signature, as did the attending nurse for the day. The letter was folded, inserted into an envelope addressed to Laurie Smith, Pinedale, and handed to Gene, where he placed it inside his shirt for safekeeping.

Gene offered a short prayer for Zack's health and for Zack's daughters wellbeing. He talked with Zack for a spell and requested that when Zack could, he keep Gene's kids in his prayers. Zack agreed he would do just that.

When Gene left Riverton Memorial Regional Hospital, he did so with a heavy heart. Seeing Zack in that condition was a real downer. All Gene could think about was he had seen Zack for the last time and Zack's daughters would in all likelihood never see their father again this side of Heaven. Gene found himself more and more in constant prayer as part of the underpinning of his consciousness while functioning on his current task. He had the added responsibility of now delivering Zack's letter to the Smith daughters while he hadn't found his own yet.

He checked with a second record keeper. There was no record of Bonnie in this hospital. Gene knew Bonnie had been in the emergency room last winter as a result of a very bad bruise on her knee caused by falling on the ice. Gene felt if he asked another person as to her location in the hospital he could find out if she had been there recently and whether she subsequently released.

His next step would be to check the remaining bulletin boards and clearing houses near to the campus near where Bonnie lived.

The dorm buildings and campus center had become squalor. Sanitary conditions had become appalling. Many of the residents fled to other locations. Others hung around for who knows what reason. Gene had an uneasy feeling and stayed ever so vigilant so as not to be surprised by a sudden mugging. He knew at his age and stature he was no match physically for most of these college young bucks and some of the girls too. He decided to make a show of checking his .357 loads and crossbow bolts for any who might be watching.

For all the social noise about the MLS being the authority who had taken over public functions, Gene saw no indication of their presence or that they had taken any steps to help the hospital or the college residents.

The day was getting on and Gene knew it was time to find shelter. He thought of the dumpster-concealed sleeping spot of the night before and considered returning. It would be better to not be a creature of habit. Repeating was a good way to invite being waylaid. Gene had kept an eye open on the way to the hospital for a likely place to stay. He saw a hidden spot, a nest-like place near the front steps of a church concealed by a huge old Blue Spruce with draping bows. The nest at the base of the tree was hidden by the low sweeping bows on one side and by the tall cement steps and exterior church wall on two other sides. In normal times, the cops would roust hobos out of it, but cops were non-existent these days. Gene watched from a distance both the lair and anything that might give away another watcher.

As daylight ebbed, Gene decided to enter and settle in for the night. He could sit leaning against the corner made by the steps and the church wall. By doing this, he could watch the opening where he crawled in. It appeared nobody had used this as a bedroom for a time.

Just about sunset, he heard two men walk up the walk, turn and climb the stairs to the church front. He could hear the key turning the ancient lock tumbler, the latch releasing, and the door opening as the two entered the building. Gene overheard part of their conversation. Apparently, there were some toughs roaming the city acting on behalf of the MLS who were confiscating any arms they could find. Someone by the name of Johnson or Johnston or Johington, Gene couldn't hear exactly, was supposedly authorized to perform this so-called police action. Gene made a mental note to watch for and avoid anything appearing like confiscation activity.

Restlessly sleeping, morning could not have come soon enough. Gene was stiff. He had made a point of being quiet and longed for the open spaces of the countryside. At least he would have some peace and privacy there, not so much here in the city. The other thing about the city was the utter lack of edible food. Gene neared the last of his rations obtained at Compound J and ate just enough to sustain his energy. He still had the care package given to him by Samuel. It was a meager breakfast. Gene emerged with his pack in place and considered going into the church. He might find out more about Johnston and the police action.

Climbing up the dozen or so steps of the old church, Gene had a feeling he was in the wrong place. It was the feeling he was slipping into or out of one of his other dream dimensions. *Darn, now isn't a good time*. He fought to maintain continuity. For a moment, he just stood and then the church door opened.

"Can I help you?" a voice said. "Fella, are you okay?"

Gene snapped back to reality. "Ah. . . Yes, I'm looking for some information."

"Please step in; you shouldn't be seen here and with the stuff you carry. You'll draw attention to yourself and to any with you," said the man as he closed and locked the door behind Gene.

The man introduced himself as Pastor Toliver. Pastor Toliver invited Gene to join him in a fellowship room where they both then sat.

"What do I call you?' he asked.

"I'm am Shaky," Gene replied.

"Come in and set, Toliver offered. "Would you like a glass of water?

"No, I am called Shakey. You're taking a big chance inviting a stranger like me into your church, aren't you?"

Pastor Toliver looked at him appraisingly and said, "In my experience, a man intending harm usually does his deed under the cover of darkness or the last half of the day. A man coming to a church door at the break of dawn usually has a mission in mind, not larceny. By your dress, you aren't from the city. You appear to be a sojourner, a traveler, not one of the typical derelicts we have seen here over the years. What is it you're looking for?"

Gene was taken aback by Pastor Toliver's observations. Gene explained his quest to find Bonnie. Pastor Toliver listened to the complete sordid story from Gene's capture by the Hoover compound until the hospital visit with Zack Smith. While Gene related his story, Toliver offered some sausage, fresh cheese furnished by some of his congeration, and crackers to Gene for breakfast. Gene thanked him and the Lord for the provisions.

"I am refreshed to see there are still some men of faith among us," Toliver proclaimed. "We talk of the tribulation and the end times and these times seem to resemble the tribulation without persecution of the Saints. I know Sam Hoover, Joe Mickelson, Mike, and John. Hoover and Joe are both good but strict men. This crisis fits Sam to a tee. He has spent his whole life preparing to administer a situation such as this last month has brought about. If any survive, it will be those under Hoover's management."

"Pastor, I'm curious. You don't seem to be bothered in the least by my weaponry. You don't seem threatened. You're as cool a cat as I've ever met. How is it you know Hoover and Mike?" asked Gene.

"Well, Sam Hoover is a member of my congregation. I have known him for over twenty years. Joe Mickelson ran an outreach for the homeless here in the city. You mentioned Johnny, or John, one of your escorts. He and I served in Desert Storm in the Special Forces together. Now if I can, I will try to help your friend Zack Smith get better care. A word spoken here and there can loosen the restraints on scarce and protected meds. You may not realize, but when you told me your name, I recognized it. Hoover's network is vast. Shaky is an unusual name and MLS has probably tagged it for more information. They will want to know what the buzz is about and what is significant about you. Be careful in its use around this city. You can check in here and if you need a haven, we have lots of room, a definite lack of beds, but room. Just be careful not to leave a trail as you come here. Don't lead a tail here."

Gene nodded his understanding. He asked if Pastor Toliver had any suggestions how Bonnie might be located. Toliver said there was a local gathering spot where the college students hung out. He felt Gene would raise suspicions if he went there, but there were people who would make discrete inquiries. He wanted to know about Bonnie, what she liked to do, what she looked like, and if Gene knew any of her friends or roommates. Gene explained about her and told of her shooting ability. Toliver looked up and scowled.

"Was she an active competitor?" he asked.

Gene affirmed she was.

Toliver launched into an expose, "I don't want to alarm you. When they started confiscating arms, the college was the first place they went. A list of Trap and Skeet Club members, the archery team, and a list of concealed carry holders was compiled by the MLS. They didn't stop there. They got lists of gun club members, hunting license holders, and gun purchase records from another list. They had addresses for many of those on the first list. My understanding is they took custody of many and interrogated them to gather information on others who owned guns. I pray your Bonnie wasn't one of them. In this part of the world, nearly everyone owns guns for hunting and personal protection. The MLS knows if their actions are perceived as illegitimate, then armed citizens will resist. The citizens' fear is if the MLS can make the martial law thing stick, then the MLS can hold a banned weapons possession charge over the head of anyone on the list. The idea is any arms that may have once been legal are now banned under declared martial law. We're not talking about the federal government here. We're talking about a self-appointed group of local politicians. They even came to question me here at the church. Can you imagine the audacity?"

Gene listened and his heart turned over as Toliver expounded. If true, things were serious and he intended to gather Bonnie and Samuel if he would come, go home and proceed to live away from the chaos.

"Pastor Toliver," Gene inquired, "would you have a spare Gideon Bible you could part with?"

"Well, that is an interesting question, Shaky," Toliver responded. "Of course I have one. Whatever do you want it for?"

"The Gideon is the scripture form I like to study and read from. I gave my last one to a guard at Joe's camp to encourage him," Shaky replied.

Chapter 9

Intrigue

G ene left by a side door after watching through a small window to see if the way was clear. Toliver had given him a signal to tap so he could get back in when he returned. Gene went to another clearinghouse and found no postings. He then went to a message board and likewise found no message from Bonnie there. He did locate one which Samuel had left for Bonnie.

Upon leaving, Gene noticed a young man pretending to study an object. When Gene moved out of sight around the corner, the young man was fast on Gene's trail. Being followed wasn't a familiar situation to Gene. He contemplated what he should do. He decided to proceed to the next message board some dozen blocks away, all the time keeping track of the tail's activities. Gene wasn't sure whether the tail was looking for an opportunity to mug him or if he was tracking Gene to see what his intentions might be. If the latter were the case, Gene would show the tail what he was about, simply looking for Bonnie. Gene knew the tail had been reading his postings. Gene reasoned, if he were going to mug him, it would be later or in an isolated location and likely both.

About mid-afternoon, Gene decided he would return to the church without the tail. He took an indirect route and did some misleading turns. The young man wasn't daunted. Gene went down an alley flanked by brick-walled buildings and stepped into a deep doorway to be out of sight. The young man walked past the alley and then returned looking disgusted. He started at a rapid pace toward the opposite open end. Just as he reached the doorway, Gene waited with his crossbow cocked and loaded. The tail realized his error. He pulled up short and stopped.

Gene casually said, "Did you lose something?"

"No, mister, I was just cutting through here to go home. Please don't rob me. I don't have much but you are welcome to it."

"Young fella, you're full of it. You should come up with a better explanation. I know you've been following me all day. Who are you and what do you want?" Gene demanded.

"Ah. . . I don't understand what you mean," lied the man.

Gene exclaimed, "That's it, you dog!" as he aimed the bow at the man's chest. "I want you to undress down to your shorts, NOW! Toss your clothes in to the trash bin there."

The young man protested a bit until Gene made a slight show of tightening his finger on the trigger. The desired action from the young man commenced, except instead of starting with his coat, he started with his shoes and pants. Instead of putting them in the trash bin, he just slid the shoes off and let the pants slide to the ground and stepped out.

"You should stop now and put your hands high in the air, just as high as you can reach," Gene stated very quickly.

Gene asked a series of questions and made a pointed statement, "Are you a cop?"

"I work for the county," the man stated.

Gene said, "Yes or no. Are you a cop?"

"No," the man said after a hesitation.

"What's your name?" Gene was terse.

"Sergio," came the reply.

At that moment, Sergio's arms had slowly lowered and Gene noted the change.

Gene stated as mater-of-factly, "Sergio, you should get those hands as high as you can. Have you ever seen what a razor broad head does to a deer or a wild hog? It kills because the target bleeds to death from the cutting, unlike a bullet that kills from shock. Would you like to try an arrow? You see, when this bolt penetrates any part of your body, sudden and rapid hemorrhage starts. When the body struggles, it causes the wound to bleed more rather than clotting up.

You become light headed just before you pass out and then die. Do you think you want to try for the pistol in your coat now?"

Gene went on, "I want you to turn around, then carefully remove your coat, being very careful not to make me think you're going for your gun. I haven't stuck anything for a week and I'm a bit nervous right now. When you have your coat off, throw it in the trash bin, then slowly turn around and with your right hand reaching high, take your gun out of its holster with your left hand, index finger and thumb only. Toss it over there into the trash bin with the other stuff. When you are done doing that, I want to see your complete birthday suit. DO YOU UNDERSTAND, SERGIO?"

Sergio complied and said nothing. When the coat was off, he revealed not only a Glock 9mm in a tie-down shoulder holster, but a smaller caliber tucked under the other armpit. Gene should have guessed, but the second gun was a bit of a surprise to him. It shouldn't have been, he carried two himself, one of which was hidden. Gene became more exact about what the crossbow was aimed at. He wanted Sergio to perceive this change. His eyes seemed to focus on the bolt with the broad head just feet from his chest. Gene carefully instructed Sergio to stay a distance beyond arm's reach for two reasons. Sergio could deflect a shot if he got a hand on any part of the weapon before the bolt completely launched. The second reason, the bolt would need to clear the bow to be most effective when launched.

Prompted by Gene clearing his throat, Sergio did as instructed and deposited his 9mm into the trash bin.

"Now, the other, and be smart, you understand? Turn around," growled Gene.

Sergio did as instructed, then unclipped his holster straps. Gene moved back and to the left just in case Sergio flung the holster at him.

"I would get that thought out of your head," Gene said. "Remember, a broad head makes a nasty cut. I've shot charging wild hogs." The information must have been effective because Sergio tossed the holster after the clothes and guns. Next came the T-shirt and then Sergio's boxers. Sergio made a remark about Gene's heritage, which Gene ignored.

"Sergio, I don't know why you were tailing me, but if you do it again, I will not, I repeat, will not be so generous. I want to know what you know about the confiscation of privately owned arms," Gene demanded.

"I don't know what you're talking about," replied Sergio.

"I will assume then you were planning to rob me and that I should treat you like an assailant," said Gene.

"I. . . wasn't," stammered Sergio.

"Sergio, you remember me and stay off my back and trail. That applies to your compatriots too. I certainly will remember you! Now, you should walk to the end of the alley, don't turn right or left and keep going into the alley beyond the street. When you feel you can outrun this arrow, you can run, hide, or throw rocks. This thing has an accurate range of a hundred and fifty yards and cuts just as well at that range as at two yards. Now, go!" commanded Gene.

Sergio didn't hesitate. He walked as if he were the drum major in a parade, every bit as proud and, Gene thought, as defiant as the compliant child who had been told to sit but was still standing on the inside. Instead of retreating out the other end of the alley, Gene followed Sergio down the alley. Sergio looked back one time and to his surprise, he saw Gene was still close behind.

"Keep movin', Sergio," Gene encouraged.

Gene stopped at the end of the alley and watched as Sergio kept walking. There was no doubt in Gene's mind Sergio would return for his goods. Gene replaced the broad head bolt with a bolt tipped with a target point. Gene raised the crossbow, anticipating Sergio's turn.

Gene yelled to Sergio, "I can reload before you get halfway back, if you get back at all. Keep going!" Gene anticipated an attempt to make Gene miss with a first shot in hopes to reach Gene before a second.

Sergio reached the next street and turned onto that street on a dead run. Gene changed his location to the end of the parallel block and watched. Sure enough, Sergio was making his way around the block back to the alley. Gene watched and picked his target. As Sergio slipped along a hedge for cover, Gene picked a cedar power pole just ahead of Sergio. When Sergio was close to the pole, Gene launched, sticking the bolt near Sergio's head with a vibrating thud. *If Sergio had been clothed, laundry would have been in order,* thought Gene.

Gene said to himself with a slight grin, "That should keep him for a while."

Gene realized he may have just made a major mistake. One shouldn't humiliate an enemy. The humiliation can come back to haunt a person. Sergio had been humiliated three times within ten minutes. Gene should have just dispatched him, but to kill without reason wasn't proper in Gene's mind.

Gene worked his way back near the church without further incident. He studied the neighborhood surrounding the church and saw nothing before advancing. Just as he stepped out to go to the side door, he saw two people watching. He nonchalantly changed his approach and proceeded to the tree-covered lair. He knew they knew he was there. They must be aware of the lair as well. He believed they didn't know he knew they were watching. From between the drooping tree limbs, he could see their movements, however slight.

After a while, darkness overtook the street and it being a dark night, he decided to venture out and around the opposite side of the church. He hoped there weren't other spies on the other side. When able to get back near the base of the church, he found a rock and tapped the entry signal series. By keeping to a discrete track, Gene made his way to the side door where he quietly tapped the signal a second time. The door opened in the dark and Gene slipped in. The door closed behind him as quietly as it had opened.

"Shaky, I don't believe they had a clue. They have been watching all afternoon," said Toliver.

"Who are they?" asked Gene.

"We think they are part of the MLS. They could be thugs scoping us out for a hit, but they seem too sophisticated for that. How did you get past them?" asked Toliver.

Gene replied, "They think I'm still under the tree out front. I slipped out and around the back of the church. I hoped you heard my first signal and they didn't."

Toliver motioned Gene to follow him to the fellowship hall, where he lit a candle.

"Have you eaten anything today?" Toliver inquired.

"A little. Food is mighty scarce here in the city. I'll be glad to be in the wilderness where a man can eat his fill," replied Shaky.

Toliver inquired about Shaky's day and whether he had found a trace of Bonnie. Gene said he hadn't found a thing and explained his time had been occupied by the tail, Sergio. Gene told of the events with a slight touch of humor in his voice. He apologized to Toliver about his amusement because he didn't feel right to be amused at the expense of another. He just couldn't help himself.

Toliver stated he knew Sergio. Sergio had been a school principal before the EMP. He wasn't sure why he tracked Gene or was carrying heat. Toliver offered Gene a small amount of wine that Gene declined. He knew his current constitution would melt under the effects of alcohol. He declined and requested more water if available instead.

"Shaky, I put out some feelers about Bonnie," said Toliver. "I think we have a lead. One of my congregation knows her. She thinks Bonnie is gone to ground around 23rd and Pichone. That's a rough part of the city now. If you go there, you should not go by yourself. We could be there before the sun is up if we leave early. What do you think?"

Gene considered, and after reviewing today's events, felt company would be good. Toliver, being familiar with the city, would be a useful guide and his help would slick the process along.

"I think the goons outside will be gone by morning. We should get an early start," said Toliver. "I'm going to hit the sack."

The day's events started in the dark before dawn. Gene was up and packed. He looked up to see the flicker of Toliver's candle as he emerged out of the church recesses. Toliver, who was already dressed for the day, turned and Gene followed him to the front doors of the church. The big door opened with a slight squeak, prompting a growl from Toliver. "Need to grease that."

They descended the steps and turned to the north. Gene watched the back trail.

"If they're there and see you watching, you'll give our surprise away. Try to be discrete. That way we can make a move at our timing," Toliver commented.

They walked for an hour and turned a corner just before the sun peaked over the mountain to the east. The street was littered with all kinds of junk and cars that hadn't moved in a month. Some had flat tires and on others, the tires were low. As soon as Gene and Toliver started down the street, heads peeked out of windows of older disabled cars. The makeshift bedrooms allowed a measure of security if one could manually lock the doors at night. Newer cars didn't offer this luxury as most of the door locks were electronic. The ultimate security would be a knife or pistol in case of break-in while the occupant was sleeping. To break in would be noisy. The one pitfall was the vulnerability to fire from the outside. One had to understand the social workings of the neighborhood to live. This system had become more finely tuned and evolved in the last short month.

If Bonnie were in the area, she would be a leader if they didn't kill her first. Her personality was just that type. She was a natural leader with a take-charge quality about her. As Toliver and Gene approached what looked to be a central point of the neighborhood, a giant of a man stepped out of a doorway to the left.

"You," he demanded. "Stop right there."

Bonnie was shaken awake by a roommate. "Bonnie, there are strangers in the street!"

It was early for anyone to be in the street. The people here had an innate suspicion of outsiders since the raids of the MLS. The MLS had pillaged anything of value under the guise of declaring martial law. These strangers were armed. They were either Gestapo or rebels. When Bonnie looked out the second story window, she gasped. The shabby skinny little old man with the crossbow looked like Daddy. Bonnie grabbed her coat and flew down the stairs to the door. Her friend Thor was bigger than a barn and a physical specimen of Zeus himself. He had been on the university football team. He played guard position and had been named All-American guard the last two years running. Thor had challenged the two strangers with the authority that the giant 6-foot 9-inch three-hundred-forty pound size possesses. He had no friendship in his demeanor or his eyes and the bat in his hand emphasized that authority.

"Thor," Bonnie exclaimed, "that's my daddy!"

Thor didn't look away but closed to an uncomfortable distance where those long arms and bat length could span the distance before Gene or Toliver could blink an eye. Gene thought the intimidation was greater than the menace.

"You don't say. Which one, the little scrawny dude, or the preacher? How are you, Preacher?" Thor inquired.

"I'm doing well, Thor," replied Toliver. "Haven't seen you in church lately. You doing okay?"

"Ya, been busy protectin' the flock," Thor flatly stated. "The Man has been leaning on the citizens a lot lately. They are some hesitant about setting foot in here these days. I don't understand why, but they have proclaimed us as outlaws."

"Come on, Thor, you know the preacher isn't my dad," chided Bonnie as she gave Gene a big hug over all his gear.

Gene could see a slight smile on Thor's face. The group of people had grown to a dozen people scattered strategically and Thor turned toward the building he had come from.

"Daddy, what are you doing here? How is Mama? Have you heard from Seth?" She bombarded him with question after question, just as Samuel had.

"I've come to take you home if you wanted to go. Mom is with Jake and Meg and conditions in the city wherever I've been are deteriorating."

He explained he had seen Samuel and Janna briefly and they were intent on staying to minister at the Salvation Army shelter.

"I would have gone there," said Bonnie, "but my being there would bring trouble to them. I've been declared an outlaw by the MLS. They don't need my kind of trouble."

"Will your return home with me? You would be better off than here in the city," Gene said with a bit of trepidation.

"Yes, if you think we can escape the MLS," she replied. "It won't take me five minutes to pack."

Thor, who had been listening patiently, finally directed his comment toward Gene, "You're taking my right hand lady, ya know. She's the best organizer in this community. But if I could go all the way home to Saint Louis, I would do it in a heartbeat. It's good you found us when you did. We're moving out to settle a new community away from the influence of the MLS. That isn't for publication, you understand. Somehow, they seem to know what our plans are as soon as we do."

"Thor, do you know a man by the name of Hoover or Michelson?"

"Ya, I know Hoover. Met him in church. What about him?" Thor replied.

Gene told Thor about the loose knit compound origination and said he would be seeing Hoover on his way out of the valley. "Hoover tells me the MLS is planting spies.

They actually thought I was a spy until a lady from my past identified me. I would consider their blueprint. I've seen it and it works better than any other society I've seen lately. Are you interested?"

"I know Hoover well, Thor," added Toliver. "I would be glad to talk with him if you want. I also know Michelson well. Both are straight shooters as I believe you to be. I can go with Shaky and Bonnie from here to see Hoover. I'll bring back word if I know where to meet you."

"Preacher, I'll tell you in secret, but you only," said Thor.

The two walked away from the gathering discussing the situation and the conditions. In the meantime, Bonnie appeared with her pack ready to depart. The bruise on her cheek started to show in the early morning light. Gene hadn't seen it in the twilight before. He lifted his tremoring hand and touched the bruise lightly.

Bonnie showed signs of physical weariness. It wasn't like her to be weak, but she was. Bonnie explained the MLS had beaten her badly when they came to search for her prize skeet gun. She didn't remember a lot following the raid. It had taken two weeks for her to regain her faculties. Thor and two friends found her beaten and unconscious. They moved her to their safe house where she was nursed. Slow as recuperation had been, she'd returned to a resemblance of a human.

Chapter 10

Pool

After finding Bonnie in such a shape from the beating the MLS had given her, they traveled slow and took long rest spells to give her time to recuperate.

Pastor Toliver led the way back to the church. Gene and Bonnie waited some distance away secluded so it would appear Toliver was alone. He entered the church by way of the front door, remained inside for a time, then emerged and walked toward Gene and Bonnie's spot of seclusion.

As he walked past them he said, "I have a tail" and kept walking.

Gene stayed quiet watching where Toliver had come from. A moment later, a man followed Toliver down the street and around the corner. Gene and Bonnie followed the tail at a distance and soon the tail became aware of their presence. Stopping, he waited casually until Gene and Bonnie approached.

"You people know there is an ordinance against people carrying arms since marshal law has gone into affect," he addressed them as he produced his pistol pointing it at Gene. "I am confiscation these and you are to come with me. Now, hand me your crossbow and the other weapons you are carrying."

Gene resisted the demand verbally even while facing a pistol that looked old enough to have been with the cavalry at The Little Big Horn. "I'm not sure what authority you believe you have, but . . . . . ."

"NOW," he interrupted.

Gene acquiesced and started uncocking the bow. He wasn't about to hand a loaded bow over to the man. The man gripped the bow and eyed it like a salivating dog. Just that moment a click from behind his left ear stiffened him like a board. As instructed, he unhanded the bow, releasing it back to Gene and along with his old pistol. Gene handed the pistol to Bonnie, who was seething. A second later, she struck the man on the top of his head with a down stroke meant to kill. The man's pistol split his own scalp and the man crumpled unconscious on the ground. A quick search yielded ammo for the old .38 and further search found the driver's license identifying the unconscious man as Leland Charles Morris. Mr. Morris seemed to have nothing of other importance. Toliver kept the driver's license, explaining the information would be added to the underground information logs. Gene hadn't heard of an "underground" or "information logs." Gene didn't ask. He just cocked and loaded the bolt for immediate use if needed.

No further incident occurred on the way to Compound J. Mike opened the gate for Pastor Toliver personally and greeted Gene as he walked through.

"Joe, we need to confab a bit," Toliver said.

As they walked away, Gene saw Toliver hand Morris's license to Joe. They talked a few minutes and then Joe and Pastor Toliver returned to where Bonnie and Gene stood.

"Shaky, Pastor Toliver tells me this is the daughter you were looking for," said Joe. "I'm glad you were successful. You also were looking for a son as I recall. Did you find him?"

"Yes," said Gene. "He and his wife are ministering at the Salvation Army Camp like you said. They're well, but they're remaining here in the city. May I ask a favor of you? Will you allow Bonnie to stay here while I go to see them? I need to assure myself they really want to remain. I also told them I would check in with them before I left."

"That should be no problem," said Joe. "The pastor here tells me she has been declared a fugitive, so she will need to stay inconspicuous until you leave. MLS is flexing a lot now and we can't have her caught here if she has been declared. You need to make your trip fast and get back."

"Thank you, I'll leave in the morning early and be back as soon as I can," said Gene.

The trio was directed to sleeping quarters and fed the same soup substance Gene had experienced before prior to retiring. This time the soup had delicious flavor.

Journal entry:

"I've been able to locate Bonnie. She's been beaten badly and is in slow recovery. The people she was with seemed to have saved her life. She is quite anxious to go home but a bit angry. She has an underlying current of anger I don't quite understand. Today, she acted with a greater viciousness than I would have ever believed possible coming from her. I believe, had she been left to her own means, she might have killed a man today."

Having left before daybreak, Gene knew the way to the Salvation Army Center. He arrived without incident and requested the door attendant to call Samuel. It took only a few minutes for Samuel to appear. He greeted his dad as if it had been months, not days, since he had seen him. Samuel, not unlike his sister, bombarded Gene with questions again before Gene could answer the first. Gene answered them in order of importance.

He explained Bonnie was okay and waiting to meet Gene when he returned. Gene explained she had been beaten and robbed, and there were people who were looking for her. She was staying out of sight. Gene inquired again if Samuel would go home with him and Bonnie. Samuel declined, stating he and Janna were doing the Lord's work here. Gene acknowledged this and then they turned to other topics.

They discussed Samuel's family and their welfare. Gene knew he would have to take news back to Jessie or not come home at all. The kids were learning servant-hood and how to make do with what was at hand. They weren't starving and they were developing a good spiritual life. Samuel apologized that the kids were not available. They had gone with Janna to the storehouse to bring back provisions for the next meal. It would be several hours before their return. Disappointed as Gene was, he understood. He bade Samuel to convey his love to each of them and to Janna.

"Samuel, I need to leave. Bonnie is waiting and she needs to be gone from Riverton right away," said Gene.

Samuel wanted to know more, but Gene explained there were details that would be of no benefit to Samuel. Many details Samuel did not want to have knowledge of for his own safety. He explained to Samuel that Samuel shouldn't tell people he even knew his sister or who she was. Bonnie's pursuers were deadly serious and knowing too much might bring peril to Samuel and his family. He went on to explain Bonnie hadn't done anything wrong, but it was what she knew not, what she had done, that was causing the difficulty.

Gene departed with a heavy heart and after a bit, controlled his emotions enough to become aware of his surroundings. He worked his way back to Compound J, where Bonnie and Pastor Toliver awaited his return. He negotiated that section of city streets back to Compound J went without incident or complications.

Bonnie was busy helping in the infirmary with a young woman who was in pain. Gene didn't know the cause or extent of the illness. He preferred to stay removed from such activities when possible.

Toliver was talking with Joe and when Gene appeared, they walked toward him.

"I've been filling Joe in on Thor's situation," said Toliver. "I'm still going to see Hoover as well, but Joe may be able to assist from this location better."

The next leg of the journey home was on the way out of town by way of Hoover's compound. Gene remembered the heavily-armed guard escort from there to Compound J and wondered aloud if the return trip would be as perilous. When he mentioned this to Joe, Joe explained the people coming in generally carried goods. The people going out of the city were generally empty of supplies and not subject to robbery as often. Going out, one didn't want to look laden.

After one more night in Compound J, the three departed before daybreak. This trek was longer than the distance from the Salvation Army Camp to Compound J. Walking would take them the better part of the day to get there. These longer early spring days were starting to get hot. Gene and Bonnie had reduced the clothing they wore in order to stay cool. This, of course, exposed Gene's .357 and the .38 that Bonnie now carried. Toliver didn't change anything about his dress. He kept his worn suit coat in place. Once Gene detected the bulge of a weapon at Toliver's back and a bulge under Toliver's left arm pit.

An interesting conversation developed when Gene asked Toliver a question. "Pastor, now that you are a preacher and not in the Special Forces, what is your opinion on carrying weapons that potentially may have to take the life of a fellow man?"

Toliver didn't hesitate a moment before answering, "If you are asking theologically, I would quote 'Thou shall not kill,' which is the Sixth Commandment. To be more precise, it says 'Thou shall not murder.' If God would have meant the translation to say 'kill,' He wouldn't have armed his armies of old and wiped out groups and tribes of people, men, women, babes, and animals. To kill in war is justified. To kill those who are innocent is murder. Killing to rob is murder. Killing in self-defense or in defense of others is not murder.

"You are a man of faith and you carry arms for what reason? Jesus said, 'He who murders in his heart is guilty of murder' and He says, 'when you break any of the commandments, you are guilty of breaking them all.' So if I covet my neighbor's wife, I am guilty of and have committed murder. We all, each, and every one, have broken one or all the commandments at some time in our life. By definition, that is why we are sinners. That is why through the grace of God we have the sacrifice of Jesus Christ to cover the guilt of those sins for us.

"If you are asking philosophically, in our society we generally think we have the right to defend ourselves and our loved ones. We teach in self-defense classes one should use the weapon needed to neutralize the threat or threatening party. Using a gun isn't always the solution. The proper weapon might be a Tazer, a billy club, rubber bullets, a beanbag gun, pepper spray, and or even martial arts training. Depending upon one's ability, an old lady may use a gun where a hulking man may only need a billy club or less for self-defense. On the other hand, if the old lady is the aggressor with the gun, the hulk may need a gun of his own for self-defense.

"Now, if you are asking as a matter of practically, it isn't practical to not be prepared for the worst possible situation. One always prepares for the worst. In all cases, judgment goes a long way in avoiding difficult situations so paramount. In days prior to the EMP, there wasn't always a cop nearby to help with an instant solution. Now, these days there are no cops close or far away. The ultimate responsibility of protecting one's self and family falls to one's self.

"Now, if you are asking carnally, some people just like packing heat because packing makes them feel tough. It's their ego kick. Packing too is like a drug that wears off. Eventually, the guy or gal looks for a bigger, better, and more exciting high to satisfy their ego. Many become outspoken and boisterous. Some of them start pushing and provoking. They are the ones who eventually get into a scrape when the situation would have been totally avoidable."

"I haven't preached a sermon for nearly a week," finished Toliver.

They walked in silence for the better part of two hours.

Toliver said quietly, "We have picked up some company."

Behind a couple hundred feet following were three men. Gene stopped and brushed Bonnie's elbow. She stopped and, watching her dad's action, stood with her back to him. He made a show of drawing his pistol, unloading and palming the shells, and reloading the .357. Bonnie followed the act plainly in sight of the followers. The idea was to give second thoughts to any watching. Gene believed the show to be effective. He believed in his heart that half of winning the battle was to assure your opponent your strength was real. It was real. The idea was akin to the Mutual Assured Destruction nuclear program. If they know you have it and believe you will use it, they might just back off.

Toliver smiled. "That is the difference between you and me. I would prefer to have them underestimate my strengths and abilities. But on the other hand, I have so many weapons and skills at my disposal I wouldn't be able to display all of them. And I have God on my side and when God is with me, who can be against me?"

Gene believed that. To trust is difficult for an average man or woman. Gene believed God also provides self-confidence, training, and other tools as part of the help He provides.

96

The three following didn't gain or lose distance. Then of a sudden, one was gone. Toliver explained the followers were about to take action. He pointed out a good rifleman could take one or two out before they safely could gain cover. The missing third man would likely be carrying instructions for such an action to take place just ahead of them.

"We have three choices," explained Toliver. "We can proceed as we are, we can change direction, or we can do the unexpected: charge those dudes behind us. I vote for the latter."

"Me too!" said Gene and Bonnie in unison.

"OK then. On three, we turn and go as hard as we can. Don't leave anyone behind." Toliver referred to Bonnie with a glance. "You ready? One. . . two. . . three!"

All three broke into a run to the rear. Their follorwers were startled when they finally discovered the charge. They hadn't been attending business and were caught off guard. By the time they were alerted, the two-hundred-feet following distance had shrunken to less than a hundred. Toliver shot with a sprint to the nearest man who stumbled all over his own feet trying to turn and escape. Without slowing, Toliver caught the man with a hand chop to the neck just above the shoulder. The man dropped to one knee, then fell to the side. By the time Toliver reached the second tail, Gene reached the first. The man now trying to rise was ordered by Gene to stay down and keep his hands in sight. Toliver in the meantime caught the second tail and simply jerked him backward by his collar, dumping him roughly to the ground. The man was begging Toliver not to hurt him. Then the questioning started in earnest. Gene in turn asked a few questions of the first man, but had little skill at interrogation.

Toliver was correct in the assumption the third man had been sent ahead with instructions for an ambush. After further coercing, Toliver extracted that the location of the ambush wasn't more than a hundred yards ahead.

The decision was made to go off-road in an irregular track circling around the attackers, keeping them off guard, and uncertain where they would appear next. Doing that was risky but safer than being predictable. The two pursuers' hands were tied with cord found on themselves. *Thank you very much.* They were gagged for assured quiet. The two being retained were to only to be released after the group passed through the gates of Hoover's compound. With them on either side, chances a so-called sharp shooter would make a try were reduced significantly. There was always the chance a shooter could be someone with training like Johnny or Toliver. There were, of course, the country boys who cut their teeth on a gun barrel. Gene himself and Bonnie were some of those as well.

Toliver lead an inexact trek between houses, over and through fences, through orchards, and in the bottom of irrigation ditches. Toliver looked with skill ahead to avoid unwanted encounters and Gene and Bonnie watched behind and to the sides. Twice, Toliver backtracked and changed direction, avoiding makeshift camps. He stayed away from the river, as most the refugee camps had located near the river's banks.

Mid-afternoon brought the party within sight of the Hoover camp. The scattered population had increased and Toliver entered via the pavement that led to the front of the compound gate. As they reached the entrance gate, the guard was hailed. Hoover was summoned and within minutes, he appeared.

"Mr. Hoover, it's Shaky and Pastor Toliver with my daughter Bonnie. May we come in?" Gene requested.

"Well, Shaky, we never expected to see you again, so we filled your position, and we have a pastor, so that position is taken too," Hoover chided. "If, however, you would like to enter as our guest, we would be pleased to have you."

The two captives were unbound and released with a warning they needed to quit their felonious activities. The next victim may not be so charitable. Toliver threw the binding cord to the midsection of the first man saying. "We don't have a need here for this."

Gene, Bonnie, and Toliver entered where Bonnie went to the nearest wall and sat in obvious exhaustion. One of the guards approached her and offered her a better resting spot around the corner. The evening meal had passed, but Hoover, seeing Bonnie's exhaustion, sent a runner to the cook shack. In the meantime, their weapons were removed by the guards. Hoover gestured toward Gene's hidden shoulder holster and Gene smiled a little at Hoover's memory, then relinquished his hideaway without hesitation. Toliver, to Gene's surprise, also relinquished two fine stainless 9mm automatics. Toliver shrugged and smiled as if to say, "You didn't ask, I didn't tell."

When the guard returned from the cook shack, he carried bowls of porridge for each of the travelers. The soup filled a hole and soon Bonnie was asleep on her feet. A lady took her by the arm and guided her to an empty cot in the woman's quarters. This wasn't without her being further searched for additional dangerous tools.

Morning arrived like always. When Gene exited the barracks, he could see Toliver and Hoover talking. Gene could hardly believe they had arisen before he had. As Gene walked in their direction, they turned toward him.

"We're making plans to contact this Thor fella," said Hoover. "I want to talk with Bonnie about him for additional background. I know I've met him but am afraid I don't know him well. If we are to offer an alliance and our working model to them as the preacher here believes we should, we need to know who they are."

"I can't say what Bonnie knows about him," said Gene. "She told me Thor and his friends found her and nursed her until she was able to do for herself. She still hasn't recuperated fully yet. Thor comes from someplace in the Midwest, maybe Saint Louis. He's an All-American football player two years running. He's huge in stature. He seems to be not fond of the MLS. Toliver knows him better I think."

Later after a light porridge breakfast, somewhat the same as supper the night before, when questioned, Bonnie was reluctant to give information about Thor. After she understood it was for a good purpose, she answered a few questions. Bonnie being a loyal person by nature seemed thoughtful before expounding on what she knew. She didn't add much over and above what Toliver and Hoover already knew. Their interest was mostly in Thor's style of management. They were reserved about helping to setup a tyrant. Bonnie described Thor as a reluctant leader who had been pressed by the community into taking charge. His decisions were thought through before he took action. Also, he didn't like being the muscle but was the muscle for obvious reasons. He of all people understood the subtleties in the use of power and force. His understanding of physical leverage was not unlike the understanding of logistics management.

Gene wanted to and was anxious to get movin'. He desired to be beyond the obscure radius of scavengers who advanced into the countryside daily to forage for food. He wanted to accomplish that before they stopped for the night. He had reservations whether Bonnie could go that far in a day. She was tough but wasn't near 100% yet. Maybe not even 50% yet. He suspected the radius had expanded in the last couple of weeks since he had first passed through. Many of the resources, like rabbit and prairie dogs, would be less plentiful in the zone. Gene was hungry—not like wanting a meal, but like not having had a steak or bacon and eggs for three months.

John and another man accompanied Gene and Bonnie away from the compound for a couple miles then broke off to tend to other business. They rested frequently before pushing on. Noon according to the sun came and went. Gene found hardened Pinon tree sap, a resin to chew as they walked. It tasted of turpentine when first chewed but after a while, it turned into a pliable gum pleasant for the chewing. Gene learned as a child Pinon gum was a resource that helped keep one's mouth moist. The other thing Gene liked very much was to chew freshly shelled wheat kernels. Wheat made a fine gum and the taste was more palatable. There, however, was no wheat to be found these days.

Gene with amusement thought back fifty years about the time a city cousin spent the summer with Gene's family at the farm. Gene had broken off a nodule of hardened Pinon gum and popped it into his mouth. At first it broke similar to chewing a bank counter sucker. It didn't taste as good, but the objectionable taste dissipated after a while. The cousin thought if his younger cousin could chew the sap from the tree trunk, he could too. He would be smarter and get some easier to chew and not so hard. The only problem, the cousin gathered softer pliable sap deposits and popped them into his mouth. The sticky substance immediately acted like glue when bitten down on. Cousin Kyle couldn't open his mouth for hours without pulling his teeth. Needless to say to expel the horrid uncured turpentine taste and fumes was impossible. Kyle thought Gene had played a cruel trick and promised to exact vengeance. The summer became considerably more interesting after that.

By mid-afternoon, Bonnie was simply tuckered. They located a campsite that concealed them from searching eyes above and below. Daylight faded and Gene hadn't seen a morsel anywhere to eat. He went hunting supper in whatever form it may be. As he stalked imaginary quarry, an occasional bird would fly through or land near his location. There seemed to be no succulent meal any place in the local.

Stopped and studying the landscape, Gene heard what sounded like a child's voice pleading. Among a thicker grove of Juniper trees, he squatted and waited. He listened and watched. A moment or two passed and he observed a big man, a somewhat overweight man dragging a girl by the wrist. He dragged her near the trees where Gene watched from. As they got closer, she was begging him not to do it again. He said nothing and just continued to pull her along. It wasn't a big task for him as he easily outweighed her more than a hundred plus pounds.

When they arrived at a place where a couple dead falls had crossed just about twenty five or thirty feet down hill and to the left of where Gene watched from, the girl pleaded, "Please, Mr. Pool, not again."

Just then, he slapped her so hard Gene thought her head might come off. She landed and crumpled near one of the logs nearly life-less. Mr. Pool hadn't noticed Gene as he moved in. This Pool fella seemed to be distracted by the anticipation of his plan. He started to unbuckle the straps on his overalls and just about the time he let them slip to his feet, Gene quietly said, "Mr. Pool, I think the young lady doesn't want that to happen again. Is that right?"

Standing there in a dirty pair of Daffy Duck printed boxers, his overalls around the calves of his legs, the startled look on his face turned to a look of hatred and anger. He grabbed at his pants and pulled them mostly up while holding them with his left hand and then pulled a hunting knife from its sheath in the pocket and started at Gene over the nearest log. Gene pulled the trigger on the crossbow, intending to catch him at the height of the hurdle over the log. Pool was faster than Gene expected and the bolt went high, catching him in the right temple just behind his eye socket embedding itself in the back of his skull on the inside. Pool took two steps toward Gene, stopped, took three staggering steps backward, and sat down hard atop the log he had jumped. His eyes were open. His breathing was no longer heavy, but shallow and even. He just sat there. He seemed to be in a trance.

Gene reloaded his crossbow with one of his last bolts and worked his way around to where the girl sat like she was in a trance. Gene inquired, "Young lady, are you alright?"

She looked at him, then started sobbing uncontrollably. Gene had not a clue what to do so he just let her sob for a long time. Gene was now suffering from tremors so bad, he could hardly keep a quiet hand and had to steady himself on a nearby tree. The adrenaline in his body now caught up with him and his trembling lasted for some time. The shaking finally subsided some just as the girl's sobs let up a bit. Gene inquired about who she was and where she belonged. All the time, he watched Mr. Pool. Pool just sat. He didn't even fall over but breathed slowly and steadily.

The girl said her name was Amanda. They were from a camp about a half mile down the hill. Gene asked if she could find her way there and she said, "Please don't leave me. He might come after me." Gene didn't believe that to be the case, but he agreed to accompany her partway to the camp.

As they traversed the hillside, Gene inquired as to who Mr. Pool was. Amanda said he had come into their camp and taken over. He took what he wanted as he wanted and he had taken her once before. He had killed one young man and scared the other men into submission. He claimed to be the camp protector. Amanda's mom had tried to protect her from him and he had beaten her badly with a threat to kill Amanda if she interfered further.

Within a hundred yards of the community, Gene watched her descend into the camp and as she entered, hardly a soul turned to watch her as she came in. It was as if she had been out on a casual hike. Gene thought he should go back to where they left Pool sitting. Then Gene could determine what should be done there.

Gene now was starting to second-guess himself and what he had done. Might there have been another way to stop Pool's attack on the girl? Did Gene really have to shoot? Would Pool have done anything to him? He answered his own questions one at a time. His final conclusion was the shooting couldn't have been avoided.

Upon nearing the two crossed dead falls, Gene couldn't see Pool anywhere and thought he must have fallen behind one of the logs. When Gene surveyed the site, Pool was nowhere to be seen. Gene knew Pool hadn't returned to the camp by the trail they'd taken. Gene could clearly see the trail as he and Amanda returned to camp.

He worked up and around the logs and Pool just wasn't there. His first thought was he might be tracking a wounded bear that could turn instantly on its pursuer and kill or maim beyond recuperation. Spots of blood had fallen on the log where Pool sat, but not much like one would expect from a head wound. Studying Pool's tracks easily seen in the adobe clay dust gave Gene an indication Pool had gotten up and started away from the log. He walked with an uneven gait, one of a drunken man. After a mile or so, Gene determined Pool was well away from the camp and probably disoriented. Gene didn't understand how a man with an arrow through his brain could continue to even function, let alone travel. Gene gave up the trail and worked his way back to his own camp where Bonnie anxiously waited.

"Where have you been? I was getting worried," she scolded.

"Well, it's a long story. It'll keep," Gene said. "Do you think you will feel like traveling tomorrow?"

"I think so," she replied. "Well, what?"

"I said, it'll keep," Gene snapped, which wasn't his usual style.

Bonnie looked at him with wonder at what must have upset her dad in a way she had seldom seen. What could be so wrong he wouldn't talk about it? Being so exhausted, she didn't dwell on the observation but dropped into a fitful sleep for most of the night.

Gene hadn't told her of the afternoon events. She would need to know eventually, but for now, in her condition, he'd rather she rested the night. He would resume tracking Mr. Pool tomorrow.

It's funny when there is little perception of any existing law, a few renegades can make things seem like they have no societal rules to follow at all. Actually, it's not funny at all. The tragedy is one must resort to self-preservation when there is little hope of a real cop being around. The danger is, in exercising one's self defense, one stands in danger of being the target of accusations and of being lawless themselves. In the old days, there existed Miner's Law and Range Law and Civil City law, and the King's Law. Which ever law it was, it was law. Now there wasn't any form of law except the strongest rule. Current law enforcement, if it existed, couldn't communicate or even travel because of the EMP. The bigger towns like Riverton had a sort of martial law but it was just a set of dictatorial sort of strongman rules. There were loosely organized vigilante groups in some areas now. These hadn't had time to solidify into a consistent structure. One wants to stay away from those areas for concern of being tagged with a trumped-up violation. That could very well become fatal.

Gene was concerned Mr. Pool had likely died as a result of aggressive action toward himself and others. Gene even felt worse because it may have been Gene who had dispatched him. Gene, however, had long since learned he would take a predetermined action in a given situation. Indecision can get a man killed. Gene learned to know in advance what he should do in any given situation when the time came. That deal with the Amanda girl and Pool coming at him with his hunting knife had been decided long past even though Gene had never seen him before.

Now came the question of what Gene would answer to God for. Gene prayed and asked his forgiveness and further guidance. Somehow, Gene felt in his heart he had acted with justification. The condition of "my soul" didn't bother Gene nearly as much as the condition of Mr. Pool wondering around in the wilderness with a bolt driven through his head. Gene had known several people who lived with nails from nail guns and re-bar, and one with a fence picket stuck in his head. They all had access to the best medical services available. Well, Gene would track Pool tomorrow and give assistance if possible or confirm Pool's fate.

Before dawn broke, Gene had awoken and laid quietly listening to the early morning sounds. One of Gene's greatest joys was listening to God's creatures without interruption from the mechanized world in the early morning. He had long since learned one can tell what the day may be like by listening and watching nature and its actions.

This summer morning was cool, very cool, enough to frost and too it seemed cooler because of the moisture held by the air. His nose was cool and there was frost on his sleeping bag.

Before Bonnie awoke just after sunrise, Gene had a small camp-fire lit with some water heating. His small gas camp stove had long since run out of fuel. They had no tea or coffee for the hot water but he'd found some Mormon tea that when dried well made an excellent brew for the morning's tea. He brewed it. Rose hips made a much better tea but they hadn't found any the last couple of days. The problem with Mormon tea was, it worked like a laxative when too much was drank and seein' how they had not eaten much the last few days there wasn't much too lax. Boy, what all those TV and Internet weight loss programs didn't know before the EMP.

Bonnie's movements were stiff and slow as now she moved about. The bruise on the left side of her face and around her left eye now had turned a faded ugly purple and yellow and shades between. She held her right arm with her left hand, rubbing it gently.

"Purty sore, aren't ya?" Gene inquired as a statement more than a question.

"Yes," she said and then with some acid in her voice added, "I know you don't like my cussin', Daddy, but if I ever see that bastard again, I'm likely to cut his ears off and feed 'em to 'im. He didn't have to beat me up like that. On top of that, he took my skeet gun, the one I won at the turkey shoot last year." She had been fuming over the theft since.

The ladies in Gene's family had always been good shots and very competitive. They were in most cases better shots than the men. These ladies were not to be scoffed at. They could hunt, fish, track, handle livestock, cook, sew, and wash pots and pans too. Now the men could cook as well, but the girl's biscuits won every time. It is interesting how there are traits that run through families and the blood born women in Gene's family. Them being able to shoot and compete was more natural than having babies, although they had babies well too. Sis still lets Brother wear the pants even if she does shoot better.

Gene said, "Bonnie, there's some very serious things happened last evening".

Gene laid out the events. She looked at him with a look of shock and surprise as he elaborated on the intended ravishment of Amanda and the encounter that resulted from the attack. He perceived the look of shock and apologized to her for being so descriptive.

"No, Daddy, it's OK," she said. "I needed to know."

Gene went on to describe how he had tracked Mr. Pool and gave up after a time. Gene explained he intended to track Pool further to discover what happened to him. Bonnie seemed overly concerned for Amanda's emotional welfare and said so. Gene told her as near as he could tell, Amanda was okay, back and safe with her camp. Somehow, Gene got the feeling from Bonnie he as a man just didn't have an understanding of the effects the attacks would have on Amanda. Well, he wasn't sure he did, but he had done the best by her he could do by rescuing her. What else could he do? What else was he supposed to do? He'd likely killed a man at that and that action had exacted its own price upon Gene's mind.

After the morning sun had warmed their camp they broke to move out. Bonnie said she wanted to follow up with Amanda and if possible talk with her. Gene was reluctant and wanted to get on with tracking Mr. Pool. Bonnie beyond any reason Gene could understand insisted on seeing Amanda, so he reluctantly agreed and they worked their way in the direction where Gene had left Amanda. On the knoll above the camp, they stopped and watched their surroundings and back trail. Some in camp stirred about, but the attitude certainly seemed to be one of the whipped and downtrodden.

Bonnie asked for a more complete description of the girl. Gene hadn't really taken notice of details other than Amanda was young, maybe sixteen, youthful and slender. His eye for that kind of detail was lacking. Maybe she had light brown hair. Like everybody else, her hair was a bit dirty, dull and greasy.

Bonnie started down through a shallow draw toward the camp and up the far side to near its outskirts. There were four or five who saw her. They just stood and looked. No one made an offer to greet or even acknowledge her presence. Bonnie approached a haggard-looking woman and Gene could see a short discussion. The old lady gestured toward a makeshift shelter on the far end of the clearing. Bonnie quietly walked to the shelter and stood a moment. Gene saw a lady come out with a solid stick ready for action. Bonnie backed away a step or two and raised her hands in surrender as if to say she meant no offense. Gene was ready to make a charge resembling the light brigade but held long enough to ascertain a calming of the situation. They seemed to talk for a time then and the lady seemed to relax her aggressive stance. Shortly, Amanda emerged from the shelter, looked at Bonnie, and then reached her hand toward Bonnie's face where the bruises were.

Gene felt as if he had seen a display of tenderness from Amanda that Gene hadn't realized was there. She and Bonnie walked to the edge of the camp, seated themselves and talked for a long time. At first, the talk appeared to be distant and then there were tears on both their parts and hugs with consoling. Gene wasn't sure who was consoling whom. Then the thought came into his head, had Bonnie been defiled too? Was that why she seemed so deeply angry inside beyond reason? Was that why she had attacked that Morris fella with such ferocity?

When they finally stood, Amanda turned and looked searching where Gene stood half-obscured by a juniper tree, then after a bit turned and went back to her shelter. Bonnie made her way back to where Gene waited.

When she reached Gene, he could see she had been crying. Gene wasn't very good with that sort of stuff but inquired if she was okay. From the look he got, he might as well have asked some other dumb question. The look wasn't one of disgust or anger or even dismay, it was one of those looks like "men folk don't understand anything." Gene did understand that look.

They worked their way traversing up and around the hill where he had last seen Pool's track. Pool's path wasn't hard to follow. He walked plainly in the open, occasionally stumbling now and again. His track was steady, but he wasn't moving fast. Now and again, he would bump into a tree or dead stump, then stand. Each time he would change direction just a little but not consistently in any given direction. They tracked him about two miles. Meanwhile, Gene expected at any time to come upon him. He trended downhill more and more like wounded animals do when fleeing after being shot. Beyond their current location lay a series of cliffs in a shelf formation above one of the big rivers leading on to Riverton.

Pool had turned toward the river in the last half mile. More and more he stumbled, occasionally falling. He now was dragging his right foot and as Gene studied a fall mark, he could see where the protruding part of the bolt had gouged a place in the soft dirt. It must still be stuck in his head. Gene just couldn't imagine any man being able to motor through this terrain in that condition. After the last fall, there were a number of stumbles, and he seemed to be walking through prickly pear not trying to avoid it. He had fallen a couple times where cactus was. All Gene could think was Pool must have been walking in the dark.

Nearing the upper cliff ledge above the river valley, Gene became careful to watch both ways along the rim. The hard rock surface along the lip of the rim would be a path on which Pool might have gone in either direction looking for a way down. There weren't any tracks to be found. A big strong man like Pool, and in his condition not likely feeling pain. He could be extraordinarily dangerous if he set upon them. Gene and Bonnie's only hope to render aid to him would be if they were able to find him down or unconscious.

Gene searched both ways along the cliff lip about a quarter mile while Bonnie watched the surroundings so as to not be taken by a surprise attack. With no success in their search, Gene returned to the last sign in the trail they had located. Pool had gone straight toward the cliff edge, but the last fifty feet was the rock cap before the ledge. About twenty feet across, the rock was a small cactus leaf just lying there. As Gene studied the rock surface, he saw an ever-so-slight scuff where Pool must have drug his foot and then there it was, a spot where Pool must have fallen with a pin-head size drop of blood just there on the rock located only three foot from the cliff edge. Gene's heart fluttered as he looked over the edge. Between boulders below Gene could see Pool's leg and part of his hand lying partially exposed. The distance was some hundred fifty feet below.

"Well, that is that," said Gene as he sat down hard. While watching their backs, Bonnie saw her dad sit. Gene believed she knew what he'd seen. Gene implored her not to look and assured her Pool wasn't going to hurt another living soul.

Gene was surprised by her response: "That's one we won't have to deal with!"

Gene asked, "What's that supposed to mean?"

"Daddy, what he did to that girl shouldn't happen to anyone. He and others like him will be hunted and their crimes will be avenged. That's what I mean," she said flatly.

"Bonnie, I've never seen you so angry or so determined. What's going on with you? What has turned your personality so venomous?" Gene asked.

"Do you think Amanda is the only one who has suffered at the hands of jerks like him?" she replied.

"Bonnie. . ." Gene started to say.

Bonnie interrupted him. Her face turned red and tears erupted out of her eyes from anger and emotion, but her voice remained steady and unwavering, "Daddy, I didn't tell you all.

When they took my shotgun, they took my pride and my virginity. I made a promise to myself I would stop them and all like them. That soldier when he slugged me didn't know he changed my life and my focus forever. Daddy, when I discovered you had only wounded the man who did that to Amanda, I made up my mind he would die when we caught him. He's lucky. I don't intend to be so hard and God knows I tried to forgive, but what that man did to me is beyond acceptable by any measure." Her steady flat voice had deteriorated into quivering blubber.

Gene knew then Bonnie meant what she said and she would not be stopped except by the will of God. She was skillful, smart, and able. Whoever the man, the soldier, was who now had her shotgun had no clue he would eat his ears or what else might be in store for him if Bonnie caught him. Bonnie had learned to skin many deer, elk, and a couple bears. She was capable and knew how. Gene decided talking to her about due process wasn't appropriate at this time. Besides, this was a lawless land at present and it might be three months into winter before anything else would change. They needed to concentrate on how to get through the next winter. Everybody seemed to be consuming all they had at present just to stay alive. Setting stores aside seemed incomprehensible.

Over the next four days, they worked their way back to Jake's ranch. There wasn't a way to approach Jake's house without stirring up one or more of five chained big dogs kept around his house. Gene had seen Jake take in any old bum, give him a lift, and send him on his way with pride and hope. Gene knew Jake on the other hand was a formidable foe professionally trained and if provoked would be very dangerous. Gene looked forward to a full night of uninterrupted deep, deep sleep.

When they arrived over the hilltop, Jessie was first to greet them. She was full of questions about Bonnie's bruises and wanted news of the Samuel and his family. There were many questions and Gene answered with the best positive light he could shed upon the situations.

Jake had no news of the Smith girls' welfare. The community had been mostly quiet, except for some missing livestock. Deer and other wildlife seemed to be plentiful still as pressure from a sparse population was light. Ranging chickens could be seen mostly near and occasionally far. They were birds unaccustomed to roaming free range. Chicken seemed to be the manna of the day. Jake still was raging war on the skunks, coyotes, and foxes. An occasional bird of prey would snag a chicken after circling overhead.

Journal entry:

"The journey from Riverton was difficult for several reasons. First, food has been scarce. Second, the social conditions have deteriorated rapidly to the point that vigilante justices may need to be implemented to keep predictors at bay.

If some semblance of judicial order can be cobbled together, it should be done. There is no room for the delays that the recent courts have embraced. Justice must be swift and sure. Society is in no condition to house criminals for years on end. If a law enforcement contingent is created, it must be dependable and not of the self-appointed ilk found in organizations like the MLS.

I feel saddened and frustrated, and yes, angry to find out the extent of Bonnie's injuries. I feel she has been deeply hurt in her soul as well as suffering from the physical damage. The physical part will heal. It seems she has embodied a driven desire to exact her own brand of justice while her injuries have yet not healed. The business with Amanda seemed to have congealed a direction of her purpose. I pray she controls this drive for revenge. She will be a formidable foe to any whom she deems as guilty of violations."

"God, please find a way to restrain her and guide her," Gene prayed.

After resting the next day, Gene started the trek up country toward the Smith ranch. He intended to deliver the letter he carried to Zack's daughters and check on their wellbeing. Bonnie wanted to accompany him, but Gene felt the climb would be overly taxing on her condition. Gene felt he needed to move unrestricted without the burden of caring for his daughter. The travel went uneventful and took longer to trudge up the hills than it took to walk from there down to Jake's.

It was late in the day, although the days were becoming summer-long, when Gene topped the drive leading to the ranch house. He stopped to observe the setting. All seemed quiet but occupied. Gene started down the curved drive the last quarter mile and just as he came around the final corner, he heard the click of a gun's hammer being cocked off to his left in the trees.

"When I was here last, I said not to shoot me, do you hear?" said Gene.

"Shaky!" exclaimed Sally Smith. "I didn't know it was you. You said to keep watch and shoot anybody who tried to take advantage of us."

"Well, now, Sally, what I said was if you need to, shoot to kill. Kill if you have to rather than be raped or get killed yourself. Try not to be caught alone. Be sure to keep each other informed of where you plan to go and be. I also told you not to shoot me," said Gene with some humor.

"I'm sorry, Shaky," she said as she came out of the brush with a Winchester 12 gauge pump. "I wasn't sure who you were when we first spotted you coming. We've been having a little trouble with chicken thieves. Sonja has a rifle aimed at your chest right now."

"What you loaded with?" asked Gene.

"Oh, a couple double aught buck loads and some number twos. My real ace in the hole is Sonja in the barn loft."

Sally turned toward the barn and waved. She walked with Gene back toward the house, where Sonja now approached them with caution.

"Shaky, I didn't recognize you. You're so skinny," said Sonja.

As Sonja turned to walk to the house with them, Gene observed the watchful state she was in. She was watching all the critical places where an intruder could appear. They had set up a system of close encounter and deterrent that would be deadly to anyone attempting to intrude their domain. Sonja explained they had several defense schemes, which they altered irregularly according to their own timing. Laurie was out checking the livestock but would be on the prowl as Sonja had erected the signal that could be seen from anywhere on and many spots around the property. Sonja had likewise withdrawn the warning signal and erected the all-clear sign. Knowing Laurie, Gene thought she would only believe the all-clear after checking things out for herself. That was the case now. Laurie stood in the door like a ghost with her rifle ready for action. It took her a little time to make sure the place was clear before she came through the door.

"Shaky, we weren't sure we would ever see you again," exclaimed Sonja.

Gene explained his foray into the city. He told of his talk with their dad and the conditions where Zack was. Gene produced the letter from Zack to his daughters. The letter was some the worse for wear having been soaked by sweat from the exertion of strenuous travel. He handed it to Laurie to read. The others looked over her shoulders as she read aloud.

Realization of what Zack implied sank in. Drops of tears now slipped down Sonja's and Sally's cheeks. Laurie also had to wipe tears from the corners of her eyes. She wiped them away and said only one word, "So."

Gene sat quietly while the young women gathered their emotions. There was a deadening quiet as they each wiped away the tears. Sally turned and went outside and Gene followed. She stood watching the driveway.

"He'll be back. I just know it. Shaky, you can tell me he'll come home. He said when he left, he'd be home in a couple days. One of us should have been with him." She half blubbered and she stomped her foot.

Laurie stood and walked out to where Sally stood, reached an arm around Sally's shoulder and stood in silence with her. Sonja sat now at the table with her face in her hands silently regaining in her composure.

Gene said nothing for the time it took the girls to come to terms with the news Zack's letter seemed to be delivering. Sonja started to busy herself with the preparation of the night's meal.

"Shaky, I assume you will stay for supper," said Sonja.

Gene affirmed he would stay. Laurie requested Gene to say grace over the meal. After he had asked the blessing for the meal, adding the request that God find favor with Zack, they ate. It was a simple food. Fried zucchini in butter, scrambled eggs, sliced tomatoes, new potatoes, and peas smothered in fresh cream sauce, biscuits made as usual from scratch with fresh churned butter and jam spread over the fresh steaming surfaces. Gene couldn't remember when he had eaten such a feast. He had eaten so little over the last month, his stomach had shrunken. This was a feast however much he ate and much better than the porridge at Compound J.

After the meal, Gene said sullenly, "Girls, I have to make a serious request of you. Bonnie experienced a terrible beating and other experiences not unlike those you had with the Gilders. She is not completely healed yet. She is deeply bitter and has a vendetta in mind. I believe she has in mind to vindicate any who have experienced similar attacks. She is aware of what Toby and Josh did here. I think she will come here to talk to you. My request of you is you try to dissuade her from her undertaking. Vengeance is the Lord's, but she is very angry deep inside."

Laurie sat for a moment and then said with some venom, "I understand why she feels that way. I will have to consider what to do. You don't realize how many times I have imagined what I would do to that Toby if I saw him again. The vision isn't pretty!"

"I didn't say anything to Zack about the incident. I didn't feel he needed the worry or the guilt for not being here," said Gene.

The girls just sat quietly for a long time. Gene hadn't intended to cause them discomfort with the comment. He intended just the opposite, but obviously his intentions had been misgiven.

Gene decided to change the subject. "I will be leaving in the morning for my place on the mountain. I want you all to understand if you need a refuge for any reason, it is there for you."

When morning arrived, leftover biscuits and fresh scrambled eggs sat on the table. Sally packaged several biscuits, four hard-boiled eggs, and some jerked venison for Gene to take with him. Before starting, he elaborated and described the secrets of how to gain access to the mountain house and where they could find specific items they might need to survive. Gene explained he planned to return to Jake's and then make plans after. He reminded them about his request for Bonnie's welfare. Then, he turned and started up the ridge that separated the Smith's valley and the next, where above and on the other side sat the mountain home.

Three hours later, he could see the property. All seemed secure and Gene approached the house from a hidden pathway. There wasn't any indication of intrusion. The property did set back and away some three quarters of a mile from the main commonly traveled roadway. There seemed to be nobody around. Gene went into the house first. He wanted to replenish his clothing with fresh ones. He needed to replenish his bolts for his crossbow. He would take as many as he could make from the supplies he had there.

He spent the next day preparing and assembling the goods he needed and spent a most comfortable night in his own bed.

Awaking in his own bed, Gene was grateful to be awake. He had experienced the most awful nightmare anyone could have ever have had. Something about world crisis and having to find his kids. . . What an awful dream. He guessed he was having another of his fantasy worlds, as Jessie called it, in his sleep. But wait, the longer he was awake, the more he began to realize with his wits about him, his dream was the real world. His heart sank and he began to weep.

It wasn't just a cry of discouragement, but a deep grieving brought on by the realization his dream was real.

It took Gene the better part of two hours to shake the despair he was experiencing. If it weren't for the goal of locating Seth, he might have just given up and crumbled in place.

He reviewed his journal. "Yep, it was real."

Journal entry:

"I thought I experienced another fantasy last night in my sleep. Oh God, would that it were. When I woke up to find it wasn't. . . Well, that it's all real, I cried.

It was time to get movin'. There would be ammo to obtain from his cache and he anticipated winter to come and go before he would return. Gene retrieved his winter Polyfill Arctic sleeping bag, his wool cargo pants, wool camo shirt, and replacement bandanas. The pillowcase he carried was replaced with a new 100% cotton pillow-case and matches as well as the last of his butane liters. Generally, his pack was properly stocked so he didn't make many changes to its contents, except he had forgotten a water filter when they departed before. He would not forget it this time. Lastly, Gene added some lightweight durable winter pack shoes to his load and a collapsible antique aluminum-drinking cup with lid.

His footwear now wore thin and after the trip over the divide, he felt the shoes would have long since worn out. Even though he was some thirty pounds lighter, Gene had gained strength and stamina. Living like a mountain man had been agreeable to him physically. The meds he took for blood pressure had long since depleted. Gene hadn't checked his blood pressure since the EMP. The opportunity just hadn't presented itself. Gene wasn't sure he wanted to know anyway. There was more than enough to be concerned over without keeping track of that.

Locking the house and storage behind him, he started back down the mountain to Jake's. At that moment he remembered Jessie might want some stuff. He went back to the house, went inside, and prepared a pack with her favorite shoes, slippers, and extra nightgown, pants, stockings, shirts, hairbrush, emery board, a bottle of shampoo, toothbrush, a small bottle of her favorite cologne, and photos of her kids and grandchildren. Gene knew this was going to be a more cumbersome load than he could pack comfortably so he made a handle around the pack and carried it like a suitcase. He likewise made up a package for Bonnie from the items she had left at home when departing for college. That too Gene carried in the other hand when he left. One difference was, Gene added two extra boxes of .38s and his spare pistol. Gene strapped Bonnie's old shotgun on his pack with the crossbow and added a box of shells to her pack. Now really loaded laden with supplies for three, he hoped he wouldn't have to leave part of the load somewhere, then go back to retrieve it. The food given to him by Sonja Smith had given him strength he hadn't felt in weeks. *Oh, yes.* He retrieved his driver's license for identification.

He re-secured the house and storage, started on his way, and slowly made his way down country. Gene hiked just over halfway when evening overtook him. He made a cold camp, ate a second egg and biscuit, drank filtered water, and settled in for the night. The filtered water was a real treat.

Upon arriving at Jake's the next day, Gene was greeted with concerns of "Where had he been?" They thought he would return yesterday. He appeased the scolding with the packages he carried for each of them. Jessie looked through the articles and exclaimed she had taken so much for granted. Now what a blessing simple things had become, to be cherished as she had never before. Bonnie too was pleased to receive the goods. She however remained reserved in her enthusiasm and simply said, "Thank you, Daddy."

Gene recuperated for three days and readied his equipment for the next leg of what would prove to be a daunting task. Gene knew traveling in the high mountains in the fall and dead of winter could be treacherous. He would have preferred to wait, Seth hadn't been heard from.

Chapter 11

Reckoning

As Bonnie went about her daily affairs, she found herself in tears. She felt there was nothing to cry about, but she just couldn't help the occasional outbursts. She had recovered physically from the attack. She was admittedly angry and promised there would be a reckoning. What she couldn't understand was why, if she had healed, did these outbursts of tears explode from her. They would happen sometimes without warning, especially if she were alone with her own thoughts or working at some mindless chore. When she stayed busy at something that kept her thoughts occupied, the tears seemed to not come as often. As time progressed and as she fought to rein in her emotions, Bonnie found herself feeling angry. The anger wasn't the "mad as hell" kind as if she'd just had a fight with someone. It was deeper, like a "gonna get even" type feeling. She caught herself beating the living daylights out of a laundered shirt when she realized she had beaten fresh holes in it. Another time she was killing a chicken for dinner when she realized that more than just cutting the head off, she had chopped the dinner bird into many pieces.

Jessie observed Bonnie for some time and one day as they walked, she asked if Bonnie was feeling okay. Bonnie asked what was the purpose of the question.

Being Bonnie's mom, Jessie said, "Bon, honey, I'm your mom. I see the turmoil you're going through. I saw you with the hen the other day. You're acting angrier and angrier. I've been praying for your comfort and peace, but you're becoming different from your old self."

Through a start of tears Bonnie blubbered, "I can't help myself, Mama. I'm feeling so frustrated that I could do nothing about those guys when they attacked me. I just want to rip one of them apart. Actually, I want to rip 'em all apart like I did that chicken. I'm sorry you saw it. You don't have to tell me what I'm feeling is wrong, but I can't help how I feel. I know God will have the last word, but I find myself wanting the next to the last word. I don't know what to do."

Jessie embraced Bonnie and held her for a long moment. Finally, after endless sobbing, Bonnie rubbed her face and wiped her eyes. She was totally whipped emotionally and drained physically. Jessie and Bonnie walked arm in arm back to the house.

Jake had been standing on the porch and as they neared, he asked, "You girls okay? I don't pretend to know all of what stress these times bring on folks, but if I can help, clue me in."

"Thanks, Jake, for the encouragement," said Jessie.

Bonnie and Jessie disappeared through the front door, leaving Jake to ponder.

A week passed and the outbursts had ceased. Bonnie had made a decision. She was going on a mission. She somehow was going to protect women from attacks like she and that Amanda girl had suffered. She was aware of Laurie Smith's situation and the thought of it made her seethe.

Bonnie started making her plans. Her intent needed to be clarified by a set of guidelines. She couldn't just go around whacking perpetrators—there had to be definable rules. Justice had to be served fairly. If courts existed to dispense justice, then she would see suspects delivered. If there weren't courts, then, she would see justice encouraged.

Bonnie spent a week planning and setting up her pack for her foray. When Jessie inquired about what Bonnie planned, Bonnie said she was going to see Laurie Smith and her sisters. She had agreed when Gene asked if she would check in on them. Now was a good time and a reasonable reason to be packing. She carefully concealed the extra pistol Gene had brought her from the mountain home. She cleaned and readied her shotgun just before leaving. Jake watched and studied her. Bonnie said her goodbyes and Jake offered a word of advice and said a prayer. Then Jessie, Jake, and Jake's wife Meg sent her on her way with their best wishes.

Bonnie made good time climbing to the valley to Smith's ranch. She had some trepidation about her goal, but she knew in order to keep her sanity she had to do something. While questioning deep within herself what her real goal might be, she topped the crest on the driveway that entered the Smith farm. Bonnie knew from Gene's experience she needed to be careful. When about a hundred yards from the house, Bonnie called out Laurie's name. There was no response. She called again, then she called out for Sonja and Sally. Bonnie approached with less enthusiasm and slowed her approach. Calling out again, a movement to her left caught her eye. It was Sonja standing there with a shotgun and a broad smile.

"Bonnie, you caught us out of position. It took us a little time to get into place. You might have walked in on us had you not called out. How are you anyway?" she asked.

"I'm good," Bonnie replied. "Daddy asked that I come see you now and again. I guess this is now."

"How is he and your mama?" Sonja asked.

"Mama's good," replied Bonnie. "Daddy's been gone a while. He went off to Metropolis to find Seth. Of course, we haven't heard from him. Mama is concerned but all we have is faith God will take care of him. We pray."

They walked toward the house and Laurie emerged from the barn. She came running to Bonnie with a hug, rifle and all, greeting her like a long-lost sister. Laurie's questions mimicked Sonja's. Bonnie's answers were the same. Sally was under the weather. She had been ill for the last month. Neither Laurie nor Sonja knew what the trouble could be. They had consulted their dad's medical books. They tried some simple cures, but nothing seemed to have an effect. The three young ladies went in and set supper made of vegetable stew and cornbread. Bread flower had long since been depleted. There was butter, water, and milk to drink, and honey for the cornbread. The Smith girls were beekeepers and could harvest honey with the best. Sugar was now nonexistent, like wheat flower.

Finely ground corn meal and honey had become the staples, as were cabbage, carrots, potatoes, and venison.

Bonnie and the Smiths sat and talked until the sundown. Bonnie was shown to Zack's room. He hadn't come home and they believed he must have succumbed to the truncated surgery or the infection. The girls agreed that this year had become a very long year. Sally made a brief appearance to eat some. Bonnie was surprised how thin she had become and how pale her face appeared. Bonnie gently began to probe about Sally's symptoms. Sally hadn't been feeling well for a month; she'd been a little lethargic and discouraged since receiving Zack's letter.

"We try to cheer her up. She's always sad now, not like before," said Sonja. "It's like she thinks there's no reason to try any longer. I think Sally is suffering from depression."

"Sally has never been that way," said Laurie. "She has always been the one to cheer the rest of us up when things got tough. She was so looking forward to going away to college and seeing the world. She wanted to travel and meet people. I think the news about Dad's condition, the assault from Toby and Josh, and the prospect of going into the world disappearing has discouraged her. Quite frankly, if I think about it too much, I could get down too."

The next morning, Bonnie asked Sally to walk with her. They tended to the chores, milked, and then walked past the barn and corrals through the pasture into the forest behind the barn and corrals. A large log lay across the trail. It had been smoothed and polished by years of animals and people jumping and stepping over it. Bonnie sat down and leaned on an adjacent tree. Sally sat on the log near the other side of the trail. This was a comfortable log. This place was a quiet place in the forest as serene as any Bonnie could think of. She had been here one other time when she stayed overnight as Laurie's guest several years back.

"Sally," she began, "what's wrong? Do you have something physical ailing you?"

"I don't know, Bonnie," admitted Sally. "I'm just so disappointed with life right now. It seems that everything has fallen apart. I don't want to do anything. What's the use? There's nothing to look forward to. Does that make since to you?

She continued. "When Josh and Toby came that day, I was glad to see Josh. He and I had been talking a lot; now I haven't seen him since. I like Josh, Bonnie. I was mad that day and would have beat him nearly to death, I was so mad. Bonnie, Josh is not like that. Toby just misdirected Josh. Josh is headstrong, but he worships the ground Toby walks on. When he's away from Toby, he's kind, considerate, funny, and a wonderful person. I don't understand why he went along with Toby that day."

Sally began to cry and as the tears trickled down her cheek, she said, "Bonnie, I think I love Josh, and now I will never see him again. Shaky gave instructions to Laurie, Sonja and me to shoot him on sight if he ever came back. I'm afraid if he does, he'll be killed."

"Sally, what he did is inexcusable," said Bonnie. "He needs to stand on his own two feet. He will have to prove he can before he'll deserve your attention. Toby, on the other hand, has always been a wild one. He was bad in school and he has that personality that will lead him to no good. If you want Josh and he feels the same about you, he will find a way. He, not you, will have to make the move. You must not make yourself available voluntarily without Josh indicating he has an interest first. If he truly loves you, he will find a way. You need to be patient and look forward to that time like you have been looking toward your future in the world. Sally, all is not lost. Regardless of conditions now, as bleak as things look, there are always hopes and dreams to look forward to."

Bonnie caught herself thinking about her resolve to exact punishment on human predators. What advice would she give to herself? Bonnie didn't want to think about it. She had too much anger, maybe even hate, bottled up right now.

"Sally, do Laurie and Sonja know how you feel?" Bonnie asked. "I think we need to talk to them."

"Bonnie, they would shoot Josh on sight, at least Laurie would," said Sally. "Sonja knows him better. I don't know if she would. She darn sure would Toby, though, without a thought. Laurie's table-poundin' mad. Without a qualm, she'd drop either in a heartbeat. That's why I haven't talked to them about Josh. I've been afraid of the explosion. Laurie may go hunting them yet if she gets a chance."

"Sally, let's go talk to your sisters. I think they'll understand," Bonnie replied.

They walked to the forest's edge, then across the grassy pasture, and to the barn. Sally seemed to be a bit more energetic, more like the old Sally. Laurie was in the barn with her rifle nearby.

"Well, ladies, did you have a good vacation? Hop, hop now, there's work to do. Winter's coming and you know many hands make work light," jibed Laurie in a half serious but light tone of voice.

The Smith girls had handcut the hay field with old scythes which had been stored in the hay loft years ago. The cut grass hay was gathered in the barn but not stacked in the loft. Sally and Bonnie made bundles, "shocks" they were called, which should have been made in the field. With a rope and pulley, these were hoisted to the exterior second story loft door, swung in, and stacked. A lot of winter feed would be required for the milk cow and other livestock. Bonnie estimated the winter need at six tons of hay. They had about two thirds of that stacked now.

Work went well the rest of the day. The hayloft was filling. Tomorrow they would cut more hay in the upper field. It would need to cure for a day or two. By the time they had cut the last of the field, the first of the cutting would be cured. Bundling too quickly before curing would cause the hay to mold inside. Too much molded hay in one spot can cause spontaneous combustion, burning a stack into a pile of ashes. If in a barn, the barn would burn. Bonnie thought there must be a special kind of knowledge required of country folks to keep all functioning properly. In prior times, people who bought milk from the store had no appreciation for the effort required to make such commodities available. Growing and producing commodities wasn't as simple as growing a zucchini in a backyard garden.

At supper, they were all tired from a hard day's work on the Smith farm. They all pitched in with the preparation of supper, table dressing, and cleaning. The food was tasteful and certainly filling. Sally had prepared the main course. She was an accomplished down-home farm cook. She could make a meal out of the available supplies and it became more than palatable.

Bonnie opened the conversation with, "I just don't understand why city folks call the evening meal dinner. They must be plain ignorant. The Last Supper is called supper, not The Last Dinner. We dine at formal meals like Thanksgiving, Easter, or Christmas. These are events which take time to enjoy and to fellowship. When we sup, it is informal. I guess people who dine at the evening meal want the pretense of being like wealthy folks who have extra time to waste every day. As for me, I think supper tonight is scrumptidelicious. Thank you, Sally."

"Aren't we quite the philosopher tonight," jibed Sally. "I liked thinking I was wealthy, aristocratic, and a cut above you commoners until you spoiled it. Now I'll have to slurp my soup with the hogs."

She made an exaggerated slurp from her spoon of venison stew. They all laughed. Sally seemed to have up cheered up this evening.

"Welcome back," said Sonja. "It's good to have you happy again."

Sally paused a moment, then with a more serious look said, "Bonnie and I had a good talk this morning. I have some things I need to say."

All was silent except for a cricket chirping his tune outside on the porch. Sally continued, "I've been just about sick trying to work things out. I wanted to tell you. . ."

Laurie interrupted, "Are you pregnant?"

"No!" exclaimed Sally, "I'm still a virgin. I haven't ever done that with anyone! But you may think just as bad of me after what I tell you next. I hope you don't. I've been worrying myself sick about Josh Gilder. I like Josh a lot and I'm afraid I won't ever see him again. I'm afraid that if he ever comes around again you'll shoot him. I don't care if you kill Toby, but please don't hurt Josh. Please."

Sally's eyes started to well up with tears. She was about to bolt into the bedroom when Sonja reached her arm and turned her. "Sally, I thought you liked Josh. After you and Jessie beat him so, I thought you were done with him. It never occurred to me you still were sweet on Josh."

Laurie just sat watching the situation unfold. She was in total disbelief. In her mind, Sally was too young to have feelings like that for any man. Laurie never imagined anything existed between Sally and Josh. Laurie sat speechless, not wanting to believe what she heard. Her hatred for the Gilder boys especially Toby was beyond her ability to express. Her shock that Sally would have anything to do with either was astronomical. She said so.

"I'm sorry, Laurie," exclaimed Sally. "I can't help how I feel. Josh is sweet and kind. . . and smart. . . and fun to be with. I was mad the day they came here and I might have killed him myself with that stick. He heard Shaky tell us to shoot either of them on sight if they came back. My heart sank a bit that day because I was afraid he wouldn't come back. I want him to come back, but I don't want you or Sonja to harm him. Maybe nothing will come of it, but I want to see him again."

The room stayed quiet for a long period. Nobody spoke. Sally turned and exited to the bedroom. Sonja looked at Laurie, studying the anguish on her face. Laurie was hurt or lost in self-doubt. Laurie got up and walked to the front door, opened it, then went out.

Sonja watched after her, then said to Bonnie, "She's been angry and hurting like you. I see it in both of you. You both want to break an egg or worse. What happened to you? Why are you so hard inside? I'm mad too, but as violated as I feel from Toby hitting me, I can't imagine what Laurie feels."

Bonnie told of the Riverton raid in general terms. She told of finding Amanda in the camp so broken in spirit. She tried as best she could to explain her feelings of not wanting to sit on the sideline. She wanted to take action. She realized she had become a vigilante, a vigilante with no authorization to act. That was what a vigilante was, one without official authorization to carry out the law. That was what she intended to do. Where would she go to get authorization, anyway?

Bonnie started making preparations for the next day's travel. She would head for the mountain house. There were some supplies and clothes there she felt she needed. Gene had been thoughtful enough to bring some stuff, but he never fully understood what Bonnie considered necessary. Bonnie would fix that tomorrow when she arrived there.

Chapter 12

The Hunt

Bonnie reached the mountain home about mid-morning. She carefully observed the property and could see trespassers had been poking about. They seemed to be present no longer. When Bonnie got to the entry, the door stood open. She withdrew her .38 and proceeded inside. Whoever had been there had taken many of the stored food supplies. The dwelling had been searched for any useful items that could be traded. Bonnie knew the guns and ammo that weren't locked up would be gone. They were. Bonnie proceeded to the shop and machine sheds. They'd been looted of anything that could be carried easily.

As Bonnie surveyed the turmoil, she heard a voice that sounded like Laurie Smith's. Again, as Bonnie listened, she could hear Laurie calling her name from outside. Bonnie emerged to see Laurie looking at the disarray.

"Laurie, what are you doing here?" questioned Bonnie.

"Bonnie, I can't let you go it alone," said Laurie. "I have a knife to sharpen too. You know what I mean. I have never felt so humiliated, afraid, and violated. No one should be allowed to do that to anyone. Something has to be done by someone. We don't have determinable laws anymore or anybody to enforce them even if they did exist. If you're going to be the enforcer, I want to join you, you hear. Your dad said you would have something on your mind to do, and I was supposed to speak to you. I feel as you do, but together we can do it right, ya hear." Laurie took a deep breath and exhaled.

Bonnie just stood and watched as Laurie spouted her words. When Laurie finished, Bonnie broke into tears, then calmed for a moment, then cried again.

Bonnie blurted her reply in one long, nearly unintelligible sentence. "Laurie, I'm pissed as hell, angry enough to kill, ashamed, frustrated at wanting to get even, and none of it is my fault, but I can't stand by and watch when girls are being taken, raped, and worse. I intend to do what I can now, right or wrong. If you come with me, I run the show. I promise I'll try to be just, but I will have no mercy. They didn't! Your company is welcome."

They stood looking at one another for a minute, studying the tears running down the other's cheek. Then, with a short gasp, both started laughing, a nervous sort of laugh, as they realized the implications of the path they were about to take together. The pact was made.

Bonnie and Laurie were headed to Pinedale. Pinedale would for now be their local center of information. They were known as local kids and could pick up information they were seeking there. First, they would stay the night at the mountain home.

In the basement, Bonnie found canned supplies that hadn't been disturbed by thieves. The two made a feast of home-canned vegetable soup, home-canned beef, and home-canned apricot juice for a drink. They could see a quarter mile of the driveway from where they sat. There seemed to be some activity Bonnie hadn't been aware of before. As she watched, she could see what appeared to be a family. There was a man, woman, and three children near the creek. They seemed to be fishing in the creek.

Bonnie said, "Laurie, cover me. I'm going to take some food to those people."

Bonnie walked out the door with two jars of vegetable soup in tow. When she approached, the people had no clue she was anywhere around. The water rushing over the rocks covered any sound she might have made. Bonnie just stood watching as one of the children caught a small fish. She thought he might as well have found the pot at the end of the rainbow. As she watched, the woman was first to see her. Shaking the man's shoulder, the woman turned toward Bonnie with apprehension on her face. The man turned too with defense on his mind.

"Hi there," greeted Bonnie. "If you are interested, I have a couple jars of vegetable soup."I thought you might be hungry and would they like a little extra?"

The man approached her with some trepidation. Studying her for a moment he accepted the offering as she reached the jars toward him. He accepted gratefully and handed one jar to the woman who proceeded to open one jar.

"Please, you should heat these before you eat them," Bonnie explained. Home-canned food should be heated before eating and the food will taste better when heated."

Being hungry, they ate it cold.

After a cool comfortable night, the ladies gathered the items they needed to travel, secured the doors, and left for Pinedale. The trek down the mountain to Pinedale was a short seven miles for those young legs. Bonnie had healed physically from her injuries. She retained deep psychological issues that drove her beyond reason. Laurie, on the other hand, although angered after her experience, resolved to stop animals like Toby in whatever way would work. She had no qualms about methods that may be needed to accomplish her goals. Bonnie, however, driven with little reasoning tempered by mercy, had no definable goal other than to punish perpetrators herself.

Walking into town was a familiar experience for the two. This was their home territory, although Bonnie had been away for some time. As they approached the town center, there seemed to be no central coffee spot as once had existed. They went to other familiar locations without finding people gathered socially as used to be the custom. This was unexpected. The old codgers always collected to chew the fat and a little tobacco. Zack Smith commented to Laurie at one time that these groups were far more efficient gossip centers than any lady's quilting bee.

Finally, as they neared the local grocery, Laurie saw Mrs. Lattimer. When they approached Mrs. Lattimer, Laurie greeted her with, "Mrs. Lattimer, how are you?"

"I'm OK," she replied. "Well, Laurie and Bonnie, what are you young ladies doing here in town? Bonnie, I thought you were in school in Riverton."

"I was, but Daddy came for me and brought me home," said Bonnie.

"How is Shaky?' Mrs. Lattimer inquired.

"The last I knew, he was good. He went to find Seth over there." She thumbed her hand toward the east. "We haven't had word, but there isn't any these days. I've heard some of the ham radio people get a little news—the ones who protected their equipment—but nothing otherwise."

"I understood Seth was on the east side," Mrs. Lattimer said.

"He was the last we knew. That's what Daddy is going to find out," replied Bonnie

"Laurie how are Zack and your sisters?" inquired Mrs. Lattimer.

"My sisters are good, but we're not sure about Daddy. He was in Riverton Memorial Hospital when the lights went out. Shaky saw him and he sent a letter home. We haven't had any further word and are afraid for his well being." Laurie didn't want to admit what she really was fearful of.

"Well, Laurie, I pray Zack is well," assured Mrs. Lattimer.

"Mrs. Lattimer, where is everybody?" asked Laurie.

Mrs. Lattimer explained the little coffee crowds had stopped gathering. They now had to spend their time working for the meals they were getting. Several had died as medical services became non-existent. The others around had started scavenging for food and supplies. A couple of the retired executive types had organized small groups and were communing for survival.

She continued, "That old Duff had been seen breaking into the grocery store and the Siever home. He has been just stealing stuff. Duff had started breaking in to Guadalupe's home and Guadalupe caught him. He ran him off at gunpoint with a stern warning. Rumor has it that Duff had been seen in the countryside with unusual supplies in his possession. The general thought is, someone will find Duff dead somewhere of unnatural causes."

Bonnie inquired about the Gilder boys. Mrs. Lattimer knew only that Josh was at home helping his dad. Toby had left over some disagreement with Josh in which Mr. Gilder had pulled Toby off Josh while he beat him with a whip. Gilder at his end invited Toby to leave. Toby left to who knew where.

Laurie inquired about other news in the community. Mrs. Lattimer chitchatted about this and that. The rumor was a militia group had overtaken the settlements in the south. They were rumored to be thieves and thugs stealing to live rather than being a productive part of society. They pumped all the gas bulk tanks and any car tank for fuel to use in the few trucks they had that were operational. It seemed nearly everybody was out of gasoline and diesel. There was no resource this group hadn't started controlling.

They captured and enslaved some families. Bonnie listened intently and inquired for more information. Mrs. Lattimer said she didn't know a lot, just what she had heard. Her source was a traveler who had stopped to work for a meal. He'd been there when the capture was made and escaped by hiding in an irrigation ditch, then he bugged out.

The girls bid Mrs. Lattimer good-bye. They departed to the south. The Gilder home was located south and Laurie wanted to confront Josh. In the meantime, they looked for other information sources that would shed further information on their quest.

As they progressed down the street, Bonnie thought about Sara, a classmate whose parents lived nearby. They detoured to the Brinkmans' home. When they arrived, Bonnie could see Mr. Brinkman in his backyard garden. He tended the nearly-planted tomatoes and was weeding. Bonnie greeted him and inquired about Sara. He had had no news of her. She had gone several states east to attend college. They had talked the day before the outage and Sara was well then. He had no news since. He was trying to get ham communication information, but the radios working were greatly overwhelmed with traffic.

As they talked, Laurie asked about news in the community and surrounding areas. Mr. Brinkman didn't have much information. He wasn't inclined to gossip or talk much about people. The only news he had was there were some toughs about. He warned the girls to be careful in their traveling. It wasn't safe for young ladies these days. Bonnie wanted to challenge that but thought better and kept her mouth closed. Mr. Brinkman offered his home for a night's refuge, which the girls accepted. They presented their rations for the evening meal and Mr. and Mrs. Brinkman combined theirs to make an ample meal. The girls packed water from the nearby creek and carried wood for the fire to boil and sterilize the water. A simple spit bath was adequate. Their canteens were replenished and they were ready for travel the next day.

Bonnie and Laurie's discussion surrounded the conversation they had with Mrs. Lattimer. If any person was enslaved by a person or group of persons, that wouldn't do. They would look into the situation. That is what they intended to do.

Morning came with the girls being refreshed. They considered themselves capable young ladies. The older generation considered them girls out of age difference and out of an attitude of being societal protectors. In any circumstance, it didn't matter. They considered themselves crusaders with a cause of right and justice.

When they left the Brinkmans', well wishes were extended both ways. Barely away and out of earshot, Laurie asked, "Bonnie, you thinking what I am?"

"Yes, I can't believe anyone should be enslaved," said Bonnie. "What comes next is inevitable. We'll do what we can to keep things right if you're in agreement."

"Let's get with it then," replied Laurie.

They agreed the best plan was to recon information, as much as they could gather. Zack had said knowing the enemy was worth a ton of arms. If you could outwit the enemy, the battle would be three quarters won.

"Bonnie," probed Laurie, "I feel like I need to make a call at Gilder's. Sally's pinin' for Josh and there isn't any way he'll know unless somebody drops a hint. We need to stop by there."

Bonnie said nothing. She wondered if Mr. Gilder knew of the events at the Smiths'.

The Gilder place was on the way to the settlements. When they reached the property entry, Bonnie could see Mr. Gilder and Josh in the side yard sawing wood with a crosscut timber saw. The older Gilder looked up with a little surprise. "Well, Laurie and Bonnie, welcome, how are you two doing?"

"Mr. Gilder, we're doing okay. Josh, can I talk with you a moment?" asked Laurie.

Josh, a bit uneasy, turned to face Laurie.

Laurie said, "Josh, come with me. I'd like to talk to you."

Josh looked toward Bonnie, then, toward his dad, then, followed Laurie down the driveway where they stood and talked, walked some distance further then stopped again. Josh at first was somewhat reserved, then became a little animated. As they talked, Josh seemed to gain a spring in his step.

"Bonnie, what is that all about?" inquired Mr. Gilder.

Bonnie replied, "I believe the explanation should come from Josh. We just came to deliver a message. If what we believe is correct, Josh will be pleased about the information."

Without stopping, Bonnie inquired about Toby. It seemed there had been a huge disagreement between Josh and Toby. Mr. Gilder had pulled Toby off Josh, as he was about to do major damage to his younger brother. Angered by the apparent lack of concern for the younger brother's welfare, Mr. Gilder had ordered Toby away. Toby, unrepentant for the severe beating of Josh, left without a word of kindness.

Mr. Gilder demanded Josh explain what was so almighty important as to make Toby set upon Josh in such a manner. Josh had told of the events which led up to the beatings the boys received at the hands of Shaky, Jessie, and the Smith girls. Gilder was dumbfounded at the tale. After some deliberation, he was shamed and wanted the full details from Josh's point of view. He had insisted he and Josh return to Zack Smith's and offer amends. Josh had insisted the danger of returning was far greater than his dad could imagine. He'd told him that Shaky's instruction for the girls to "shoot to kill" should not be taken lightly. Gilder considered these events. He left word with several mutual acquaintances of Zack Smith and himself that they needed to meet at Zack's earliest convenience. When he saw Bonnie and Laurie, he had anticipated that was the purpose of their visit.

Bonnie said it wasn't, but there was purpose for their stopping. She felt Josh would explain when the time was right. She assured Mr. Gilder there was nothing ill or bad if the explanation came. She told Mr. Gilder Zack hadn't returned from Riverton yet.

When Laurie and Josh returned, Laurie motioned to Bonnie to leave with her. As they advanced away from Gilder's home, she explained to Bonnie she believed what Josh told her about the events at the Smiths' that day. Josh had followed Toby there knowing Toby had "bad" in mind. He had tried to stop him, but Toby, being larger, could not be dissuaded. Josh had held Sally back to spare her from harm in tangling with Toby, as Sonja had experienced. That's when Shaky had intervened, not knowing the full circumstances.

An argument between Josh and Toby over an unrelated matter escalated into an altercation between the brothers. Words had been exchanged. As a jab at Toby, Josh threatened to disclose to their dad the Smith events. Toby had set upon his brother with intent when the elder Gilder intervened. After the intervention, much to Mr. Gilder's shame, the beans were spilled. Mr. Gilder, being a humble man, was not a weakling. He was resolute and strong with purpose. Amends in his mind were to be made.

They walked away without talking for a couple hours toward the settlements. Bonnie stopped and turned toward Laurie. She had been considering their quest. Discussing the desired goals, the young women confirmed their resolve to eliminate unjust savagery, especially on women. They decided to enter the town discretely, find shelter and nose about. They knew risk existed so decided on a preliminary plan to recon apart while keeping each other in sight. They looked for a cache site for spare weapons and goods. When a cache site was found, it concealed their access as well as protected the cache.

Late in the day, they saw movement of small squads who seemed to be removing articles of value from unprotected groups along the river. One of these particular groups had taken two young women in tow and proceeded to raid another camp. When the raiding squad walked in, the leader shot the first man who stood. Laurie leveled her shotgun at the man's side as he was close, within twenty yards. Bonnie touched her on the arm and indicated she should hold. Bonnie was going to slip to the far side of the camp for a crossfire advantage and to detain escapes.

"Give me five minutes," she whispered and then dissipated into the trees and undergrowth along the river.

The squad possessed good quality weapons. Nothing more complicated than hunting rifles and handguns. Laurie trembled with nerves. A hunter would call it buck fever. She didn't know if she could wait five minutes and wasn't sure when five minutes would be up. Waiting that long seemed to take forever. In the meanwhile, the pillagers ransacked the camp and struck people at will. As one older woman started to object, the leader started to point his pistol at her head. He never heard the shot. The others looked up in surprised that they would be challenged. From the other side of the camp came the roar of a 12 gauge, toppling the second of the five-man squad and wounding a third. Laurie fired at the fourth and dropped out of sight. The fifth man dove for cover when the older woman and two others set upon him with sticks and cast-iron frying pans. Laurie watched a bit and tried to think what to do next. She shook and her knees seemed to lack strength to move her. Where was Bonnie, and what would she do? Should Laurie approach the camp or should she to stay out of sight?

As she watched and collected her wits, Bonnie quietly said, "Laurie, it's me."

Bonnie might as well have yelled it in her ear. Her heart skipped a beat as she nearly wilted.

"Laurie, let's get out of here!" Bonnie commanded.

They moved quietly away unseen and within half a mile stopped to gather themselves.

"Bonnie, I never shot anybody before, but that man killed that man. He was about to shoot that lady. Bonnie, I think I'm going to be sick. Oh Bonnie, I don't know, I. . . ." she said as her voice trailed off into a whimper.

They sat a few minutes and then discussed the event and outcome. They had not been seen and as near as they knew, the camp people were now in control, the captives freed. At least for now, the captives would be safe from whatever.

Chapter 13

The Judge

Bonnie and Laurie discussed the battle they had with the camp invaders. They were almost euphoric about the outcome. They now had the full realization as to the seriousness of their endeavor. They both understood how lucky they had been in not being shot or seen by the residents or the raiders. Identification hadn't occurred to them until after the deed had been done. They needed to plan rather than be impulsive. They needed to retain their anonymity and yet get the message out that people would not be abused, especially the girls and women.

"Laurie, I intended that we deliver the bad guys to justice. I didn't intend we should deliver justice itself to the bad guys," said Bonnie apologetically to Laurie.

"Bonnie, that's what I had in mind, but when that man was shot pointblank with no provocation, I couldn't stand by and watch others meet the same fate. I needed to do what I could because I could. I don't apologize for that, not a bit," replied Laurie. "Bonnie, we need to maintain our original purpose. If we have to modify it periodically, I'm OK with that."

"It took all my willpower and was all I could do not to go in blasting," said Bonnie resolutely. "We did it right, I think. I still think we should deliver the bad guys, not the justice. I don't want to be a real outlaw even though that bunch in Riverton put a price on my head. I just want to help the less able and the girls to protect themselves."

They located a site for a dry camp that night. They split their sleeping location so as not to be easily caught together. In addition, each could watch the other's back for protection. After some discussion, they worked out a set of silent signals in case audible language became inconvenient. Having been around each other many years as kids, each easily grasped the meaning of the agreed private sign language based upon earlier youthful activities.

Dawn came after the two were launching into the day. The events of the day before had been thrust all too suddenly on them. Now was the time to start the planned reconnaissance. They would start with questions from local people. As agreed, they stood and walked apart, all the time keeping the other within reach upon an instant's notice.

They watched their surroundings at all times, their back trail at all times, and what they were walking into at all times. Spread apart as they were, each could see things the other wasn't or might not be aware of. They practiced their signals for better communication. Bonnie was the first to locate the campsite. She indicated seven visible people, nothing threatening, but all seemed aware and fearful. Laurie edged around to see at another angle. She motioned Bonnie to hold her place a moment. Another person had appeared at the edge of the camp. Laurie and Bonnie both knew her. She had been a competitor from another community in the skeet competitions in which they had all participated. Her name was Gretchen Conroy. She lived in a home near this area but acted as if she were living here. Bonnie and Gretchen had been fierce competitors and had some amount of animosity toward one another.

Laurie, on the other hand, had gotten along well with Gretchen at the meets. Laurie motioned Bonnie to stay while Laurie approached the camp.

"Hello in the camp," Laurie clearly and loudly called out.

The eight scattered out of sight instantly. No person remained visible.

"I mean you no harm. Please, I would like to come in," Laurie announced.

As she walked carefully with her hands in full sight and away from her visible weapons, she entered the edge of the camp. No one offered a greeting. Laurie reassured anyone who could hear she had come in peace and intended no harm. From behind her she heard Gretchen's voice telling her to raise her hands. Laurie complied.

"Gretchen, I thought that was you. What are you doing here?" asked Laurie, trying to ease the tension.

"Laurie Smith, I might ask the same," fired Gretchen right back.

"Gretchen, my friend and I are looking for information," Laurie explained. "We thought some of the locals would be able to help us."

"What friend?" asked Gretchen.

"Me," said Bonnie as she broke the silence just feet behind Gretchen's left shoulder. "We mean nobody here harm and we do need information, Gretchen."

"Bonnie, how did you know where I was?" growled Gretchen.

"Gretchen," said Laurie, "we didn't know you were here until we saw you just now. Gretchen, give us a chance, please!"

"What do you want?" Gretchen stated angrily. "Just go away and leave us alone. Things are bad here. The gangs rob us. The next gang takes what the last didn't get. That so-called Martial Law Service from Riverton confiscates everything and makes captives of the girls. They have tried to take me twice. I escaped both times. I hear screams coming from their camp at night. I can't do anything about those bastards!"

Bonnie later remembered thinking, *Pity the man who tried to lay a hand on Gretchen.* Gretchen, while five-foot four-inches tall, was stocky, not fat, weighing one hundred sixty pounds. She was as skilled a marksman as Bonnie and Laurie, but in addition, she possessed martial arts training from before the time she started grade school. Bonnie wasn't sure of the discipline but had seen Gretchen take down the biggest jock in a neighboring school after a sporting event. Gretchen wasn't to be underestimated.

Stay at a distance, Bonnie my girl, Bonnie thought.

Laurie turned to Gretchen and after some quiet conversation with her, requested they all discuss the current events and conditions. After a tentative agreement, others emerged from the background. Some were armed with machetes, one with a rusted pistol, and another with a staff. Bonnie stayed within earshot but out of sight at the edge of camp.

They learned in fact the MLS had taken over the area one group at a time. They were making people serve them or starve until they submitted. They confiscated anything of value. They raided, raped, and took captives. Gretchen had experienced capture firsthand. She got quiet for an uneasy time. She studied Laurie and looked in Bonnie's direction analyzing the two. The others were still enumerating the transgressions of the MLS when Gretchen broke in with a matter of fact statement.

"Last night one of the MLS squads was enforcing rules on a camp down river from here. They shot a man and then all the squad was killed by an outside force. No one saw the group who killed them, but it is believed that there has been volunteer home militia formed rebelling against them."

Laurie didn't blink or flinch. She hoped she didn't have a tell that would give her away. She simply listened and asked Gretchen, "Who do you think it was?"

Gretchen studied Laurie longer than a moment, then, she shrugged, "I don't think I know. The rumor says three were killed with shotguns, two were beaten to death. Two girls escaped. They went underground, as have their families. The MLS put the word out that anyone helping these would be 'dealt with.' They offered a reward of ample food for a year for information leading to apprehension of the ones in the outside force. If I knew who they were, I would join them in a heartbeat!"

Laurie gently stood and said, "Thank you, Gretchen, for the information."

She turned and walked out of the camp with purpose. It was all show. She hadn't expected their actions would stir such a hornet's nest. They must remember in the future unintended consequences can result from strong actions.

Gretchen stared after her. Moving away a distance, Laurie knew Bonnie was shadowing her as she walked away from the camp. Bonnie signaled her to stop for a powwow. When they converged both were speechless. Some powwow. Neither had a word to say, but each looked at the other for a comment. None came.

Later, Bonnie explained what she knew about the MLS to Laurie. She enumerated her experiences with the MLS. She related events from the first raid up to Thor's community when Shaky had appeared. Laurie hadn't realized the depth of the conflict within Bonnie. They now had become committed!

The next two recon trips yielded additional information about the MLS and about a couple local gangs who had been robbing the people. They collected names and events. The concealed partner wrote in a notebook. Dates, places, and coded names were written down. As hard as they tried to find it, there seemed to be no official law enforcement, judicial authority or cops in the community. They started inquiring as to who were the latest judges for each of the local courts. A Judge Millner had been the US Magistrate for the area. They started trying to locate Judge Millner. He was believed to be located some twenty-five miles away near a small town called Lumberton, where he'd lived when the lights went out.

If they could talk with Judge Millner, maybe they could get instructions for the process to stop all the madness. They left early the next day. Two days later they neared the home of Judge Millner.

On the road near Lumberton, a man Bonnie had stopped to speak with asked why she was so interested in the Judge. She explained she wanted to locate Judge Millner for information. He then wanted to know what business she would have with this Judge.

"He's the US District Judge," she explained. "He should have answers for questions we have."

"Young lady, any attorney can answer legal questions. There is no court or law enforcement over which Judge Millner presides these days," said the man.

"Mister, that needs to start now with him," retorted Bonnie. "He's the only authority left locally who has any power to start the process unless he likes this anarchy style of society that now exists. If you will so kindly direct me to Judge Millner's home I will hear from him what can and what cannot be done."

The man studied her, and then asked, "What would you do?"

"I don't know. I want instructions from someone with knowledge and authority, so we can turn this thing around," she retorted. "He's the only person of legal authority we can locate."

After a lot of questions and short answers, the man said, "I'm Judge Millner."

Bonnie fell all over herself apologizing for her brashness. Judge Millner graciously accepted her change of countenance. Bonnie introduced Laurie and they talked for an hour about the demise of society, the solutions to the problems, and the consequences of failed efforts. Bonnie explained the ideas for her plan to bring criminals to justice. The Judge listened and when Laurie brought out a notebook, he asked to see the book and then, it was as if a light went on in his head. He inquired why these two just-out-of-school girls thought they could enforce the law.

Both looked at each other and Laurie said, "Because it's right and has to start somewhere. We're willing to start it, but we need authority to do the job right. We'll bring them in for trial when possible. You're the Judge. These are exceptional times. It will take exceptional measures to turn this thing around."

The Judge studied both thoughtfully. He invited them to his home for a simple meal, then sat to write an appointment for each, making them appointees of the United States District Court with law enforcement authority to back it up. They would be appointed as US Marshals. Local people knew who he was and would recognize his authority as the US District Magistrate. His instruction to them was stern about respecting individuals' God-given rights. His instruction included a warning that Bonnie and Laurie themselves especially were subject to the law. He would not tolerate unwarranted deviation or give favoritism just because they represented his court. They each were to have the authority to deputize others as needed to detain and enforce the law. They would be responsible for the actions of those they deputized. The regulations would be simple: no murder, rape, theft, or beatings. The accused would be faced by any accusers and witnesses with any compelling evidence to be presented. There would be power of subpoena and there would be punishment pronounced as applicable based on the law as the Judge deemed and based upon the evidence provided.

"If you encounter a duly-elected County Sheriff in your activities, you'll respect him or her as the top law enforcement authority in the county. I do reemphasize duly-elected," he emphasized. "You will be respected as Federal Law enforcement by my appointment as well."

This would be an imperfect application of justice at best, but for now it would be the best available and certainly might not have been recognized by any preexisting law. It would be a new place to start.

"Please understand," he went on, "you as well as I may be held as criminals at some future time for the actions we are about to undertake. You can still withdraw now before you get in too deep. I would understand if you do."

The Judge then insisted both young ladies go through a crash course on criminal law about what was acceptable and what was not. The basic education took the better part of three days.

During this schooling, the Judge enlightened his students about what had convinced him to make a decision to enforce the law. There had been news of a militia out of Riverton who by all accounts were raiding, robbing, and killing indiscriminately in the name of martial law. Their notebook and Bonnie's experience in Riverton stood as further information to confirm those suspensions. As far as he could discern, they had no authority to rule over people and certainly not to kill and rob. The Judge issued warrants for the apprehension of one Sergio Campella, one Max Simpson, one Toby Gilder, and an open John Doe warrant for any who could be proved collaborating with them in their questionable activities. When Toby's name was stated, Laurie paled. The Judge, seeing the change in her face, stopped.

He waited for the color to return to her cheeks, then asked, "What?"

Bonnie quickly intervened, using the explanation they knew Toby Gilder. He was a hometown boy, and not a nice one at that. The Judge seemed to accept the explanation, but Bonnie was convinced he suspected there to be more to the story than what was just given. Bonnie in that moment gained a little insight as to how deep Laurie's feelings toward Toby went.

Bonnie thought to herself, *Toby should hope someone finds him before Laurie does.*

They discussed Gretchen and decided to bring Gretchen in as an appointed deputy if she would be willing and so requested the Judge write a letter of appointment like theirs for her. He did so with instructions that either Laurie or Bonnie have supervisory authority over her and responsibility for her actions. He said after he met her and had time to evaluate her character, he might change those limitations. When they left the Judge's home, the gravity of their responsibility hit home. They both became apprehensive and had second thoughts about that to which they had committed.

Chapter 14

Gretchen

Bonnie and Laurie didn't speak most of the day. When evening came, they found an empty barn for shelter. The usual protocol was to keep one near the front and one near the back where they could keep a tab on the other's circumstances. The Judge had given provisions to each for a week, so they ate and settled in for the night. They now were starting to function as complementary parts of a single unit. As they ate, they each found reality to be nearly overwhelming.

Laurie thought, *This will go away after sleep tonight*. In the time that followed, she wished Zack were there to give her some answers. He would point her to the Bible for wisdom, she knew. At the thought, she began to cry silently with tears slowly edging down her cheek. At first they sped over the edge and fell into the vastness below. What were Sonja and Sally doing right now? She cried silently longer in her aloneness.

Bonnie was as scared unto near panic as she had ever been in her life. No particular reason except if she dwelt on what lay ahead, she would go screaming into the dark like a raving lunatic. She didn't sleep, wishing her dad was there. He would know what to do. "*Oh, Lord, where is he now? Is he okay or lying dead somewhere in those vast mountains? God, please protect him*," she prayed.

The second day brought them close to the settlements, where the MLS now ruled. People were moving like refugees away from the area. When asked, several said conditions there had become intolerable. The MLS terrorized the people. If brought to court, would they testify against the leaders and accomplices? No one seemed to believe justice would ever happen again. They had genuine fear of reprisal for such actions. The belief was, there was no law, no cops, and no one who could stop the debauchery. All this seemed to be a common and well-held belief among the groups Bonnie and Laurie encountered. The people's will had been broken!

Opposite the feelings Bonnie had in the night the night before, her "mule," as Shaky called it, arose like a flag in the midst of a raging battle. Her resolve strengthened. Shaky and Jessie knew spanking this child as a child was to no avail. She refused to cry no matter how much the spanking hurt. The boys weren't the same. The mule in her was still alive and well, she could feel it and now embraced it. That mule had carried her through the attack and beating in Riverton. She suddenly realized it now. Well, mules are smart and tough as well as stubborn. It would be to her advantage. She all of a sudden felt invincible. She would need to guard against that. What was happening to her now? She considered herself as even-keeled as any person she knew, but she had been to both ends of the spectrum emotionally within the last eighteen hours.

Bonnie looked at Laurie who exclaimed, "You look as if you had just been anointed by some great power. What in heaven's name is going on in your head, girl?"

Bonnie explained to Laurie the euphoria that had come over her which was brought on by the thoughts and feelings of the previous few hours. Laurie listened, then, admitted her own fears from the previous night. They both were astute enough to understand the emotional trauma brought on by high levels of stress. This was life and death stress.

"Bonnie, I think we need some long guns," said Laurie. "These shotguns won't be any good in a long-range firefight. When I have a chance, I'm going to cut my barrel off. I read in one of Daddy's magazines a scatter gun carries much more authority close range than any pistol. Our shotguns are useless at any distance over fifty yards. What do you think?"

Bonnie considered Laurie's statement and nodded her head in response.

Their next plan was to find Gretchen. When approaching the camp where they last saw Gretchen, they saw no indication of activity. The camp appeared to be in disarray and shambles. There seemed to be no indication the occupants had abandoned the site voluntarily. Studying the sign Laurie, found signs of struggle. Someone had overrun this small community. When searching, Bonnie found tracks of several people being herded away. Some tracks were steady, but a couple had been dragged, showing intermittent footprints between drag marks. Following in their typical spread style, the Marshals started on their first quest.

Moving quietly on the trail of the captured, Laurie was the first to hear the sounds of the group they followed. Signaling the discovery to Bonnie, Laurie flanked the group on the left. Bonnie did likewise on the other side. There some two hundred feet away were the former occupants of the overrun camp. In sight among them were five armed men driving the captives. Bonnie spotted an additional drag guard watching the back trail. That made a total of six. She slipped around the drag who had dropped behind some hundred feet. Bonnie was now ahead of the drag and behind the main body. As he followed the trail and rounded a curve in the path, Bonnie cocked her shotgun and told him not to move. He froze. He dropped his weapon as instructed and disrobed as instructed. When Bonnie was sure he had no other place to hide a knife or other weapon, she ordered him face down to the ground. With Bonnie's pistol to his head, Laurie tied his hands and feet, then bound his bent knees and feet to his hands after gagging him to silence. They said nothing to the captive. One down, next!

They split again and continued their pursuit. The next opportunity came when one of the guards stepped into a grove of trees to relieve himself. Laurie laid the end of her shotgun on the base of his neck with a reassuring shhhhhhh. She disarmed him the same as Bonnie had the drag. He was tied, gagged, and left for collection later. Two down!

The bonus with this captive was his weapon. It was a .223 caliber Savage model Axis XP Stainless rifle bolt action with a 4 to 9 variable scope. There was a box and a half of cartridges in the package.

As the captives were directed toward their destination, Bonnie and Laurie were not able to apprehend other captors before the compound destination was reached. At least the young Marshals knew the camp location. They beat a hasty retreat to their own captives, where one at a time a separate interrogation was commenced. Neither had experience at this technique or, for that matter, at many other things having to do with police activities.

The Marshals discussed what to do with what they suspected to be low-level personnel. Keeping them would be debilitating to their own activities. Taking them to the Judge would take them out of the game. They couldn't be shot now that the girls were upstanding citizens. They left the men tied except for their feet. There was left just enough gap in the prisoner's hobbles to allow them to walk but not run. They were tied together with a length of rope from one neck to the other's neck. Bonnie led and Laurie encouraged with the business end of her shotgun.

Camp this night was cold with the prisoners tethered on two sides, hands tied, and their shoes removed. The neck ropes remained in place. The girls spread to either side of the captives at a distance with a stern warning that mercy was in short supply and, "by the way, you dudes are under arrest by authority of United States District Judge Millner." They were being charged with unlawful detainment of persons, kidnapping as it were, and would be presented for trial at Judge Millner's pleasure.

Let them sleep on that this night, thought Bonnie.

The next day the prisoners griped and complained about due process.

"The laws are different now," said Laurie. "There will be no trial delays, no appeals to a higher court, no appointment of defense council, and there will be swift punishment upon sentencing. Think about that, you thugs. We are the witnesses to and accusers of your crime. Boys, you are screwed, blued, and tattooed. Now, on the other hand, if you can give us something we can work with, we might put in a good word with the Judge for you." Where that statement came from she had no idea. It just came out.

Near midday, they stopped for water and a bit of food. A bit was all the Marshals would spare. They didn't want the prisoners with strength. Leaving one tied and barefoot, they took the other away and asked questions with a promise of legal favor. He refused to tell them anything. They tied him and took his shoes.

They returned to the other and put him through the same routine with the added slight hint the other had accused him of other crimes. He demanded, "What other crimes?"

"With a little help, we might be persuaded to overlook them. How about it, what do you know about the MLS?" queried Bonnie.

He spilled his guts. Laurie took notes and the man signed the statement with names, dates, and places. It worked on the other prisoner as well and he signed too. Each confirmed the identity of the other and that was that. Both separately were warned not to say a word to the other about their statement. Two days later, they delivered the men to Judge Millner.

Judge Millner convened court immediately. Judge Roy Bean would have been proud. Both men were sentenced to death by hanging or firing squad. The sentence was set aside and each was placed on probation, having been given credit for the sworn and signed statements presented by the marshals. If any word should come that either was involved in any other crime past or future in this district no matter how minor, or if they associated with known felons or suspected felons, the probation would be revoked and the death sentence would be carried out. They would be executed on sight. They were to be fined of any possessions except the clothing and food they carried. They were instructed to leave the territory immediately. The Judge released them with instructions to get moving.

Judge Millner complemented the Marshals on their first arrest. He then sternly instructed them on some of the finer points of his law and warned them they were making deadly enemies. They left for the settlements again to find Gretchen.

Five days passed before they had any news of Gretchen. It seemed she had been injured when the raid on the camp took place. She had escaped to be tended by friends until she could function. Bonnie remembered how long it had taken her to recuperate when she had been beaten. They located Gretchen some miles away in the country where the MLS seldom ventured. When Bonnie saw Gretchen, she actually swore.

Gretchen told of the raid on their camp. The men had been beaten into submission. The women had just been beaten. When Gretchen resisted, she had been slugged at the back of her head and left for dead. She awoke with blood having run down over her face. The camp was empty. She recovered enough to make it to the camp of some friends.

"We found the camp, Gretchen, probably just after you left," said Bonnie. "We weren't able to stop all of them, but we caught two of them and returned them to the Judge. They turned state's evidence against the MLS and some of the leaders. We're going after them next."

Gretchen said, "I'm in. When do we leave?"

"Not so fast," added Laurie. "There are some conditions. First, you need to understand the rules."

"What rules? They don't have rules," retorted Gretchen as her head throbbed.

"Gretchen, Laurie, and I have been appointed as Marshals by US District Judge Millner," said Bonnie. "We have all the authority we need to do what we need without being outside the law and breaking the law. In fact, we have to abide by the law. We can bring these bums down legally. No, now wait, he has with our recommendation written a letter of appointment making you a deputy US marshal. Until he can meet with you, he placed you under our supervision. That's the way it is for now. You interested?""Hell ya!" exclaimed Gretchen. "I know who to take down first."

Laurie said, "Gretchen, we have restraints on what we can do. Understand we need to work together, OK? That's the way it's going to be!"

The trio discussed the plans and who to focus on. They wanted to take the leaders and the worst of the now named outlaws. They showed the written warrants to Gretchen to help her focus on the project. She just stared at the appointment letter.

"I always thought I might like to be a cop someday," Gretchen finally said.

The next week was spent discretely reconnoitering the MLS encampment. Gretchen stayed recuperating where she was. The marshals observed the site from all sides first at a distance being careful not to give away their presence and intentions. They closed gradually to a quarter mile, then to two hundred yards, then to less than a hundred yards. Occasionally, depending on the wind direction, noises could be heard, and once distinct words.

Laurie could see clearly the entrances of shelters occupied by some of the captives. Twice she saw what appeared to be an assault on the young women therein. On the next foray, Laurie spotted Toby Gilder barking out an order to a captive tent. When a response didn't come, he entered and began dragging a girl from the entrance. At that point, Laurie lost control. A calm resolve overtook all reason in her. The next thing she knew, she had placed a shot perfectly located along the front of Toby's pants about crotch level. The bullet grazed the skin on the right leg, cutting a deep furrow in the front of his left leg. What had been hit in between she knew not, but she knew what she intended.

Toby screamed, dodging backward and falling to the ground. When he rolled over, the front of his pants were blood-soaked. Laurie ducked out of sight watching Bonnie's direction and then executed on their planned retreat. After running half a mile through Tamarisk scrub, she broke for their planed rendezvous. She paused to catch her breath before proceeding.

Chapter 15

Molly Brown

A voice from behind her quietly said, "There are three men closing on your left. Follow me now!"

Laurie nearly wet herself at the sound of a voice so close. She whirled to see a tall, large-boned woman about forty years old crouched in the brush.

"Now, honey, if you want to live!" she repeated.

They took off, with Laurie following the woman. When they stopped, Laurie thought about Bonnie. "*Where is she?*" Some time passed and so did the pursuers. Laurie thanked the lady and was about to make off to find Bonnie when the lady introduced herself. Her name was Molly Brown. As it turned out, as Laurie and Bonnie had been watching the encampment, Molly had been watching them.

"You ladies are setting yourselves up for grief," said Molly Brown assuredly. "If you keep doing what you're doing, you'll get wiped out. I speak from experience. I did a tour in Iraq and two tours in Afghanistan. If you're going to exact damage on those bandits, you need help. I can help you."

"Well, Molly, we would welcome help in the right circumstances," said Laurie at last. "How do we contact you?'

"You don't. I'll contact you," she said and disappeared into the brush.

Laurie, still concerned about Bonnie, worried if Bonnie would be caught trying to find Laurie. She first went to the rendezvous location. Bonnie had been there. She had left a discrete indicator. Laurie followed the sign and after a time walked right into Bonnie.

Bonnie whispered, "Laurie, stop!"

She signed there were men ahead just yards away. After observing, they decided to abandon this battle. The odds were poor at best. They were outnumbered four-to-one. As they spread and slipped away, night fell. When they settled in for the night, Bonnie demanded an explanation from Laurie. Laurie didn't have one. She simply explained her rage and if she would have been in the camp, she would have killed him in defense of the girl, period.

Bonnie said nothing for minutes, then commented, "He may bleed to death anyway, the way you shot him. I saw the results. I believe you got his attention. If he thinks a little, he'll know it was you. Nobody else can shoot like that."

On a different topic Laurie said, "Bonnie, we've been watched."

Laurie told Bonnie about her encounter with Molly Brown after the shooting. She explained what Molly had told her. Bonnie again listened and sat without saying anything for some time. Bonnie was feeling like they were losing control. Too many people were getting involved. Yet on the other hand, they needed people, tough experienced people, people who could bring their A-game to this conflict.

All the next day the MLS swarmed like a plague through the vicinity, turning over every camp and beating any who resisted. They shot two and tortured several others maliciously. When the day of terror was over, refugees fled the area. The settlements had now become ghost towns, and most houses were abandoned. Even Bonnie, Laurie, and Gretchen packed their camp and headed for new parts. On the trail out, Laurie saw Molly Brown standing watching them. She signaled Bonnie with their silent language. Bonnie observed Molly until they reached the place she stood. Molly smiled at Bonnie and acknowledged Laurie briefly. Gretchen stood to one side, prepared for action.

Laurie introduced Molly Brown to Bonnie and to Gretchen. They stood sizing up and evaluating Molly. She was an imposing person.

"I saw you take down the thugs who raided her camp," said Molly, indicating Gretchen with a point of the chin. "I saw the shot she took at the man in the camp." She indicated Laurie with her nod. "That wasn't a misplaced bullet. It was perfectly on target. You ladies are lucky—dumb and lucky. Trained personnel will eat your lunch. You just haven't encountered them yet. When you do, you're all done unless you learn some stuff first. You aren't enough: not smart enough, trained enough, disciplined enough, or mean enough to pull this off. If you try to start your own gang, you'll become just as they are and I wouldn't be part of that, but if you want to do it right, I'm looking for people to join with and you are the best I've seen lately."

Bonnie resented the implication about their ineptness. She blustered, "And how do you know so much? You think we want to start a gang of our own? We have a right to go after these criminals and bring them to justice."

Clearly, Molly Brown had pushed a button. Bonnie had bitten, hook, line, and sinker, proving in part Molly was right. As put off as Bonnie was, she knew Molly to be right about their abilities. She explained they had been appointed United States Marshals by a US District Judge and were the only existing law enforcement for this area. The County Sheriff's office had been wiped out to the man by the MLS in the first encounter. The local settlement's city police department had vaporized in the face of such daunting forces.

Molly was surprised and requested that Bonnie repeat what she said. Bonnie, sensing Molly's disbelief, did and now her mule rising inside curtly offered her letter of appointment as evidence. Molly waved her off, then questioned how they had come by such an appointment.

Laurie jumped in to slow the turmoil, "We asked for them. We have an axe to grind, but this governs our ire. We knew that unchecked we would unjustifiably start vengeance and maybe wouldn't stop. We talked about it and decided this was best. The Judge agreed and he needed to start some form of order. That's when he appointed us. Do you see, Molly, how it is? We have a chance to stop the riffraff who are brutalizing the people with legal justification."

"Just the three of you. What do you think you can do?" asked Molly.

"Within the last two weeks, we have signed confessions and two convictions. We have warrants for the apprehension and arrest of

151

the leaders and authority to appoint others as deputies. With all that said, we are restricted," said Laurie.

"Are there others or is it just the three of you?" queried Molly. "You are outmanned, outgunned, and that Commander Campella is ruthless. If you go head to head with him, you will lose. All you can do is pick off stragglers. In the meantime, the MLS gets stronger and the word is there are sizable reinforcements in Riverton if he needs them. He's been sending pillaged supplies back to Riverton. The word too is they are going to start raiding the outlying farms that haven't been touched yet."

Bonnie's first thought was of Jake's and her family. MLS would have a scrap if it came to that. They had to warn Jake before MLS surprised them. Her thought escaped her mouth before she could harness it. All looked at her in surprise.

"Explain," said Gretchen.

"We need to warn the outlying farms and ranches," said Bonnie. "One alone can't hold off this bunch if surprised. If warned, they can make a good stand. If the marshals get on the MLS's tail, we might discourage them a bit."

"Bonnie, it would be suicide to go head to head," said Molly. "Now listen to me. I have experience in this stuff. What the hell do you think I did in Afghanistan? I was a logistics specialist. I saw what the Taliban did to the mighty United States military. Had we not had far superior air power, firepower, night scopes, body armor, and millions of dollars' worth of guns, the Taliban would have kicked our butts right into the sea. We were good because we had technology. The MLS doesn't have that. If we fight a Taliban-style guerrilla war against them, we will wear them out. They don't have a cause and will fold. Then you can arrest to your heart's content. Listen to me, we hit and run, hit another place and run, strike at unexpected times and fade away. They can't defend against that and a sniper shot occasionally will demoralize the hell out of them. Laurie here started today. You need to understand there will be casualties. You will need to grow the guerrilla forces and keep tight discipline on them. That in and of itself that will be a monumental task."

Bonnie thought a moment and said, "We need to think on it. This may be beyond our authority. I want to talk with the Judge. Will you go with us and explain what you told us?"

"Yes, I will," Molly replied.

"I must warn the farmers from here to Jake's and have them spread the word," said Bonnie. "On the other hand, they might take the MLS on just for a Sunday outing. Better yet, I believe Gretchen's friends could carry the word and our message. They need a place to go and our letter would be a great introduction for them. We will go see the Judge."

Bonnie sat down and composed a letter to Jake and one to her mom.

"Dear Uncle Jake,

The most current information is the MLS, an outlaw para-military group, may be headed your direction. You and your neighbors need to be prepared for an MLS raid on your homes and farms. The MLS is ruthless. Don't give them any quarter, not any. Laurie Smith and I have been appointed US Marshals to enforce the criminal law in our area. We have a project that requires our attention before we can come to help. If possible, we'll be along in a week or so, nipping at the heels of the MLS. Don't mistake us for enemies. We intend to catch them in a crossfire if they engage you in a shootout.

Love,
Bonnie"

She wrote her mom a short note expressing her love. She inquired about her dad and whether he had been heard from. If someone could check on Sonja and Sally, she would appreciate it, she added. Both letters were addressed, folded, and placed with the woman who had cared for Gretchen. The lady knew Jake and the location of his ranch. She said she would be there in two days, maybe three at the outside.

The foursome started for Judge Milliner's. Two days later, they arrived, where they were challenged by a contingent of men guarding the Judge's home. Bonnie identified herself and the three others. One guard crossed to the dwelling and moments later the Judge exited the house.

As he approached the gate, he greeted Bonnie and Laurie sternly. "You don't tie your prisoners anymore, I see."

"Well, Judge, if they were prisoners, they would be hogtied hand and foot. You see they would be more dangerous than any we've taken to date," Bonnie replied tongue in cheek.

The Judge, not to be outdone, quipped, "So far all I've seen from you is small fries." He paused. "I trust your being here must be important."

Bonnie introduced Gretchen and Molly. Quickly, she outlined the situation involving the MLS. The Judge listened and then indicated he already had most of the information. Additionally, there were reinforcements coming from Riverton to reinforce the newly hatched plans of the MLS.

Molly stepped forward, addressing the Judge as "Your Honor," and proceeded to explain the purpose of their report. They planned to raise a fighting force to harass the MLS as it attacked the civilians. She went through her creds, told the same story she told the Marshals, and requested he appoint her as commander of a militia force for defense of the population.

"Miss," Judge Millner responded, "I don't have authority to appoint an army. I will consider your theory and see if there's a way we can legally set up a military-type force. If we can contact the governor, there may be a way, but not right now. In the meanwhile, all I can do is appoint marshals and allow them limited discretionary law enforcement powers. Bonnie here or Laurie can deputize you. With that, you have the right to protect the public if they are under attack. You will have authority to apprehend as needed and deliver to me any you arrest. You will not murder, steal, beat, or torture any prisoner. Beyond that, we are as near to Old West law as we have ever been. We probably are more 'Old West' now than the real Old West ever was. The difference is, there is no chivalry or chivalrous fast draws now. I long for the days of real law and order."

With that, the four women departed across country straight toward Jake's. In the evening camp, they outlined what would be required in a defense posse to defend the population from gangs and the MLS.

The settlements lay at the confluence of two medium size rivers. The trail cutting cross-country from one to the other formed a triangle. Jake's ranch lay about three miles north of the far north east corner of this triangle. Between the two rivers was a large expanse of semi-arid land with irrigated farms sporadically spaced. Many of these had been abandoned as the public domestic water services had long since quit functioning. Lacking an alternative other than the remaining brackish water running in the adobe-lined stream beds, the tenants moved. The local water was not drinkable for man or beast. The people had moved closer to the fresh water sources of the rivers.

The four Marshals traversed this arid land and found shelter in deserted homes. It was at times easier to just sleep outside than to evict the spiders and other creatures that had set up residence inside. But when it rained, the sacrifice of shared shelter with bugs and mice had to be made. There was nothing in the world like walking through a doorway with a spider web draping across one's face, sticking stubbornly to one's hair and cheek.

Three days brought the four near Jake's ranch. Bonnie laid out the approach so as not to disturb any of the five big dogs Jake kept chained near the ranch headquarters. It was late in the day and like her dad Shaky had done, Bonnie didn't want to approach the farmstead in the dark.

As night passed, Bonnie had a feeling there was a problem at Uncle Jake's. There seemed to be no light at night in the house, no smoke from the cook stove, and no people moving about.

Morning came like always with the coldest part of the night just before the early sunrise. Bonnie had lost track of the seasons. She thought it was about late summer. It seemed the cottonwood leaves had lost that fresh growing green sometime in the past month, but it had been a hotter shorter summer than she felt it should have been. Now the nights were cooling in earnest. Bonnie approached the house, but she wasn't seeing the activity she was accustomed to seeing. The dogs were not where they normally had been chained and there wasn't smoke coming from the chimney. Bonnie's reaction was near panic. She raced to the back door, the normal entry used by the residents. She entered with her heart pounding so hard she thought it would beat right out of her chest. The house was silent. It hadn't been abandoned a long time, but like most abandoned dwellings, there were cobwebs starting to form in the doorways.

After studying the setting and conditions, the marshals' collective opinion was the household residents had packed up and moved suddenly. Bonnie started looking for signs her letter had arrived to Jake and her mom. She found nothing.

"Bonnie!" exclaimed Laurie. "I've got to go home; the girls are in danger!"

Bonnie was torn. Where was Jessie and where was Jake and Meg?

They searched the surrounding grounds for sign and tracks. There seemed to be newer military vehicle tracks on three sides of the grounds. Molly found two dog carcasses and Gretchen found a third. Each had been shot multiple times. They apparently had been released by Jake from their chains to attack intruders.

After some discussion, the Marshals collectively made the decision to rapidly go to the Smith Ranch. The trip had taken Gene the better part of two days. It took the Marshals every minute of five hours.

As Laurie approached the house, which appeared to have been burned, she heard Sonja whisper, "Laurie, Laurie, it's me. Where have you been?"

"You wouldn't believe," Laurie replied. "Why are you so quiet?"

"There have been marauders who robbed the house," Sonja explained. "Sally shot two, Daddy and Josh got a couple more. I was hidden when the robbers retreated. They came back with a bunch more and ransacked the house before they burned it. Daddy, Sally, and Josh are hiding out in the trees. The bandits finally left."

"Sonja, you mean Daddy is alive and here?" Laurie asked.

"Yes, he's been awfully sick but was better when he come home. Josh had been here helping with the work when Daddy came in. They hit it off right away," she explained.

"Sonja, did you know any of them?" asked Laurie.

"No, I don't think they were from around here," said Sonja. "The way it sounded, they didn't seem to know the country. I heard one mention Toby's name. I think he sent them. When they came back, they had a truck. Where'd they get gas?"

"We believe this bunch have been pillaging all over from Riverton to the settlements on the river. They're called the MLS. We're going to stop them, and do it legally," Laurie declared. "How long has it been since they were here?"

"The last of them left about noon yesterday," Sonja replied.

Gretchen and Molly appeared, causing Sonja to turn, ready to fight. Laurie calmed her when the women approached. Then Laurie introduced them to Sonja. She explained that Bonnie was covering their rear. She would be along shortly.

When Bonnie joined, Laurie called a war counsel. Up to this time, Zack, Josh, and Sally had been out of sight. When the discussion started, there was a variety of ideas as to the plan of attack. When all had been said, they agreed guerrilla tactics would be best: snipe, hit, and run. If they could catch the MLS red-handed, then they would shoot to kill. The first part of the plan would be to disable the transportation, then eliminate one or two at a time, taking their arms until the militia became weary and retreated. Molly reminded them they shouldn't move too fast to confront the MLS directly. Direct confrontation only should take place when their arms and numbers were superior to those of the MLS.

Having lost track of the intruders at Jake's due to the many paved roads obscuring the departing tracks, proceeding to the Smith's had been the next most important priority. Now that they discovered the Smiths were burned out but safe, the group started the return to find Bonnie's missing family. There was no lead, nor was there any news from the infrequent contact with the citizenry.Bonnie separated and detoured to stop by the home of Jake's daughter. Mike and Cindy had been raided according to a neighbor. Cindy put up a fight that would have made an Indian fighter proud until Mike arrived. Together they lasted through the balance of the day and most of the night. By early light, the invaders had outwitted the defenders, killing both in a flurry of shots during an on-rushing charge. Their home had been ransacked and burned to the ground. Cindy had taken her toll of nine and Mike added his charge of five more to the attacker's expense before the end.

Bonnie was infuriated to the point of tears and frustration. Her resolution renewed, she returned to the neighbor's for a written statement. He was reluctant for fear of reprisal. Bonnie explained the law being enforced by the US district Judge and the appointments of Marshals to effect arrests. She explained the need for evidence and witness statements to strengthen prosecution. The neighbor skeptically declined to cooperate.

Returning to the posse, Bonnie described her findings. Josh was quiet, white with anger, and conjuring a scary resolve. Mike had been a favorite relative. Bonnie believed she saw a change in his demeanor in that moment, a hardening in his spirit. They were at war and there was not a question as to their purpose.

First, they disabled several of the MLS's vehicles covertly, nobody being the wiser. Over the next cooler couple months the small contingent spied on, collected information on, and harassed the MLS, along with arresting and delivering many to Millner.

The MLS had been reinforced with men, arms, and supplies from Riverton. None of the Marshals saw evidence of Jake's family. They seemed not to be captive in the MLS encampment. Having no sign of Jake added to the fears that Jake, her mom, and the others might have perished.

Forays of MLS squads would go and return in a daytime. Occasionally a squad would take two days, but those were not as frequent as the twenty-four hour trips. Twice, a group of twenty soldiers would leave by vehicle and be gone for three days. Both times they returned with captives and goods pillaged from the out-lying populous.

After observation, plans were set for an ambush of one of these mechanized outgoing forays. The observer would flash coded signals to outlying observers as to direction and numbers when a mechanized contingent departed. The signal would be protected so detection by the target wouldn't occur. The signal in turn would be passed along to the disbursed Marshals. They would collect at predetermined points, depending on the direction and speed of the MLS contingent. A long-distance sniper would take out the driver at a hazardous point in the road hoping to wreck the transportation and as many soldiers as possible with it. Then the retreat of soldiers would be ambushed with design to capture or wipe them out completely. Arms and supplies were to be collected and the Marshals would melt into the landscape, covering their trail as they retreated themselves.

The system worked perfectly the first two times. With no contingent returns, the MLS was left wondering. Somehow, a scout sent out found the second ambushed contingent and reported undetected by the Marshals back to the headquarters. The third attempt was met with fierce resistance and unbeknownst to the Marshals, a follow-up force followed the first. It nearly caught the Marshals off balance, and they rapidly retreated into the landscape with trackers on their trails.

The plan was to retreat in pairs spread many yards apart. Pursuit while in retreat had been anticipated as an eventual possibility. Molly was the first to be trailed. She watched her back trail and discovered four trackers. She shot one, wounding his leg, hoping to slow them. They treated him and left him. Molly's partner, one of the new deputies, hearing Molly's wounding shot, set an ambush from the high ground and killed the first man through the opening. The two partners retreated while Molly worked around the back trail waiting for the remaining two to appear. They did but were on the partner's trail too far for a good shot. Molly knew her partner being in jeopardy placed a shot as close as she could guesstimate. When she shot, the distance must have been four hundred yards. She held and squeezed. One of the trackers slumped and fell face down in the cold adobe dirt. As Molly watched, the last tracker jerked sideways, falling headlong into a tangle of juniper stump. Molly heard the report of the rifle shot just milliseconds after the man went down. Neither man moved. Circling the fallen men, Molly found her partner stripping the arms and ammo as well as binoculars from the bodies.

Backtracking, they gathered the first kill equipment and liberated the wounded man of his equipment. He was in such shock from the leg wound, he offered no resistance. Neither said a word but left with his equipment, leaving him only a canteen of water.

When gathered with the others, Josh was surprised by one of the rifles Molly had collected. The rifle was one that belonged to Mike.

It had Mike's livestock brand burned into the stock. He and Mike hunted deer together with it. Josh sat a long while and then quietly walked into the dark. Sally knew he grieved hard as Mike wasn't only relation but a life-long friend. Sally went searching for him and after a time found him sitting on a stump, having wept his eyes dry.

Two times, the MLS commenced attacking an outlying farmstead. The residents' resistance was solid because of forewarning. The resistance was bolstered because the Marshals surprised the MLS with crossfire from the rear and sides.

During the first attack, several MLS soldiers had been killed while several others were wounded before the others escaped. During the second attack, the soldiers were surprised again but suffered a resounding defeat. Several escaped. Three were captured and tied, while the rest of the dozen were slain in heated gunfire.

After intense tag-team interrogation, Bonnie, Laurie, and Gretchen started another of the three-day treks to the Judge's for criminal delivery and prosecution. They traveled along the small river on an ancient Indian trail toward the Judge's headquarters. Two times the prisoners attempted escape, but their efforts were foiled. One made the mistake of slipping his ties and grabbing Gretchen from behind. After kicking the living daylights out of him with long practiced skill, she proceeded to quietly and quickly rebind his hands and feet before he regained his senses. The second event occurred when nearly at their destination. The tying of their feet together in a rope shackle served to restrict their movements.

Laurie, while suspecting some form of activity on the prisoner's part, stepped out of sight, watching the prisoners all the while. Two of the three slipped the shackle ties and started running. Their hands still being tied impeded their speed. Laurie, being quick of wit and used to wrangling quick calves, grabbed a long dead stick and as the first went by and thrust the stick between the steps of the first, causing him to trip with tangled feet. While Gretchen proceeded to keep him down, Laurie caught the second. She simply picked up a river rock just larger than a lemon and pitched it like a fastball that toppled the escapee, leaving a goose egg on his topknot. Before he could recover, she hobbled his feet designed for a short step. Without mercy, she drove him back to the original escape location where Gretchen had delivered the first. The rest of the journey went as planned.

As usual, the Judge held a quick court. However, the Marshals couldn't testify to a specific death caused by the captives other than those killed in the attacks and the association as part of the MLS. The Judge pronounced a suspended death sentence with a warning that any of the three caught in this district would be justifiably shot on sight. They were instructed to leave the district immediately.

Bonnie delivered a report of the activity on the MLS and what plans had been implemented to apprehend them. Judge Millner listened to the report thoughtfully and at the end gave warning. Reinforcements from Riverton were expected to arrive before the Marshals' return to the settlements. Word had it that the MLS acquired ordinance and supplies from the National Guard Post in Riverton.

"You are to gather as much intelligence on this as you can and in three weeks report to me with your information. They mustn't know what we know," the judge instructed.

He released the trio to return to the settlements. Bonnie now was frustrated, as she hadn't been able to follow up on the disappearance of her mother, Jake and his wife. They had simply for the present disappeared. The Judge's orders for observation would help them gather information, if there was any, on the Jake party. There had been no sign of them.

Spying for two weeks revealed the expected. The MLS had reinforced the settlements with men and weapons heretofore not seen. The activity according to Molly was one with the demeanor of a military outpost. Numbers were counted as well as supplies estimated. No attacks were made and few forays sent out after the last ambush. Molly felt the MLS was readying for a military campaign. Josh discovered a single scout returning from the direction of the Judge's headquarters. Josh captured him after cold cocking him with a club. Gagging and tying him in an obscure location, Bonnie, Josh, Laurie, and Molly returned to question the scout. After persuasion, he spilled his guts.

On the way to make the report to the Judge, Bonnie and Molly took the captive with them. The Judge was pleased and their report confirmed the MLS intended a direct attack upon the Judge and his court. It would be coming within the week.

"Marshals, we are going to vanish before the snow falls," instructed the judge. "I suggest you consider doing the same. Devote yourselves to gathering winter supplies. I will send word where you are to report when better weather comes. Don't make the mistake of leaving tracks in the snow any child can follow. You still have authority until next July. Here is your extension of appointment for you and the others. Again, I warn you not to take the law into your own hands. Good luck to you." He turned and walked inside.

Knowing the Judge's quarters were likely under surveillance, Bonnie and Molly left in the opposite direction from which they had come. They circled some five miles out of their way into what had been designated Bureau of Land Management holdings never settled by anyone because it wasn't desirable to live on. It for the most part was barren wasteland, or not the preferred usable lands for grazing or farming by the homesteaders of the late 1890s and early 1900s.

Chapter 16

The High Ridges

I t is said time passes quickly when you're having fun. Gene wasn't having fun and time seemed to be flying. All he could think about was getting to Seth so far away. Every day was a drag no matter how much progress he made in that day. The obstacles Gene faced in addition to hunger and fatigue were the avoiding of other people and the locating of a functional route over the Continental Divide. The city where Seth lived in was a suburb of a densely populated metropolitan area. Gene could only imagine Metropolis would be in chaos without local law enforcement.

Before he reached the halfway point, the late summer monsoons had commenced. They seemed to be never ceasing. The late afternoon storms could be treacherous this time of year. The rain seemed to be colder and more penetrating than Gene could ever remember. The thunder would approach mostly from the west and Gene would find shelter under a rock ledge or a smaller spruce or pine tree until the storm passed by. Gene was careful not to sit under a tree with split bark. Split bark was an indication lightning had struck there before. If a big storm approached, Gene would go so far as to set his metal equipment down a way from himself until the storm passed. Several times he laid his metal equipment aside some distance as a large storm would pass to avoid attracting a possible lightning strike.

In years past he had ridden out many lightning storms by being smart. He wouldn't hold up under a big tall tree. Sheltering under a large tree was equally an invitation to disaster and death. His preferred choice when available was a thick clump of short trees that hopefully would not attract a bolt from the sky.

He watched the ground for indications of iron-impregnated soils that might attract lightning. He watched the tree trunks for signs of prior lightning strikes, split bark, or shattered wood. He was ever so careful where his feet were, not in the water or damp ground if he could help it. Being hit by lightning in this country was certain death without help from modern medical response services. A lightning strike from a storm could knock a man literally half off the mountain.

These wet rainy days seemed to bring out a myriad of mushrooms. These varied in shape, size, and color. White coral-looking ones, white toadstools with red highlights, large yellow scalloped toadstools, and puffballs of all sizes were nearly everywhere in the conifer forests. Gene had no clue what he could safely eat and what he could not. He mused he could try two different varieties a day until one killed him. That death wasn't appealing because death from mushroom poising is a painfully excruciating death. *Oh, well, no exotic dinner this week.*

Grocery stores had three days or less of food supplies at the time the EMP occurred. Some three or four months had passed since and Gene knew under the best of circumstances another three or four weeks would pass before he could get to city outskirts. Seth lived on the outskirts of Metropolis and commuted some forty miles to his work. Seth was an engineer working for a highly secured defense contractor. He traveled extensively and often for his job. There was a better than even chance of Seth being out of town when the EMP occurred. If that were the case, Seth wouldn't be around. But Gene had to try at any costs.

The closer Gene got to Metropolis, the more people he started seeing. There were many small bands that had made forays into the mountains in search of food and goods. A person by himself was vulnerable. Gene considered joining one, then decided he was better off not becoming part of a roving band. He felt that depending upon one's self was far preferable to depending on others in a group.

To join a group of people takes some thought. If the group is strong, then there's some protection in mutual association. If the group is made up of weak members and that have banded together because they feel there is safety in numbers, then there may not be protection in a mutual association. The old saying "a chain is as strong as its weakest link" is a misappropriation of metaphors for this situation. An unordered association of people is nothing more than herd mentality, where the strongest of the herd survive while the weak attract and are consumed by predators. Gene was not one to become part of a herd. He felt considerably more secure depending upon his own abilities and trusting his own survival abilities rather than coupling with others who may or may not contribute at critical times for survival. Gene would rather be alone and self-dependent than vulnerable as part of the herd.

So it had come to pass Gene had several opportunities to join up with groups of survivors but those were dismissed by Gene. He wasn't confident in relying on others' decisions for his own fate. In addition, their goals did not mesh with Gene's objective of locating the oldest son so far away in the north and east. So as it went, Gene took the next step literately and figuratively to achieve his goal.

Day after day, Gene covered as many miles as able in the high mountains. Time was taken to catch snowshoe hares, whistle pigs (ground hogs for tender feet), squirrels, fish, raccoons, a porcupine, grouse, and even a skunk for the next meal. *Talk about smoke revealing one's presence, a skunk will announce your presence like a siren. The difference is people generally don't come huntin' you when you smell like a skunk unless they are very hungry.* Catching these meals were not daily events but occurred often enough that Gene hadn't starved. He lived like a mountain man without further thought except for his goal of finding Seth, his oldest adult child.

These high mountains were cool this time of year. The mornings now were below freezing, but the skies when they were clear allowed the sun to quickly warm Gene's side and front as he hiked higher and higher in the mountains. There had been some early snows, but those had readily melted from the sunny days.

Gene's footwear didn't wear as well as he had hoped. He could detect the sharper edges of rocks penetrating pressure against his foot sole as he stepped on them. He hoped with care they would last until he returned home.

There were old mines in this high country. Their locations were given away by telltale tailing slides running down the hillsides below them. Gene had never been very comfortable inside these old diggings but would use them as shelter during inclement weather. He never went in much past the portal face. Several times he discovered occupants of the human kind possessing these shelters before he could get there. He would turn away and seek another, maybe higher on the hillside, where many wouldn't try to go.

Two times Gene thought he had traveled far enough to have crossed the Continental Divide only to discover another range of mountains ahead of him. He had forgotten how many mountain ranges and sub-ranges there were between Pinedale and Metropolis to the east. Before the EMP in an automobile over paved four-lane highways, they seemed of no consequence. Now they were monumental.

Summer by Gene's estimate was nearly over now and he would need to push on if he were to cover the 300-plus miles to get to Seth. Always in the back of his mind was the extra care he would have to take to not become disabled or injured. At Gene's age, a fall or injury could be fatal where a younger man might survive such an event.

Skirting around the traveled roads taken by wondering refugees hoping to find some way of reducing their plight, Gene often would traverse hillsides and climb ridges above the valleys to stay away from these groups of people and the more traveled roads. These people had become more and more desperate seemingly by the week. Looking down from above on small bands, he had seen attacks more than once where one band would pillage the others and plunder their belongings. Gene had seen utility vehicles twice along the roadways loading and gathering people. When loaded, they would drive away oftentimes leaving their meager belongings behind. Gene wanted nothing to do with either, nor did he care who the victim and the victor might be. Gene focused upon one thing: getting over the mountains to where Seth should be located. To be caught up in a refugee compound would be unthinkable.

Gene had hiked around one hillside, then another and at midday, he decided to consume a meager ration of dried and cured porcupine he'd packed away. He missed salt for the cure. He would have to scrounge a supply somewhere if he could find a source.

Gene spotted a resting place near a large rock just below a fallen tree. As he started to sit, some off-balance from the weight of his pack, something hit him. It toppled him over. He had been shot, but with what? The slight pain in his left shoulder blade wasn't bad, but it was very real. As he tipped over from the impact, he tried to shed his pack, but it seemed to be pinned to him on the right side. He shed his coat with pack seemingly attached, unholstered his .357, and looked up the hill from behind the downed tree for a sign of where the blow had come from. Looking quickly back at his pack, he saw an arrow stuck at the location just where the pack rested on his shoulder blade. On the inside of his coat there was blood, his blood, not a lot but enough to know he was bleeding. All this took him only a second or less. As Gene looked up the hill and to his left toward a movement about seventy feet, a man drew another arrow in his bow and pointed it directly at Gene's position. Gene quickly pointed the pistol and squeezed off the shot. Gene didn't hear the shot go off but did see the arrow release and fly above his shoulder a foot or so; he heard it hit a tree far down the hillside. A split second before the archer released his shot, the .357 slug hit him three or four inches below his left nipple, and he fell backward with the bow clattering on the rocks nearby. Gene surveyed the surrounding bushes and trees for other assailants and after a bit saw nothing that remotely looked to be a threat. Gene circled back to the left around the hillside to cover that was near and watched. Gene shook almost uncontrollably. After watching and listening from his concealed spot, he then ever-so-carefully moved in on the archer. The archer seemed to be lifeless and his eyes had the clouded over look of death.

This is one bushwhacker who won't bushwhack again, Gene thought.

As he stayed watchful for the moments that passed, Gene again began to tremble. He wanted to make sure there weren't others there, then he felt the trickle slide down his back. He wondered if it were nervous sweat or blood. It was too cool to be blood, although the stress and adrenaline of a moment like this could cause a man to perspire all over. The answer to the question didn't need answering: he wasn't sweating.

Gene was low on bolts for his crossbow and the arrows carried by this archer would do mightily when trimmed and weighted. This chap had no more use for them. Gene didn't bother to check for anything else on his body.

Gene slipped down to where his pack lay and looked with great interest. The broad head on the arrow had penetrated the pack and the aluminum frame enough that the broad head protruded through the frame so as to cut half an inch deep into Gene's skin and shoulder blade under his shirt. The full impact of the arrow had been taken by the pack frame, toppling Gene while he was off balance as he sat. Gene tried to pull the arrow out, but the head was wedged tight. He turned the shaft counter clockwise, unscrewing the shaft from the broad head and pulling it back out through the backpack as if extracting it from a bail of straw.

Funny thing, he thought. His coat had flopped loosely around the pack. The arrow had pinned the coat on the outside of the back-pack while he still wore it, making it difficult for him to shed the coat and pack.

The archer must have misjudged the kill spot based upon the location of the coat. His coat had been pinned to the frame on both sides. Now, the problem remained. The broad head still penetrated the frame just where Gene's back rested against the pack when in carry mode. Gene took his pocket tool and pulled on the obstacle to no avail. Gene picked up a rock about the size of a softball and hammered against the point. Part chipped off and part curled.

Time was of the essence. He didn't want to be caught in the open if the archer had companions. Gene needed to be moving and quickly. Gene struck again and the point loosened, but the part that curled had clinched the point in place so it wouldn't back out. Gene struck it again, bending it enough so it wouldn't puncture his back, and then he packed up and rapidly made tracks, or in this case tried not to leave tracks, as fast as he was able.

The cut on his back was starting to sting and Gene could feel the blood. The irritation was lessened by folding a multipurpose pillowcase and placing it just below the wound to make space and thereby lessen the rubbing irritation. The majority of weight in his pack was carried by his hip belts.

Gene covered a couple miles and picked a location with cover and a good exit where he could rest. He could watch his back trail for about three hundred yards. He chose a sheltered spot in which to hold up and kept his possessions nearly packed in case a quick exit was needed.

If someone followed, they would have to cross a series of clearings and slide rock patches to get to where Gene was. Slide rock travel is slow and if one steps on the wrong rock, it can upturn, causing the traveler to fall or be pinned by the tipping or tumbling rocks. Gene used this knowledge of slide rock treachery to his possible advantage. A man on foot can cross with care but horses most generally have to go around, not across.

Gene now needed to accomplish two things. He needed to treat his wound and he needed to remove the broad head from his pack frame. For the first act, he felt he needed to disinfect the cut. He carried a small bottle of coal oil for many reasons. It helped as a fire starter in wet weather. It would clean and lubricate metal parts in a pinch, but most of all, it was a great disinfectant, an antiseptic, and healing agent. As a child on the farm, his family used coal oil to treat and medicate cuts and scrapes, unlike the neighbors, who used iodine and Merthiolate. Coal oil was the best when cutting and doctorin' livestock. Gene couldn't remember a steer or a hog getting an infection ever. It was one of the main ingredients for a concoction called Black Oil, which was used to heal wire cuts on horses. Gene's memory of the formula was dim. However, he did remember Black Oil worked miracles on deep flesh wire cuts.

As he started removing his shirt, he discovered the shirt stuck to the wound. Gene contemplated the situation. The location on his back was difficult to reach. Gene took a dry air-exposed stick about three quarters of an inch in diameter and wrapped some cleaner cloth around it. The cloth was soaked in coal oil and Gene dabbed the oil on the wound until he felt the area had been thoroughly soaked. The shirt gently pulled away and bleeding started again. Gene placed a patch of cloth soaked in coal oil over the wound but had no practical way to secure it. He leaned against a tree trunk for a spell, pinning the cloth between him and the tree, but he wasn't sure if the dripping he felt was oil or blood. Whatever the case, the drip wasn't bad and when he felt behind and below the wound he perceived blood diluted by coal oil. With that determined, he proceeded to figure out a way to bind the cloth in place. In as awkward a location as the wound was, to dress it himself was next to impossible. Gene decided to don his shirt and tie a strap as high on his chest as possible. It likely wasn't a good solution but was all he could figure for the moment.

The second task was to remove the broad head from the pack frame. Removing it turned out to be no trouble. Gene bent the curled end with his pocket tool pliers. Now the object loosened and he pulled it out backward. The razor sharp blades were broken, but the screw-on feral would be useful as a small game arrow tip.

The damage to the pack frame was bad. The hole had weakened the frame considerably. If Gene could get some rawhide, he could make a reasonable repair with a rawhide wrap and a splint. Dried bone would work well as a strong light splint and there were many dried and bleached deer and cow leg bones in the hills. The rawhide might be harder to obtain. If Gene could find an animal carcass where the hide had dried stretched over the rib cage, the task could be completed. The thought of obtaining hide in that way would be most repulsive to the average person, but one uses the resources at hand.

The old timers made rawhide by throwing a freshly skinned hide in a creek for three weeks or a month. The bugs and enzymes in the water would cause the hair follicles on the hide to rot. The hair would turn loose with a little encouragement, leaving the rawhide ready to use. Gene had made two bull hide rawhide skins as a youth and subsequently braided a Mexican riata with one. Nasty job, that removing of the hair. A stretched hide over a carcass would be a much easier and faster way for Gene to obtain the rawhide strips he needed.

Gene discovered the arrow had cut a hole through his spare shirt in four places. Also the waterproof pack bag had two holes as well. There was the hole in his coat in two places and the shirt he wore was ripped and blood soaked. Well, a day of sewing would be needed but the quantity of thread he carried wasn't enough. Resupply would be in order if he could locate a spool of cotton thread. A quilter's lair would be ideal. Quilters use cotton cloth primarily for their art. Cotton cloth is the absolute best material to make char tinder out of. Polyester fabrics do not work. Quilters also use cotton thread, so any shrinkage of the cloth and thread will match when the assembled quilt ages.

Gene liked to keep extra thread just in case he needed to stitch a wound. He had sewn wounds up several times in his life on himself and on wounded animals. As a youth, fifteen miles back in the wilderness he had sewn a badly cut finger by using a very cold mountain spring to numb the hand. That time, an antibiotic ointment had assisted to detour infection. All healed well with only the sheath of a tendon being partially severed.

Gene hadn't made a journal entry for some time. He used blank paper space sparingly these days. As Gene thought on the events of the day, he considered how very lucky he had been.

Journal entry:

"I have been very lucky today. A man shot a couple arrows at me. He gave no warning and didn't state his purpose. I believe he was attempting to kill and rob me. I did suffer a slight wound but escaped without further damage to my equipment or self.

I am still some hundred miles from Seth's location. Fall is setting in and there are considerable mountains left to cross. I could be in the snow before I get over the top. If all goes well, I should be there by the end of next month."

Gene's mind wondered back over the day. He now worked on a lunch of roast porcupine, which he had intended to eat near the fallen tree earlier in the day. The archer was intent on killing Gene and Gene didn't have a clue until after the arrow hit that he was in any danger. This event was the second test of his skill in live action. Gene couldn't help but wonder who and what the need was in killing an unsuspecting traveler and what would be accomplished from it. People's values have slipped, actually disintegrated. Gene just couldn't believe all the law enforcement of the past modern world had kept humanity in check. Then again, he had to consider the tyrants of late modern Africa, Somalia, and the Arabian deserts.

171

He also considered the Godlessness of the American public in the last few decades. Gene felt the chickens must have come home to roost. Maybe man wasn't so inherently good. With the thought on his mind, he laid back to rest for the balance of the night.

Arising before dawn again, the soreness, stiffness, and utter pain in his shoulder nearly made him pass out. The temperature had been colder the night than before. The combination of the wound and cold was nearly overwhelming. Gene realized if ever he needed self-determination, it was now. He needed to get moving and he needed to drink water. The second would be easy. He would need to get fresh food. As he walked, he saw the Orgen grape plants so very close to the ground that had a few berries. Some choke cherries were dried and shriveled on the brush and he saw service berries. The rose hips had set on. He picked and consumed a handful of each of these. The choke cherries were so so tart they were actually bitter. The service berries were full of little seeds, as were the rose hips. Gene thumped a rabbit with a rock and with a small fire roasted the meal. He had pepper but no salt. *Salt would sure make life more pleasant*, he thought. *So would an orange.*

Chapter 17

Meat

D ays passed without further event after the archer incident. Gene saw a couple other people, but there seemed to be no threat from the encounters. Twice he saw bears feeding ravenously, preparing for the winter sleep. A bear was much larger than he felt he could eat or even wanted to handle. The fur hide would be nice if he would have to spend the winter in these mountains. He didn't have intentions of doing that, nor did he have the time to treat it appropriately. Then again, he questioned, where would he spend the winter? He began to think some about that and became more uncertain as to what his plan should be for the upcoming season. He had tools neither to build a cabin nor time enough to do it. He might keep an eye open for a suitable cave or an abandoned mine. He might have to evict a bear after all or a knot of rattlesnakes. He preferred the bear if it came to a choice.

If he were to spend the winter in the mountains, he would have to make snowshoes, which meant he would need more rawhide or additional para cord. He would need a supply of firewood. A winter alone in the hills would be lonely, very lonely, to the point of going mad. But to spend the winter with masses of refugees would mean the loss of his equipment and arms.

"Well, that decision has just been made," he said to himself under his breath. "But what if I can't find a suitable cave?"

His wound had healed without problem on the outside, but the shoulder blade was sore and when he moved wrongly, the pain notified him with no uncertain terms. A knot had developed at the wound location and it was sore to the touch. He resigned himself that if he were have a chance at medical assistance he would have the thing looked at.

The grueling trek carried on for days. Gene had lost track of the date, but by the length of the days he knew, winter had approached. By Gene's reckoning, he thought he was more than three quarters the way or better to Seth's last known location. The high mountain forest and meadows were fresh and clean, unlike the squalor Gene had experienced in the refugee camps near the settlements and other places. It would be tempting to just stay there away from the poverty in the settlements. The towns and cities had reverted to mere encampments, houses used as simple shelters without regular facilities, as opposed to organized towns and cities that once existed some three or four months past.

The problem with staying in the high mountains would be surviving the winter. Without shelter, heat, and food stores, a man would succumb to the elements. Staying would mean being stationary for a long spell. Gene felt he didn't have the time for that option.

Early one morning high in the mountains on his way off the easterly slope to the plains below, an elk, one of few left, grazed its way through the clump of trees where Gene watched from. Several days had passed since Gene had enjoyed a good eat. In studying the situation, he decided elk meat jerked was as good as a Micky D's Quarter-pounded and far more likely plentiful these days.

"Thank you, Lord, for your provision," Gene gratefully uttered a quick prayer.

Knocking the bolt in the crossbow, Gene picked his shot, squeezed the trigger, and let fly. The elk had not a clue until the bolt split the hair just behind the top joint on the right side leg. The elk jumped, turned, and took off, tearing across the nearby meadow. Just beyond the far edge of the meadow he stopped, wavered a little, and dropped with a thud to the ground.

Gene approached the fallen animal with caution, then prodded the animal with a stick. Determining the elk was done for this world, Gene proceeded to cut the throat and turn the carcass over to clean and field dress it. After twenty minutes, the gutting was completed, and Gene set up to skin the animal as he boned out the haunch meat, shoulders meat, and the tinder loins. Skinning and cooling the balance of the carcass, Gene roasted those parts over a slow-cooking fire.

All those choice meaty cuts he cut in thin strips. The strips he draped over freshly cut quaky saplings suspending the meat in the smoke above the fire for curing. These smoke-stripped pieces made great jerky and were as good as any jerky made pre-EMP minus modern jerky flavorings. Gene used four small fires for this purpose. He stretched part of the hide so it dry-cured in the smoke. Part of the hide he cut into thin strips and braided, forming a stout rope. Part of the green rawhide strips he used to repair the aluminum pack frame. The rest he wrapped lengthwise on a forked stick for storage and packing. The curing and braiding activity took the better part of two days. Gene had dried over two hundred pounds of prime elk steak. He had eaten five and saved cured heart slices for a change of taste. With rawhide rope he packed two thirds the jerked meat in the cured hide bag, sprinkled the balance of what pepper he carried to discourage the insects like flies and hornets and then hung the bagged meat as high above the ground he could. He placed a quaky log in a tree fork above head high, then tied the package to the end of the quaky log. By levering down on the other end, the package lifted some fourteen to fifteen feet above the ground. That would be high enough to keep the dumb bears out. A smart one on the other hand would eat well. So would a lucky human. The pine martins, as few as they were, would eat well regardless. Bobcats, if persistent, could get to the cache as well.

Gene would leave the cache for his return trip if he could find it again. He was being optimistic of course, but he had enough confidence to know a food cache such as this could make all the difference in hard times.

Just as he finished tying off the levered cache, he caught sight of a man crouching in the brush watching. Gene pretended he hadn't seen the man and went about his business. Keeping his eye on the stalker, Gene readied his pack to go. Gene expected the man to wait for him to depart before he robbed the cache. Instead of waiting, the man stood carefully and waved to Gene. Instantly, Gene suspected a trap and quickly surveyed the brush and cover behind himself and to the sides. There seemed to be no threat, but such a distraction was suspect and definitely not unheard of. To protect himself, Gene moved sharply and quickly to the side. If he were to avoid an attack from the rear, he needed to be where his rear wasn't vulnerable to attack. The man stood and watched for a moment and approached carefully. Gene in the meantime kept an eye peeled for possible assault from him or others.

"Mister, I didn't mean to startle you," said the man. "I just wanted to ask if you would share some of your meat with me and my family. We haven't been as successful as you."

Gene, still watching his own back with one eye and the stranger with the other, was surprised by the question. All the stranger had to do was wait until Gene was out of sight, then he could cut down the cache, but instead he had made a direct request.

"Well, stranger, I can't eat it all right now and if the wild animals don't get it, someone will. If you are in need, have some. How many are you?" Gene asked.

"There's just my son, daughter, and myself. I was out looking for food when I smelled your meat cooking. That was a distance down the stream, but there was no mistaking the smell like that when you are hungry. You might as well have been on the street corner saturating the air with the greasy odor of burgers and fries. I sure appreciate your generosity," the stranger said thankfully.

"Why'd you ask? You could have waited until I was gone," commented Gene.

"Mister, it isn't right to steal a man's provisions even if we are hungry, not if we can ask."

"You said you had kids, where are they?" Gene observed as he kept his eye on his side and back.

"They're at our camp," the man said as he approached Gene.

Gene perceived the stranger intended no harm but watched the stranger's eyes for telltale signs that would give away some lurking enemy. The eyes never indicated other threat.

"My name is Sullivan," the stranger said.

Gene, although reluctant, replied, "They call me Shaky. Sullivan, you can help yourself to the jerked meat. If you would be so kind, leave some for my return when I come back through. I'll help you retrieve it if you'd like. They went to the low end of the lever and lowered the cache. Sullivan made a sling out of a plastic canvas and packed just over a third of the jerked meat into the package. They re-secured the cache and levered it high into the place where it had been.

Sullivan said, "Shaky, is there anything you need? If I have it, I would be pleased to share."

Unlike other encounters, Gene felt at ease with this man. He thought a moment, then decided he would accompany Sullivan to his camp. The time alone had been just that, alone. In conversation, Gene quizzed Sullivan about the circumstances thereabout. He queried Sullivan's knowledge about the cities and the conditions there. He asked more personal questions about how and why Sullivan was in the mountains and not the city where he was from.

Sullivan had been a teacher with two teenage children, one of each gender. He had fled the city for the mountains when conditions got ugly. Stores had been looted and ransacked, defenseless homeowners had been robbed and as time progressed, things grew worse. Sullivan was an avid yet inexperienced outdoorsman. They donned their packs and headed out of town. The first couple weeks were hairy with threats at every turn. Things got better the further from the city they progressed. It took them another couple of weeks to find a camp location they felt safe at.

When Gene arrived at the Sullivan camp, he was surprised at the setting. It lay on a bench above a creek bottom. A small spring oozed from the hillside near the shelter. The shelter was rock on three sides. One wall was a natural rock wall and two were tightly stacked rock barriers. One stacked wall had a fire pit built into it and the fourth side was constructed of logs. Sullivan had placed a ridgepole about fourteen inches in diameter between the natural rock wall and the wood wall opposite. Upon the ridge log, he placed log pole rafters running from the ridge log to the parallel walls. He placed grass thatching atop a stretched plastic tarpaulin laid over cut willow sticks, which were in turn laid cross ways on top of the log rafters. The cut grass thatching was laid over the tarpaulin as much for camouflage and insulation as for moisture repellent. Sullivan had spent a large amount of effort on this dwelling. As Gene studied the setting, he saw the location could not be seen from above or below. It was ideally located out of the frequent avalanche runs and roundabout there existed plenty of fuel for a winter heat. Sullivan had already started collecting and stacking it.

Among the most valuable tools Sullivan possessed was a small portable crosscut bow saw. Gene commented on the saw and saw little sign of axe marks on the wood construction. Sullivan explained the sound of an axe striking wood could be heard miles off, so the axe use was restricted to very special times.

Sullivan explained that food procurement and storage had been a difficult challenge for them. He said he had watched Gene while Gene processed the elk. He doubted he had the ability or means to kill an animal of such size. He didn't have a gun. He had a good quality knife and he had fishhooks, pole, and line only.

Gene explained to Sullivan about the many brook trout in the beaver ponds below. He explained how to catch many, and then dress and smoke cure them over the fire just as Gene had done with the elk meat. Gene showed Sullivan how to make a figure-4 trap to catch whistle pigs, squirrels, and snowshoe hares. While out scouting the area, Gene found a porcupine and demonstrated how to kill the animal with a one-inch stick by striking it on the end of the nose. One swift blow was all it took. Afterward, turning it over while avoiding the pointy quills to dress and skin it was simple.

"These are a greasy animal," Gene explained. "The energy from the fat that drips off while it cooks can be a welcome source of energy if you're hungry. There aren't a lot of sources for olive oil here. Whistle pig's fat when cooked can be used the same."

Gene demonstrated how to spin a two-inch stick through the air above a walking grouse to knock it out of the air as it flushed. If Sullivan and his children were going to survive the winter there, they would have to catch and store a considerable amount of food. Gene had an extra wire snare made from a guitar string and offered to trade it to Sullivan for three fishhooks and a length of line. The deal was made. Gene didn't need a pole.

Gene felt pressed to continue his journey, but the wound in his back was troublesome. He mentioned it to Sullivan and Sullivan listened.

"I have some experience with wounds," he said. "Before I was a teacher, I worked in an inner-city emergency center. If you want, I will look at it."

Gene considered the offer and agreed. Sullivan watched as Gene removed his coat, shirt and 9mm. With Gene's back to Sullivan, Sullivan looked at the surface-healed wound. Sullivan prodded the tinder spot just a bit and stated he believed Gene had a pocket abscess under the skin, maybe caused by a foreign object or just an infection. He suggested it needed to be opened and drained. However, without antibiotic to combat infection, there was a danger. Gene still had an ample amount of coal oil in his flask. Gene explained the antiseptic properties of coal oil to Sullivan. Sullivan was skeptical at best, but if Gene was that confident in the stuff, he would consider using it as an antiseptic agent.

A single-edged razor blade was heated with one of Gene's butane lighters for sterilization, the lump was swabbed with coal oil, and Sullivan made the short deep incision. A semi-liquid yellow substance oozed out. The incision hurt Gene like sin. Sullivan put pressure on either side of the lump, causing additional liquid to erupt that dripped down Gene's back. The wound was sore. Sullivan swabbed the incision liberally with coal oil and bandaged the surgery, as crude as it was.

"That needs to heal from the inside out. You should pause your trip a while to let the thing heal," said Sullivan. "We should apply a hot compress on it for several days to draw out the poison and aid the healing."

The cloths that caught the ooze were placed on the fire. Gene donned his pistol, other shirt, and coat. His wound was very tender, but the deep soreness he had been experiencing was gone.

He would spend one more week at the Sullivan camp. They needed to learn about berry plants and how to save them as food. The Indians made pemmican out of a mixture of pounded meat, wild grain seeds, and dried berries. Gene told of the cattail root that could be eaten. There didn't seem to be cattails around this location, but the information would be good for Sullivan to know. Gene talked of how Indians used the cattail heads as a form of insulation. When the heads were shelled, broken, and fluffed, they became every bit as useful as goose down. Willow bark in a pinch could be chewed for pain relief. It had a nasty sour taste, not unlike letting an aspirin dissolve in one's mouth, but the result was effective and similar.

Sullivan's children, Ivan and Nattily, became excellent students and learned the information rapidly. They each quickly pitched in, putting into practice what they had been learning. Gene instructed them on how to weave baskets out of plant fiber.

Gene's incision continued draining and after the hot compress treatment, coal oil was applied each time. The oozing stopped and evidence of healing was present. Gene made plans to depart. In those days, the Sullivan family made determinable headway toward lasting through the winter.

Gene departed on a crisp sunshiny morning. There were light dew droplets on the long grass, which soon dissipated in the early morning sun. Gene's pant legs from the knees down were wet. They soon dried, cooling his legs as morning went on and the sun rose in the sky. Several times Gene observed small bands of people as he descended through the mountain valleys. He carefully avoided contact with them by sound or by sight. These encounters became more frequent as Gene descended in altitude. Gene observed that encounters with wildlife had become more infrequent as he closed in on the population centers. He became even more thankful for the jerked elk and smoked fish in his pack.

Chapter 18

Vets

Both Bonnie and Molly made mental notes of the land they crossed after leaving Judge Millner's headquarters while working their way back to the predetermined Marshals' newly relocated camp. Arms had been cached at locations handy to any marshal or deputy marshal from any of their camp locations. Three modern compound bows had been obtained along with arrows. Gretchen was the expert and Bonnie a close proficient second. They hunted game and procured several deer for winter supply. Someone always watched the MLS camp from one vantage point or another. A week after the two arrived back at the Marshals' camp, the MLS moved out toward the Judge's headquarters. They were likely to find them empty when they arrived. Bonnie hoped the Judge would cover his own exit tracks.

After three days passing, Bonnie made a decision to probe deeply into the remaining MLS encampment. Scouts were advanced to watch for the MLS battle brigade returning from the Judge's headquarters.

Gretchen and Bonnie moved in to the perimeter of the MLS compound. After months of close observation, it was like they knew the camp, its nooks, and crannies as well as their own. The audacity of the MLS was such that the camp was completely devoid of guards. The will of the remaining inhabitants was such that escape was not considered. Slipping in under the cover of evening darkness, the Marshals were able to gather detailed information on supplies and stores. It was tempting to scorch the camp, but the captives there needed that food and shelter, as poor as it was, for the winter. Both confiscated as much ammo as they could carry and Bonnie disabled a number of AK47s and other weapons by filing the firing pins. That discrete alteration would not likely to be detected until the weapon was used.

Nearly all the resident captives were broken in spirit and existed only for the meager provisions provided them. If one didn't work, even those provisions had been withheld. There were few able-bodied men and none of spirit. Most men had been extinguished during the capture raids unless their appearance was such that no threat was perceived and it appeared that they would be more productive than a burden. The shelters were minimal and even those were crowded. The crowding was most likely what kept hypothermia from killing the bulk of the inhabitants.

Bonnie observed many people, a couple of whom she knew saw her but seemingly didn't register in their eyes who or what she was. There was simply no reaction to her presence. Bonnie looked for the familiar face of family but saw not a one. If Jake or her mom were there, there seemed to be no sign of either now.

After their recon, Bonnie and Gretchen compared notes and no additional light was shed. Enroute to returning, they kept separated at a distance, as was their usual mode for travel. The Marshals encountered a single man, an old-timer sitting in the open on a stump. Gretchen saw him first, or so she thought. She signaled Bonnie with their usual travel sign and they approached from opposite sides.

When Gretchen approached within ten feet of the lone stranger, he said, "Marshals, I would like to discuss matters of some urgency with you."

Gretchen froze where she stood. Bonnie on the other side froze as well. His statement was clear. He'd said "Marshals" plural, so he knew there was more than one. He knew they were Marshals. *Is this the Judge's messenger? Well, we'll find out, thought Bonnie.*

"Who are you?" demanded Bonnie.

"Well, Miss, my name is Bobby," he calmly commented. "I've been watching you both for the evening. I don't know what you're hoping to find in there, but I would lay odds you didn't find what you were after. If you'll give some of your time, we need to talk."

Bobby went on to explain he was a resident of the outlying farming community near the adobe hills and the badlands. Bobby was a vet of Vietnam who decided to settle as far from society in as isolated a location as he could find. He wanted as little to do with the civilized world as he could reasonably get away with. He was angry and felt deserted by the government and society in general. He and many others from Vietnam and the Gulf Wars were scattered through the isolated landscapes of the country.

He wasn't a messenger from the Judge after all. Bobby had been observing the circumstances from the perimeter and there were dozens of others like him, vets who had loosely stayed in contact with each other scattered across the countryside. They were becoming fed up with the raiding and pillaging of the populous. All were armed to the teeth for who knows what reason.

The general idea for each was to gather arms for self-defense, but truth be known, they armed themselves as a comfort activity. Arms and weaponry is what they knew from training and what they were comfortably familiar with. Like people who eat comfort food and gain weight, a lot of weight, many isolationist vets gain armament weight as their feel-good habit. Bobby was one and knew many others in their loosely-connected network. The challenge here was so many of them had very poor health conditions as a residual condition of military service, and those health conditions limited their effective impact. Since the power outage, many had passed from lack of proper meds and treatment based upon that required electrical service. There were still however, survivors and they were ready to act under the right structure and direction. Bobby had come to talk with the Marshals about the authority they possessed.

Bobby explained the Marshals had been under close observation from the sidelines. Intelligence had been gathered and their authority had been closely questioned before the Vet Militia decided to make contact. The Vet Militia had no central leadership except for one possible man and most of these vets were as independent as a heard of cats. It would take a solidifying purpose to align them into some coherent force. The other problem was there were other vets who had joined the MLS. They might be called renegades because they seemed to condone the raids, pillaging, and murder of captives. The holdout Vet Militia did not condone these activities in any sense of the word.

Bonnie and Gretchen listened and explained to Bobby there was more to the decision than could be made at the moment. They wanted to confer with the others and think through any action before making a decision.

Oh, what the hell have we gotten ourselves into? thought Bonnie, *I pray Molly knows what to do with this.* Bonnie's frustration with recent events and lack of solutions was affecting her demeanor and responses more lately. Her frustration was now being revealed in her thoughts and verbalizations.

Arrangements were made for a follow-up meeting with Bobby and his companions. Bonnie, Molly, Laurie, and Gretchen's powwow was an uneasy one as they realized the decision was far beyond the scope of their authority. The discussion ranged from how nice it would be to have a real army with combat experience to apply to the situation to why they didn't have the right to take such action. Their euphoria was tempered by a nagging feeling that something wasn't right. What if this was a trap to catch them all together unsuspecting? What if they did ally themselves with this group of vets and lost control of their legal authority?

The closest military strategy experience Bonnie possessed was three days in a ROTC exploratory class at Riverton. This was beyond her scope, interest and desire.

"Molly, I don't even want to consider the implications involved in working with Bobby and the vets," exclaimed Bonnie. "I have no clue and no interest in commanding a full-on military assault."

"Bonnie," commented Molly, "I've experienced more in the line of chain of command than actual combat, although I've been there too, but only two times which was two too many. These ex and retired military will be like gathering dandelion seeds blowing in a high gale. They'll follow if the need is proven and once committed will not be stopped. Until the need proven, getting their commitment may be tough. Most of them have been independent too long." She went on to suggest, "I believe they can be utilized in three ways.

They make a resounding show of force, whether or not they are ever used. They have experience that can be tapped for any eventual conflict, and we can draw upon their training and experience to strengthen ourselves." She went on, "Bonnie, you will need to be firm in your continence and resolve. Be firm, and show no weakness in your presentation. If you want to appoint me as the marshals' liaison, the law enforcement commander so to speak, we could use this to our advantage."

Laurie and Gretchen listened without comment. All had become vetted battle personnel. Each was aware of the gravity of such a move, including veterans from seven decades of foreign conflict.

Gretchen finally, after being unusually reserved, exclaimed, "We don't have the right to start an army. I understood we were strictly law enforcement for the safety of the public."

The others stopped and looked at her for a long, uncomfortable moment.

Bonnie finally flatly stated, "Gretchen is right. We can deputize marshals, but if you remember the Judge specifically stated he has no authority to appoint an army, only to enforce the law for civil order."

"I don't mean to be so paranoid," said Bonnie, "but the MLS would do anything to wipe us out. That includes an irrefutable offer from wayward vets who we don't know, who we might desperately want assistance from. I smell a rat!"

"How do you plan to deal with the vets?" asked Molly. "We still have to decide if this next meeting is a setup or not and how to deal with it. "We pick the next meeting location, one that can be covered by the others, one where we can exit with cover, and one where we can watch the vet contingent arrive. Any ideas?"

"How about Elder Creek down at the narrows? We can cover both sides from the bluffs above and see any approach," said Gretchen.

The discussion considered alternatives, but Elder Creek seemed the most logical and strategically the most advantageous. The approaches to Elder Creek could be watched from the bluffs above, which in turn would be observed from other vantage points. This would take the complete marshal and deputy contingent to a man the operation.

The discussion continued over the course of two days. Bobby hadn't waited around for an answer, but he was to re-contact the Marshals in three days. When the time came, he appeared instantly.

Bobby had been instructed to bring the Marshals to a meeting site on the day after tomorrow. Molly and Gretchen, suspecting a trap, were having no part of it. The only Marshal who showed up was Bonnie. Along with Bobby were several others decked out in combinations of weaponry and tattoos.

"So, where are the others? I thought we all were going to convene today," commented Bobby.

"Yeah. . ." said Bonnie. "They're around. We need a better understanding and we need to know a bunch more about the vets contingent before we expose our assets. Do you know the confluence of Willow and Elder Creeks? Our next meeting will be tomorrow evening there. Bobby, if we are to have any form of coalition, this is how things are going to be. We call the shots from the law enforcement side. Your military operation will be of your own volition, but understand it will be for self-defense only. If your guys go on the offensive without reason or legal authorization, you will be no better than the MLS and will be treated as they are. This will not be a vigilante force. We will not command you, but you will remain under the strict civil and criminal authority. When we meet tomorrow, we will outline the structure at that time. See you then."

Bobby burst with an expletive, then added, "What the hell. Why the change? Bonnie with a shrug eased out of what had become a circle and walked away. The circle indicated to her there wasn't a structured hierarchy in the group. She, however, was careful not to let any get behind her during the talk. Those conditions in and of themselves were encouraging to her that this meeting wasn't a setup. She was paranoid and self-conscious about it, but, on the other hand, had a deep desire not to be trapped.

Watching her back trail, Bonnie met two others and they made their way back to the base camp, where she briefed the others on the meeting. The fact the Marshals had been unaware two times before of watchers, secret observers, namely Molly and now Bobby, deeply concerned her. The Marshals needed to be more vigilant. If Molly and Bobby had been able to spy on them undetected in the past, then what could the MLS with trained scouts do? That fear nearly drove her to distraction. Taking Laurie aside, she expressed her fears, her obsession, and her vulnerability and inadequacy about being so unaware of those circumstances.

"Laurie, we need to be more careful," Bonnie exclaimed. "If they can't take us out together all at once, they'll start picking us off one at a time. Our buddy system has worked well, but it hasn't been fully effective and it hasn't been fully tested. What can we do?"

The ladies sat in silence for twenty minutes, then rose without a word, slipping to their respective sleep locations.

The sunrise came as a gorgeous array of black sky faded into a myriad of hues, gray mixed with light blues, shades of salmon, and a spot of light orange peeking around a late summer cloud. The sunrise was well behind the contingent making their way to Elder Creek and the overlooks above. Again, only two Marshals would be at the meeting if it took place. The others would be looking out from above and others above them. It took the whole Marshal contingent to man this operation.

The constant "rek rek rek, rek rek rek" of a small flock of magpies working on a carcass was heard off in the distance. From that direction was where Bonnie expected the approach of the vets. Funny, her brother Seth used to call them flying skunks when he was a small boy. The idea had never left Bonnie's mind. What a wonderful time it had been growing up under Shaky's instruction about nature. How she missed her daddy. Just now, she longed for his insights and guidance.

Bonnie knew when those birds spooked, the meeting would be close at hand. Nature was a most valued ally in these conditions. She gathered herself and looked toward Molly's direction. Molly signaled her understanding of Bonnie's thoughts. She and Molly both had the greatest confidence in the spotters on either side above, but there was an unspoken nerviness about the events about to unfold.

Spreading out and waiting in place, Bonnie and Molly heard the flock of magpies take flight. *Well, here they come!* thought Molly.

There were nine in the vet contingent. Bobby walked beside an old-timer who must have been in the Korean War. The others strung out for a hundred and fifty feet to the rear. They now were traveling in squad fashion with arms neither woman believed legal to be owned and possessed by civilians. Molly knew the equipment, but Bonnie had no clue about most of it.

"Well," said Bobby with a little animosity in his voice, "now we're here. I hope you have something worth our while. We spotted one of your lookouts on the bluff up there. What's the idea anyway?"

"Bobby, I apologize for any misgivings we may have projected, said Bonnie. "You of all people must understand if the MLS can bag us all in one play, they wouldn't hesitate to do so with deadly force. If they should try, there will be a huge price and hell to pay. I don't believe I have met your people. By the looks of this man, he has been in the pre-Gulf War conflicts."

"This is Colonel Whitmore," said Bobby. "He was a battalion commander in Korea. He has agreed, reluctantly I might add, to direct our operations. All vets who sign up for this operation will be directly under his strict command."

"Now, wait a minute," exclaimed Bonnie. "What operation are you talking about?"

Molly stepped in. "Hi, Walter, ah. . . Colonel Whitmore, I am so pleased to see you with these guys. You realize our skittishness about unknown blood. Every unknown is suspect to us unless proven otherwise. Your presence here is a great relief."

Bonnie looked at Molly as if she had an extra head but said nothing.

"Colonel and Bobby, here is the position we hold," said Molly. "We are appointed by Judge Millner to enforce criminal civilian law in the absence of any other legitimate agency. We are US Marshals under his direction. We have no authority to appoint a temporary or standing army as much as we'd like to. We need to tell you that if you act without authority as a vigilante force, we will pursue and arrest the same as we do the associates of the MLS. On the other hand, if you need to band together to protect your homes and property from gangs and outlaws, that is your prerogative. We would encourage it but will not condone unmeasured and unrestricted armed activity."

"I know Judge Millner," said Whitmore. "He is a fine man and lawyer. He contacted me by courier this week and requested assistance. He has been under siege from the MLS. Now we come to the crux of the matter. Our vets are fed up with the activities of the raiding, robbery, and pillaging, which this gang called the MLS has rained on us. By Millner's direction we will stop them! My understanding is you don't have the training for a military engagement. Ergo, we will confront the MLS directly ourselves with or without your help and with Millner's blessing. You are to continue your law enforcement activities."

Bonnie's blood flashed when she heard the description of "raiding and pillaging" that came from Whitmore's mouth.

"Colonel," she started to say but was cut short by his demeanor.

"Young lady, we all of us who have served, have sworn an oath to these United States of America to defend Her and the Constitution by which She is governed," stated Whitmore. "We are now doing just that. We don't need your permission or your authority to do that."

As Bonnie's face flushed, Molly stepped closer to her and said quietly under her breath, "Cool it!"

Whitmore continued, "We are now in continual contact with Judge Millner and he is who made us aware of your authority. We might not have known except he knows you're not big enough or strong enough to take on the MLS. They have been getting continual reinforcements. Those supplying them are not aware of the savagery of their rule. Millner has been trying to get word through to the governor, but up to this time hadn't made contact. This week the governor responded but has little to offer in way of assistance.

"Your Marshals have had the tremendous effect of forcing Sergio Campella to concentrate activities here in the settlements region, taking pressure off the Riverton people. He believes once he cleans you out here, he can return to Riverton and do the same to the several holdout societies there. Now, understand, our purpose here is not to receive your approval, but to build an alliance military to civilian law enforcement and that is where you come in. We possess the right under the second amendment to own and bear arms specifically for reasons we now encounter. We are protecting our country, our homes, and our lives. We can catch them. You arrest them and deliver for prosecution. You got it?"

Bonnie stood stunned as she tried to assimilate all the colonel had said. She felt she had just been chastised and was shaken to her core. She had lost control and she didn't like it at all but didn't know what to do next.

Finally, Bonnie slowly said, "I see." But she wasn't really sure she did.

"Bobby here will be our liaison to you and he will keep you informed of our progress. That will be all." The Colonel spoke as if dismissing a lower rank.

The vets turned and left the way they had come. One even had the audacity to wave to a lookout above.

"You know him?" Bonnie asked Molly.

"Yes," said Molly, "he's a friend of my uncle. They served together in Korea. When I saw him, I knew we were okay, but I didn't have time to let you know."

"I am so pissed," growled Bonnie. "I feel like we've been ambushed. Why didn't Millner let us know? I feel like a pawn now."

"Well, we are not pawns, we are far more important than that. We aren't the king or queen either, but maybe a rook, bishop, or more like a knight in the scheme of things," encouraged Molly. "Let's regroup and make sure of what our goals are."

They left and collected personnel at prearranged locations on the return to base. All were anxious as to the outcome. Bonnie was tight-lipped, so Molly laid out the prior events and possible implications as she saw them. She encouraged the others to contemplate and come back with their observations and ideas in the morning. Bonnie said nothing, then jerked up part of her equipment and purposely walked out of the camp. Laurie, aware of Bonnie's stress, grabbed her equipment and followed with instructions to Gretchen to give cover at a distance.

Bonnie walked for half an hour in a nondescript direction before Laurie was able to apprehend her.

"Bon, do you have a clue how much danger you are putting us in by this erratic behavior?" pressed Laurie. "You aren't paying attention to your cover. You may give away the rest of the Marshals by being stupid."

"I'm done, Laurie," exclaimed Bonnie. "I have lost total control of everything. I can't do it anymore. I'm going it alone from now on."

"Wait a minute, we're in this together if you remember, or have you forgotten all we've been through?" pleaded Laurie "You just can't dump me, your friends, or the purpose of our lives right now. Remember what it meant to you and to me to have purpose? Are you going to just throw that away? Bon, you can't!"

It dawned on Laurie that Bonnie was threatened by the apparent loss of status as the boss, the one who pulled and pushed the strings. Their previous conversation about Bonnie's insecurity made sense now. Bonnie knew she hadn't the ability to command an army, and that option had only been just a myth in Bonnie's mind. At any rate, the myth exploded by meeting with Whitmore. Not only did the Whitmore meeting validate that, but it validated Bonnie wasn't the most important piece in the game. Whitmore had such a commanding air about him, it made Bonnie feel deeply inferior. In her mind it humiliated her. The meeting confirmed she was not the center of this conflict and Bonnie would now have to come to grips with this painful realization.

"Laurie, I need to be alone. Please leave me alone. Please," pleaded Bonnie.

"'K," squeaked Laurie, fighting back a flood of tears.

They each turned in separate directions and departed. Gretchen was close by as Laurie topped the near rise. Gretchen pressed as to the nature of the problem. Laurie indicated Bonnie needed time to work out some problems in her mind. She desperately hoped that was the only thing she needed to do.

Bonnie walked aimlessly for two days and a night and became so fatigued she began to stumble. She walked like a zombie in her wanderings, being distraught and broken. She wondered into the scrub-covered foothills. Once she saw a person at a distance who watched as she passed. She topped a hill and the opposite side was steeper than she perceived. Falling, tumbling, she landed near the bottom. There she lay too tired to rise and with no will to go further.

Chapter 19

Wounded

Night fell and the late summer evenings were becoming cool to cold. The chill brought Bonnie to her senses as she realized she was shivering. Not knowing where she was, her former survival caution kicked in enough to prevent her from building a fire. She curled into a fetal position to conserve heat. When morning broke, Bonnie had stiffened and became nearly immobile. She stretched out her stiffness and began to shiver all over again. Recovering took almost more energy than she could call upon. Bonnie began to ascend the hill behind her toward a sunlit spot where she could warm. The warmth of the sun rays seemed better than a hot cup of mocha. She still shivered but now gathered her wits. Bonnie wasn't familiar with her present location. There seemed to be a green meadow and stream some distance to the northeast. Bonnie made progress toward it, but she hadn't forgotten how angry, confused, and discouraged she felt. After four hours through the brush and trees she reached the edge of the seemingly undisturbed oasis. Collapsing at the water's edge, Bonnie drank and drank again. This must have been her first drink since she left two days before.

Yes, I had left, I'm done! she thought. *And I'm hungry, yes, hungry.*

Bonnie found some rose hips and some wild onions. She rocked a chukar partridge. She had dinner roasted with the fixings. Sitting on a log, her grief overwhelmed her. She didn't understand why, it just did. Sobbing uncontrollably, Bonnie sobbed ten minutes and continued to cry for forty-five minutes. Finally, after a time, her emotions exhausted, she moved about to explore her surroundings.

Bonnie in her despair was thinking back to her childhood days when a friend had taken her favorite kitten without asking and how her heart had been broken when Daddy said to let it go. Bonnie truly loved that kitten and was brokenhearted to find the kitten lost to the friend. She felt that way now. Losing it was a deep disappointment and it had affected her then just as losing control affected her now. Mama had encouraged her to pray, to ask God for some comfort. Bonnie hadn't done that for years, even after the attack in Riverton. She turned to a nearby log and began to weep again. Blubbering her simple plea to the Lord above, she asked for the answer to all that was wrong in her life that made her feel so bad.

From behind her, a withered old voice gently said, "Young lady, is there a way I can help you?"

Startled, Bonnie was on her feet with weapons poised to kill. It was an old lady.

Older than Methuselah, Bonnie thought. *She's so shabby.*

"Who are you?" Bonnie demanded.

"I'm Nell," the woman said. "I heard you crying and that tells me you are hurt, lost, broken, heavyhearted, or afraid. I don't want to pry, but you are drawing attention with your goings on. There are people watching up there. They haven't been here before and you brought them. Let's move out of the open, come now. Come, come!"

Bonnie scanned the hills and saw nothing that might indicate spies. She reluctantly followed Nell to an obscure path, which led to a modest old fashioned dugout dwelling. Nell went past the dwelling and climbed a hill to a vantage point where they could see movement across the valley. Bonnie couldn't make out the identity of the followers, but Nell indicated Bonnie's path to the meadow.

"I'm sorry, Nell, to bring this on you," said Bonnie. "I have been thoughtless in my actions. I believe there are people tracking me—maybe to kill me."

Bonnie explained her station and circumstances to Nell. Nell inquired as to the cause of her distress. Bonnie, now embarrassed, was ashamed to answer, realizing her self-centered concerns were just that, self in focus, a needless pity party. Nell encouraged and listened to Bonnie's story until Bonnie finally came to grips with the real problem.

Bonnie was having a delayed reaction to the attack in Riverton and had been baring the emotions with the facade of being in control where she hadn't been before. Losing control at the meeting made real the inability to control the events of the attack in Riverton. The meeting with Whitmore had undone the superimposed cover. Now Bonnie was realizing reality with the encouragement of Nell. Nell explained some fifty years ago she too had a bad experience.

She explained, "The wrong of it never goes away. The beast of humiliation, shame, anger, and inability to right the wrong can be faced and dealt with. You cannot do it out of vengeance fueled by frustration. You have to recognize and own the feelings. They are not wrong. What you can control is your response in predetermined action and activity if you don't bury your emotions. It isn't your fault and you have to understand that. Rape by definition is without consent. Until you face it, it will control you, break your heart, and undermine your life. After you recognize it for what it was, with time the pain will subside some. There will be times when it tries to return. Use the same process as you did before. No one can slay that dragon for you. With God's help, you have to do it yourself."

Bonnie and Nell sat down to a small bite of mountain greens smothered in butter served with goat's cheese and buttermilk.

"Where on earth did you get butter?" Bonnie exclaimed.

"Oh, that came from Sally," said Nell. "She milks good every day. Ya know, when I was just a girl, we milked thirty goats every day on my grandma's ranch. She used to like ta sell it in town, but we were nine miles from town. That was too far to pack all that milk, so she dumped it in the creek. They call that creek Milk Creek to this day."

"I know where that is," said Bonnie a split second before she jerked violently backward.

She never heard the sound. But Nell did and instantly knew the shot was a long-range attempt to kill Bonnie. Bonnie lay bleeding from the shoulder between the collarbone and the neck. The hole was small on the front, but there was a gaping hole in the coat just above her shoulder blade like a big game rifle leaves when the bullet hits flesh and then exits. Nell was a cool-headed old hide who didn't much get shook up in a crisis. She grabbed Bonnie and shoved her behind a fallen log which had been used for seating just as another bullet struck it. The rifle shot report followed this time indicating to Nell an approximate distance of the sniper. She hurriedly grabbed a towel, applying it to the back of Bonnie's shoulder, placing Bonnie's right arm across her chest and hand over the towel and the wound. An instant later, she had a pump 12 gauge short barrel shotgun and disappeared into the foliage with a warning for Bonnie to stay down. Another shot splattered the rocks just behind them.

Had the sniper been smart, he would have vacated after his first shot. When he rose to see the movement to his left, he was met with a full load of double 00 buck spread from his belt line to his armpit. There was never a more surprised look on any dying man's face than his when he saw a shabby old woman wielding a short barrel shotgun. He rolled to his right side, head back, mouth agape.

Nell turned and scurried back to Bonnie's side with the sniper's rifle in tow. Bonnie reclined against the log hidden deeper in the foliage. She paled and had become semi-delirious. Maneuvering Bonnie back to the shelter, Nell tended Bonnie's wound by irrigating it with fresh boiled clean water. Bonnie winced from the pain when Nell applied the Iodine. Later she applied a bandage-layered poultice made of boiled wild carrot root mixed with juniper needles to the exit wound in back.

"I don't have anything else for your pain," said Nell. "I'll cut some willow bark for you to suck on. It tastes awful, but should help the pain a little." Bonnie shivered, so Nell covered her and placed a soft fur under her head.

It was time to bring Sally to camp and milk her. She left quickly so as to return as soon as possible. Nell anticipated a long night ahead. When she returned, a stranger sat with Bonnie. Nell paused and watched while she herself was being watched from the brush by another set of eyes. There seemed to be no animosity from the newcomer toward Bonnie. Nell advanced, leading Sally as she went. Laurie looked up to see Nell and the goat.

"I didn't expect an additional guest, but if you're friendly, you can stay," stated Nell.

"I'm sorry. We didn't mean to intrude," said Laurie. "We were worried about Bon here. They were after her. We found that guy up there. Did you do that?

"He stopped shooting at us, didn't he?" retorted Nell, "You said 'we.' Who is 'we'?"

"Her and I," said Gretchen quietly as she eased from the brush.

The Marshals introduced themselves and the purpose of their quest. They had discovered Bonnie's trackers, all three of them. One they captured. The second had a heart attack when Gretchen got the drop on and startled him. He died presumably of heart failure on the spot. They hadn't closed on the third when the shooting started. When located, rigor had set in and nothing more was to be done. Their first captive had been tied and bound to a cedar tree for safekeeping. Now their concern was Bonnie and how serious her wound was.

The three talked as Laurie comforted Bonnie as best she was able. Bonnie's pain set in and she was intolerably miserable most of the night.

The sun came up, with Bonnie alternating between chills and profuse sweating. Her condition didn't change for two days. The cool rags were applied to Bonnie's forehead and cheeks when she became feverish. She was wrapped in blankets when she had chills. At last, Gretchen decided to retrieve her captive and would return him to the base camp. He would be handed off to another Marshal and delivered for trial. The Judge had become less tolerant of the bad guys. Gretchen would return with medical supplies as fast as travel would allow. She left the site via a different exit than the one she used to enter.

Laurie and Nell became fast friends. They knew the same people but somehow had never become acquainted. Spelling each other off in turns for Bonnie's care, both worked intermittently to lay up supplies for Nell's winter survival. Nell was an excellent teacher and possessed an immense knowledge about natural herbs and foods. This information she freely offered Laurie for her own use. Bonnie seemed improved: walking a little and eating portions that facilitated her healing. The wound wasn't infected. Nell would change the bandage with various poultice dressings. She boiled the old dressings and sun dried them in the open air, then repeated the process several times.

Gretchen and the camp medic appeared mid-afternoon two days later with supplies. The captive had been delivered emaciated to the base camp, where he promptly was whisked off to the Judge's new headquarters. Upon her arrival, two circulars awaited issued with the Judge's seal. The first was a warrant for the apprehension and arrest of named persons. The second was a declaration of parole violations punishable by execution upon site and/or capture.

Whereas the following named persons heretofore have been found guilty of felonious crimes punishable by death and had their death sentences conditionally set aside; and

Whereas the following named persons have violated said conditions of their parole by associating with the Martial Law Service and other designated outlaw elements,

Therefore, each named below shall be detained and returned to this court for parole violation review. If such person or persons resist said return, then he or she shall be immediately subject to the sentence of execution. This execution to be carried out by any person or persons upon detainment and/or capture.

The following are subject to this:

- Andrew Adams
- Charles Ackerman
- Jerome Caseau
- Zackery Hollister
- Henry Hotts
- Holly Stokes
- Paul Smith
- Ebinizer Balensky

I hereby certify this order by the power vested in me by the United States of America Judicial Authority

Alford C. Millner
United States District Judge
5th Judicial District

Judge Millner had now authorized the vets commanded by Whitmore to execute the deferred death sentences on parole violators. The list was exact. Among Whitmore's contingent included several former special forces personnel. Among those were trained snipers proficient at their skill. Millner released them as one would dogs on a cat hunt. Bonnie and Laurie both earlier expressed their reservations, but neither possessed the knowledge of the validity of authority or legality in the matter.

There was a third document offering a bounty issued by the MLS with the names of the Marshals and Bonnie's dad, Shaky. Gretchen kept this back from Bonnie but secretly showed Laurie. Now the Marshals would need to be doubly careful of their associations. It named Alford C. Millner, Toliver, Thor, and others not known to the Marshals.

Chuck Simpson, a newer addition to the marshals' force, had accompanied Gretchen. Chuck had been an EMT with emergency room nursing experience as well as a medic in the army. He looked over Bonnie's wound and seemed pleased at her progress. The hole in the back would leave a noticeable indention and scar after healing. Chuck presented an assortment of pain pills, Ibuprofen, acetaminophen, and stronger narcotics. Where they came from wasn't disclosed. In his stash, he carried several disinfectants that may have been needed. Painkiller was the order of the day. Bonnie was healthy, strong, and had the mule in her makeup for determination. She willingly partook of painkillers when offered.

Meanwhile, back in camp, the Marshals started spotting lookouts at strategic locations to monitor the MLS activities. At predetermined times, gathered information was delivered for compilation. Several MLS scouts had been apprehended weeks before, so an impending raid against the Marshals was known from interrogations.

Before the four arrived back at base camp, word had come the MLS planned an extraordinary night campaign against the Marshals' headquarters camp. A plan conceived some time earlier in the event of such an attack had been enacted. Before morning came, the camp was vacant. They scattered before Bonnie, Gretchen, Laurie and Chuck had returned. Molly and Sam went as runners to warn them and made contact prior to their return. The buddy system now was in full mode with each group being in sets of three.

Molly and Gretchen moved out with the third deputy, Sam, earlier while Bonnie, Laurie, and Chuck departed as a squad, the last to leave base by some two hours. Just before their departure, a dispatch from the Judge arrived with instructions for the Marshals to temporarily stand down their operations against the MLS. Whitmore's troops were to engage the MLS. The Marshals were now for the time being to enforce civil law only. The conflict with the MLS had now become a military operation. All marshals and deputies were to be notified. Molly and Gretchen, having left earlier, were not there to receive the word.

Leaving camp to avoid the near pursuit from MLS operatives, Bonnie, Laurie, and Chuck traveled hastily for three hours. Spitting moisture turned into snow as the air cooled to a brisk temperature. Soon the snow stuck to the shady patches not warned by the day's sun. Those places and soft dirt were avoided so as not to leave tracks that could be followed. While traveling apart using hand signals to communicate at a distance, they backtracked in serious fashion to throw off any trackers who might be following.

The trio headed for cap sand rock on the high desert mesas, where they might not leave tracks for fractions of miles. An occasional hint purposely was planted to mislead. Coming to the end of a cap rock flat, they would leave a barely discernible track leading away from their true direction that lead to an indefinite dead-end. Backtracking a mile while utilizing game tracks, downfalls, and shale beds to mask their true purpose, the three vacated the location by miles before they stopped at a defensible site.

High up on the sloping mesas, their back trail could be observable in several places. The snow now had become a hindrance to secret travel. Holding up in an ancient Indian cliff site became most beneficial as it offered protection from the snow, wind, and chill. Facing the southeast, the morning sun warmed the temporary camp with bountiful sunshine. The site sat just under a high point, which afforded a superb lookout of the country below to the north, east and west.

Molly, Gretchen, and Sam, short for Samantha, broke hard for the canyons. Gretchen was intimately familiar with this territory. The territory was considered "badlands" among the old-timers. The thousands of outcroppings overlooked the valley trails, which linked and forked like tree limbs as they ascended upland. If necessary, their positions would be defensible from almost any place in these meandering canyons. Obscure trails led up to the tops of ridges and hidden trails came off the ridges from above. The outcropping rock formations afforded clear views for miles.

The outlaws of old headed first thing successfully to these lands to escape posses. Only one time was Gretchen aware of one outlaw who had been apprehended when he fled there. He drank himself into a stupor, was caught up with, and tried to shoot it out with the posse. His body subsequently had been displayed for photos while propped up by boards against the wall of the local feed store in the settlements. The old Robbers Roost, where they now headed, allowed clear views down the valley for several miles. The escape route out the back to the south offered a vast forest wilderness in which to run.

The current winter storm was problematic. The three could obscure their tracks, but the sandy soil they traveled in was bad and left telltale signs and a trail for followers. If it stormed hard enough, the tracks could be covered over with snow or washed out by runoff.

When they came to a small creek at an angle, they approached and entered the creek, turned down stream at a hundred degree angle and went. All took care not to step on a sand or mud bar where a track would remain. Sticking as much as possible to the gravel bars, the three found a solid rock outcropping nearly half a mile downstream, where they could exit without excessive telltale signs. These rocks were solid for some hundred yards perpendicular to the stream away from and on the opposite side of the common valley trail.

Keeping to the opposite side of the ascending ridges where their tracks couldn't be seen from the trail below, the three covered another half mile before the snow started accumulating over their tracks.

Another mile put them within sight of Robbers Roost. All three were near exhaustion when they topped the ridge. The trail around the bluff face leading into the hideout was a sideling path and treacherous in the wet weather. They were all soaked through, feet tender from walking in water, and famished. Setting up camp, Molly started a small fire of dried sagebrush sticks long since gathered by some hunter or an outlaw. It heated hot tea and a small hot meal and dried their garments. The shoes and socks steamed as the heat drove moisture into vapor. There wasn't danger of the wisp of smoke from the dry wood fire being seen as the storm intermittently obscured the valley and landscape for miles around.

Chapter 20

Metropolis

A dozen days had passed since Gene had left the Sullivan camp. He could see the High Plains below as far as any eye could see. Gene looked for landmarks he might be familiar with. He hadn't realized when he exited the mountains before in an automobile how much he'd depended upon the industrial smoke and steam plumbs to locate landmarks. Upon topping the last hogback above the plains, Gene was able to study the landscape below. Once oriented, he could make the decision as to the course and direction he should take. The canyons and ridges had diverted Gene off course several miles. Gene knew a division would cost him time. The effort of dealing with human obstacles and social structure encounters was a major delay. Who would know what set of regulations and what groups might be in charge of society here? He had no desire nor was he willing to find out.

He decided a direct route to Seth's would not be in his best interest. He could see smoke arising from scattered camps. He could also see a wasteland where a large portion of the older city had burned. Through his binoculars he studied an area that appeared to be a large refugee camp. Shelters there seemed crude, ranging from pup tents to makeshift cardboard box quarters and every combination in between. The slums and squalor he had seen in Calcutta could not have been any worse. On the outskirts were military vehicles. This camp looked like a prison camp, not a refugee center.

Gene requested, "God have mercy on them."

He studied other areas further away. They were too far to make out in detail but seemed to have the same characteristics as the camp closer at hand. He then turned his attention toward the terrain that led to the north. He picked out a more sparsely populated route in the foothills whereby to make his way toward Seth's. Gene's attempt to see miles from his location was of no avail. He couldn't discern the objects and movements of the inhabitants. The effort was fruitless from this distance.

Without the satisfaction he wanted, Gene reluctantly started his journey on the route picked from the ridge top. All went well and he avoided contact with anyone for the rest of that day. A campsite was chosen more for the seclusion it offered in a dry wash bed than for the shelter it provided. Camping in a spot like this was risky if a rain storm started. Gene knew he could lose everything to a sudden flash flood. But he needed as much anonymity as possible and would have to accept the calculated risk for that reason.

The cool of the evening told him fall was in the air. Often this part of the country would have an early frost and an early snow-storm, then clear up for five to eight weeks in an Indian summer. Gene hoped for his sake and for the sake of the local human kind, that would be the case this year.

The next day went without incident and Gene found another dis-crete night camp. The nights now dipped into the low thirties while the days still rose to temperatures in the low eighties. Gene desired to have a very small fire for two reasons. He had gotten very cold the previous night and he had rocked an unsuspecting raccoon. The coon had been pillaging an old rubbish heap where earlier discards were plentiful. Gene wanted to cook the newly acquired critter for a change of flavor from and to save his jerky supply. In examining his surroundings, he didn't see a place his small fire might be spotted from, so he started it and cooked the food. Putting out the fire, he abandoned the site and moved some half mile further before settling down for the night.

Morning came with heavy frost on his coverings. Gene waited for the sun to dissipate the frost and the moisture residue before packing. He disliked getting such a late start, but his gear needed to be taken care of and thus preserved. He felt he was only a couple days from Seth's residence now. He needed to traverse some inhabited areas to get to his destination. He encountered some outlying camps, but no one said a word, they just stared as he passed by. He would now have to be careful he wasn't ambushed or followed and waylaid. He had come into perilous territory.

Near one such camp, a large man shabbily dressed looked at him and came walking toward Gene. As he approached, he started moving faster the broke into a dead run, a charge. Gene quickly raised his crossbow and aimed at the man's chest. The man pulled up short. The others sitting around a fire watched, then they got up. Nobody said a word. Gene held a hand up with one finger in the air signaling to hold a moment. He drew his .357 and a moment later shed his pack. Watchfully he opened his pack and started to withdraw a pack of the jerked meat. One man yelled a rebel type call and charged from behind the big man. Gene fired one shot and the man spun and dropped in his tracks. The others come to an immediate stop, then started advancing. Gene dropped a second man, the biggest and meanest looking among the lot. There were five left. Gene laid the packet of jerky on a nearby rock, slid the backpack over his shoulder, picked up his crossbow, and backed away from the group. Moments later, a quick glance over his shoulder told him they hadn't flanked him. He moved swiftly away as the pack had converged on the jerky. The last he saw of them, they still brawled over the meat. Gene made a mental note to be more careful before exposing himself to an unknown situation. Next time he might not get out.

Like in Riverton, Gene observed people living out of cars and vans. They had forted up and many watched with a suspicious eye as he passed. Gene, now in the suburbs of the area, was in the neighborhood where Seth lived. The last two days had been uneventful except for the gang who intended to accost him. Gene was weary. He didn't want another incident like the one of two days past. Funny though, or maybe not so funny, Gene wasn't nearly as upset by the last incident as he had been in the two prior encounters. In his mind, not being as concerned worried him. Hopefully he wasn't becoming callous about taking a life.

Gene had driven to Seth's dwelling, a row home, many times in the past. As he approached, there were only a few of the former population of the neighborhood who appeared to remain. Gene didn't recognize any on his approach to Seth's block. Gene rounded the corner where the house was located and he was surprised to see a virtual ghost town. Smaller limbs had fallen in the street. Leaves piled against porch steps and some front doors stood open. Automobiles sat where they had been parked or where they had quit running after the EMP. For all intents and purposes, Seth's home looked as abandoned as the others.

Gene approached the steps of the front porch and could see the door stood ajar as if it hadn't been fully closed by some previous user. Gene carefully pushed the door open far enough to see no activity had been happening there for some time. Gene shut and locked the door behind him. Knowing the layout, Gene cautiously checked the interior for unwanted company and when finding the house clear, went to the basement where Seth kept his sporting equipment and emergency supplies. The garden level window had been broken and intruders had liberated anything of value except Seth's gun safe. It had been battered and beat but still was intact and bolted to the cement floor and wall from the inside.

Returning upstairs, Gene started looking for any sign of Seth. Gene checked the bulletin board and various scraps of paper now scattered on the floor. A calendar caught Gene's eye. He picked it up and there on the checkered date grid for the week of the EMP, the squares were X'd out. The note read "Orlando." Gene knew Seth's company had headquarters in Orlando and Seth flew there for training events on a regular basis.

Gene sat on a chair, thought a moment, then he made a decision. Gene returned to the basement gun safe and opened it with the combination Seth had given him. He placed the calendar in the safe with a note reading, "I was here. I'm not sure of the date, but it's early fall. If I am reading the moon right, it must be late September or early October. I'm going home to Pinedale. Love, Dad".

In the safe was a light caliber hunting rifle, ammo for it, Seth's shotgun and ammo, Seth's handguns, and gold and silver coins. Gene removed a gold coin and a handful of silver coins. Gene closed the safe and spun the combination closed, tested the handle, looked around once again, and departed. If Seth were to return, he was more likely to find the calendar there in the fireproof safe than in any other place.

Gene departed by way of the front door, carefully locking it behind him. A lady's voice caught him in mid-stride going down the front steps. "Find what you want?"

Gene, startled, stopped and turned to face a familiar middle-aged female. Gene replied, "No, I was looking for my son Seth. Have you seen him?"

The lady was a neighbor from across the street. Gene had met her a couple times when he and Jessie had visited. The lady recognized Gene and indicated Seth had left a couple days before the blackout. She, Barbara, hadn't left the neighborhood, as she expected her own children to come for her. She had been a prepper and was living on the storage she had put together. Her home was fortified now and she was armed with an AK 47 and a sawed-off 12 gauge pump Winchester. She drank filtered water from swamp water in the green area. She would stay until her children came for her.

Gene inquired as to the news about authority services. Rumor had it that refugee camps long since started turning people away. Things were bad in the city. People had ransacked the suburbs for survival goods and had long since gone away. They depleted any stored goods people had and now there was no reason to return. An occasional wanderer would come through but if undisturbed would keep moving, looking for a treasure around the next corner. Barbara suggested Gene leave the front door open just as he found it. A locked door here aroused the curiosity of a scavenger. Gene went to the back where the garden level window had been broken, entered, climbed the stairs, unlocked the front door, and left it slightly ajar as he first found it. Barbara watched Gene's action, then expressed her approval.

"Barbara, is there anything you need I can help you with?" offered Gene.

"No, if you could bring my kids, that would be enough. Otherwise, I am set, safe and secure here as long as the hordes don't discover me," she replied.

"Where are your kids located?" Gene asked.

"They were living in Shanksville, west of here," she replied. "I would call if I could."

"If you would write a note, I could try to deliver it to them as I make my way home," Gene said.

She wrote a note with non-detailed information. If the note fell into wrong hands, it wouldn't betray her location or circumstances except to let her children know she was alive and waiting, hoping for their company. The address on the envelope read to Johnny Plaster, Shanksville.

Gene nodded and said, "God bless you and the best of luck to you, Barbara."

He turned and started his return to Pinedale by way of Shanksville. Accomplishing that would take a greater effort and more time than Gene could possibly imagine.

Gene carefully avoided the areas where he had encountered people on his path coming in. Most of his route was without many people. There were, however, sections where people had concentrated. Those he would go around to avoid contact whenever possible.

Gene's thoughts wondered back to the men and to the place where he had thrown a good share of his jerky stores. Gene knew the mob, if that was what seven men were called, would have robbed and maybe killed him. At the very best, he would have been left defenseless, starving, and maybe maimed. That is no condition to be in, especially in this day and age.

Walking had worn his hiking boots thin and now the seams were starting to split. Gene didn't want to start wearing his winter gear so early in the season. As soon as he was able, he would find replacements. He wasn't keen on breaking in new shoes on a long trip. He had resupplied his sewing and cotton needs at Seth's, but there was no footwear suitable in Gene's mind. *Seth always wore a form of sandals or thongs, pardon me, flip-flops.* Well, Gene was having a time of it breaking old habits and mindsets.

Thinking back about the landmark details of the trip coming in, Gene remembered one of several factory outlets centers that dotted the state, which he had seen from a distance. He had glassed the area with his binoculars. Most the stores had been ransacked. The thieves had long since taken anything of value. They, for the most part, left items that wouldn't be useful. As he approached the complex, he had a foreboding feeling that stopped him in his tracks. He located a vantage point from where he could watch the east side and one of the alleys. The complex, which had appeared to have been abandoned before now, had occupants. The appearance was not that of squatters, but of an organized group. Maybe not official, but nevertheless, the group had the appearance of hierarchy. Gene recalled his capture before being introduced to Hoover, which encouraged him to check his surroundings regularly, carefully, and to remain quiet.

"Maybe, I don't need to resupply as bad as I thought," he mumbled under his breath.

Ya, maybe not, he thought back.

Gene moved away and located an abandoned loafing shed on a nearby farm for a resting place. As large as it was, it was nearly full with piles of discarded, parked equipment and old hay stored. Like so many loafing sheds across America, it had been abandoned from its original use as a shelter for livestock and inducted as a quasi-enclosed storage building. Gene located a nook where he could be out the back through a hole in an instant if happened on by an intruder.

The night turned cold and Gene broke out his cold weather poncho, a woolen blanket he had slotted to fit over his head like a poncho. The smell of the air had that of snow. Gene had hoped to be back in the hills before snow came. "Too late!" was his self-chastisement. Sometime before midnight, the temperature warmed and then came the snowflakes with little swirling and intermittent gusts of wind. Gene knew at times the air temperatures raise before snow falls. He'd experienced this phenomenon many times throughout his life. Gene was grateful for the shelter.

The dawn just seemed to filter into daylight gradually. He could see a wet heavy snow causing the still-leaved tree limbs to sag, many of which were braking from the extra weight. Even at the crack of a once healthy limb, the sound was deadened, lost in the heavy, white, wet and insulating blanket.

Gene considered. "Today might be a good day to set tight, repair what needs to be repaired, and rest." He realized he was starting to talk to himself lately. Had he become one of those crazy old coots who mumbled all the time to themselves? Answering only came when he needed assurance what he was doing was the right thing to do. He talked to God most of the time, but God so far had been quiet with audible responses. God did on occasion give Gene an inkling or a hunch. Those proved to be more valuable than anything he could think of or would hear.

Gene worked on his bolts and fletching. He made mental notes of what supplies he needed to restock. His footwear was okay but lacking. Now would be the time to start using his winter foot gear, which he had carried all those miles. Gene decided that he should appropriate a walking stick for now. It had to be of strong wood, an inch and one quarter in diameter and six- to seven-feet long. This would serve to stabilize him when walking in the snow. He must keep his eyes peeled for growth appropriate to make snowshoes out of.

Over the years, Gene learned large wild rosebush shoots worked very well for the kind of shaping he needed. Rosewood was strong and had pliable properties. If it were large enough in diameter, he could drill it to run webbing through. If it were green it would be pliable and once cured would hold a shape strong enough as needed for the snowshoe. As he didn't have quite enough rawhide, nor varnish to treat the rawhide with, he would use parachute cord combined with rawhide for webbing. Most wild roses could be found near water sources. The thorns on these large shoots pop off easily, allowing a smooth surface to remain.

If the snowstorm would continue and the wind would blow a bit, Gene's tracks would be wiped out for most anyone who would pursue him. On the other hand, Gene could read tracks and their age in nearly any condition. The biggest deterrent to travel was not discovery, but the amount of energy required to buck through heavy snow. Snow like this causes total exhaustion for one who challenges its passive force. Snow by sheer volume will defeat the strongest of men and the largest of equipment. Yet the slight warm sunbeam will drive it into the ground without seemingly putting forth an effort.

Gene cleaned tools, found an old Hudson hubcap and heated snow into boiling for a light bath, made some broth with jerky and enjoyed the comfort of the warm liquid. He had to be careful the fire didn't get started in the decayed old manure. The manure could smolder for days, stink like sin, and eventually burn the buildings and equipment to the ground. Gene had no desire to destroy property in such a way. He had too much respect for the skilled handiwork and labor of the craftsman who built this structure. He kept the fire small so as not to disclose his existence to anyone. He saw no one and heard even less. The deadening silence caused by the snow blanket was absolute.

Having cleaned, repaired, taken inventory, supped, napped twice, and bathed, Gene rested beyond what he thought was even possible. Too much of this, and Gene thought he might become soft. Oh for the opportunity to try.

The second morning arrived and with it, a bright sun that reflected sharply off the snow. His eyes hurt from the brightness when he didn't squint. Contemplating the equipment he would need, Gene had forgotten about eye and skin protection in the snow. He found a curved dead cottonwood limb about two inches in diameter. Gene carved it to fit around the contour of his eyes and nose. He hollowed it to leave room for his eyes to blink and then carved very narrow slits horizontally to see out through. Gene attached some of the bailing twine he found to hold the eyewear tight to his head. Next, Gene fashioned a head covering from one of the pillowcases he retrieved from Seth's home. It covered his neck, face, and ears from the direct rays of the sun and from the snow-reflected rays. He had known people who sunburned their eyes and became snow blind. Sun blindness literally was blindness with eye pain that was excruciating.

Gene hoped he didn't run into people. He felt he must resemble the look of a clansman without the pointy top. It couldn't be helped, sunburn without appropriate treatment could make a man sick, very sick. As a youth while hunting stray cows in the high country on the snow-covered hills, one of Gene's coworkers suffered sun fever. His lips became swollen and cracked badly, and he couldn't eat at all for a week and not well for two. His ears and nose blistered on the undersides. The upper part of his face was shaded by his broad-brim cowboy hat. The rest of the experienced crew knew and used their bandanas to cover their faces. And yet with all care taken, they too burned some. They looked like a bunch of outlaws getting ready to hold up a stagecoach.

The snow had stopped. The air cooled considerably after the storm. Gene's camp was a most agreeable location and shelter. Tomorrow he would move out. Gene slept well that night. He liked the cold better than those scorching hot days of summer.

The sun came up and was blinding bright. Gene donned his goggles and hood. He entered a wonder world covered in white everywhere. The snow had frozen on top and had a crunch as he walked. Gene had to lift his feet extra high to get above the crust for the next step, which immediately broke through. This was tiring in short order. Gene would need to find material for his walking equipment as soon as possible.

Locating a drainage which appeared to cut across a field, Gene made his way toward a bushy area. There were thick willow stands, Russian olives, and other species of tree Gene wasn't familiar with. Gene started his search for a staff. He selected a spindly tree about ten- to fifteen-feet tall. He used the saw in his pocket tool to cut the tree down. Rather than stripping the bark, he just trimmed the limbs. He cut it to length.

Snow in clumps of willows is treacherous to walk in, so Gene skirted as much as he could while searching for rosewood. Near a fence line, he found what he was looking for. The largest rose canes were in the center of the clump. Gene parted the bush with his staff and reached four large canes. They weren't as big as he desired but would work if wrapped rather than drilled. When cut and extracted, Gene popped the heavy thrones off and flexed the canes for shape. Now he needed cross-section pieces to bow the canes around.

The goggles restricted Gene's vision considerably. He necessarily would check his surroundings often, more if the line of sight distance was short. Gene considered returning to the loafing shed. It was a comfortable location and somewhat secluded. He had no idea of what lay ahead for accommodations. Gene started his return to the shed. He didn't like staying too long in any location. This was pushing the limit. On the flip side, few people would be out in these conditions, so if they hadn't found his prior night's camp, they most likely wouldn't find it today. He returned by the trail he had broken getting to where he was now. The sun had melted the snow considerably and a clear sky tonight would allow the temperature to drop considerably, freezing a heavy crust atop the snow. The day heated some, but the sunlight reflected all day off the snow instead of warming the darker surfaces. The loafing shed was a welcome sight.

The balance of the day was spent fashioning crude snowshoes from rosewood canes, a pine board split for cross sections, and parachute cord woven in a proper weaving pattern. Gene chose the Bearpaw snowshoe pattern rather than the traditional tail-drag style. The Bearpaw worked very well on crusted snow, while the tail-drag worked better in powder snow. Gene calculated his weight distribution as best he could. The size of the snowshoes for him wouldn't have to be as large as for a big man. He used the split pine board for the cross sections. Wrapping the cording under and around the frame in the traditional hex pattern, the netting was completed and tightened. The foot harness was made from doubling cord. The balance was good. The shoes seemed to be strong when Gene tried them on. He went to the snow and the shoes kept him from sinking more than four or five inches. Tomorrow after the surface froze, these would keep Gene from breaking through like he had done today. Gene ate a piece of jerky and settled down for the night.

The moon was full and the canines vocalized. Dog barks and howls were different from coyote yips. Gene awoke to hear dogs howling and a hound baying at the full moon. They seemed to be coming closer. It was cold enough that the snow had already crusted and lighter dogs didn't break through the crust. Gene quickly rekindled his small fire, reached for his staff, and checked his bow and .357. Gene listened and watched as the pack drew closer. All of a sudden, a large shepherd dog appeared around the end of the loafing shed. The dogs had tracked Gene's trail back to the shelter. When the shepherd barred his teeth, another mongrel dog rounded the corner as well. Gene lifted his staff and shouted. The dogs backed away for a moment, only perceiving minimal danger from Gene's stick.

Gene picked up the crossbow instantly. He aimed carefully as the shepherd advanced. Gene didn't want to lose a bolt under the snow. The shepherd jumped to avoid the arrow, but it was too late, as the bolt penetrated at the hollow of his neck. He yelped, turned, and fell backward as he flipped away from the shelter into the snow. The mongrel, a cross between pit bull, Rottweiler, and something else, had started at Gene when the shepherrd didn't stop and Gene shoved the crossbow up and forward to protect himself from the dog's snapping teeth. The impact nearly knocked Gene to the ground. The stirrup on the bow hit the dog square in the growling mouth. He pulled back, but instead of fleeing, he tugged at the bow stirrup, trying to take it from Gene. Gene drew his pistol, turned loose the bow, pointed, and fired. The slug caught the mongrel on the left side between the shoulder and neck. He yelped, turned, and went down, lying on his side. The beast struggled to get up, kicked, half rose, and then fell a second time. Kicking and thrashing for a time, he finally lay still while life fled from his body. Gene could hear the others in the pack in the dark. Gene hoped the shot hadn't been heard. On a still night like this, a shot sound could carry literally for miles. The frozen snow would reflect the sound of a shot like a mirror. The other dogs seemed to stay just out of sight in the darkness. Gene didn't sleep again, waiting for daylight.

When daylight came, Gene examined the dogs closer. They both were starved to skin and bone. Gene extracted the bolt from the now-stiff carcass and wiped it down. These dogs had fleas, and Gene was ever-so-careful not to handle the remains any more than necessary.

Gene had been so intent on recovering his bolt, he hadn't paid mind to his surroundings. Watching from a short distance from under a stored tractor was a Bluetick Coonhound. When Gene saw him, he just lay with his head down, his eyes darting back and forth watching Gene's movements. There seemed to be no threat from the dog. Like the others, he was skin and bones. As Gene studied the tracks from the night before, he saw where three more dogs that had swapped ends all of a sudden at the sound of the shot. Two had returned after their fright and had milled around. Finally they left. The Bluetick, on the other hand, lay just watching.

Packing his belongings, strapping on the newly-made snow-shoes, putting the goggles and hood in place, Gene set out over the crusted snow. He took a different route from the prior day. Checking his back trail occasionally, he could see the hound following at a distance. The dog didn't seem to be threatening, more like looking for companionship. When Gene had reached about half a mile distance from the loafing shed, again checking his back trail, Gene saw a couple people where he had spent the night. Watching, they seemed to be studying the scene, camp, dogs, and tracks. Gene was anything but camouflaged in the white background. The hound waited, crouched by a stump.

Gene was nearly out of sight over the brush-covered ridge but stayed still, not moving. Most people, unless trained to spot an object, will not see the object without a giveaway movement. Gene became a stump momentarily. The other problem, if there was one, was Gene didn't know what awaited him over the rise. He didn't want to ease up to a position for observation over the rise until the people behind had gone. Moving might give him away. He felt certain they wouldn't follow. Breaking through the snow crust would stop most people. He waited. Gene could see the pair poking around looking for clues, then they went to where the snowshoe tracks led away from the shed. Gene could see them looking in his direction, but there wasn't an indication they would pursue him. They seemed to study the area where he stood, abandoned that, and looked at another location to Gene's left. Gene slowly turned and carefully surveyed that location. He could see what appeared to be a coyote sniffing a mouse or mole. The animal leapt in the air and speared his nose into the snow. Gene couldn't tell if he had success in catching his meal. When Gene returned his attention to the shed, the inspectors had vanished. Gene stayed still for five more minutes. Most people will give up watching an object if it doesn't move within that amount of time.

Time having passed, Gene started moving over the crest of the hill. There hadn't been any sign of the camp inspectors for some time. Approaching the top of a hill was done with care every time. What lay on the opposite slope could be good or could be detrimental. In this case it was neither.

The sign on the fence read, "Department Of Energy, Trespassers Will Be Prosecuted."

Gene thought tongue-in-cheek, *That's a new twist. I bet the feds have unseen functioning equipment all over the place they need to keep secret.*

Gene turned parallel to the fence boundary for a mile to the south. The hound paralleled Gene's track some two hundred feet out and slightly to the rear. Midday neared and the snow crust was softening. The snowshoes worked marvelously as designed. The snow seemed to have settled from the original sixteen inches to a twelve-inch depth. The crust was softer now on the east slopes of hills. By mid-afternoon, the crust would be soft everywhere. It would take immense effort to trudge across an expanse in these conditions. Gene wondered how far this boundary went before he could turn back to the west. Another mile and the snow had grown soft and wet. The fence continued. The hound tracked and kept pace, although he now started breaking through the snow. His raw paws left spots of blood from ice scrapes and cuts. Gene wondered what kind of dedication the creature must have had to stay with him so far. If he were waiting for the meal Gene would be when he dropped, he would have to wait a long time.

Gene could see a corner in the fence. From that distance, it appeared the corner was an inside corner. That meant Gene would have to trek back to the east. Studying the fence line, it appeared the easterly leg was a bit more than a mile long before it came to another corner, an outside corner. Studying the terrain from where Gene was to the outside corner, Gene could see a brush-lined ravine, what appeared to be a creek with live water running in the bottom. His decision had been made then. He changed direction to cut across to the outside fence corner. The sore-footed hound was already halfway to the brush.

The snow in the brush was a soft, fluffy crystalline powder. It hadn't crusted like the snow in the open. Gene sunk into the powder even with his footwear on. When he approached the ravine, there didn't seem to be an easy way down, over, or across. It wasn't deep, but if one fell that distance getting down to the bottom, injury would surely result. Following the rim edge, Gene looked for a break in the rim. All the while he looked for a path up and out of the other side. He found neither. He did find a large boulder facing the edge with a lip large enough to shelter the ground where snow hadn't covered the ground. The overhang provided was an excellent shelter from the wind. It faced southeasterly to catch the warming morning sunshine. A smart outdoorsman takes advantage of such good opportunities. Gene did just that. He checked his back trail, scouted as far as he could see on both sides, and observed the rim of the ravine across as far as he could see.

"Hmm," he muttered, "no sign of the hound. Well, he must have strayed away somewhere."

Camp that night was similar to many of his other camps. Comfortable it was, although the evening showed signs of turning into a very cool night. He would spend many other cold nights he knew. Using the snowshoes and pack as a barrier against possible observing eyes from across the ravine, Gene settled into a sound sleep. He often slept well when out, but he had a keen sense and would wake in an instant at the slightest disturbance.

At early dawn the sky was clear without a cloud in sight. Gene opened his eyes, listened, and watched what he could see from his bed. As he stirred, he caught a glimpse of a shiny rock. It was an arrowhead from some wondering nomad of times past. It was a finely-crafted piece chipped to a razor-sharp edge and the shape was exquisite. Of course, it made sense an Indian would have sheltered here. He must have lost this perfect specimen during his camp activities. What a loss that must have been for him.

Dog, I smell dog! he thought. *Had the smell of the dogs I killed got on my cloths in some way? No, this smell is of fresh alive, wet dog and is nearby.*

Gene sat up and looked past the backpack and snowshoes. There, with head down and eyes darting back and forth ever-so-watchful, was the hound. There wasn't a threat in those eyes, but the look of a dog waiting for a scolding or a reward from a master.

"Dog," Gene said quietly, "did you come to be breakfast, lunch, or supper or did you expect something to eat?"

The hound didn't move. Gene cautiously got up to meet the day with one eye on the hound, stirred the small fire to life, and heated some water. He pulled a small piece of jerky out of his pack and bit off a section, tossing the remaining part to the hound. His head came up instantly to snatch the morsel midair. He chewed it a bit and swallowed, laid his head back down, and resumed his laidback awareness without moving a paw. Gene drank his hot water and packed.

"What the heck," mused Gene. Thinking further, *it's good to wake up with some company, but how'd the hound do it, slipping right into camp without being detected? He'll have to earn his own keep. I can't carry feed for the both of us.*

Current task at hand, Gene resumed his search for a way off the edge and up the other side. The snow intermittently was crusted in open areas and crystal frozen powdered in the sheltered and shady spots. Further along the edge appeared the spot Gene had been seeking, a sloughed-off break in the rock rim. If he had to, he could get back out of the ravine just in case the bottom and opposite side offered no other way out. Gene scanned the other edge for a similar passage. He didn't see one. He decided to follow the near rim further before descending into the ravine. He knew before descending into the canyon he should have a plan of exit. Now he noticed the ravine had deepened and had grown into a small canyon.

Reversing his direction of travel, Gene followed the rim the opposite direction upstream. He passed last night's camp and the point where he had come to the ravine. Three quarters of a mile further up the stream, the ravine disappeared. The stream fell into an icy pool below, where the head of the ravine started. Above that, the ravine did not exist.

"What a place for a deer hunt," he said or thought. He wasn't sure which.

This problem solved, Gene turned toward the location of the outside corner of the government fence. It was as far away as when he first started for it. The hound again had started shadowing Gene's movements.

The snow was firm and walking went well. Gene covered two miles when he came to the corner. The fence just stopped. It went nowhere beyond the end point. Gene pondered the surprise, then decided to proceed south toward his original destination. Four more miles he covered before the snow grew soft. The hound was off sniffing this track and the next. He was also breaking through the crust with nearly every step. Gene could again see the telltale spots of blood from the dog's cut feet on the trail where the hound had been.

There wasn't a sheltered campsite to be found that night. The land was open and barren, except for an occasional scattered dwelling. Gene knew they approached the northern edge of an old small town now incorporated into the city suburbs. He would have to skirt around as best he was able and hold the course he had picked for the foothills. The hound flushed a rabbit and with some effort, Gene chased it to a hole. The hound was still breaking through the softened crust so was not able to give chase. Gene found a willow cane, cut it and split the end four ways. After working it into the hole, he could feel the rabbit. Twisting the stick like a crank, he could feel the fur ball tangle in the forked split. Carefully withdrawing the stick, he could feel the rabbit being dragged out all the while making a shrill squeal. Now, having fresh meat presented a problem. Being so near civilization, a fire to cook the rabbit could be a giveaway. But he and the hound were beyond famished, so a small fire was risk. The rest of the night they remained in a cold camp with no barrier from the wind except for the pack and snowshoes.

The suburb now loomed. With single mindedness, Gene's choices were to backtrack some two or three miles or go through a strange community. After considerable deliberation, Gene elected to cross through the hamlet. When he approached, he came to a paved road that turned into a street going through the middle of a subdivision. He studied the street and surroundings. He could see the other end where the street exited the town. There wasn't a choice. Gene started down the street toward the far end as quickly as he could. A man stepped out from a covered porch, watched, and didn't make a move or attempt a salutation. Gene waved a casual greeting and kept moving. In the next block, two more and a woman watched as Gene passed.

One of the men hollered to Gene, "Hey, dude, where do you think you're a goin'?"

Gene didn't answer, feigning he hadn't heard. The man stepped into the street and approached Gene from the side. "Hey you, I asked you a question. Where you think you're a goin'?"

Gene turned with the crossbow lifted and growled, "Nowhere you want to be. Back off."

The man stopped and instead of leaving started circling to Gene's right side.

Chapter 21

Laurie's Awakening

To Bonnie's surprise, the trackers were inept. She felt their skills in hiding their trail were not that good, but it seemed to have worked. In the inclement weather, the MLS trackers didn't seem to have heart enough to dedicate their resources to catching up with them. One time when Chuck was on watch, he gave the signal. There were men hunting far off in the distance. They seemed not to have a clue what they looked for. Bonnie could see their tracks in the waning snow. That was a good thing. The more they mucked up the landscape, the harder it would be to find the Marshals' tracks.

Bonnie's wound had scabbed over but at times was still painful and at most times uncomfortable. When she carried her pack, most of the weight was shifted to her right shoulder. She had stabbing pains occasionally as she moved about and as healing progressed. The scar on the front healed in a circular raw spot. The wound in the back of her shoulder was tender, and every time she reached with her left hand, a shot of pain ran into her neck and down her arm. She hoped that would go away. Chuck kept a close eye on the condition of the wound and dressed it regularity. The old Indian shelter was adequate. She now understood why the ancients chose spots like these. She academically knew, but now she practically understood.

All were concerned about the welfare of the others. Bonnie and Laurie knew Gretchen intended to head for the canyons and a place she called Robbers Roost. She had spent many of her young years hiking and camping in the area.

I pray to God they got there, thought Bonnie. Samantha was game but had little or no experience as near as they knew. She was very young and physically not matured to full strength. Molly was a determined trooper by nature and training, and Gretchen was just Gretchen. Boy, how much more Bonnie respected Gretchen now compared to during the youth competitions where they first met.

The several light snowstorms during the week left little accumulation and by week's end, the adobe soil had dried into semi-fluffy clods of dirt on top of where the sun had shown in the open. Under the scrub cedar, there remained patches of snow where cottontail tracks could readily be seen. Laurie and Chuck foraged about catching rabbits for dinner and finding Mormon tea for a hot drink brew. The problem with the dried soil was it left tracks when walked on as plain as if they had walked in the snow. On the bright side, there hadn't been trackers sighted for several days. Now, Laurie expressed a wish for footprints to move around on top of which she might use for cover to disguise her own tracks.

Then they appeared. There were three spread out, searching and scanning the ground. They crossed the tracks left by the previous trackers, turned, and followed cautiously. Not knowing they were tracking their own men, they continued until out of sight.

"Bon, this is my chance to deliver the Judge's instructions," said Laurie. "I can find the others without leaving tracks from here that are obvious. I can get on their tracks; no one will be the wiser. When the time is right, I'll make my way to Robbers Roost. We went there once with Daddy when I was about ten. If they're there, I'll find them."

After some discussion, they agreed to the venture. Laurie would leave as soon as possible so her tracks over the new trackers' trail would be as fresh as theirs. By reckoning, Laurie calculated they were some thirty or thirty five miles from Robbers Roost to the west. Leaving, Laurie made a careful trek down to the trail so as to leave as little sign as possible of where she had come from. For a while she disguised her footprints by walking in the exact tracks left by the trackers. Her footprints were smaller than two, but the third had a smaller track and stride, which made it easier to disguise her existence.

Carefully listening as she progressed, she heard no sound for the next two miles. All of a sudden, a deer came bounding from the direction the trackers were heading. About a hundred yards away, the deer dropped as a series of three rifle shots echoed, rebounding off the hills. Laurie slipped behind an old burned-out cedar stump and watched as two cleaned and dressed the deer. They skinned and cut out the flanks and shoulders. Each packed haunches down the slope, where they met the third. All disappeared into the ravine and ensuing canyon below.

Laurie slipped to the remaining carcass, where the choice cuts of tenderloin and back-strap remained. It took Laurie all of five minutes to strip out the tenderloin and other cuts suitable for fine dining that remained. She carefully recovered the carcass with the stripped-off hide and just as carefully made her way away and back toward the Indian shelter.

Meeting Laurie on one side hill over from the shelter, Chuck joined her, then waited in seclusion, watching her back trail.

"Laurie, thank God, we worried you had been shot," said Chuck. "I was on my way to come in shooting."

Laurie explained the events and the surprise she had for them. Some good protein wouldn't hurt Bonnie in any event. That night it snowed, covering all tracks made the previous week. They ate roast venison steak with great enjoyment that evening. There was some twenty-five pounds of meat. They cut a couple ample steaks each and jerked the rest. Laurie would leave on the second day to find Robbers Roost, where they believed Molly, Gretchen, and Sam to be held up.

Laurie waited two days for the snow to melt before she started to Robbers Roost, but the cold never rose above freezing. The sunshine caused the snow to melt even though sub-freezing weather persisted. The snow crusted and the sound created by walking on it seemed extremely revealing to any who might be within earshot.

The journey of Laurie's life started just before daybreak. She checked and double-checked her guns. Laurie would have preferred one of the late model compound bows and good fiberglass arrows they had in camp before the bug out. Those had been stashed for future needs. Shortened days made her travel less effective distance-wise than it would have been in early to mid-summer. The bigger challengers were the three big canyons between the Indian camp and Robbers Roost. The first was Regan Canyon. Being some fifteen hundred feet deep and forty miles long, it started in the high plateaus. The second was Sanchez Gulch. Sanchez Gulch was as long as Regan Canyon but only cut a crooked path around the buttes on palisades with offshoot canyons branching left and right. Many of those were box canyons, some of which fed upon cascading falls, which evaporated into a mist before reaching the canyon floor. The third canyon was McDougal Canyon, which had a respectable length as well. Two major branches formed the bulk of the abyss. High above the confluence between the east and west fork was where Laurie remembered Robbers Roost to be located.

Laurie had been there one time when a young girl with her family on an Easter Sunday outing. She was confident she would find her way back, even though her approach came from a different direction. Her first night was cold, restful, and like most others, with peaceful dreams. An hour after daybreak, she wondered in her mind where everybody was and what they were doing. All of a sudden, Laurie became overwhelmed with loneliness like she had never experienced before. She deeply missed her dad and sisters. She petitioned God for comfort and the overwhelming loneliness eased. If there ever was an end to this social unrest, she told herself, "I'll go home to raise baby calves for the rest of my life."

Lost in her thoughts, Laurie suddenly realized she needed to be more vigilant. There weren't many people in the badlands, but there could be a hunting party or MLS trackers casting about. As she walked around a log, there in the snow lay a large lion track. It was fresh and she knew the big cat had seen her. People don't see the lions often. They, on the other hand, see people quite often. By the time she reached the rim of Regan Canyon, she had seen three such cat tracks. Each differed because of the track size and the stride. It was unusual to see so many lions in such close proximity of each other. Deer and small game animals had been depleted by starving populations in the valleys below around the settlements. The cats were moving higher in the hills, where the game was more plentiful.

Zack had once related the story of when he tracked a big cat to the base of a twenty-foot bluff. The cat in two bounds cleared the top of the bluff to avoid Zack. When Zack worked his way around to the top where the cat went, he saw where the cat had been watching from above all the while. Zack decided to let matters be and gave up the pursuit.

Laurie decided to find a staff heavy enough to use as a club but light enough as not to be a burden. She found some Tamarisk brush, a form of dense salt cedar with a straight branch an inch and three quarters in diameter. She cut it with the pocket tool saw to a length of six feet. Peeling the bark left Laurie with a stout staff one and quarter to one and a half inches in diameter. She wanted it six-foot long so as to be taller than she was. To fall on a sharp pointed spear as this could be deadly. Being taller than she would afford some safety in a slip. Sharpening the smaller end to a point, Laurie would harden the point with her next fire. Should she come face-to-face with a cat or bear, it might lead to a full-on attack. She could shoot a predator, but the sound of a shot would reveal her existence and position. Prophesy is the foretelling of events to come and Laurie's thoughts, even though she didn't know it, were prophetic.

At the rim of Regan Canyon, few breaks existed in the rim rock over which Laurie could descend to the bottom. Crossing an old uranium prospector jeep road, she found a game trail that worked along a steep hillside proceeding downward toward the canyon floor some fifteen hundred feet below. About three hundred feet into the dissension and edging around a bend along the bluff, she saw a wilderness road bulldozed into the formation off to the north of her location. She thought it must lead to the prospector's road she had recently crossed. The contemplation of backtracking and walking down the easy way was interrupted by the unmistakable sound of ATVs. The first in front came tearing up the road like a lunatic. The other two were not so exuberant. Only the MLS had fuel for equipment and ATVs.

If I had one of those, I could get to Robbers Roost in half-a-day, she thought. *I could string a wire and close line the first one, take his machine, block the road on a blind corner, forcing the others off over the roadside cliff, and be done with them. It would be simple.*

Her thoughts and her nature just wouldn't let her harmfully engage men and leave them suffering to die unmercifully, even if they were the MLS. Besides, the noise their machines made would keep her informed as to their location, when and if they stopped. She proceeded in her descent toward the bottom, much to the ignorance of the three ATV riders.

Near the bottom, Laurie found more cat tracks and saw very few deer tracks. Even porcupines were less plentiful than normally would be expected. Having scouted the far canyon slope as she descended to the canyon floor, Laurie chose a likely route out of the canyon to the mesa on the other side. Zack Smith always said there was more to being a mountaineer than climbing some obscure rock face. She was capable of those feats too. More important than those skills was the ability to select a route from one location to another without taking undue risks in the route. Sometimes it meant going miles out of the direct line of sight path to achieve the eventual destination. Laurie's route was one of those which changed direction and traversed the canyon face switching back and forth to the higher elevation to the top directly above her. Nearly at the top, she heard the ATVs returning down the prospector road. They stopped as if looking for some unusual sighting. Laurie froze, not moving a muscle. She felt she was obscured by scrub Pinyon and buckbrush. One of the onlookers pointed toward the bottom near where she had been. Then he traced with his outstretched arm a path similar to the one she had taken. One of the others loaded a rifle and pointed in her general direction. She saw the muzzle blast and heard the bullet impact some hundred feet to her back trail. They weren't shooting at her but something else. She studied the area and saw a mountain lion scampering up the rocks to a concealed location. The cat had been stalking her. The chills which ran up her spine nearly wilted her. Those shooters unknowingly must have saved her from being the next meal.

After a time, they remounted their ATVs and rode on down the road. Still shaken by her near encounter, Laurie worked her way up and over the rim top. This was a land where few white men had trodden. Maybe a few occasional deer hunters, uranium prospectors in the mid-part of the last century, and cowboys seeking stray critters. This was truly wilderness, not by designation, but by fact.

Laurie crossed the mesa top in about three hours, approaching the rim overlooking Sanchez Gulch. The country below was rough and rugged. Crags and crannies existed everywhere with no discernible path to proceed on. There were many side canyons to study. Easing her way over the rim on a game trail, she looked for a secluded campsite she could defend against predators. About a hundred feet around the trail she followed was a cave. It wasn't natural but a hand dug cave. There were two entries large enough for a small man to squeeze into. When inside, Laurie realized this was no ordinary cave. It was in fact a flint mine hewn out by the ancient people for flint with which to make spear points, arrowheads, and skinning knives. There was an old fire pit, the embers of which had been long-since extinguished. The temperature was a warm fifty-two degrees, some warmer than the night air outside would be this night. What luck it was to find this shelter. The mine was long enough for her to stretch out in but not tall enough to stand upright in. Looking out the second entry, Laurie could see over the adjacent cliff. While looking out the entry she had crawled through, she could see four or five miles down the canyon. She would need to be careful. Her smoke could be seen from that way as well.

Building a small smokeless fire of dead cedar and dry brush would keep the late summer bugs away and would detour predators as well. Laurie slept well again that night, only to wake to six inches of fresh snow on the ground and a white wonderland beyond. Traveling in this terrain in such conditions was not something she would have chosen to do in ordinary circumstances. She preferred not to now but would have to keep moving to reach the Roost.

Laurie spent her time the next two days resting and repairing. The mine was stale from years of animal dung accumulation. Laurie found a bump just where her hips rested when sleeping. She felt around and found a piece of flint about five inches in length. Tossing it aside, she rested like a dead man the whole night until dawn. Her fire had died out. She was comfortably warm and ate jerked venison and drank creek water from her bottle. She rested. Stale as the air was inside, breathing fresh air from the entry, she spent time studying the wrinkles and bumps in the landscape below her from the cave opening.

The piece of flint in the cave discarded during the night had been worked to a fine knife-edge. It was a fine spear point, large but fragile, and would break on any rock the spear tip might strike. It could be useful as a lethal extended knife in battle. Laurie considered it as a tip for her staff. After consideration, Laurie left the piece there, choosing the fire-hardened wood point as readily replaceable. As was the usual practice among the Marshals, Laurie left a sign of her passing. The system was simple. One rock was placed atop another with a stick in between, perpendicular to the direction of travel. About eight- to ten-feet opposite the direction of travel, a long stone or tapered stone fragment pointed to the exact direction of travel. These were left at any major change in land feature, like a creek bottom or canyon rim. If there was a significant change of direction, a sign would be left clear to those who knew. For the unknowing, the stick between the rocks would indicate a direction ninety degrees away from the true route. Laurie left these at regular sites where the others could locate them if needed.

Her drop over the edge became slippery and she left a deep muddy trail in the soil, rocks, and snow. She would have waited longer but felt no hope the conditions would change for several days. As near as she could determine, there would be more storms on the heels of the last. Her hope was the coming storms would mask her disturbing of the mud.

All the morning and much of the afternoon she consumed descending to the bottom of Sanchez Gulch. She had decided to work up-valley toward a trail she'd observed that led up and out of a side canyon. This evening found her in a box canyon seeking shelter. To her surprise, she stumbled into a cultivated marijuana patch. These were dangerous places. These were places to avoid if a casual hiker wanted to see the next day. Drug growers jealously protected their operations. Caution shot through her mind as the adrenaline awoke her body. If the farmer had seen her, she would most likely have already been dead. She froze in place, concealed herself, and watched. There was nothing stirring about except a squirrel and some small birds.

The setting seemed funny to Laurie after studying the plants. They hadn't been harvested or even cut. Whoever the tender or tenders were, they appeared to have abandoned the project. Skirting around the side to the far edge, Laurie could see black plastic pipe used to irrigate the plants that now were well over eight feet tall. Edging past the small stream, she came to an overgrown trail, which at one time was well worn. The mist from the waterfall above rose as the steam was interrupted by falling over a sand rock cliff. The mist caused many plants not found other places to flourish here. Laurie found wild grapes small, succulent, and ripe, and some dried like raisins. Ones the squirrels had not eaten were still on the vine just ready for the tasting.

On edge as she was, Laurie habitually stayed attuned to any sound around, but suddenly she realized there was no sound. No fluttering or bird chirps, no squirrel chatter or rustling—then she heard it, almost too late, the slight snap of a twig and the staring of rotted vegetation. Whirling in the nick of time, she saw a lion make two bounds toward her and it covered the last twenty feet airborne. Laurie could later confirm the statement "time slows in times of peril." As she instinctively dropped to one knee, setting the large end of the staff in the earth, she directed the sharp end directly toward the cat. Twisting in the air as he came, the spear point penetrated under the left front leg at the pit and projected out the back between the ribs and shoulder blade. It was not an immediately mortal wound. The impact knocked Laurie's tin cup over the teakettle. The collision momentarily knocked her senses from her.

Wounded animals have ferocity equal to none other when first stricken. Laurie experienced at close hand that violence as it exploded. The cat thrashed, biting, clawing, and tearing at anything close by, especially the staff spear. The wound not being mortal would likely cause eventual death, but in the meantime, the danger this cat projected was terrifying. Laurie instinctively back treaded for some twenty feet, grasping at what to do. She should shoot the animal, but with its thrashing, a clean shot would not be likely. Three or maybe four might do the job. Those in turn could bring unwanted two-legged company. Laurie now trembled from her toes to her shoulders. If she were to try to put the cat out of its misery, she probably wouldn't be able to shoot straight anyway.

Biting and clawing at the spear, the cat snapped the wood like a toothpick. The amount of power exhibited in those jaws was astounding to her. In snapping the spear, the cat regained its feet, bounding off with the pointed end protruding skyward from its shoulders. Laurie shook, then cried for fifteen minutes before she could regain her composure. She returned to the spot of attack, gathering her scattered equipment as she went.

"Laurie, girl, you ducked a big one just now," she squeaked to herself. "Thank you, God."

Moving back up the trail, she came to a makeshift shelter. It was in disrepair, but it would be serviceable for her needs. Packrats had frequented the makeshift shelving and canned goods had been pushed off the shelving to the dirt below. Laurie cleared a spot for sleeping but slept very little that night. Her fleeting naps were interrupted by the violent sounds of the cat thrashing about in her mind.

Exhausted at morning's arrival, Laurie set about taking inventory of the camp. It had been recently a serviceable shelter. She found cans of tuna, clams, beans, and three bottles of beer, and a half empty bottle of Wild Turkey bourbon. There were other goods, but none she would trust her life to. Cautiously scouting the area around the falls, she picked a handful of those dried grapes. They tasted like candy. She hadn't remembered when she had had such pleasant taste in her mouth. Laurie forced herself to track the cat for a distance. Much to her dismay, it had taken the path up the side canyon where she intended to go. She returned to the shelter, confident the lion wouldn't return that night; although wounded, it could be a menace to man or beast who might have the appearance of easy pickings. Selecting a stout hardwood staff, Laurie proceeded to make another staff with a fire-hardened point.

The night had been cold and the small fire warmed her. Refreshed, Laurie located other wild grapes and proceeded on the trail out where the lion had fled. Up the trail three quarters of the way to the top lay the front two feet of her old staff. It must have worked its way out of the cat and fallen in the path. Laurie could see the blood spots and the tracks where the cat had begun to stagger. This was one sick pussycat. The trail wound along the hillside and topped out on a low mesa. The sun up was warm and welcome and there seemed to be no other living thing within miles. Off in the distance east of Regan Canyon she heard the faint sound of ATVs. At the top of the rim, the usual rock sign was set, pointing her intended destination up and around a long ravine which bisected her direction of travel.

Melting snow and unfrozen soil provided a medium for tracks a blind man could follow with a cane. The mud balled up around Laurie's shoes so her tracks looked like a giant's track with a short stride. There was nothing to be said or done. It was what it was. All Laurie could count on would be the remoteness of the location and hope the enemy wouldn't discover the tracks. She held her path to as many of the washed runoff bottoms where a storm of any kind would wash away most her telltale tracks as she could. Working up around the head of the ravine, Laurie avoided the cap rock where mud from her tracks might remain much longer than the impressions in the wash bottoms. Her remoteness didn't allow for a lapse of care. Being careless here could be a fatal mistake.

Midday the following day, Laurie reached the eastern rim of McDougal Canyon. Having miscalculated the location of her desti-nation, Laurie came to the realization she would have to maneuver up canyon some ten miles to reach Robbers Roost. Viewing over the canyon bottom, Laurie could see evidence of recent vehicle traffic and the actual movement in an organized personnel encampment. Observing a moment longer, she saw that not only did they have ATVs, in camp were half a dozen horses tethered on the far side. If the girls were in Robbers Roost, they might outrun mechanization in the deeper snow of the mountains behind, but they could never outrun horses. Horses could travel miles through belly-deep snow that would stop any ATV or 4 x 4. Laurie had to get to Robbers Roost far ahead of the contingent below.

Studying the canyon roads in the bottom, she could see branches to side canyons. One of those roads led up the branch nearest her location. She could see a switch back that apparently topped out on the mesa she was on. That road crested some two miles beyond her and between her and the location of Robbers Roost. Being careful not to leave any signs, Laurie edged her way toward that destination.

She could hear the low-throated rumble of an ATV ahead of her. What she really wanted was one of those horses. Horseback was her eliminate. Even though an ATV could outrun a horse on roads and on a trail and over a distance, a horse would cover territory ATVs couldn't. Horses could eat for fuel. When the gas ran out, the ATV was finished.

Laurie's pressing thought was to get to the Roost as soon as possible. The soil was still moist and tracks were difficult at best to conceal. Muddy patches would preserve tracks forever. To not leave her footprints, an alternative method of travel would need to be found. The most convenient option to accomplish that would be to ride an ATV, which would leave a plain but indiscriminate trail. Until the trackers realized they weren't tracking one of their own, it might buy time via confusion, especially if they weren't aware the opposition drove the machine.

Working her way to the location of the ATV sound, Laurie spotted the man and the machine. As his machine idled, he watched the canyon from above as a lookout. He smoked some foul-smelling cigarette. Now was decision time. She needed to be decisive and do the deed. Take him out without an alarm reaching the contingent below. There was too much open distance between him and her location. She couldn't shoot him. The sound would alert the others. She thought back to the earlier encounters with the ATVs on Shimmers Mesa. Backing away, she made her way up the two track trail, where she found a place she could string a cord. Her plan was to show herself far enough away that the man would jump on his machine and tear full speed toward her last location, consequently clothes-lining himself on the stretched parachute cord. If this worked, he should be knocked senseless, allowing her to take command of the situation and ATV. She would prefer to commandeer a horse, but that was far too risky given the number in camp.

The trap had been set. She reviewed in her mind the what-ifs, the variants to the event, all the things that might go wrong. She watched until he arose and was looking in her general direction, then sprang into action, allowing him a fleeting glimpse of her as she darted into and then out of sight. He drew a pistol and without a target to shoot at did just as expected, climbing on the machine, gunning full throttle, and accelerated it in her direction. When he came to the tightly-stretched rope, she was waiting close out of sight. He hit the outstretched trap with a gasp just before he was ejected off the back of the ATV. The impact with the ground, instantly stopping from some thirty miles per hour, was devastating. The man never stirred. Laurie approached carefully to discover his neck broken. The ATV had run into a stump, overturning then dying from the upset. Laurie uprighted it and backed it around to the body.

He was heavy, but she loaded him on the cargo wrack cross ways of the machine. She retrieved her cord, which had broken and brushed awaythe tracks, the only sign left by this event. Shutting off the ATV, Laurie listened for sound of others. Not hearing any, she proceeded up the dirt road for a mile. Stopping occasionally to listen for other sounds, she proceeded carefully. It occurred to her others may be riding the road and if encountered could be problematic. She located a cap rock where part of the road crossed. Turning, then following the cap rock trying not to leave tracks, she left the beaten path. Off-roading was slower travel, but she was not as likely to find unwanted company.

She stopped some dozen times to sample the mountain sounds. They were just that, mountain sounds undisturbed by the world of engines on the ground and jets in the sky. An estimated six or seven miles up the mesa, Laurie could see Robbers Roost setting on the point at the convergence of the two main tributaries of East McDougal Creek and West McDougal Creek.

Her dilemma now was what to do next. Should she hide the ATV for future use? She needed to bury the dead man just out of humanity. To do so would be difficult at best given the time of year and the temperatures. Another option would be to find a cliff or precipice where the ATV could be made to run over the cliff, making it look as if the lookout had an accident. That might hide the fact she had been anywhere around. This plan was the most logical when push came to shove. Having passed a steep precipice some half mile back she turned the machine around and paralleled the canyon rim. The point she wanted was straight in front of her.

The ATV throttle was set at a speed fast enough to cause the machine forward progress when Laurie released the brake. Over the edge it went, just barely scraping and tumbling past the rocky edge. The precipice some twenty feet deep welcomed the machine and man. The evidence had lodged in the crack at the bottom. Shakily, Laurie brushed away any sign of her prescence and followed the rim rock away toward her destination. Now she had to descend into East McDougal Canyon and get to Robbers Roost. It would be dark before she could descend a third of the way.

There seemed to be little cover with which she could conceal herself for the night. Any travel in the dark of night would be foolish. Laurie needed all the light to help her avoid leaving a discernible trail and to avoid a misstep. She opted for a dry cold camp. There was no sleep. There was risk of cat attacks at night, and her conscience lashed her for the deed she had completed. She tried to justify the act with logic, but in her heart, guilt still engulfed her. She sobbed quietly for a long time. Exhausted, she rested lightly and prayed for the morning to come early. It didn't. She prayed to God for forgiveness and vowed to go home and raise baby calves. What she desired was to live a quiet life raising calves. They all grew up to be cows, but even cows begat more little calves.

When the sun broke the crest of the ridge, Laurie descended, well on her way over the side on a game trail. She wanted to stay in the shadow of the hillside as long as possible. Moving carefully and watching for onlookers, Laurie reached East McDougal Creek just before straight-up noon. Filling her water reservoirs, Laurie picked a trail ascending the hillside to the Robbers Roost access. There seemed to be no sign of human life here. She saw wildlife tracks, but no deer or elk tracks. That seemed unusual in this location. There were many deer and elk that would escape the constant pressure of year after year hunting season.

Nearing the ledge where the Robbers Roost trail traversed the cliff face, Laurie saw some faint evidence of small human tracks. Were they here? Soon she would know.

"Laurie, I almost shot you about ten minutes ago," said Sam. "If Molly hadn't told us not to shoot, you would be stretched out under that cedar over there! She saw you in the bottom filling your bottles. She was so excited I thought she was going to stroke out."

Laurie, surprised, nearly wetted herself. She stared at Sammy with round sleep-deprived eyes. Samantha grinned from ear to ear, all the time watching the trail behind Laurie. Laurie said nothing.

"The camp's over there. Gretchen is resting from her watch last night. I think she'll be overjoyed to see you," said Sammy.

Laurie stumbled up the incline into the camp, collapsed near the fire, and slept. When she awoke, a blanket had been placed over her. Gretchen poured a hot cup of funny-tasting tea. Laurie guessed it to be rose hip tea. It was good and a strip of jerky tasted like a T-bone steak.

"You know, Laurie, you didn't have to sleep in the kitchen," Gretched stated blandly. "We do have a designated bedroom and the living room is just over there by those rocks."

Laurie quipped back, "At least I didn't fall asleep in the bathroom."

They looked at each other for a split moment and both started with the giggles. They would almost regain control, then each burst out into uncontrollable titter for another round. Finally exhausted from the episode, they regained their composure. Laurie wasn't sure if the episode was a result of relief for being there or simply a release of tension building from the circumstances. Whatever the reason, both were relieved at the end of it.

Two were always on guard at offset schedules, eight on, and eight off. At no time were they all together in camp at the same time. The relief lookout always relieved the duty lookout at the lookout site and the other would return to camp to rest for the next shift. They were all tired from the routine. It would be a relief for just one more to share the task. Laurie explained her discoveries to each in turn when they came together. At the start of the second day, she took her turn at the posts. Molly and Gretchen had observed activity a long way down the bottom of McDougal Canyon below the confluence. The activity seemed to be more frequent as of late.

Molly had seen people on the rim east of East McDougal Canyon, opposite their location, seemingly watching the Roost. She quizzed Laurie about her observations as she had come from that direction. Laurie, quiet for a spell, not wanting to tell them about the man and the ATV she had taken, finally told there had been an encounter and the man and ATV were concealed, hopefully without a sign of her involvement. After much discussion, they concluded there would be an attack on their site soon. If the MLS had good information, they would know escape out the back from Robbers Roost was possible. Gretchen, listening, surmised the horses would be used to get behind them in a flanking maneuver. They would have to ride some ten miles up the west ridge of West McDougal Canyon to get behind them, then add another four or five miles from west to east, but that was easily doable in a few hours on horseback, and so the preemptive response was quickly agreed upon.

They all became possessed with the thought of the horses and the idea of a raid, Indian style. Sammy was an accomplished horsewoman, as her dad broke horses as a vocation along with his farming operation.

Sammy Samantha Juanita Ochoa. She was some twelve years Molly's junior. She joined the Marshals after a raid on her father's farm by the MLS. The MLS killed her dad, her older brother Juan, and her younger brother Jose. Hidden in a false fireplace wall, she was found sobbing by Gretchen when she and Bonnie arrived. They had tried to get to the Ochoa farm to stop the raid but were an hour too late. With nowhere to go, Sammy joined the Marshals at Bonnie's insistence she not be left to fend for herself. She was a surprisingly capable sixteen years old. She had the skills of an older woman taught by her mother.

The raid on the camp below to liberate the horses was a risky idea, but all would be faced with an eventual attack from the squad below. From Laurie's report, there appeared to be little doubt of an inevitable attack. If they took no action, the horses would be used to circle behind their position and pin them down unto death.

Their raid was now planned. It would be a night raid during the first quarter of the moon. There would be just enough light to raid and escape while not proving good targets in the dim light.

Chapter 22

Tennis Shoes

W hen Gene's eyes opened, his head pounded and his sight blurred. He lay in the snow between buildings, as near as he could tell, two houses. His face was wet from the hound licking it. He struggled to sit and he could hear the blood rushing through his head with a rushing sound. Gene scooped some snow and held it on his neck for a moment. As his head cleared, he started looking for his stuff. It was gone—the crossbow, his pack, his coat and his .357. They took the pocket tool and the sun goggles were nowhere to be seen. Gene could feel the 9 mm tucked safely in his armpit. The leg knife Mike in Riverton helped him to rig was not there.

These thugs had seen him coming literally and figuratively. He'd walked into it like a dumb rookie. As Gene struggled to get to his feet, he first saw the blood on the snow, *his* blood on the snow. He felt the right back corner of his head and the clotted blood stuck in his hair over a knot as big as the proverbial "goose egg." His sight ranged in and out of focus as he unsteadily kept upright. Gene could see where he'd been dragged from the middle of the street. He leaned against the side of the nearest building, giving him some moments to clear his head. As he studied the scene, the hound's tracks came from opposite the street and he could see something near where he fell in the street. It appeared to be a piece of wood. They were his goggles and closer in the drag mark was the pillowcase he used as a screen from the sun. They had dragged him feet first between the two houses. His hood and goggles had subsequently come off during the drag. If they had lifted him by his arms they would have found his hideaway.

"*That's a fine thing*." he thougt. He had very little now, certainly no food, no fire, and little in the way of tools to survive with. He knew with a knife he would have a chance. The year he'd spent overseas had put him through a survival course with less. It wasn't winter then. He unsteadily walked to the pillowcase and then to the goggles. They were both intact. Studying the tracks, he could see four sets, then he saw them: his snowshoes had been thrown to the side, apparently considered useless. That thought hurt his ego some, but was also a means to rejoice. Admittedly, they were crude, but they had been serviceable. Well, the first thing he would need was shelter for the night and some heat. There wasn't sign of any activity—no tracks or other signs of the activity one would see in an occupied community. This town seemed to be a ghost town, abandoned for lack of potable water.

Why did I not see it before? he thought. *There wasn't a physical sign of tracks in the street snow or on the steps entering the houses. Oh, ah. . .* His head hurt.

"Well, Lord, I'm in a pickle now," he muttered.

Gene turned to the nearest open door and gently eased it open. Maybe he could find a blanket and some matches. Others bent upon destruction had ransacked this house. There was a ragged leather woman's coat still hanging in a closet. Gene found tools in the attached garage. There was nothing of any value. He eased out of one house to the next and again found nothing useful. Now he looked for an out-of-the-way dwelling.

The one he spotted was a small dwelling set back some two hundred yards and on a tree-covered knoll in the middle of a small acreage. It was so quaint. From a distance, it nearly looked like a shed. It appeared unkempt and in some disrepair. Gene moved in toward the little log house around the near left side. There weren't any tracks or sign of inhabitants around the house. Gene could see what appeared to be a rifle barrel sticking out of a window. It appeared to have been propped there. He worked his way to the back of the house and tried the doorknob from the side of the door. The door was locked, but Gene could see the latch slid into the brass striker plate through an opaque glass. This door wasn't tight. He found a wood splinter and slipped the point against the latch, easing it backward. He pulled the door tight, causing the latch to jam. One more time easing the latch backward and it released, allowing the door to open.

The moment the door swung open, Gene knew he had struck gold. There was hunting equipment all around and through a doorway he could see a second room in the cottage. It was so unspoiled. Gene expected a shot to take him out instantaneously. None came. There was that sickening pungent sweet odor of the dead, which filled the stale air in the house. After letting the room air clear out, Gene looked around and closed the door, locking it behind him. He peeked into the second room where he found a body slumped near the window holding the rifle Gene had seen from outside. Near the body was a short barrel shotgun. The skeleton had dried skin and clothes holding it together, the flesh long since having decayed and been eaten by those small creatures designed by God for such a purpose. That explained the undisturbed nature of the place. He must have had a reputation of, well, being a grouchy S.O.B. and the odor must have repelled any would-be intruder.

Gene shut the door to the second room. He took a mental inventory of what he could see. Somewhere here would be everything he would need. For now, this quaint log home would do as a place to hold up for a recuperative night. There were canned goods and packaged food for a meal. Some would do as trail fare. The hound had laid down on the backdoor stoop. Tomorrow, Gene would get his equipment back. He had become accustomed to it and wanted none other. They had even taken his journal.

The cabin contents furnished Gene with a shotgun, ammo, food, matches, cooking gear, and blankets. Gene discovered a nearly-full box of sugar cubes. The resident here must have liked sugar in his coffee. One lump or two was unclear. This would make a fine gift for the Sullivans when Gene arrived there. The footwear found there was too small for Gene's feet. Gene fashioned a loose-fitting poncho from an old wool army blanket to replace his lost coat. There was an old World War One vintage army pack. It worked well but lacked the supporting hip support straps found on modern backpack frames.

Gene made padded hip straps from old belts found on the tie rack in the bedroom.

It was almighty funny how fast sixteen inches of snow could melt in places. Bare patches of dirt appeared, turning to mud then ice when it froze. The paved areas seemed to soak up the heat from sunshine and the snow receded faster in those areas at the edge of the pavement. Gene was a capable tracker, having learned as a child in the high country hills. He soon discovered the hound was better. The four sets of tracks were clear except when they mingled with tracks of other people. The sun had melted them enough to make them obscured among the others. The hound, however, wasn't confused at all. He tracked until the four sets separated distinctly from the others. This hound would track them in the air if he had to. That saved Gene hours of circling to find where the tracks went. The tracks consisted of two medium-size tracks, one larger track, and a smaller track that must have been the woman Gene had seen. The track movements were not those of a child, even though they were small. One of the medium tracks wore tennis shoes and seemed to be heavier than the others. He probably was stocky or carrying a load. When Gene and the hound came to the first camp made by Gene's assailants, the tennis shoe track seemed to lighten up. The track didn't make as deep an impression as before. Where these four were going wasn't clear until Gene came upon another scene of robbery. There was blood but no bodies. There were signs of scuffling and imprints where a couple had fallen rolling in the snow and mud. These thugs wandered randomly, spying on people, overlooking camps, and seemingly striking their next victim by surprise. That would stop if Gene had anything to do with it.

These thugs meandered to and fro. Gene developed a feel for their habits and characteristics. Each time they stopped, they left more information. Gene could see where two bedded together, tennis shoes and the woman. The big man and the fourth man slept separated from the other two. Gene could see where the crossbow had been propped against a small tree. There was no evidence of any long guns or shotguns that might have been set in the snow where thugs like these may have rested them on their butts propped against a tree or rock.

Gene was getting closer to their location. He would pick his time. He would need to be careful they didn't stumble on him as they backtracked. Late in the evening, a shot echoed over the snow-strewn landscape. Guns all have a distinctive sound and Gene knew the sound of a heavy handgun when he heard one.

When Gene and the hound came upon the thugs' camp, he could see new evidence of these people's nature. Tennis shoes lay face down in the snow. A small dark bloodstain in the middle of his back at the spot where he had been shot faced skyward. There also was the stain of bright blood red snow under the man's chest that had oozed out. His tennis shoes faced sole-up, heels on top. Gene could see his own Sharp-wool winter socks peeking out above the tinny-runner tops.

"Darn," said Gene. "There were a lot of things I'd do these days, but taking my socks off a dead man isn't one of them, darn!"

Gene studied the camp setting. It appeared the woman had been standing behind Tennis Shoes when she'd shot him from behind. Tennis Shoes fell to his knees, then to his face, without even trying to catch himself with his hands. He must have been dead instantly. Gene could see the man had been sunburned badly from lack of protection. His lips were cracked and his ear skin was peeling and scabbed from the burning. He was gaunt from lack of food and his clothing fit loosely. He was middle-aged with some auburn-gray hair. Now he was dead.

It appeared from the tracks, the smaller of the remaining men with hiking boots on had picked up the crossbow, the woman had Gene's .357 and the big man now packed Gene's pack and supplies.

Tracking the three remaining thugs wasn't hard. Gene advanced carefully, knowing he and the hound were only hours behind. Gene wondered what he would really do when he caught the bunch, except his head still throbbed now and again and again. He gave thought to trying to steal his possessions back, but idea made his head hurt. Stealing his stuff back could be dangerous, considering the woman had his pistol and the man had his crossbow. In addition, the big guy was twice Gene's size.

The thugs held to the high ground, stopping to look over various groups of people. Evening was coming and Gene decided tonight would be the night. He scouted an escape route after the raid.

He located their campsite at the edge of a clump of trees; it would be easy to slip in on unseen. They had set up the fire close to the trees and had bedded down on the opposite side in the open. Looking toward the fire, their eyes wouldn't see into the dark past it. The crossbow had been propped against a sapling about five feet from Hiking Boots. The woman was off by herself some fifteen feet away. The big man was closer to Hiking Boots than the woman. Gene decided he would grab the woman first, extracting his pistol, thereby retaking possession of it. He would use it to cover the men and move them back while he gathered his pocket tool, pack, and crossbow. He would then lecture them on the virtues of not robbing people. He might even disable them to keep them off his trail.

As he slipped in from behind the woman sleeping on her right side, with his 9 mm drawn, Gene reached down with his free hand and covered the woman's mouth, at the same time pressing the barrel hard against her forehead, and said, "I want my .357 back, you thief."

She started to struggle and Gene emphasized the pressure of the 9 mm hard against her forehead.

He told her quietly and carefully, "Take it out with your left hand and lay it behind you."

She did as told, then Gene signaled to her to be quiet. He rolled her on her stomach and bound her hands to her feet and doubled behind her with parachute cord.

The big man now was sitting looking not at Gene, but into the dark. He was about to reach Hiking Boots to wake him when Gene heard a deep growl coming from the dark. Every time the big guy made a move, the growl resurfaced. Gene turned to face the two men directly with his .357 in his left hand and quietly suggested they stay where they were.

Hiking boots exclaimed, "B. . . S. . .," then made a lunge for the bow. To Gene's surprise, Hiking Boots never made it. The hound had him.

"Call him off," the man screamed. "Call him off!"

Gene said, "I don't tell him what to do; he's not my dog."

"Call him off. He's breaking my arm!" the man screamed.

"Dog," Gene said quietly between growls, never taking his eyes off the big man.

The hound released Hiking Boots but stood close and snarled at any slight movement he made.

Gene motioned to the big man to roll over on his stomach where he bound him the same as the woman. Gene did the same for Hiking Boots with no consideration for the dog wounds. Gene went to the crossbow, picked it up, and slung it over his shoulder by the sling. He then went to his pack and did a quick inventory. Much of his stuff was missing. There were also extra items, which he quickly discarded. Gene asked the big man where the pocket tool was located. He said nothing. Gene's adrenaline had become pumped and without warning, he kicked the big man in the ribs. He had heard the muted snapping sound before. The man grunted out an obscenity and groaned. Gene asked again, and this time the big man responded, "She has it."

Gene moved to her, stopped, and said, "You're next. Where's my pocket tool?"

"It's on my belt," she replied. "If you take my pants off, you can get it."

Gene thought about how far this person would go to get her way. He reached down to her belt buckle, unlatched it, and started to pull.

"Aren't you going to untie me first?" she questioned.

"No, I'm not going to untie you at all," said Gene. "I saw what you did to your buddy in the other camp. I should string you up with a noose."

The pocket tool fell off the belt as the belt unwound from her pant loops. Gene picked it up and dropped it into his pack. He located the crossbow bolts Hiking Boots had and collected them.

"One of you left a knot on my head with the help of the others," Gene said as he thumped the first soundly on the side of the noggin. Each received the same treatment in turn.

Putting all remaining cartridges in the pack, he picked it up and exited into the dark. The last quarter of moon reflected on the snow enough that Gene could see to make good headway back to his own camp. He remembered as a child hunting rabbits in the full moon. It was nearly as easy to see as hunting on a cloudy day. It would be a while before the thugs would be after him if they didn't freeze to death. Gene had tied each so they couldn't reach either of the others. The raid hadn't taken over twenty minutes from start to finish. The trip back took an hour, time enough to burn the excess adrenaline out of Gene's body. There would be six or seven hours of moonlit dark until daybreak. Gene bedded down and slept with a smile on his face and in his heart.

Gene packed and made quick inventory early. There were several items missing from the pack he wished were in there. The thugs apparently didn't have the same opinion. His poncho was there, but his spare wool socks were back on the trail worn by a dead man. His can of coal oil was gone and so too were his butane lighters and fire tinder. Fortunately, he was wearing his wool pants and the wool camo-shirt. His Polyfill winter coat had been stripped from him, but he'd found a blanket poncho replacement at the home of the dead man. Gene also collected enough canned food supplies, heavy as they were, to last two weeks if stretched. He had the sawed-off shotgun, which in his mind was as much of a burden as an asset. He replaced the old pack with his own, which he'd recovered from the big man.

Gene knew to make tracks without making tracks and covered his trail. He purposely did so by walking in leaves, careful not to turn them over. He stayed on rocks whenever possible and away from muddy spots so as not to leave easily discernible tracks. Walking on areas where small rocks were, Gene was careful not to upturn smaller stones. Gene knew the dog had no such mind set and hoped he would not leave a telltale trail which could be followed.

Gene's thoughts wandered back over earlier events. *Well, Lord,* he thought. *I messed up again. I know vengeance is yours. I just had a failing and took things into my own hands. I thank you for deliverance. I seem lately to be falling into more difficulties. I've always considered myself the master of my own destiny. I pray it isn't false pride. I'm starting to miss what I value most: Jessie, family, and my home.*

Journal entry:

"This trip has gotten rough. I was waylaid and robbed. A hound has adopted me and we've traveled together for a spell. When I went to recover my belongings, he came to my rescue without hesitation.

"I'm some disoriented, but it probably doesn't make any difference. I have a letter to carry to Shanksville for an acquaintance, if I can find Shanksville. I'm going to try to locate the folks I met on the trail on the way here. I could use some amenable company just now."

He had written on the remaining pages the thugs hadn/t torn out and used for fire starter or TP.

Two days of travel gave Gene confidence the thugs were not following. He was still watchful of his back trail and changed directions several times so not to be predictable.

As near as he could reckon, Gene thought Shanksville lay further to the west up the valleys, but he wasn't sure. He shied away from talking to people at all costs. He also shied away from public roads and highways where directional signage might be found. Gene hadn't had time to consider Shanksville with the events of the last few days.

After one change of direction, Gene came upon an open valley meadow. It had been a hay field or large pasture about ten acres in size. Wider at the lower end it funneled in to a canyon below. The pasture narrowed at the top from where the valley above flowed into the wide valley. The valley pasture was flanked on the northeast by peaks, which deteriorated into slide rock fields covered in snow. Near the west upper side sat a dwelling and out buildings. Gene watched and there seemed to be no inhabitants. This ranch stead brought flashes of the Smith property to Gene's mind. Gene wondered if there was a Zack, a Laurie, a Sonja, or a Sally waiting hidden with a shotgun, or some fearful protective owner hidden undetected. Gene watched a good period without seeing an indication of any occupant. Wild creatures scurried about the machine shed and barn. The barn door stood ajar and seemed unattended. Gene decided to approach the house from out in the open. He kept his crossbow slung over his shoulder and kept the sawed-off hidden under his blanket poncho.

As he approached he hollered, "Hello, in the house!" Again, he hollered, "Hello! Anybody home?"

There was no response. When he walked to the front door, it had been broken down and the interior was ransacked. There seemed to be no one present, nor had there been for some time. Gene took stock of the contents and saw little remaining he considered of value. The cupboards were empty of food, as was the pantry. Some eating utensils had been scattered about, but most cooking supplies one would see in any kitchen, simply were not to be seen. They had been packed off. Gene took stock of the barn and machine shed. Normal farm equipment and tools sat where they had been parked for storage after the last use. Hand tools like axes and saws, however, were missing. Around the side of the barn stood a fuel tank on a head high stand that seemed to be half-full of stale gasoline.

Gene continued up the valley to the narrow entry at the base of the canyon above the dwelling, having decided he wouldn't benefit from lingering at the homestead. The dog sniffed around and laid down watching as Gene snooped and poked about. He followed up the valley for a distance, then at some time disappeared. Gene figured he would show in camp the next morning as he usually did after he wondered away.

The good road which led into the homestead came from the lower end of the valley. It extended up the valley as an old wagon trail usable by Jeep or ATV. Gene followed this track.

Camp that night was simple as usual. The air had a chill that had the feel of snow to come. Gene located a spruce tree with blue-green-tipped bows thick and heavy that provided shelter from the windward side against falling snow flakes. Fallen tree needles beneath were thick and fluffy—fine and dry for a soft bed. Gene was careful to keep the fire small and out of the needles and duff. He scratched with a stick down to bare soil and lined the fire pit with three rocks. Over this, Gene roasted the contents of a can of Spam found at the dead man's home. The rest he wrapped in some plastic wrap he had obtained there. He would save the foil he'd gotten there for more important purposes.

Contemplating his location, Gene knew he needed to go south to reach the Sullivan camp. He wasn't sure about Shanksville. He would address that when he exited the valley where he could find his bearings.

Sleep was cool but good. Morning brought a blanket of white on everything. Gene checked his snowshoes and after a light bite to eat started up the trail to what he hoped would be a topping of the ridge above. The fresh snow was the heavy wet kind and stuck to his foot gear like adobe mud to a boot. That made progress slow and Gene felt he had covered only three miles the entire morning. The effort didn't bring him close to any summit but did bring him into the direct path of a cold biting wind. The dog hadn't appeared anywhere. Gene was surprised by the thought that he actually missed the hound's company.

Gene could see upland for a long distance. He was miles, maybe thirty, away from any summit and his exact location wasn't clear in his mind. What he was sure of was he needed to go west and south to get back home. Another thing he was sure of was he needed to find the location of the Sullivan camp. He had found a high mountain cave before but wasn't exactly sure how to get back to it. Gene would keep going for a couple hours and then try to locate adequate shelter out of the wind and blowing snow.

One full day of travel brought him to camp in the snow without comfortable shelter. He started the next morning on the same path. Soft-blowing snow tends to harden when piled in drifts. The snow now was of the dryer kind and drifted. Gene found the drifts easy to traverse and the near-bare places on the ground were easy to cross. The softer unblown snow was easy to sink into. The wetness had dissipated and that didn't allow the snow to stick to the snowshoes as much now. Travel was easier the next couple of hours and he was intent on making some distance. He failed to see the encampment ahead until a slight pause in the wind opened up a wispy window. He stopped instantly. He studied as much as he could see.

Gene was in the open under cover of blowing snow until it momentarily quit blowing. He was covered in snow but was not out of sight. His movement might be detected from any careful sentry. All Gene could do was try to get out of sight while the gusts of blowing snow covered his retreat. He turned and started away like a buck deer attempting to keep the nearest obstacle between any observer and himself.

About a hundred feet away from tree cover, Gene heard a shout from the camp, "Hey you—you out there in the snow! Stop!"

Gene kept moving, pretending not to hear until the air-splitting shot sounded over his head. Gene froze in place, then toppled into the nearest snowbank as if shot. He quickly shed the sawed-off and the crossbow, hiding both under the snow. That accomplished, he arose to see several men bucking the drifts running toward him with weapons. Gene struggled to his feet, raised his hands, and moved several steps away from the hiding place. Gene made note of the approximate location. The men rushed up near Gene and demanded he remain where he stood. Gene was prodded to advance toward the encampment. He moved reluctantly but didn't have as settled a feeling as he had when captured by Hoover's men.

Two men flanked Gene, one on either side, and there were two at his back. Gene was guided to a spot near a fire. The men stripped Gene's pack and took the .357. They found his 9 mm and the hide-away leg knife. Gene tried to protest and was sharply jabbed with a gun barrel in his right side for the effort. That doubled him and he wasn't sure he wasn't ruptured. He tried to straighten, but the jabbing pain was excruciating.

"Well, mountain man, what you doing out there?" demanded a voice out of the dark. "Did you think you could sneak in here and steal something or what?"

"No, I'm trying to go home," responded Gene. "I have my own supplies in my pack. I don't need to steal stuff. I even have a small amount of goods for trade," he added, thinking of how to explain the .12 gauge ammo.

"You better have. We don't have food for ya here," the man said. He commanded Gene to be bound to a tree and left for the night. The night was very long and cold.

Gene's side ached badly. If he hadn't had the padding of the woolen poncho and heavy shirt, he surely would have been punctured. His feet were cold and his hands numb from being tied. In addition to that, he needed to drink some water and had to pee badly.

Still dark and cold, Gene thought the morning couldn't come soon enough. The pain in his side had nagged him all night long. The sky had cleared sometime about four o'clock and the cold set in as the wind died. The temperature must have been below zero by daybreak. The guards warmed themselves by the fire. Gene couldn't understand how they saw him if they had been near the fire before his capture. But they had seen him anyway.

"Hey guy, I'm about to freeze to death here and I need to pee," Gene said.

"Later," said one of the guards.

"Come on, I need to go bad," Gene pleaded.

The guard turned and looked for a time, seemingly considering the circumstances. He finally came to Gene and released the rope. Considering the obvious, the guard released Gene's hands so he could complete his task. Accompanying the release came a stern warning not to try a stupid move.

Gene assured the guard he wouldn't and thanked him for the relief. Gene said, "I don't understand why I've been taken prisoner."

"We don't like strangers," said the guard. "The boss will want to know what you're doing and what you know about the area. You might consider that before questioning starts. You need to be helpful, and if not, consider yourself wasted!"

Gene considered for a bit and said, "I will help all I can. What do ya need to know?"

"We will get to that," said the guard.

Gene requested he be allowed to warm at the fire. The guard pointed to a place near the fire. Gene gratefully took it.

Gene sat and warmed, trying to make sense of this camp. There seemed to be no women or children. Probing, Gene said, "My wife and daughter are waiting for me to return home. I've been looking for my son in the suburbs. How about you guys—you got family?"

The guard didn't reply. He simply turned away and another flatly stated, "You need to clam up for now."

Gene did.

Morning didn't come too soon. A voice from the dark barked some orders to men in the other bivouac. He could be heard throughout the camp. This was no ordinary camp. It resembled a military compound. There seemed to be a military hierarchy. Gene watched and studied the events as they revealed themselves. There was a mess and a makeshift latrine. He wished he'd not stumbled into this.

The camp commander walked up to Gene with demand in his demeanor. "Old man, I want to know who you are, what you're doing here, and why I shouldn't shoot you here and now!"

"My name is Shaky," replied Gene, "I'm on my way home. I've been looking for my son in the city. I didn't find him, so now I'm headed home."

Gene did not respond to the comment about being shot. The commander demanded to know where Gene had been, what he had seen, and about any groups of people he'd observed and where. Gene answered, starting with seeing the people at the factory outlets. He told him about the group of four who had dry gulched him and their spying on camped groups without telling of the reckoning. The commander seemed interested in any resources Gene had seen, like food, fuel, and other supplies.

"I found a country homestead a ways from here, a few miles back," said Gene. "It seemed abandoned. There was a tank of fuel behind the barn."

"Where and how far from here?" the commander barked.

Gene offered to draw a map but requested in return he have his pack returned. The commander growled that Gene wasn't in a position to make deals; Gene would tell the location. After some explanation and some frustration on the commander's part, Gene offered to lead a contingent to the farmstead. The commander said he would consider returning Gene's pack when the goods were delivered back to this camp. Gene explained the trip would take several days by foot and survival gear would be required if the contingent were to complete the trip. Gene would rely on his own gear but would require some food supplements to get there and back. The question came as how he expected to survive if he hadn't found them. Gene indicated he would survive as he always had if he had his guns and knife.

The commander turned and walked away. After a time, one of the guards brought Gene's pack and handed it to him. It was in disarray due to the search. Gene was weary of people going through his stuff but said nothing. Gene's snowshoes were returned and two five-gallon jerry cans were placed before him.

"Don't worry, mountain man," said one of the guards, "we all will have them. These two are your share."

248

Chapter 23

Escape

Gene's pack had been liberated of ammo. It was lighter now. His canned rations had been removed, but rations for two days had been added back. Now the detail was on its way to the abandoned farmstead. As Gene lead the way, he carefully took a route away from the spot where the crossbow and shotgun lay concealed under the snow. After a start, with rest breaking the pattern of travel, the end of daylight was near. Gene settled down under a deformed squat ponderosa pine for shelter. The five others located a level place free of deep snow where the wind had blown the snow to another location. Gene knew the wind would blow in that location all night long. His spot was void of snow due to its sheltered nature from a tree. *Well, they're big kids*, he thought.

The next morning came. Gene could see the five suffered from the cold, sunburn, and exhaustion caused by bucking drifted snow. Gene built a fire and heated water for consumption and hygiene. Several accepted the hot water to drink but none attempted to wash.

The snow that had softened during the previous day had crusted from freezing during the night. They didn't have the advantage of snowshoes like Gene possessed and broke through the crust where snow had piled with nearly every step. Gene's snowshoes disbursed Gene's weight, keeping him from breaking through. The effort they expended was exhausting beyond belief. Just before noon, the leader called for a rest. Gene knew they were all in. Gene told the leader the farmstead was just a half day ahead. This information seemed to pep up the exhausted men.

Gene came across tracks he believed to be the dog's. Where the dog had been was beyond Gene's imagination. He was considering when a proper time to escape would be. These men were tired beyond normal physical limits. Gene was tired too, but the snowshoes conserved energy in these elements. Gene decided he would wait until the men had seen the farmstead, hopefully near the end of day. Gene spent effort encouraging them each, telling them the farmstead was close.

At last light, the farmhouse loomed in the dusk. Gene encouraged the men, telling them there was a fireplace in the dwelling and inside would be warmer. He knew that to be true and wanted to enjoy the comforts with them. He also knew, however, this was his best and last chance to escape. Tired but believing they were too exhausted to pursue him very far, he feigned exhaustion and dropped to his knees in the snow. The others staggered past him one by one. Gene pretended to follow but lagged, widening the distance slowly.

When the first reached the dwelling, stumbling around the front and through the door, he yelled in a hoarse voice they had made it. The others seemed to be encouraged and one by one disappeared around the front. Gene, pretending to be winded, which in fact wasn't hard to do, slumped over. When the last of the five turned to look, Gene put on a display of effort to proceed. When the last of five turned the corner out of sight, Gene bolted away out of their sight as fast as he possibly could. He drove himself toward the trees to the other side of the drainage bottom opposite the trail. He reached cover and turned in a direction he thought the detail would least expect. He circled the farmstead from another side behind the barn. He set his pack down, extracted the sugar cubes, and approached the fuel tank. Shedding his snowshoes, Gene climbed to the top filling cap, quietly unscrewed it, and dropped a dozen sugar cubes into the tank. Gene screwed the cap back on and swept the snow with a branch where his tracks had been. Now a bit of wind would do to help cover his tracks further. Darkness had nearly enveloped the scene. Gene was nearly to the edge of the timber where his snowshoes had been deposited when a man rounded the corner and looked up at the tank.

"I found it!" he called out.

The others came around the corner. One started tapping on the tank, determining the amount of its contents.

"Good, half full!" he exclaimed. "The boss will be pleased."

Gene thought, *Not when those cylinders freeze up. That should keep them off my trail for a while.*

Gene considered what his next move should be. He could divert his direction and go around the encampment. He would be without any arms. He could try to get back to his crossbow ahead of the detail. He could follow the detail at a distance and pick up any discarded arms they might leave behind when they became totally exhausted as he expected. . He didn't remember seeing any abandoned weapons at the farm.

As of now Gene intended to make tracks down the valley, away from the anticipated path of the five. Gene would make a cold camp this night. If the wind blew the right direction, he might build a small fire at daylight. He moved quietly after the men left the tank to find shelter for the night. After half an hour, Gene found a large tree, which had fallen over a worm fence. Underneath there was a sheltered bough large enough to sleep in comfortably. The snow had drifted over the back side, enclosing the exit with a layer about six inches thick. Gene took stock of the surroundings, then climbed in. This was as good as any snow cave. He slept like a baby, warm and comfortable and out of the wind that came in gusts.

When early light finally erupted, all was quiet. Gene's tracks seemed to be obliterated by the wind as far as he could determine. In the timber where the snow was soft, the wind would cover them except to an experienced tracker. In the open, the drifting wouldn't cover his tracks but very little. He thought back on the previous night's activities. He should keep moving down and away from their anticipated trek back for a day. His clothing would stick out in this snowy world badly. Unless there was a good melt, he had no hope of being camouflaged. The thought struck him that if the farm had some white bed sheets, he could use them.

Listening for a long time, Gene could hear the clanking of the gas nozzle on empty jerry cans. So they were filling the cans to be carried back. He counted eight he was sure of. He knew there were a dozen cans, including the ones he had carried. He was sure one man couldn't carry more than ten gallons and that would be with great discomfort. A strong man might carry twenty gallons, but not through this snow, even if they followed the broken trail and tracks they had left coming in.

A stray thought caught him. Was one man detailed to track him down? That would account for only eight cans being filled. Gene eased out of his lair and started down country over snow he was sure a normal man on foot would break through. The effort would tire him greatly, giving Gene the advantage. But Gene needed to get with the program now!

Gene found a snow-covered slide rock field. The crust had frozen on top, but if a man broke through, death from a broken leg or worse could very well be his fate. Gene carefully started across the field with baited breath, and eased to the far side before pausing to rest and take a long breath. Gathering his wind, he proceeded through the trees straight away as far as he felt his trail could be seen from the rockslide. Deep into the trees, he turned toward a dip in the terrine, where he hoped to be out of sight from any pursuer.

Advancing, paying careful attention ahead as well as behind, he covered another half mile in a semicircle. When the opportunity allowed, Gene started circling across the valley from where he could watch parts of his back trail. The breeze blew erratically one way, then the next. It would be hard to kindle a fire and if started, the smoke might give away his location.

So much for a warm breakfast, Gene thought. He didn't have food for breakfast anyway.

Gene picked an obscure spot where the sun poured through the openings. He settled where the sun warmed his poncho. The dark of the wool blanket soaked the sunrays like water into cloth towel.

Warmth: what a pleasant blessing of nature from God, Gene thought.

Having picked his next route that would be concealed from a possible tracker, Gene watched to see if there was a tracker and suddenly there was. Gene saw him just as he edged the slide rock. Gene's trail hadn't been hard to locate, nor had it been hard for any man inexperienced or otherwise to follow. Now one was following it. Gene decided to hastily take to the predetermined trail.

The tracker had crossed halfway across the slide rock field and by now about a quarter mile from Gene's location. Gene moved toward the new track when he felt the rip at his poncho near his right hip. He reached down to pull it free of the brush, but there wasn't any brush. Just then he heard the report of the rifle; a moment later the crack of the deep throated roar of the avalanche flowing down the rockslide above the tracker. The man had started to run but fell through the crusted snow twice before the powdered flow engulfed him. Gene saw nothing more of him after that.

The sight was discomforting. Gene knew he had played a part in the man's probable death. If the man had been closer, surely Gene would be dead. If Gene had been fifty pounds heavier, he would now be wounded. He now suspected there were orders for his execution if separated from the group. He needed to be careful. Again, Gene reviewed in his head the options available. Those hadn't changed.

Gene moved toward the homestead from another approach. If the men had started to the encampment, they would need two days with the weight they carried. A half-track could be back in three or four hours. Gene needed to move quickly. He pushed toward the west side of the hay field, being careful not to leave tracks that could be seen from the farmstead. Let them believe he had been swept up by the avalanche. Certainly, his tracks would lead into the avalanche flow. Within about a hundred yards of the dwelling, there seemed to be no activity. As he watched, the dog came out of the door. If the men had been nearby, the dog wouldn't have been.

The dog started sampling the air with his nose. Gene realized he was upwind from the dwelling and the dog must have been sensing his smell.

Gene untied his snowshoes, worked his way to the house, and carefully stepped into the open door. There wasn't much orderly about the recent guests. They left trash strewn about. In the kitchen, Gene found a good quality butcher knife, a sheath for it, a sharp kitchen knife of good steel, and a small whetstone. In the bedroom, Gene found a folded white sheet, double bed size. Gene quickly poked around and found a white pillowcase with embroidered daisies around the open end. The daisies were pleasant to the eye, but not of much practical use at present. He found sewing supplies including safety pins. Gene rigged the sheet over his wool poncho, pinned it with a hand full of safety pins he found in the house, then proceeded to cut eyeholes in the pillow case. Now he felt somewhat camouflaged in the white. Gene made haste to exit back to his snowshoes. The dog followed.

"Well, dog, I sure don't know if you're welcome or not right now," Gene muttered. With that said, he encouraged the dog to leave. He left.

As Gene proceeded to follow the remaining four men, he could see they struggled with their burdens. He knew he would need to be careful not to come upon them by accident. They would be three or four hours ahead and traveling not half as fast as he could when taking a stroll. The jerry cans he had dropped lay where he'd dropped them.

Following carefully so as not to be detected, Gene moved parallel to the trail where the men now traveled. Gene didn't want to be spotted. He knew the men would be watching for the fifth missing man to join them. As they progressed, Gene listened carefully for the sounds the group made while struggling with their burden through the crusted snow.

A little after noon, he heard the distinct sound of jerry cans bumping each other. Gene edged up to the top of a rise over which he could see the detail. They were strung out over a distance along the trail. All appeared to be exhausted at midday. The question now was would they hold up soon or push on? Gene discretely continued to watch from the timbered ridge and waited. One man seemed to have already discarded his weapon. The others still retained theirs.

The detail's progress was slow at best. If the encampment perceived a delay in their returns, they might send out additional personnel. Scanning the back trail, Gene looked for signs where the man may have deposited his weapon. Backing away and down over the rise, Gene studied the back trail foot by foot. He could see the dog on the trail sniffing as he poked about. Watching, Gene saw the dog follow a short side trail. Gene studied the spur from a distance, looking for a yellowing stain of urination. He could see it when the dog sniffed at the end of the short track. Watching to see if the dog indicated the presence of other deposits, he saw none. Retracing backward along the track, Gene looked for a sign of a fall. After a hundred yards, he saw what he was looking for. A fallen tree and a trail in the snow led to and from it.

Eureka! thought Gene as he studied the possible cache. A man wouldn't have picked that spot to elevate. He was going there to hide something and Gene had an idea what that that something was. Whichever man it was had approached the downfall in two places. Gene knew he would need to conceal his own path and investigation. He picked a path that would cover over when the wind blew. The first search yielded a Remington model 700 30-06. The clip was not the in the rifle, nor were any bullets. Next Gene looked at the second entry and after feeling about under the log came up with the clip loaded. Further search yielded seven additional rounds wrapped in a handkerchief.

Slipping out of the cache, Gene swept the snow in an effort to cover his backdoor entry. With luck and some wind, his tracks would cover over. Sweeping the snow with an evergreen bough for a hundred feet, Gene then traveled to the top of the rise where he had observed the detail from before. They had advanced out of sight of that vantage point. Gene picked another route, which would take him around, flanking them on the south. He again listened for telltale sounds. Soon they came. The men had advanced another half mile strictly sticking to the trail they had broken when going to the farmstead.

The detail had bunched, all setting on their cans. Two chewed on rations, while two were asleep on their feet, or in this case, their butts. Their progress had moved them barely five or six miles from the farm. They had another seven or eight miles to go.

Gene no longer concerned himself with following the group. He now considered how he would retrieve his crossbow and sawed-off. The frisking had removed the 12 gauge cartridges. The bolts for the crossbow were in the attached quiver. Gene considered the loss and determined he would have to forget the equipment and move on. There was a great chance of exposure at the cache. He turned away, struck out away from the detail's location, and set a course south away from the encampment.

Gene had put miles between the encampment and himself. He was some twenty miles and at least one full day south of their last known location. He'd not seen sign of followers and so felt secure in his escape. The area he now was in looked similar to the area where he'd killed the elk. The snow made it look different, but it was familiar in many ways. As he entered the next valley, he studied the area closely. Turning to the west and up valley, Gene walked two days. The snow started to recede. Indian summers weren't uncommon this time of year. The days warmed and the nights were freezing cool. Gene caught two snowshoe hares and a grouse. He cooked these and stretched them into a week's worth of meals. He had one of the rations issued by the para-militia but saved it for emergency.

Gene camped the third night in the valley near a stream. The water was good and there were fish, although not as many as Gene might have expected. He ate two and that overly filled him. He smoked six more and packed them away for later. The sun seemed to come up later each day. The days were shorter and left less time to travel. On the other hand, the nights were longer, which left more time to keep from freezing. To make camp this time of year, one had to pick early and securely. Gene had done just that every night since his escape.

He left his campsite before daylight. The moon was still in the sky and gave ample light in the snow-covered landscape to move slowly along the trail. At midday, Gene broke into a clearing that seemed familiar to him. He crossed it and on the other side he stumbled across the cache of cured elk meat hanging in the tree. Gene realized he must have walked within hundreds of feet of the Sullivan camp. He retrieved the remaining meat. It had been reduced to less than twenty-five percent of the last tallied amount. He then struck off for the Sullivan camp. Upon reaching the edge of the bench where the shelter was, Gene called out to the Sullivans in the camp. A head peered out of the door and said something to the inside. Sullivan recognized Shaky at once.

"Shaky, it's so good to see you. Come in, come in," said Sullivan.

They shook hands and Shaky could physically feel in Sullivan's hand the loss of weight. The children were thin as well. After inquires as to their welfare, Shaky perceived all had not gone well since his last visit. A bear had pillaged their considerable food stores. It had returned twice, but Sullivan had driven it off.

Sullivan had been able to replenish some of the fish, but there weren't as many in the stream now. Finding and catching small game was not often successful. They in fact were slowly starving. Winter was long ways from being over. The shelter was adequate, but the fuel supply grew low due to the lack of physical ability to cut and gather. Gene determined if these folks were to survive the winter, they would need help.

The Sullivans had little idea of the surrounding conditions. They had made two trips to the cache, leaving the last for Gene if he returned. Gene made up some elk jerky and fish soup for the camp. They had allowed themselves to dehydrate. Gene said so as he checked the 30-06 and readied for a hunt.

The first day Gene scouted the valley and saw a few deer tracks but nothing that would indicate a threat from man. He made a second trip the next day, cutting a single deer track. He tracked slowly and spotted the animal browsing at the edge of some willows. The deer's head came up as it looked across the creek and then it slowly turned before bounding away. What had the deer seen?

The deer had seen a black bear, fat and ready for hibernation. *It should be in hibernation by now*, Gene thought. It would be a great piece of meat and a source of energy for the camp. The bear ambled toward Gene at an angle. He stopped at the stream edge and dug for a snail or toad or something. Gene took aim with the 06 and fired. The bear turned, ran twenty feet up the stream bank, and stood looking at Gene. Gene fired a second shot directly at the bear's chest. The bear sat down where he stood, then fell to the side with a thud. Gene waited where he could see the bear for fifteen minutes. The animal didn't move. Gene cautiously approached the animal, well aware a wounded bear could kill a man instantly. Loaded and ready to shoot again if need be, Gene approached the fallen animal. He was dead. Gene proceeded to gut and dress the smelly creature. Gene remembered his dad having told him if Gene ever shot a bear, he could dress it by himself. Dad wouldn't touch such a stinky creature. Well, as it was now, Dad wasn't helping with this one.

Dressing such a compact heavy animal takes time. When he completed the gutting, Gene spread the chest cavity and propped it open with a stick to allow air to circulate, cooling the carcass. Gene skinned the haunches first then worked to the ribs, back and shoulders. At the neck just below the ears, Gene cut the hide to free it from the head. Gene was exhausted now. Dragging the carcass over a fallen log evelivating it off the ground allowed air to circulate around the carcass. Doing this facilitated cooling. The meat would cool in the night air very well. If left laying in the snow or the insulating skin, the meat would sour from the trapped body heat. He knew there would be some loss to birds and other scavengers overnight, but nothing could prevent that. Gene cut off the largest flank muscles and fat. He hefted them in his pack and started for the Sullivans'. There would be a feast tonight. Slicing, smoking and jerking the cuts of meat would be left to the Sullivans'. Gene would retrieve most the rest of the carcass and hide tomorrow as time and strength allowed. The third day would be easier.

The second day was filled with packing labor. Ivan felt strong enough to help carry Gene's rifle, freeing Gene's hands for balance. Ivan was weak but game. He didn't complain but became every bit as exhausted as Gene before they got back. The fourth and fifth trips would be on the third day. The hide was as heavy as any one of the loads of meat. It would make a fine bed this winter for someone.

With all usable parts retrieved, Gene set about rendering the ample fat into lard. Bear grease while not quite as tasty as pork lard, but it served the same purpose in cooking. Bear grease when rubbed into boots or heavy material served every bit as good for waterproofing as commercial mink oil. As a young child, Gene's family used bear grease exclusively as their winter waterproofing for boots and chaps. The horses didn't approve much, but eventually they accepted the odor.

Using a hide bag made from the remaining elk skin, Gene sealed the stitching holes with cold grease. Then as he rendered the bear fat in the small kettle, he would poor the resulting hot oil into the bag. When filled, he constructed a second bag and repeated the activity.

The third time the process was repeated and so on. The pungent odor of the lard was almost repulsive and would become more so as it aged and became rancid. This would be especially true when the weather started warming. In the meantime, this substance could be used as bait for fur-bearing animals. Their hides could be used to supplement coats and replace the threadbare clothing.

Journal entry:

"I caught a bear last week. It was a heaven-sent supply. My friends here were in peril from lack of provisions. I would not be surprised if brother bear was the one who raided their supplies. We've been able to rebuild their strength and many supplies. The honey from the bee tree was most exhilarating. We've lost track of the date. It seems by the phase of and location of the moon it should be about October. That doesn't change anything; survival is paramount."

Sullivan and the children seemed to be gaining strength. The bear fat gave them great energy and nourished them. They set out to gather additional wood for the winter fuel. Work went well, but the more they gathered, the more evidence they left of their presence. Gene made further forays into the surrounding areas. He became familiar with the trails, the routes taken by animals and the locations to avoid when deep snow came. He tried to snare a mountain sheep and failed. He feared shooting the 06 because he knew the sound would carry for many miles, exposing their location. He decided to construct a bow and make arrows fletched with grouse feathers. Ivan accompanied him from time to time. He was a quick study. He also constructed a bow and made arrows. They each shot grouse and Ivan killed a snowshoe rabbit. These bows weren't nearly strong enough to bring down large animals.

Weeks passed while the Indian summer lingered. Then it came. The storm was bad. Heavy deep snow, raging wind, and following the storm came cold from the bowels of the Arctic. The shelter entry drifted nearly full and had to be dug out. The fuel reserves were buried in drifts and the familiar trails disappeared. Gene had anticipated winter and they'd constructed snowshoes earlier for everybody. They discussed the danger areas where avalanches would likely come and the conditions that could start one. The need for fresh food hadn't changed. There were many rose hips available. Gene located another wild beehive. Even though he could raid it in very cold weather with smoke as an anesthesia, he still wanted his head and hands protected. There were a lot of honeycombs full of sweet, sweet heaven. They was placed in containers, which they had woven from water grasses covered with pitch. There was more honey than containers. Nattily ate herself sick.

The bees wax while still very eatable was saved, melted down, and let to cool into pan-size ingots. It would have many uses throughout the coming months. The days had grown noticeably short. When possible, they would recover more firewood and fresh meat or berries. They passed what few spare hours they had playing games. Most were made up because no one could remember any that didn't involve a computer or deck of cards.

The weeks turned into months. Gene reckoned it must be near the start of December. Nobody was sure. They had started marking days just after the bear was shot. Now there were seventy three in all. What date the tally represented no one knew. They decided to use the full moon as the start for their month. That seemed to work well and gave a meaningful relationship to the passing time. Gene had been there two and one half-moons and wondered if he would ever see Jessie and the kids again. He wondered if they had the same thoughts about him. He wondered how Bonnie was doing and if she had calmed. Oh, how he longed to be home.

He caught himself now thinking of Sullivan, Ivan, and Nattily as family. He felt a little twinge of guilt, as if he had betrayed his real family. Well now, wasn't that silly. His love for his family wasn't threatened in any way by events here. This situation only further assured his survival and sanity as well as Sullivans' throughout the winter. That he knew to be a fact. He realized as long as he had been alone, he needed to care for someone, if even temporarily.

Chapter 24

Night Stalking

The plan for the raid had been made. Laurie and Sammy would slip into the remuda, liberating as many of the cayuses as possible.

Sammy teared up a little as she related, "Papi always called the horses 'cayuses.' He liked the sound of the word and the way it rolled off his tongue as he said it."

They would leave camp with a slow-burning fire to indicate their presence, then make the fifteen-mile loop to cross over and around to the west rim of McDougal Canyon. Following an old drover's trail, they would follow the decline, descending to the encampment below. While Laurie and Sammy made the raid, Gretchen and Molly would set an ambush at an advantageous site, where they could capture and arrest any pursuers that were sure to follow.

The trek was difficult as the loop around the canyon head led into deep snow. The progress through the snow was slow and tiring until they broke into the lower elevations of these badlands. Gretchen located an ideal ambush site that funneled any traveler through a gauntlet. Tracks were deliberately made by the Marshals down along this path with unmistakable travel signs in place leading back up country. The plan was to lead any who followed behind the raid back up through same trail. Several vantage points from which they could ambush the trail were established. Each became familiar with the site, knowing what their position would be when the time came.

Leaving Molly and Gretchen, Laurie and Sam moved down most of the remaining four miles to within striking distance of the horses. They would wait until after midnight before they raided, hoping all would be sleeping, including the guards if any had been posted.

A stranger entering a camp at night would most likely disturb the horses. By Laurie's reckoning, there had been enough cats and coyotes around that slight disturbances among the animals wouldn't be perceived as unusual. Sam agreed and was confident she could get in without detection. Having observed her talents and the new skills Molly had taught her, Laurie knew she could pull it off.

These early winter days were short and the wait until post-midnight seemed almost intolerable for Laurie. Both had adrenaline building, which at one point made Laurie quiver, jittery and shaky. Sam, on the other hand, seemed as cool as a cucumber, but like a coiled spring ready to release on a moment's notice. Her mama before her had passed on and related stories of the olden days when her maternal great grandfather raided horses from the settlers in New Mexico and Arizona Territories. Sam in her mind was reverting to days of old and the glory of the legends. She intended on doing her part if not for the glory, for the sake of Papi, Juan, and Jose. She saw herself as inhabiting the heritage passed down from her ancestors.

The moon and stars told Laurie the time had come. They worked their way down the trail near the camp. They would have to skirt the tents to approach the animals. There seemed to be no guards posted. What would this camp have to fear? They were the hunters. Laurie held her breath as Sammy casually moved to the makeshift corral. One horse snorted a bit, then with Sammy's assurance calmed. She truly had a way with these animals. Finding a short rope, she secured one halter, then a second, and silently letting the gate pole to the ground, mounted the third horse. Casually working her way almost to Laurie, she led two and the other five followed.

Someone in the camp realized the horses were out of the corral, swore, and shouted for others to lend a hand. They didn't have a clue what had happened. At that moment Laurie grabbed a hand full of mane hair and swung up bareback on the nearest horse as he came by. He shied to the side, then settled, following the others. The raiders were away. Riding two and leading two, Sammy led the way up the stock trail at breakneck speed, which in the semi-dark was dangerous at best. Laurie's mount, on the other hand, was night blind and stumbled more than once. Two of the other horses followed the leaders.

Shouts from the camp erupted and a great commotion started. One man followed up the trail some distance, then gave up the effort. When daylight came, the entire camp would be on their trail. Sam had counted eight. She rode one horse and led two. Laurie sat one and the straggling horses had trailed off as they rode up the trail. They made the ambush site by early morning. Molly and Gretchen waited in their assigned spots without even a hint of their presence.

"It went off like we planned! I don't understand what was so bad about those old Indians stealing horses," exclaimed Sammy.

"Well, girl, we're not done yet," said Molly. "They'll be along, and we'll find out how easy it was then."

They tied their horses beyond and above the ambush site. All the while Laurie grumbled about how she could have picked such a night blind, stumbling, piece of crow bait. She would have shot the beast right then and there, but she'd never eaten horse and they needed him in the worst way at this time.

Just before noon by the sun's time, the fall of horse hooves could be heard trailing hard upon Sammy and Laurie's tracks. Four mounted men were coming. The lead held his rifle across the pommel of his saddle. He tracked with his head and eyes to the ground. The others followed in single file, carrying head gear to lead the lost horses back to camp. Molly and Gretchen stepped out in sight enough to have clear vantage of the riders.

"Hold it where you are," declared Molly, clearly and flatly. "We are US Marshals and you are under arrest."

"The hell ya say!" The leader raised his rifle for a shot. A big man by stature, he was one of those with the attitude of a brute and a bully. His finger never so much as tightened on the trigger when Molly's shot jerked him sideways, tilting him out of the saddle. The others, following the man's lead, started pulling pistols and long guns to join in the battle. Gretchen and Laurie's shots stopped the next in line as abruptly as the first. Sammy, on the other hand, missed her shot and the horseman put one round into the tree just behind Gretchen's head. Molly prevented a second shot from being launched. He fell over the rump end of his horse to the ground, causing the horse to spook up the trail, taking the other two with it. Sammy shot the fourth man and as he tried to turn his mount, Laurie jumped from a high bank, grabbing his collar as she went by. They tumbled to the side of the trail. The man didn't get up. Sammy's shot had wounded him gravely. As Molly and Gretchen watched the back trail, Laurie and Sammy caught up the spooked horses.

Gathering the dead riders to a conspicuous place in the trail, the Marshals left their bodies where followers would find them. That would serve to take the heart out of others who would come. First aid was rendered to the wounded man. The man was in great pain and there was nothing to be done for him. Leaving water and a small amount of food, they made him as comfortable as possible. Men on foot tracking the horses were sure to come upon him where he rested within the hour.

Gathering gear and horses, the four Marshals were out of there. They headed for the high country, where the snow depth was enough a normal man wouldn't be able to follow on foot for very long without snowshoes. After two days, there seemed to be no evidence of a tail. In places where they could see their back trail, no one followed.

Working their way down in elevation some two thousand feet, traveling became easier. The horses no longer had to buck and lunge through the deep snow. They headed for the Indian site, where Laurie had last seen Bonnie and Chuck. Several times they had ridden upon a small herds of elk. Catching one group in a shallow ravine and just after a fluffy snowfall, Laurie dropped a yearling with a single shot to the neck. The snow around her filtered off the spruce bows in bright shiny cascades of twinkling crystals in the sunlight. A quarter mile away, Sammy and Gretchen heard the shot. It was so muffled by the snow and timber, it was a mere faint sound shadow of the bright report given off by the rifle shot from where Laurie stood. The next two days were spent feasting, jerking meat, and repairing clothing, blankets, and gear.

Making crude pack gear for the horses of the elk hide, gut string, and tendons, Laurie loaded the supplies on one of the spare horses. They had ridden some twenty or thirty miles in order to position themselves above the Indian site where Bonnie and Chuck should be located if they had not moved. When within ten miles, Laurie and Gretchen went afoot, staying spread out to find the site and using their signals for commutation. Molly and Sammy found a secluded camp site with passable forage for the horses.

Easing their way down the ridge, there seemed to be no sign of life at the cliff dwelling. Gretchen, keeping watch from a high point, encouraged Laurie to recon the area. Laurie, being more familiar with the location, would understand how to approach. When she arrived, Bonnie and Chuck were not there. There it was: two stacked rocks with the stick. The direction indicator pointed at a thirty-degree angle toward Signalman's Point, a ridge that lead to the high country just east of where Molly and Sammy now were camped. Signaling Gretchen to parallel her, Laurie became the tracker. Bonnie and Chuck left a difficult trail to follow, but Laurie was up to the task.

Near sundown, they made cold camp, and cold it was. Laurie had seen no sign of anyone besides Bonnie and Chuck. All she could guess was Bonnie and Chuck now looked for more suitable digs and maybe supplies. The second day Laurie found another marker. This one pointed off to the west, closer to where Molly and Sammy were waiting. The third afternoon, Gretchen signaled she had spotted something ahead about a quarter mile off. It was a line cabin, one of those line camps used as housing by range riders when checking fences and summer grazing. Warmth seemed to be emitted from the cabin and it appeared welcoming and cozy.

As she approached with some stealth, a branch popped up from the ground, rattling a tin can with a rock inside. The world went quiet. When one is in the forest or wilderness, there are natural sounds. If one spends significant amounts of time in those conditions, one learns the quiet has a whole concert of sound all in its own. The tin can broke every sound barrier known to Laurie in those conditions. It must have done the same for somebody else. The door opened and a quick shadow darted to some cover beyond. A second person went the other direction from the opening. Laurie carefully stood and cautiously walked into sight where she could be plainly seen. She heard the click of a rifle hammer being relieved to a resting position.

"You're not too good at sneaking up on things, are you?" questioned Chuck as he rose from his position.

"Well, that jury-rigged alarm sure enough caught me by surprise," she replied.

Chuck held his arms open wide to greet her as Bonnie emerged from her spot. It wasn't at all from the location where Laurie thought Bonnie had exited to. Bonnie moved undetected to a better spot more protected and better to guard Chuck's position from. Gretchen hadn't said a word, she just appeared from behind Chuck and Bonnie and silently stood. Chuck and Bonnie were so relieved to see Laurie, they started firing questions machine-gun style.

"Did you find the others?" they asked.

"Yes," Laurie answered.

"How did you find us?" quizzed Bonnie.

"You left a trail plain enough a blind man could follow," she lied.

"Are the others okay and where are they?" they asked.

At that moment, Gretchen decided to chime in. "Try asking us."Both Chuck and Bonnie jerked around, startled to hear the voice from behind.

"Kill us with a heart attack, why don't you?" Bonnie exclaimed.

Gretchen was some amused by the surprise although she stymied her euphoria at having gotten another one over on her old competitive advisory. She even felt a little bad for the outcome, although not too much. Sometimes this game of cat and mouse was even fun.

"This is the best Christmas present anyone could receive," exclaimed Bonnie, "tomorrow is Christmas according to the calendar on the wall. It's right for the phase of the moon, so it must be Christmas."

They settled in without a great celebration but with salutations for every other.

Chapter 25

Christmas

Gene set a snare made of barbed wire strung between two trees. He had seen many deer with their hind legs entangled in fence top wires after not jumping high enough to clear the top wire with their back feet. Using that idea, Gene made a fence across a well-traveled deer trail. Using brush to funnel the deer toward the snare, he'd force the deer to jump the barrier where the wire had been strung tight. Gene caught a buck. The event seemed to be pure luck, but it provided food for another month. Daily, the party fished through holes in the ice up and down the stream and in the beaver ponds. Some days yielded food for all and some nothing. They hadn't starved up to this point in time. In Gene's mind, the Lord had provided.

Gene sat in the shelter across from the fire weaving a larger utility basket. He looked up occasionally and in front of him was the day's tally.

"Do you all know what three days from now is?" he asked.

"Who knows?" replied Nattily, answering his question with her own.

"In three days, it will be Christmas Eve," he said convincingly.

"No. . ." said Ivan. "I haven't even thought about holidays. We have been out of it so long. . . Well, I guess we just dismissed having holiday celebrations all together."

"Well," added Sullivan, "Christmas in my way of thinking is the top of the new year. I have always looked forward to the New

267

Year starting from Christmas. I think it's a fine time to celebrate Christmas. It seems the days are becoming just a bit longer and when that happens, Christmas is close at hand."

The following three days were spent in secrecy. Each hid their activities and their plans. Gene kept prodding Nattily about what she was keeping so private. She wouldn't tell. Ivan, on the other hand, sent glances warning Gene not to ask. Sullivan knowingly smirked every time Gene challenged either. Sullivan himself wasn't any more cooperative than the other two when Gene tried to strike up a conversation with him. The mood being light, it was almost giddy during those three days.

The designated day arrived. Sullivan had cut a small tree, setting it up just inside the entry. The decorations were comprised of long grass stems draped over the bows for ice cycles. Someone had found small pine cones and used them in place of decorative glass balls and hung them using grass as string. On top of the tree was a small origami dove folded out of a piece of a torn space blanket. Gene couldn't remember a Christmas tree that meant so much made of such simple items.

He, like everyone, was like a kid waiting for Santa to come in the night. No one slept that night. Everybody awoke early except Ivan. He slept longer than normal because he hadn't slept the night before. Nattily was about to have a conniption waiting on Ivan to wake. She finally lost it, shook him, and demanded he wake up. He shook the cobwebs from his head and slowly became conscious.

Gene opened with, "You all know how I feel about my faith. It's not just a religion with me. Part of what my faith is about is the Christmas story. Do you know the story?'

"Jesus was born," said Nattily.

"Yes," said Gene. "Do you know why?

"No," she replied.

"The Bible says, 'God so loved the world he gave his one and only Son that any who would believe in him would not perish, but have everlasting life,'" quoted Gene.

He went on, "God sent His Son Jesus to earth in the form of a human. This was so man could relate to him. The story goes like this. A couple thousand plus years ago an angel named Gabriel appeared to a young maiden girl named Mary. She was frightened and the angel told her not to fear. He carried a message to her from God Almighty. Mary had been chosen above all others to bear the Son of God, the Christ. His name was to be Jesus."

Gene continued, "Mary said, 'But, sir, I have not known a man, how am I to have a child?' Gabriel said, 'You will rest and the spirit of the Lord will come upon you.' When the angel left, then the spirit of the Lord came upon Mary who became with child.

"Mary had been betrothed to Joseph before the angel came. Joseph did not want to make a spectacle of Mary's condition now that she was discovered with child. He had it in his mind to quietly put Mary aside. That is to say in our language, disassociate from her."

Gene continued, "Gabriel the angel appeared to Joseph in his sleep and spoke to him saying, 'Joseph, Mary is innocent of wrong-doing. What is conceived within Mary is from the Holy Spirit. She will have a boy child who is the Christ. You will call him Jesus.'

"In that day and time decrees mandated all citizens return to the country of their birth to be counted and to pay taxes. Joseph and Mary made the long trip to Bethlehem, where Joseph was from. They arrived in the evening, but there wasn't a place for them to stay the night. They finally checked in at an inn where the proprietor said there was no room. The only place available was in the stable, where the boy baby was born.

"Great sounds from angels in the heavens singing alerted shepherds in the region that a wondrous event had occurred. They left the flocks they were attending and went to the stable to see the newborn Christ Jesus.

"Sometime during the next three years, Magi or 'Wise Men' as they were referred to, came from the east being led by and following a bright star. They carried rich gifts for the baby Jesus, the King of the Jews. Inquiring of King Herod where they might find the King of the Jews, Herod in his jealousy determined to have the baby killed, for Herod believed he was the only king and there should be no other. The small family fled to Egypt to escape Herod's wrath.

"After returning to Israel, Jesus grew into a man and at the age of thirty started his ministry of miraculous signs and teachings. He healed many in the name of God and at the age of thirty-three surrendered his life as the final sacrifice to atone for the sins of all the faithful of humankind.

"You see, historically under Mosaic law, God required the shedding of life blood from an animal to atone for the sins individuals committed. Those atonements were only temporary for each sin and needed to be repeated for every new sin committed. Jesus's sacrifice was the final and everlasting atonement for all sins committed by the faithful. Because a sin is a personal action by an individual, the atonement Jesus made for each person's sin is personal.

"After Jesus's death on the cross, he was buried in a tomb. The Bible prophesied in the book of Hosea, 'On the third day he will restore us that we may live in His presence forever.' He rose from being dead, having victory over death and sin on that third day. Many saw him alive and gave witness of it after the entombment. That is why we talk to Him as God now, because he is alive after being slain.

"One needs to recognize by asking Jesus to be Lord of one's life and becoming faithful, one will be included in his atonement. Any person can become one of the faithful by just by asking forgiveness of their sin and by asking Jesus to be Lord of their life. His or her personal sins will be forgiven through the sacrifice of Jesus, God's gift.

"You see, God gave us His gift, and in some small part that gift is represented by every gift we give each other at Christmas.

"Nattily, this is the real Christmas story, a story of the most valuable gift anyone could have given so another could live forever," finished Gene.

With that told, Gene presented three small pine needle baskets to the others with three sugar lumps in each. As shaky as Gene's hands were, he controlled the trembling when addressing tasks that required fine motor skills. The condition was similar to a man who stutters badly being able to sing without a misstep in his song, and so it was with Gene's tremors.

Nattily also had been secretly shopping. She had made smoked trout with real salt. She found reed leaves near the creek and wove them into a mat, which she folded to enclose and wrap the delicate morsels in, then tied them with long strips of split reed fiber closing the packages. Ivan wanted to be next. He had found some rusted wire, which he'd fashioned into three tiny deer and a sleigh. The front deer had a miniature rose hip for a nose. A real work of art it was.

Sullivan, nearly overwhelmed by the wonders of these gifts, had fashioned four whistle flutes from the larger reeds gathered from the edge of the beaver ponds. He presented each in turn. "We now can have a flute quartet and can make music the rest of the winter."

The kids took to making music immediately. Gene fumbled out a Christmas carol and then Sullivan started playing a harmony part to the song Gene slowly perfected. Soon all made such joyous sounds Gene knew God must be pleased. The scripture says God loves a joyful sound.

Another sixty days passed. The group had been able to find some salsify roots and other tubers that seemed starchy, which made an addition to jerked deer and bear. During this time, Gene was able to present salvation and the gospel of Christ in measured amounts. Gene explained about the "grace" of God, the forgiveness of our human shortcomings. Sin needed to be forgiven, regardless of how slight or how evil it had been. He explained a person had to request of God to be forgiven, like we would ask each other to forgive us. Then a person needed to ask Jesus to become Lord of one's life to obtain grace and salvation to attain eternal life in Heaven.

Ivan was the first to accept salvation and became euphoric for several days. Gene had made his worn Gideon Bible available to all so they could study as the spirit led. Ivan had read the book of John twice through before the light dawned. When it did, his countenance changed literally overnight.

Nattily, although very interested, had many questions. She was one to justify only when logic exhausted itself. Gene knew until one became steeped in the full word of God, logic made it difficult for the average person to work through and come up with a sound answer. Gene had confidence she would eventually work through to the answers. He explained Proverbs 3, Verses 5 and 6 says, "Trust in the LORD with all your heart and lean not on your own understanding. In all your ways submit to him, and he will make your paths straight."

Sullivan himself had knowledge from some prior time. He was, as Gene termed it, "a passive backslider." He was open to Jesus as Savior and not opposed to Gene's presentations. He had some difficulty with the religion thing due to prior negative church experiences.

Gene stated, "Christians and churchgoers aren't perfect. They too are sinners, but they are forgiven and still as much as any person need the Lord for guidance and salvation. Romans 3:23 says, 'For all have sinned and fall short of the glory of God.'"

Sullivan considered it over and over.

Gene directed Sullivan to another scripture which had resonance with him. In the book of Acts, it says, "Salvation is found in no one else, for there is no other name (meaning Jesus) under heaven given to mankind by which we must be saved."

With so much time passing, Gene became anxious to be headed on his way toward home. He was satisfied the Sullivans wouldn't starve the rest of the winter and spiritually would not perish. He decided to start for Pinedale very soon. He worked on a new pair of snowshoes that offered greater buoyancy. He would leave the old ones with Sullivans along with his Gideon. Announcing his intentions one early morning, he was met with shock and surprise. The kids were beside themselves begging him not to leave.

"I must," Gene explained. "I have a family of my own waiting for me to come home. It's a very long way and I need to start while the snow is still firm or wait until late spring."

"You are welcome to come with me," he offered, "but I'm not sure you have the strength to make the journey. It is long, rough, and without the convenience of shelter or stores."

They objected, then finally gave up when Sullivan confirmed they had been blessed to have Shaky's company for the time they had it. He needed to be about his own business. Gene prepared three more days, then said farewell to each. With Nattily's tears on his collar, he turned to go, feeling a drop of moisture run off his own cheek. He kept going and only turned to wave after he was far enough away the telltale tears on his own face wouldn't be seen.

He turned westward toward Shanksville. Sullivan had offered general directions to Shanksville. He believed it some ninety miles to the west.

Over the next week, traveling in the high mountains especially this particular year was very difficult for Gene. The snow drifts and bare patches of dirt were intermittent and interspersed with each other. Gene would have to don snowshoes to get over the drifts and then remove them again to walk the bare dirt and rocks. The weather would be cold, even colder with wind, and then high wind chilled to the bone. Gene found shelter daily, but some were not to his liking. Others were more than adequate, offering protection from the wind and occasional snow flurries. He pressed on and on and on again.

When he located a road sign, it indicated he had passed Shanksville by ten miles. He debated with himself whether to go on or go back. *Do it right*, he could hear his inner voice telling him. He turned and advanced back to Shanksville.

Gene located a natural shelter some hundred feet above the valley floor where the road snaked its way through the canyon. He could see a group of travelers trudging their way away from the small hamlet. None looked healthy and all appeared weak from malnutrition. A cold camp would be in store again tonight. Starving people could be ruthless in their desperation to survive, especially if their will was still slightly intact.

The morning following, Gene worked his way toward town by way of unused retired back roads. These roads generally were easy grades to travel and most other people were unfamiliar with them, especially if they had come from somewhere else. Staying on these roads in fact lessened the chance Gene would run into strangers. Gene knew these old roads existed nearly everywhere after the days of modernization and nationalization of the federal highway systems.

Near a corner where the grade of the road reduced some, someone had established a permanent campsite. Gene watched the occupants, who seemed to be three or four at the most. In studying the location, Gene could see a fresh spring and decent latrine facilities. As he observed, camp activity seemed to revolve around the fire pit. It had been dug down into a bank of clay soil with an air channel from the lower end. The pit was lined with rock as an additional barrier for containment. The main purpose of the rock positioning was intended to reflect heat for effective baking and cooking.

Gene weighed the chances he could make contact safely. He analyzed circumstances while resting and decided he should at least hail the camp.

"Hello in the camp," he called out. "Can I come in?"

A voice from his left rear said, "If you are friendly, you can go in."

The hair on the back of his neck rose with goose bumps. *Darn, I must be getting careless and old. How had this person gotten behind me?*, he thought.

Gene turned to meet the watcher, who appeared to be unarmed. Gene suspected a hidden person with sights trained on his chest or his back or this man was a deadly force wrapped in a human body. Gene guessed the former was likely the case and that could be far more dangerous if the hidden power were to misconstrue Gene's actions. Gene moved carefully as if under gun point.

"Well. . . hello there," Gene casually stated. "My name is Shaky. Might I ask if you know the residents hereabout?"

The man seemed cordial enough but kept moving to Gene's right as Gene moved right. In Gene's mind, the action confirmed there was a second person concealed with armament aimed at him.

"Who are you looking for?" inquired the man.

"Do you know a family by the name of Plaster?" Gene asked.

"Maybe," the man replied, which indicated to Gene he did. The cloaking of the answer also indicated not only the name known, but also there seemed to be no animosity in his familiarity with the name. Gene could be misreading the response, but he didn't believe so.

Gene proceeded with, "I'm carrying word for them."

"You can tell me," said the man.

"Well, that would OK if I knew you were the right party. Would you mind telling me who you are?" stated Gene.

"Yes," the man replied

"Well. . . Again, what I have is for a specific person. Do you know the whereabouts of the Plasters?" Gene again inquired.

Gene realized this new society had fostered a new kind of distrust between strangers. This distrust was not an unwarranted condition. Survival depended upon caution with strangers. These sociological conditions were tenuous at best and not at all consistent between stranger groups.

They had come to an impasse. Gene wouldn't give up the information and the man wouldn't reveal his identity.

"Can you direct me to where I can find Plasters?" Gene asked.

"I can," replied the man, "but they ain't there. They're gone."

"Gone where?" queried Gene.

The man studied Gene for a moment before he answered, then flatly said, "Here."

Gene needed to take a chance and the only way he could figure to loosen things up was to mumble under his breath like an old codger just loud enough for the man to hear, "Barbara sure wanted this information delivered as soon as I could."

Gene watched to see if there a response in emotion showed or a physical tell that would indicate recognition at the mention of the name "Barbara." There was.

The man said, "What's that you're mumbling about, old man?"

"Oh, it's nothing. Just a friend asked me to transmit a message, nothing more," Gene said.

Getting a little more excited and a little agitated, the man said, "I heard you say something about Barbara. Barbara who and what about her?"

Gene had all the time been maneuvering to keep the man between him and whoever was on the hill.

"Mister," said Gene, "before things get complicated, would you mind calling in whoever is watching from the brush? That way they can understand what's going on here and I won't mistakenly be shot for some misunderstood reason. Do you think that would be OK? Besides, I'm tired of trying to keep you between them and me."

Gene had made the last statement to ease the tension and soften the ice a bit.

The man called out, "Scott, come on in here. You can watch this dude from here. Now, mister, you say your name is Shaky. What the hell kind of name is that anyway? I didn't catch all you had to say about Barbara. I want to know Barbara who and why you are looking for the Plasters."

"Are you a Plaster?" asked Gene. Then he went on to state the Barbara he referred to was a neighbor of Seth's in the northern suburbs.

"No, I'm not a Plaster, but they are my relatives. Barbara Plaster is my sister, so what about her?" the brother demanded.

Scott, who had been in the brush with a Winchester model 94 30-30 carbine, now stood close but off to the side, listening to the conversation.

"I have a message for Johnny Plaster," Gene said. "Do you know where I can find him?"

"Johnny left last month to go get his mom," he replied. "We haven't had any word nor did we expect any. So what have you got for Johnny?

"Well, it seems you are as close to Johnny as I am going to get and I plan on resuming my trek to my own home at Pinedale," Gene matter-of-factly stated. "I'm carrying a letter to Johnny from Barbara. She's waiting for him. She was well and well-fortified with supplies the last I saw her. That's all there is to it."

With that said, Gene handed the letter to the man, turned and left by the way he came. *This bunch wasn't any too hospitable or even friendly for that matter*, thought Gene.

That was the basic reason why Gene avoided groups of people as much as possible. People were with good reason distrustful and standoffish these days. These evil times had made things hard at best.

Gene had walked so many hillsides left, then right, he knew the knots he tied in one leg or the other to shorten them were about to wear them out. He did so so he could stay vertical on the hillsides and would have to be interchangeable next week with the knot in the other leg. He wasn't sure he could walk upright on the level any more. Maybe that was the reason why most folks stayed with the state constructed roads. These thoughts tickled him as he wished he had someone to tell this yarn to.

Chapter 26

The Head of the Snake

Two weeks later, Gene thought he may be halfway home. He'd stayed away from the high country with the heavily melting snow. The runoff in the streams was high, cold, and treacherous. If he would fall into water as cold as these streams now were, hypothermia could be the result. He was anxious to get home to see his family and relax with Jessie, but not at the risk of an accident. His thoughts wondered. He hoped Bonnie would be near home but was concerned she might go on a rampage against men who had abused girls and women. The thought often tugged at Gene's heart as he inched southwestward.

Catching food was difficult at best. He had a simple bow and arrows to shoot grouse, squirrels, and rabbits. He had been successful every couple of days and he came across an occasional beaver dam teaming with brookies. He would fish as long as he could through the unfrozen open surface, sometimes catching as many as forty or fifty of the small fish. Smoked, they were a lightweight wonderful source of protein and sustenance. Gene hadn't fired the 30.06 since he'd killed the bear. He'd only seen a few people since he left the Sullivans'. That was the Plaster clan. Life in these high mountains and deep snow was laborious. He began to think he was one of the last men on earth. There had been signs left where others had been. He saw shallow graves often and twice he came across human remains that had been picked clean by scavengers, both animal and human.

Gene could see the fresh green of early spring in the large valleys below. The green was the bright shade of fresh spring grass as it emerged from the bare patches. Gene thought he could see the yellow of new spring dandelions in a pasture far below. He would work that direction. Dandelion flowers were tasty. He could cook the leaves like spinach except there wouldn't be any butter, salt, pepper, or vinegar for added flavor.

Gene tried not to allow himself the luxury of relaxing by letting his guard down. There were times now when he was just plain tired. He wanted to relax completely. The winter had been long, the food sparse, and he had dropped a lot of weight. His shirt hung like a rag over a scarecrow. His pants were held up with a piece of twine found near a makeshift corral on a discarded bale of hay in the mountains. His shoes were now scraps of hide laced together with other twisted thin strips of hide from heavier skin animals. His cloaks had becoming ragged, his hands chapped and cracked, which he tried to heal with animal fat, and he smelled worse than the boor bear he had shot and skinned at the Sullivans'.

Because he had abandoned the relatively safety of isolated high country, he now was exposed to encounters with many groups, much to his dislike. He wanted to go home. Funny, he wanted an orange.

Unbeknownst to Gene, the MLS from Riverton had expanded its influence radius by a hundred miles. Additional information he didn't know was alliances of resistance groups were in full revolt against their tyranny. Leaders like Toliver, Joe, and Thor had been resisting with a guerrilla war in the ideal theory and perfect fashion, hurting the MLS where they lived and pushing back against the spread of their lawless tyranny. Gene was unaware because he contacted no one, nor was he contacted by others. His appearance when seen left the impression of a harmless scrawny creature who wasn't worth a second look. How mistaken they were. Their misgivings were as monumental as Gene's ignorance of current regional events.

Following the ridges downhill and staying out of the valleys where residents were led him eventually to waterway confluences as the ridges sloughed into valleys. The closer he got to his home country, the larger the waters became. At the confluences, Gene had to find bridges to cross due to the stream swelling from springtime snow melt. He disliked being funneled to a bridge just to cross. He didn't seriously consider changing his direction of travel because the drainage ran the wrong direction for his purpose. Changing would take him perpendicular to the most direct path home, so he stayed the course.

One indistinguishable early spring afternoon, Gene found himself on an outcropping that overlooked the next valley he would need to cross. He sat studying the landscape for a path to his next destination. In the valley below, he could see small bands of people moving about. Their movements seemed not to be those of a random settlement, but more like a military compound or prison camp. The more he studied them, the more he believed this to be some form of concentration camp. Gene wanted nothing to do with it. He'd experienced that already and would avoid it at nearly any cost. He felt himself lucky to have escaped the last time.

Gene resurveyed his probable routes and chose one that appeared to be more obscure than his first choice. It was longer and appeared to be more difficult to traverse. *Oh well*, he thought, *anything to stay away from a settlement like the one down there.*

As he moved along his chosen route, he would move cautiously, stopping more often to check his surroundings. All seemed well, but this wasn't a time to become careless. The other thing he scouted for was a secluded shelter for the night. Even though springtime had arrived in the low country, the night temperatures were still near freezing and the night temperatures up on the ridges were below freezing. A good shelter was most desirable.

Gene skirted a large hill and traversed a slide area. Barren and much to Gene's dislike, it was in sight of the settlement below. He moved slowly so as not to draw attention even though the camp was more than a mile distant. Once across, he slipped into some scrub oak brush and out of sight. The problem with scrub oak was it was difficult to get through unless you were a deer or coyote. It grabbed and clung to every part of his equipment and clothing. It didn't have thorns, but it may as well have had fingers to pull and hold onto his stuff. Gene remembered when as a youth gatherin' range cows, they had worn thick horsehide chaps to protect their legs. Some of the cowboys even wore gauntlets on their forearms to protect from brush scratches. A good cow dog was best for rooting cow critters out of the brush.

Gene was not pleased with any resting place he so far had located. Daylight ebbed and he needed to find a spot to settle into. Just as he was about to give up, he came across a little draw with a finger of Quaking Aspen that had crept down the valley. A stream trickled with fresh cool water through one of those pockets where an ancient landslide had pulled away from the hillside above.

Gene always liked these types of spots. They were secluded and the game liked them as well. He made camp and ate a meager meal that settled in for the night. The night sky was crystal clear and the earth surface heat evaporated into that sky. It was a cold crisp night and when morning came, a heavy frost covered the tree branches and grass stems from a fog that had moved through during the early morning hours.

At the first crack of dawn, he rolled his bedroll and ate. His food supply had become as depleted as he was. He was on the hunt. The problem was there seemed to be a scarcity of wildlife in this location. He checked his bow and the two arrows he had newly constructed. The grouse feather fletching was securely attached with small sinews from rabbit gut. They were almost ready to use, but the tips were green and unhardened. He had intended to harden them with his next fire. It just hadn't happened yet. The knock end had been wrapped with sinew to resist splitting when the arrow was launched. These arrows were straight and thin although made out of a heavy hardwood; Gene didn't know the name. He liked the wood, as it cured in time without cracking.

Packed and ready for the day, Gene moved out to a location where he had some visual advantage. He could see a couple hundred yards ahead and to the side. He'd stopped to survey the slope in front of him and below and that's when it happened. They moved up the hill toward him as fast as they could negotiate the brush. They had spotted Gene and their intent was to overtake him. Gene quickly reversed his direction to a more easily traveled path and broke into a dogtrot, putting distance between him and the others. Gene found an obscure game trail that broke off at a steep angle and took it without leaving behind a trace of his presence.

Three went past him without a clue. Gene could hear the noise of a couple more ratting around in the brush behind. As he watched and listened, it seemed as if one of the rats was getting closer. Gene quietly edged away and circled the sounds without seeing his pursuers.

A large man studied the ground for tracks. Watching hidden from the brush to his relief he saw the man miss the trail where Gene had turned from the path he had been on. The man kept carefully studying the wrong trail until out of sight. A second man was paralleling the big man on the downhill side about two hundred feet out. When they had moved some distance past Gene's location, Gene started sneaking tentatively away. When he believed he was beyond sound giving him away, he increased his speed of escape.

If there was one thing Gene had tried to impress on his kids, it was if one is moving, one is not likely to see what he is in pursuit of. Likewise, if one is being pursued, he or she is most likely to give his or herself away when moving more than when staying quiet. He should have remembered that lesson now, but it was too late!

When Gene saw him, the man stood above and to his left with a clear unobscured shot at Gene. His rifle was leveled at Gene and apparently had been for a few moments when he said, "That's far enough. Drop your gun and the sticks! I'll shoot you if you try to run, you understand?"

Gene's heart flip-flopped then started to race as he knew he had been had. Gene wished now he'd have deposited the 30-06 in a hole somewhere. He was tired of salting the earth with weapons for retrieval later, but now it was too late.

The man motioned for Gene to advance away from his rifle and bow. When just yards were between them, Gene was ordered to lay face down. The muzzle was placed at the base of his neck. The captor let out a mountain whoop not unlike the ones Gene's mountain relatives used when hunting and locating each other. Gene remembered the Swiss yodeled in a similar fashion to communicate through the hills. That mountain call gave Gene hope, as there weren't many others besides relatives who used this mountain call to communicate.

"Well, cousin," Gene said and was interrupted instantaneously.

"Shut up!" ordered the man.

The other hunters came trickling in one by one over the next fifteen minutes. There were nine in all. Gene had missed seeing several. They frisked him thoroughly, stood him up, and demanded to know who he was.

Gene said, "My name is Shaky. I'm headed home over the mountains yonder."

A skinny man about Gene's height and age exclaimed, "That's one of them, boss. We have a warrant for his arrest. He's one of those outlaws associated with the defense militia over in the south river basin region. The chief is going to like this."

They grabbed Gene's arms and bound his hands behind him. One man pushed roughly on Gene's back, jolting him forward. In the next two hundred feet Gene stumbled twice and fell flat to his side. They would grab him, jerking him to his feet and pushing him onward down the hill toward the community below.

It was a very long mile. The captors had no compassion and seemed to go out of their way to make walking more difficult. That mile was as exhausting as any Gene had traveled in the last year. Upon the group's arrival into the camp, Gene's hands were tied to a tree with his hands lifted behind himself so he had to stand bent over. He had been tied high enough that there was no respite from the anguish in his shoulders and back. If his knees started sagging, the stress on his shoulders caused pass-out pain. It seemed like hours before anyone paid him any mind. People carried on with daily tasks, but none seemed to notice his presence or even looked his way.

Near mid-afternoon when he was most thirsty and after his arms, shoulders, and back had lost most of their feeling, a man accompanied by two others came, grabbed Gene by his thinning hair, and jerked his head upward. The pain shot down his neck and through his body. "They tell me you're the legendary 'Shaky,' the one who's organized this band of resisting outlaws. What do you have to say about that?" he demanded as he jerked a little harder on Gene's scalp.

"I don't know what you're talking about. I've been over east of the Continental Divide for most of. . ." He didn't complete his statement before being slapped hard alongside his head.

"Let's try again," the man demanded.

"No, I'm just an old man wondering in the mountains," he blurted. "I don't know anything about outlaws. I don't know who you think I am, but I ain't him."

"Do you deny knowing a Bonnie or Thor?" the man demanded again.

The light went on in Gene's head, as rattled as his brains were from the heavy slap. *What have Bonnie and Thor been up to?* Gene thought. What he said was, "I don't know anybody named Bunny or Tor.".

They slapped him hard twice more and much to Gene's relief, he passed out and sank, hanging by his arms behind him. When he awoke, he laid on the ground under some sort of makeshift shelter, which for the most part would not have passed for shelter at all to most folks. It was better than some Gene had used in the last year. He was bound hand and foot, tied to opposite sides of the shelter supports. He couldn't rise to sit either from weakness or by tolerance in restraint slack. His head pounded. His eyesight blurred and his shoulders felt as if they had been pulled from their sockets. He thought he might die and was afraid he wouldn't.

A young bedraggled waif of a girl came to his side with a bowl of ditch-water-tasting broth and spooned a little into his mouth. As bad as it tasted, it was the most welcome meal he could ever remember partaking of. He was thirsty and she helped him sip some cool water from an old porcelain coffee cup. It hurt to swallow, but swallow he did. He felt as if he could drink a lake, tadpoles, and all.

Gene had more visits from the man who had questioned him at first. Gene ascertained this dude was called Hank, or the Commander. The Commander thrust a paper in front of Gene. Gene tried to read as much as possible before it was pulled away.

"Old-timer, this is what that Bonnie witch, the daughter of a man called Shaky, what you claim your name is, has done to us," he growled.

Whereas the following named persons heretofore have been found guilty of felonious crimes punishable by death and had their death sentences conditionally set aside; and

Whereas the following named persons have violated said conditions of their parole by associating with the Martial Law Service and other designated outlaw elements,

Therefore, each named below shall be detained and returned to this court for parole violation review. If such person or persons resist said return, then he or she shall be immediately subject to the sentence of execution. This execution to be carried out by any person or persons upon detainment and/or capture.

The following are subject to this:

- Andrew Adams
- Charles Ackerman
- Jerome Caseau
- Zackery Hollister
- Henry Hotts
- Holly Stokes
- Paul Smith
- Ebinizer Balensky

I hereby certify this order by the power vested in me by the United States of America Judicial Authority

Alford C. Millner
United States District Judge
5th Judicial District

"My name is on this list, thanks to US Marshall Bonnie Tucker. If I figure out you are related," he snarled, "I will skin you alive inch by inch and I may do it anyway."

For his effort, Gene received bruised ribs and a black eye. His head hadn't fully recovered from the first beating. Shortly after the last beating, others had been allowed to release Gene from his bindings. Gene was filthy and soiled. The stench after the first week was overbearing. A stranger tethered to Gene and Gene were directed toward a gravel bar in the river where they were instructed to bathe. They were forbidden to speak with each other.

The water was icy cold. Gene tried to wash his clothing as well as his body. He had no replacements, so he carried his wet clothing in his arms buck naked back to the camp to dry. He had chilled through from the icy water and shivered the full distance back to the compound. Seeing his reflection in a glass as he walked past, he was shocked to see himself. It appeared he was nothing but skin stretched over bones. The vision did a number on his mind. He had seen photos of starving people of third world countries before the EMP. He had seen starved people here too, but he never visualized himself as one of them, a skin-over-bone scarecrow.

Chapter 27

Oliver

Resetting the tin can alarm, Chuck joined his group for jerked elk stew with real salt and a shared can of beans. The cabin had been well stocked with supplies. Outlining their circumstances, Gretchen indicated the others were some ten miles to the west. Sammy knew people at a far outlying and isolated ranch to the northwest, where she felt they could hold up for the winter. If they were lucky, there would be winter feed for the horses. This ranch was some thirty miles south and west from the settlements by rough and arduous roads.

Resting another full day, the four secured the cabin and started for the horse camp. Snow that fell hard that night caused travel to become exhausting. Two days later, they arrived near the horse camp but couldn't locate its exact location. The fresh heavy snow had wiped out all sign of any trail or track.

Making a plan, Gretchen and Bonnie set out in opposite directions, circling where they believed the camp to be. Gretchen returned late in the day with no discovery. Bonnie arrived at camp shortly after with Molly, Sam, and eight horses in tow. There was no open grazing. The horses pawed the snow to retrieve what grass there was, but it was little. The next morning all mounted and headed down country to where Sammy's acquaintance Oliver Saughterhill kept his ranch.

Each marshal had a horse to ride. Four of the six sat saddles and complained of the saddle sores. Riding downhill seemed to make those worse. Sammy preferred bareback, so she and Laurie, being the most experienced rode without a saddle.

Laurie remembered thinking it was warmer in the cold to ride bareback. Horses project a lot of heat when moving at a steady pace. She said nothing. Sammy knew too.

Staying out of sight, the others watched as Sammy approached the ranch house. A tall, somewhat stooped man stepped out from the door with a shotgun in his hands. Bonnie could see another person through a second floor window watching the action from above.

"Mr. Oliver, it's me, Samantha," Sammy said.

"Samantha Ochoa?" he replied. "Child, what are you doing here, and at this time of year?"

"I'm with some friends; we need help," she replied. This must have been beyond stressful for her. Saughterhill could hear the strong Mexican accent in her voice as a result of her nervousness.

Not knowing what to make of it, he asked, "Who are your friends?"

"They are Marshals, appointed by Judge Millner to keep law and order," she replied.

"Are they good people, Samantha?" he quizzed.

"Yes, sir, they saved me from the MLS," she went on. "We could stay in the barn and help out with the chores. We would work and fix things for you. . .: She was near tears as she spoke.

"Samantha, I know Millner well," Oliver Saughterfill matter-of-factly stated. "Al and I went to school together as kids. Later, he was one of my parishioners. He's top notch and a straight shooter. Good lawyer too. I lost track of him after his appointment to the federal Judgeship."

The others emerged upon Sam's signal and approached the ranch owner.

"Well, there's a bunch of you and stock too," said Oliver. "I won't have enough hay to winter them. They can survive in the canyons on the south-facing slopes. But it won't be handy to catch them there if you need 'em fast."

"That would be OK," said Bonnie. "We don't use horses a lot anyway. They're too noisy when we need to go unnoticed most of the time."

"Tomorrow, I'll show you where to turn them loose and how to get there," replied Oliver. "As for right now, there will be room in the corral and some hay so they will know where home is."

Oliver inquired after Samantha's papi and her brothers. With forced composure, Samantha related the events that led up to her being with the Marshals. The rancher stepped all over himself apologizing for resurrecting such a horrendous memory. He later stated how he admired Papi for his extraordinary skill in training of the caballos.

The older women were housed in the large second-story room where four beds had been arranged. Oliver explained hunters in the past used this as a dorm during hunting season. Sam was shown to the guest room off the kitchen on the main floor. Chuck drew the short straw for the barn loft.

Running water was a luxury none had seen in three quarters of a year. The water wasn't always hot but could be heated on the wood stove when wanted. They all pitched in to gather wood for the stove, clean, sweep, wash and cook. They took turns cleaning the barn and repairing general maintenance. Milking time in the morning and night had been commandeered by Laurie. Oliver exclaimed one day, he had never seen any person who liked to milk like Laurie did. She told him when this unrest was over she was going home to raise calves forever. He smiled and watched her milk a while as she squirted one of the cats in the face with one straight stream of white. The cat jumped sideways and licked its chops. Laughing under her breath, she thought the day would never come when she couldn't hit a cat's face with a squirt of milk.

During an evening after supper, Oliver was asked why the MLS had left him alone. He replied they hadn't. He wasn't sure they knew he was here. They were a long way from the settlements and there wasn't a lot between there and the ranch to draw them his direction.

"There had been an old Willy Jeep come up the road," said Oliver. "I heard him coming and he stopped just around the bend by the barn. The pot-licker bagged two of our best hens in a gunnysack. I stood around the barn corner watching. When he threw them in the back of the Jeep, I hollered at 'em to stop. He shot at me twice while gunning it. He took off like a shot and while recklessly fleeing, he lost control, rolling sideways over and over, then off that cliff yonder. I have hardly ever seen anyone come out of a Jeep wreck in good shape. He didn't last two hours, but before he died, he said the MLS would come looking for him. We gave him a good Christian burial up in the plot on the hill yonder. Shame too, he never did accept the Lord as Savior before he died. If he'd asked, we'd have given him food. He didn't have to steal it. But what's done is done. God rest his soul." We never heard or seen anybody else until you came."

The Marshals had set up a system and rotation for the watch. Once every two days wasn't bad, at least not like the recent eight on and eight off routine.

January came and went with no adverse activity. The occasional sound of ordinance drifted up from the settlements. There was the sound of war in the far-reaching valley below. Oliver said in the past, on a quiet night, one could hear the coal trains as they moved up and down the valley some thirty miles away. Those train sounds had stopped and were now replaced with distant explosions, a constant reminder of the strife below. It would be easy to forget about the real world in this place of isolation so far away.

Laurie noticed Bonnie's demeanor had changed and Chuck seemed more attentive, agitated, and more closely watchful of her. Without seemingly noticing the looks between them, Laurie saw Gretchen observing discreetly the same events. This change in relationship wasn't lost on Oliver and his wife Minnie, either. While milking one night, Oliver made a comment to Laurie, which was as much a question as a statement. Laurie out of loyalty to Bonnie said nothing.

Oliver offhandedly added, "I see. Well, that answers that question."

At dinner grace, Oliver prayed at the end of the prayer, "Lord, we thank you for the beauty of relationships. Please give these young folks the wisdom to make sound decisions. If I can be your instrument another time, let it be so. Amen."

Laurie watching Bonnie saw her flush redder than she had ever seen at any other time. Coming back from her watch the next evening, Laurie encountered Bonnie.

"So. . . What's going on?" Laurie inquired.

Bonnie flushed again, and then said, "Is it that obvious? He's a wonderful guy. He's smart and kind, and he looks out after everyone."

"So. . . Are you involved?" asked Laurie.

"God, no, Laurie. How could you think such a thing? He's a gentleman of the highest order. He is too good except, he doesn't, well... he's not a believer. What I'm trying to say is, he doesn't have salvation. We talk, but he thinks he is a good person and thinks being a good person should be enough to get him to the right place if he dies. Laurie, what am I going to do?"

"Bon, we can talk to him, but you know he has to make his own decision," said Laurie.

They talked about these new confusing feelings and other things. Chuck, it seemed, was also confused. If Bonnie had such a belief as she claimed, *How can she be killing, capturing, and involved in such violence?* he thought.

His understanding was one of the commandments said a person wasn't to kill. Bonnie tried to explain the proper translation was a person wasn't to murder. Murder is the act of taking a life of an innocent, a defenseless, or otherwise helpless, person. What they were involved in now was war and even God backed Joshua and King David in war. God didn't allow King David some privileges he may have otherwise had because he was a man of bloodshed and war. Chuck was of a mind that Bonnie was justifying what she was doing, but he still wanted her hand, "to spend his life with." Now the situation had become a problem between them. The scripture plainly said two were not to be unequally yoked. Chuck was dismayed, confused, and didn't understand, but he was persistent.

At the next milking, Laurie laid the situation out to Oliver. Oliver seemed to have a second sense about the nature of people. Breakfast was eggs, venison, and fried mashed potatoes.

Oliver said to Chuck, "We should check the horses in the canyons. If you'd like to go with me, I'd appreciate the company."

"Sure," said Chuck, absent of thought without a further reply.

They grabbed the equipment needed to walk a couple miles atop the frozen snow-covered landscape. Reaching a good vantage point above the pasture location, the horses could be seen scattered over a square mile grazing. They showed the hardship of winter and would be ready for spring grass when it came.

"Chuck, I don't mean to butt in, but what's going on between you and Bonnie?" Oliver casually inquired.

"Ah, sh—!" exclaimed Chuck, "That obvious, is it? I don't know. We hit it off real good. We talked a lot and dreamed what we could do after this conflict is done. I thought both of us had the same idea and wants. She's great to be with, then when I mentioned we should get married, she started backtracking. She gives me mixed signals. She says she loves me, then she acts confused. Her religion is frustrating to me. It gets in the way. She wants to get married, but she keeps saying something about being unequally yoked. When she starts that stuff, I get frustrated and sure as hell don't understand."

"Chuck, have you got time for a story, one that may explain the confusion?" asked Oliver.

"Sure, we aren't overwhelmed with a workload," he replied.

"Before I relate a tragic experience, may I ask you a couple questions?" inquired Oliver.

"I guess so," replied Chuck.

"Well, the first thing I want to ask you is, if you were to die today, where would you go?" asked Oliver.

"I don't really know," mused Chuck. "I guess I would go to Heaven. I'm not that bad and try to do good when I can."

"And so, have you ever done anything bad? I don't mean serious stuff, but just stolen a candy bar or told a little white lie to stay out of trouble?" asked Oliver.

"Sure," replied Chuck "hasn't everybody?"

"Yes," said Oliver. "That includes me. So that in and of itself keeps each of us from being perfect, right?"

"I guess so," agreed Chuck.

Oliver continued, "If we assume God is perfect in all ways, He has no faults and doesn't sin. That would make Him perfect and pure, wouldn't it? If we assume God is perfect in every way and we are not, why would we be allowed in His presence? If He is perfect, just our association with Him or being in His presence would taint His pureness, causing Him to no longer be perfect. He can't be in the presence of the imperfect like you and me. So why would God allow us in His presence? Why, if we are almost good, would we be allowed into Heaven where God is? We would need to be pure to be there, don't you see?"

Oliver continued, "Ya know, the scriptures tell us, 'All have sinned and fall short of the glory of God, and all are justified freely by His grace through the redemption that came by Christ Jesus.' Jesus also said, 'I am the way, the truth and the life. No one comes to the Father except through me.' That's why Bonnie, Laurie, Sammy, and I call ourselves Christian. We profess Jesus Christ as our Lord and our Savior who saves us from the rewards our sins have earned us. We have accepted his sacrifice for our sins to make us purified."

"So what's that got to do with this 'unequally yoked stuff"?" quizzed Chuck.

"Well, here's the story I was about to relate earlier," said Oliver. "When I was twenty years old, I met the love of my life. I was a young seminary student and she was a waitress at the corner malt shop. We dated for about six months and then I ask her to marry me. Long to short, my seminary advisor counseled me to proceed with caution. He told me there was nothing good that would come of me marrying a non-believer. Chuck, I was incredulous, not the least to say, angry. I took matters in my own hands and chose to marry her against the advice of my esteemed and wise advisor. Our marriage went along pretty good for about three months. She became restless and dissatisfied with what we had. Before long, she was drinking and eventually, she drank to excess. As hard as I tried, I encouraged her to seek guidance from Godly people and the Bible. She flatly refused, saying this religion stuff was just a bunch of rules dreamed up to ruin having fun. By that time, I had advanced to an associate professorship and had become entrenched in my teaching position.

"She, on the other hand, now stepped out afternoons and nights to the bars, coming home later and later. Some nights she didn't come home at all. By this time we now were having heated arguments on a regular basis. I was losing substantial amounts of sleep, which affected the quality of my work and my performance at school. You see, Chuck, she wasn't a born-again Christian and didn't have the same values I had. She wasn't influenced by the God's instruction, but by her own wants and desires. We simply were unequally yoked.

Chuck, if you hook an ox in yoke with a donkey, they pull unevenly. Eventually, disaster ensues. What most people don't understand is getting salvation through Jesus Christ is not a limiting event but a freeing event," Oliver finished quietly.

He went on, "When we confess our sin and invite Jesus to be Lord of our life, we aspire to live a lifestyle guided by the instruction set down in the Bible by God because we want to do our best as if doing it unto the Lord. We don't do good works to get to Heaven, but we do good works as best we can in appreciation of the salvation God gave us by Jesus's sacrifice on the cross. If we attach to a person who is not of that same mind or like mind, it is similar to an ox in a harness with a donkey. The pull is uneven and generally counterproductive. That is what the scriptures mean when they say, 'Do not be yoked together with an unbeliever, or unequally yoked. For what do righteousness and wickedness have in common? Or what fellowship can light have with darkness?'"

He continued, "Chuck, you said yourself you weren't perfect, that you had stolen and lied. You want to be pure, but in our human condition, we, all of us, just aren't. The only way we can be pure is by recognizing Jesus took our sins upon himself to make us pure so we could be in the presence of God, not tainting Him with our impurity. Now that doesn't mean we still don't fail now and again, but it does mean every time we call upon the name of Jesus, we are cleansed.

"What Bonnie means is she wants you both to be guided by the same instructions so you each don't start pulling in separate directions. When working in harness together, you influence each other for the better good and there is a synergy that is gained."

Asking Chuck if he would like to ask the Lord's forgiveness for his shortcomings and to invite Jesus to be Lord of his life, Chuck responded he would if that was what it would take to gain Bonnie's approval. He did as led by Oliver.

They walked back to the ranch headquarters, where Chuck wandered off by himself to a spot away from the house. Bonnie watched, then started toward him, when Oliver intercepted her.

"Bonnie, girl, you should let him be for a while," instructed Oliver. "He has a lot on his mind right now. When the time is right, he will let you and us know."

Bonnie wanted to run to Chuck to find out what was going on, but instead stared at Oliver and bit her lower lip, reluctant to ignore his instruction. Supper time came and Molly stood watch, so she was absent. Chuck hadn't returned, either. Bonnie was extraordinarily quiet yet fidgety while eating. The others around the table talked in meaningless quiet conversation while Bonnie stirred at her plate. Sammy, Laurie, and Minnie cleaned up the dishes, washed, and dried them so they'd be ready for the next meal. The crew retired as dark seemed to be coming early, as it had been doing all winter. The days, however, were getting slightly longer.

Bonnie watched anxiously for a day before Chuck walked to the house. He wasn't moving in any way except relaxed. Bonnie watched and wondered what was going on with him. He approached her without saying a word to her, put his hand on her cheek momentarily, and then went into the house for supper. They all sat and Oliver offered the blessing for the bounty. This time Sammy stood at watch. Molly, Gretchen, Laurie, and Minnie said nothing while events took their course. There was a deafeningly quiet to Bonnie's ears, but she bit her tongue to keep it that way.

Chuck slowly broke the silence, "So. . . Why so quiet around here? Has something happened I don't know about?"

"No," Oliver offered. "We all were just waiting for you to return. After our discussion yesterday, we weren't sure you would come back. This last day has been suspenseful."

"Oh, I just had to think some things through since I prayed that prayer with Oliver," said Chuck, looking around the table.

Minnie in her own quiet way asked, "What is it, Chuck, that you're thinking so hard about?"

"This is all kinda new to me, and there's a lot I don't quite understand," replied Chuck. "I'm a little confused. I have had some weird sensations too, like all yesterday I never seemed to be alone, ever. I would look around and that sensation never changed. It wasn't bad, a little like knowing you had a friend watching your back all the time, or who was just there beside you, not saying anything, but just being there with you and yet you're never able to see 'em."

Chuck elaborated on his awaking experience. Bonnie was nearly beside herself, hardly able to contain her excitement. Laurie reached for Bonnie's arm to calm her before she exploded. Molly and Gretchen sat eating their meal, politely observing, and not understanding fully what was taking place. Over the past year there had been frank discussions of what "being saved" meant, and what "having the Holy Spirit" was about, but Molly gently tolerated the topics and shrugged them off. Gretchen had been "churched" as a child and had gone to vacation Bible school, so she had some knowledge of the faith. Molly, on the other hand, was self-directing clueless. In her mind, she was a "pretty good person."

Dinner concluded with Bonnie gazing at Chuck over her coffee cup, and he self-consciously glancing up to her gaze. He cocked his head toward the door and both excused themselves from the table. Bonnie nearly tripped over a tapered chair leg getting away from the table. Laurie and Gretchen burst into laughter as Bonnie flushed red from her neck and ears and into her hairline. She and Chuck linked arms and exited.

Outside, Chuck didn't say a word as they strolled, arm in arm, toward the barn. They turned at the path that led behind the corrals.

"Bonnie, I suppose Oliver told you about his and my conversation the day before yesterday?" Chuck stated.

"No. . . He didn't say a thing," she replied. "He did make me leave you alone. When I pushed him as to why, he just said you needed some time alone. I was beside myself with anxiety wondering what was going on."

"The other day, Oliver explained some things to me," he said. "Some about your faith in Jesus, some about being partnered with an unbeliever, and some about just being good and doing good things isn't good enough to get to Heaven. Bonnie, did you know Oliver is a preacher?"

"No. . ." she replied.

"After he explained all that stuff, he asked me if I wanted to say that prayer with him," explained Chuck. "I said I would. He told me what to pray. Bonnie, I don't know how to explain the feeling

I've had the last two days. Oliver gave me this little Gideon Bible and said if I really wanted to know who and what Jesus was about, I should read the book called John. I did, twice, and it's amazing how different I felt. I'm not sure I understand what's happening, but if it means I'm a Christian, that's okay. If you feel this way as a Christian, that's great too. I believed calling yourself a Christian was subscribing to some social association. I don't feel that way at all now. It doesn't have anything to do with what anybody else thinks. It's how and what person feels inside."

Bonnie listened while he talked, sensing his need to express his feelings. He asked questions of Bonnie to understand her angle on a number of topics. Her answers on topics, while the same as Oliver's, varied a little but didn't conflict with Oliver's precepts. He came to the "unequally yoked" topic and, laughing a little, said he didn't want to be the donkey.

Bonnie, not knowing the analogy, smiled uneasily, then quipped, "Well, I've been a horse's patoot before, but why a donkey?

"Well, Oliver said a Christian marrying a non-believer was like an ox being yoked to a donkey. I don't want to be the donkey. Bonnie, what I'm getting to is, you mentioned the problem with being 'unequally yoked,' and I need to know from you if there is any other reason we can't be yoked?" Chuck half-asked and half-stated.

"Yes, I mean no, there is no reason I wouldn't be yoked with you!" she exclaimed and threw her arms around his neck with unreserved caresses and kisses. After Chuck underwent one of the two most wonderful events of his life, he was at a loss for what he should do next. He wanted to shout, he wanted to jump in the air, but he just stood there with Bonnie's arms around his neck, feeling euphoria from the events of the last several moments and days.

"Bonnie, do you think since Oliver is a preacher, he would marry us?" Chuck asked.

"No, silly, he's already married to Minnie," she said as she giggled.

"You know what I mean! Besides, you're more my type than he is," retorted Chuck.

"Let's go ask," said Bonnie as she pulled on his hand toward the ranch house.

The conditions of social chaos were all but lost to either of them in their present state of mind. "The bad guys be hanged." Bonnie and Chuck had other things to concentrate on at the moment.

Not one of their friends was surprised by the announcement of their intended nuptials. Oliver would be pleased to "officiate" the ceremony by the powers still vested in him. It had been a long time, but he thought he could remember enough to make it official.

They agreed the following Wednesday would be a good day to tie the knot.

Chapter 28

Salt

Gene's recuperation was slow and the poor quality food didn't help. His shoulders and back ached from the strain and he thought he would never be able to lift his arms again. He became aware of three souls in the camp who had perished. The spirit of the captives here had been broken. There appeared to be no try left in these people. Gene tried to piece together in his mind the implications of the questions he had been asked. All he could conclude was his daughter and her friend Thor had been designated rebels. Gene's mind was barely able to focus on one thing at a time, and then not for any length of time. He suffered from repeated and nearly constant headaches.

One evening just before the sun set, one of the honcho guards jerked backward with the side of his skull blown away, and then came the report from a distant rifle shot. It must have been a long distant shot like a sniper would make because the timing from the impact to the report of the sound was separated. All the guards ducked for cover and did not come out until after sunset.

The commander, while staying undercover, convened a meeting of all captives. He simply said for every one of his personnel that were sniped, he would kill five of the captives. He picked one of the strongest young girls and ordered her release with that message to deliver to the snipers.

The next evening, another of the camp personnel was hit dead center of the chest. The report timing was the same as before. Five of the closest captives immediately were lined up, shot on the spot, and in plain sight of what the commander thought the sniper could see. They consisted of a middle-aged man, three women, and the preteen girl, the waif who had first tended Gene. Gene's heart simply sank in despair. He would never understand how a person could become so fond of a bedraggled little girl like he had this girl in such a short period of time. What hurt, more than anything, was he didn't know her name. It was as if his own daughter had been killed.

Oh, where's Bonnie now? he agonized.

Gene now understood for sure these captors were outside the law and if Bonnie was opposing this kind of inhumanity, she was fully justified.

Gene started looking for anything he could use as a lethal weapon or a way to acquire one. His 30-06 was long gone, as were his knife and other tools. He found lightweight cords he could use to strangle, but he didn't have strength enough left to use them. Gene had never been very strong, even in his youth. He located a piece of rebar about ten inches in length driven into the ground to hold his shelter in place. He still wasn't satisfied with what he had, but as a last resort, it would make an effective club.

The sniper must have received the message because there were no more shootings over the next three weeks. The commander revisited Gene a couple more times with similar results. Gene didn't have knowledge of revolutionaries and their leaders. The sniper attacks that came were in the evening but now had ceased. Then it happened, just after sunrise. The Commander had risen, ate breakfast, and walked his morning inspection of his camp, as was his usual habit. The impact drove him forward and he ran several steps before crashing into the side of a makeshift shelter just as the rifle report arrived. When he rolled over, his face had disappeared, leaving a mass of mangled blood, bone, and other semi-recognizable cranium parts with blood pulsing from the gaping wound.

Gene expected the lineup to come, but the brutality of the commander's death had militia and captives alike in shock. When a head officer started lining people up, the sniper dispatched him as well. The captives, now having come to their senses, started resisting and fleeing the now-demoralized guards.

The guards had become reluctant to reveal themselves while many captives started slipping away from the camp. Gene, seeing the disorganization of the guards, took this opportunity to quickly commandeer a small caliber rifle, some cartridges, and a sack of meal. Corn, maybe, he wasn't sure. Had he had time, he would have preferred fishhooks and a knife, but he had what he had.

Gene in his wildest dreams never experienced such barbarism in his entire life, including Calcutta, than that which he had experienced in the last two and a half weeks. The extremes of pain, hunger, cold, and sadness were beyond anything he could have imagined. Now he had flown the coup. He wondered where the others had fled. Most wounded animals and humans flee downhill as the natural reaction of the flight response. Gene, determined to not be swept up with the others, turned and started uphill to the ridges that he was more comfortable with. When he took inventory of his possessions, there was the .22 rifle with eleven cartridges, the clothes on his back, his bare feet, and the bag of cornmeal. This would be the ultimate test of his survival skills.

Gene located a secluded ravine with a bench just above the bottom where he could build a small fire to stay warm by. He ripped part of his shirttail to make a strip for a bow and drill to kindle a fire. With some effort, he started a fire. He located a small dead pine tree just large enough to make a spear, combination staff or club, and walking stick. Using his fire, Gene burned off the limbs and ends to a comfortable length. He used a nearby rock to sharpen the point by rubbing the end, alternating with fire treating to harden the tip. His feet were his next concern. Old bare feet, even though tempered by months of extended travel, were still tender when stepping on a rock or bur wrong. Gene looked for some loose bark to make sandals from. He located a pine tree that had been struck by lightning. The tree had been blown apart by the energy instantly injected into it from the lightning. Parts of bark, shards of wood, and scraps were scattered fifty feet in every direction. Gene found two thick bark chunks and a long splinter that made a better spear than he had already crafted from the small tree. Using more of his shirt tail, Gene laced wraps to hold the bark to his feet as sandal soles.

Easing his way back to the fire, Gene procured a snowshoe hare with a rock. He was rich; he had food, shoes, and a fire. Gene found an adze-shaped rock and a flint left by some Indian in times past. He chipped the flint to a sharp edge to use as a knife. Skinning the rabbit, Gene made covers for his sandals. At least his feet would be warm. He used the gut to make strings for sewing and lacing. This night was cold, but not any colder than any of those of the last two weeks. The snowshoes had fleas.

"I would sure like an orange," Gene exclaimed aloud. "Well, there's none available," he instantly answered himself.

During the night, Gene wondered who the sniper may have been. He was disappointed there wouldn't be an orange. He wondered if the captives would be recaptured. He sure needed a knife. He drifted off and then he became cold. He rekindled the fire and then dozed off again. Before dawn, he awoke, rekindled his fire, and prepared for the day. When the sun broke over the ridge, Gene found a sunlit spot and soaked up every ray of warmth it could provide. He had smoked half the rabbit and now slowly consumed his breakfast.

Coming to the top of the ridge, Gene found he overlooked a small meadow. Gene could see where cattle had been the year prior. He thought he could see a salt lick. If it was a salt lick, there might be a salt block, which would have been placed for cattle to lick and consume. Working his way down the hillside, he found a partial unconsumed salt block at the salt lick. It was the remains of a white block, not one of those red mineral blocks most often used by cattlemen for supplement. Gene chipped off a piece and sucked on it until he was nearly sick from the taste of salt. Breaking off several pieces with a rock, he pocketed them for future flavoring.

Spring weather was bringing out the whistle pigs, ground hogs to the tender foot. Gene decided to expend a .22 cartage to capture one. He did and the sound of the shot seemed loud enough to awaken the dead. Dressing the rodent, Gene roasted it over a discrete fire. The grease of this particular species bubbled, boiled, and dripped into the fire. Gene caught some of the fat, and mixed it with some of the meal from the sack and water, making a cake. He baked it on a flat rock. This fatty meat contained a lot of energy. Gene cooked the entire animal, smoked the hide, and made a bag of it to contain the cooked meat and some extra cakes with real salt. Yes, real salt. He stretched the gut to a long, thin ribbon, which might work for lacing to hold his flimsy footwear together. If needed, he could use a length of it for a bow string as well. Now all Gene needed to be temporarily content was an orange and a coat.

As Gene was extinguishing his fire, he caught a movement out of the corner of his eye and to his right. There were two. Gene had had enough and would make a stand. They may even have a knife and warmer clothing. Gathering his .22, he nonchalantly moved to cover. The men split their path to approach him from angles that made it difficult for Gene to watch and defend at the same time. At no time did they try to conceal themselves. They just kept coming until they reached earshot.

"Mister," one called out, "we don't mean you any harm. I have a little food if you're interested. I'll leave it here on this rock and then I'll back off aways."

"We just want to talk a bit," he continued. "We heard your shot and decided to investigate. There aren't many who have guns these days. The Martial Law enforcers are confiscating all they find. When you shoot, you are inviting company. We've watched you a spell and you aren't one of them. We'd like to know who you are."

Gene was understandably skeptical. The man must have sensed his hesitation. He stopped, took a piece of food from the supply on the rock, and ate it. He then walked away about a hundred feet. The other just stood off a good distance watching. Gene realized if they meant harm, they could have dispensed with him before he knew they were there.

"OK, who are you?" inquired Gene.

"We are part of the People's Militia," he replied. "We're fighting those so-called government forces that are tearing up our people and countryside."

"Who is your boss?" Gene inquired.

"His name is Thor, if it's anything to you," the man replied.

"Is this Thor a big guy who played football for Riverton State?" Gene asked.

"He's the very same," said the man.

"I've met him," replied Gene.

"Would you like to meet him again?" asked the man. "We're headed that way now as we speak."

Gene contemplated the possibilities. If he could be resupplied, his trip the rest of the way home would be considerably easier. These guys seemed to be straight up, but Gene had become distrustful.

"I could use the food," Gene said finally. "But I'll travel alone. I would like to see Thor again and catch up on some news." Gene was feeling old and tired.

It would be nice to be among friends, even casual friends, he thought.

"If you don't move too fast and stay together, I'll follow. I won't be captured again," Gene flatly stated.

"Very well, we're two days out. If you need more food, we have a little we can share. We'll be on our way," he said and he turned to join the other. They went.

Gene followed, thinking all the time whether he might be being trapped or not. He was not captured and had no fight. The odds were things were legitimate. He continued and the food from the rock had a good taste. It seemed he could taste honey and orange. Oh, how he wanted an orange. He must be losing his mind. He was obsessed with having an orange.

Evening came and the travelers had set up their camp. Gene found a rock overhang to camp under but passed it by for a distance. He made pretense of setting up camp near a stream, where he ate cakes and some cold whistle pig meat for supper, then washed it down with a cool drink from the stream. After dark, he moved back to the overhang.

This evening wasn't much different from a dozen others, except the air seemed to be slightly warmer. Gene's thoughts began to wonder over meaningless recollections and ideas. He thought about his heritage and of his kids. Gene was a descendant on his mom's side from the Scotch-Irish settlers of eastern Kentucky and Tennessee. One of his great-great-great-great-grandfathers had been one of the over-mountain men who whipped the British at Kings Mountain and the Battle of Cowpens. They were a hardy lot, those mountain men, and had generations to hone the skills required in living daily. Gene could now more than any other time appreciate those skills required to stay alive. Gene didn't believe his survival skills to be genetic, but there must have evolved a genetic trate to such abilities in his bloodline. If genetic traits existed, they must be in this manner.

Generations after that, being displaced by growing populations and a need for spreading of the wings, became part of the Oklahoma land rush and were "Sooners" in the Indian Territories of Oklahoma. One whole clan had moved to Oklahoma with the promise of free land for the grabbing. Some of them succeeded and some didn't. Gene's grandfather had punched cows from the Oklahoma-Missouri border to the Big Bend on the Rio. Granddad had been a bull whacker driving six yokes plus one of oxen pulling a freight wagon. Gene had seen the old tintype photo.

Gene's dad's family was a hardy bunch as well. Out of five brothers whose grandfather crossed into New York State from Canada, four went on to settle and establish frontier towns in the West from Montana to Nevada. Gene's granddad landed in the high Colorado Rocky mining camps, where he barbered and was an incurable prospector with the fever. Another uncle trained to be a Methodist preacher and an engineer. All were men of determinable character.

On Gene's dad's maternal side, the South did arise. Gene's great-grandmother traveled by covered wagon from Southeastern Tennessee through the Oklahoma territories. They too survived after tragedy, loss, and suffering. *Yes*, Gene thought, *American strong; if they could do it, I won't quit now!*

Daylight found him back near the fake campsite watching for any unwelcome activity. None came. He could see the others breaking camp ready to travel. Gene shadowed them at a distance where he could see their progress. He would be able to evade any trap that might be set for him. The day progressed uneventfully, except Gene's bark sandals now were disintegrating. Near an abandoned dwelling, Gene saw an old saddle that had been placed on a rail fence as a display. He went to the house to find it had been stripped totally of everything of value. There were no knives of any kind, including kitchenware. He found a small sauce pan but no shoes. There was an old broken guitar with strings attached. They became unattached, quickly being liberated to become snares. There were wire coat hangers, one of which Gene removed, and he found discarded bailing twine in the barn. That would work for shoe lacing or moccasin stitching if Gene could find rubber or leather. He found an inner tube in the barn and a pair of chaps, which would work nicely for moccasin leather. He could make shoe sole from the old saddle leather and moccasin tops from the chaps. *What a shame to cut up a good pair of chaps*, he thought. His need for another use was real. If he were careful, he could make a pack with the other unused leg. Stuck in the rafters, he found an old hand scythe.

Well, now, that's nearly as good as a knife, he thought. *All I need now is a stone or file to sharpen it with.* He set to work, sharpening the scythe with a fine-grained marble rock found near the front door. He then cut saddle leather and chap leather to fit. An old nail and a rock served to punch lacing holes for the moccasins.

Night came upon Gene before he was ready. He slipped into the barn loft and bedded down for the night. The cooked whistle pig now was depleted. He started working on the food left to him by the others. As was his habit to say grace over his merger fare, it hit him. He had been so intent upon putting together footwear that he'd forgotten to be grateful for the bounty placed in his hands. He made apologies and asked forgiveness, then slept. Up before daybreak the next day, Gene completed his footwear and pack.

He knew his distant companions would miss him as a follower. If they kept going, they would be nearly at the headquarters by now. If they stopped to wait for him, they would be somewhere ahead nearby. Either way, Gene was going to follow at a distance.

Leaving the ranch stead, Gene worked his way toward the last location he'd seen the two men. He found their night camp and the trail they left. They weren't being very careful about leaving tracks. Gene figured they wanted to blaze a trail plain enough for a blind man to see. Gene didn't think he needed it, but if they were who they claimed to be, he appreciated the gesture.

His paranoia and suspicions came to the forefront of his mind. Gene broke from the trail and circled it some hundred yards on the high side. If anybody were laying a trap, Gene wasn't going to be a participant. He followed most of the morning until the trail dropped over a steep narrow edge. The trail was hardly wide enough for a horse. This would be the place if an ambush were to come. Gene pondered a bit, then scouted the rim on both sides of the trail for half a mile. He found nothing unusual or suspicious either way. His vantage from a point overlooking the trail revealed the camp below sitting on a plateau above the river.

There were watchmen and people working on their daily chores. This was an orderly camp like Gene had been in at Riverton. The people seemed content and not downtrodden like the last camp he had been in. As Gene observed the camp, one man pointed in his direction.

Have I been spotted? he thought and so pulled back from the rim some. The next thing Gene saw was a huge black man step out of a tent and start looking up to where the man pointed. Thor, yes, sure enough, it was Thor. So this is where they had relocated to. It was a big distance from their prior location in Riverton.

Descending the trail into the camp, Gene realized he had been in plain view of a lookout across the narrow gorge. He had been so intent upon watching the camp, it never dawned on him to look across the canyon for other danger. "Lord, I must be getting old. I keep messin' up so much lately," Gene mused aloud. "It'll have to be in your hands from now on, Lord. I can't trust myself to stay alert all the time anymore."

He was some hundred feet from the edge of the camp when a sentry blew a whistle. The whole camp froze in the instant, looking about at the disturbance to see what was going on, then resumed their activities. Others immediately were at the ready and two approached Gene with some measured caution. Thor poked his head out the tent door and studied Gene as if trying to recollect where he had known him from.

Two of the watchmen had spread to either side of Gene and a third watched the trail behind him. Gene saw a fourth casually watching the surrounding terrain for signs of unusual activity. Thor walked casually up to Gene, towering over him like a redwood tree. Gene hadn't remembered Thor being so huge, but then again Gene felt he had shrunk several inches in the past year. *That must be it*, he thought.

"Well, you old buzzard bait, there isn't enough meat on your bones for a buzzard to starve on," Thor commented.

"Well, sir," Gene said. "It's a long story. I'll be brief and too, I would like some news if you have any about my daughter, Bonnie."

It appeared as if the light clicked on in Thor's head. *That's where I've seen this man. He's much smaller than I remember, but it's the same person indeed.*

"Shaky, isn't it?" inquired Thor. "I thought you were over in the big valley south of here. What are ya doin' in these parts?"

"Yes, we met when you accused Toliver and me of taking your right hand man — or woman in this case — last year. I took Bonnie, my daughter, home," Gene replied.

"Yes, how well I remember," Thor said. "Speaking of last year, how has Bonnie been?"

"She was better the last I saw her. I haven't seen her for three quarters of a year," Gene stated. "I was hoping to get some news from you. I was captured by a dude called Hank up the river from here. He was in command of a labor camp. When beating and questioning me, he referred to you and my daughter by name in the same sentence. I came here to get news specifically about Bonnie from you."

"We need to talk," bluntly stated Thor.

That comment and the way Thor stated it brought a lump into Gene's throat. Gene followed Thor to his headquarters tent, where offered a chair. Gene wasn't confident he knew how to use a chair anymore. The conversation began with what Gene would have called a debriefing and he gathered little information in return. Thor was looking for names, dates, and places. Gene had very little he could offer, except his experience in the last labor camp.

It was now Gene's turn. Thor said there were always rumors. It had been rumored that Gene himself had been dispatched on the other side of the Continental Divide to summon help from the National Guard. Another rumor was that Bonnie had divided into three persons hitting the MLS in gorilla style warfare effectively to force their retreat back to Riverton. Another rumor said a Federal Judge had recruited Bonnie to a law enforcement position so they could stop the marauding, pillage, and raping. The concrete details were that Bonnie had acquired an appointment as a United States Marshal from a Federal Judge. She was taking names and numbers and kicking butt along with running the MLS ragged. They had communication runners who brought word of events and Bonnie had become top priority with the MLS.

Thor commented, "I wouldn't doubt any of it for a minute. You know her, Shaky."

Gene was now deeply concerned. When he left home, Bonnie's state of mind had been questionable.

"Please, God, I hope she halted her rage," he prayed.

Having talked with Thor about the events of the labor camp, Gene inquired of Thor who he thought might be responsible for the sniping of Commander Hank.

Thor was noncommittal. "I can't reveal all of what I know about that. I can tell you the command staff was targeted. We misjudged the resolve of 'Hank,' as you call him. The agents didn't make that mistake the second time as you know. They weren't aware of your presence. They did know there was a new captive whose identity wasn't known, but whose interrogation might compromise any operations, so they acted. Please understand we didn't have a direct hand in those activities but were made aware of impending events."

Gene was fully grieved to think eight had died just because of his presence.

Chapter 29

The Alkali

G ene left Thor's camp provisioned with some smoked fish and supplied with equipment and a warm coat. They offered him new sneakers to replace his moccasins. He politely declined, saying if he ever gained weight his feet would be too fat to fit in them, in which case he would just have to throw them away. Gene requested a notebook to write his journal entries in. He was presented with a college ruled spiral three-subject notebook. *That's just fine*, he thought.

He asked meekly if there might be an orange to be had, he sure would do about anything to have an orange. Thor burst out with a deep rumbling laughter from the depth of his guts as a response to Gene's request.

"Shaky, all this wandering around in the hills must have made you a little touched!" Thor exclaimed. "There isn't a soul here who has seen an orange for nearly a year. We had some of those little canned Mandarin oranges a while back. That's about as close as it comes."

"I know," replied Gene. "But I had to ask. I sure would like an orange!"

With that said, he turned toward the hundred-mile trek home. This some hundred miles to home wasn't unfamiliar to him. There was some difficult terrain between here and there. With decent spring weather, he hoped to cover the distance in two weeks or a little more.

Gene left, climbing out of the valleys toward the first of the large ridges that separated him from his home valley. He was cautious in his travels, having grown suspicious of anything that seemed unusual. He watched clearings before he entered them. He made his trail in places where he could watch it. He just seemed to be slowing down. The pack seemed heavier and his shoulder joints hadn't recovered from being hung in the tree. The thought of home was ever so much more alluring. Those thoughts were enough to drive him on otherwise he might have just given up and stayed where he was.

In the days when there was transportation, Gene could cover this distance in a couple hours, not so now. He saw for the first time in great detail the locations he thought he was familiar with.

Choosing his night campsites with care, Gene left very little sign of his passing. Amazingly to him, he saw no human activity. There was no sign of other people this side of winter any place he traveled. Once he came upon a dwelling that appeared abandoned. It looked to be a probable night shelter. Entering a slightly ajar door, Gene discovered four bodies. They had decomposed considerably but were still in a semi-frozen state. They had wrapped in blankets and huddled together just where they died. Gene speculated they froze to death sometime the previous winter. The nights had been cold and still were in these higher elevations. The snow was deep in the places shaded by trees and buildings.

Shaking his head in dismay, Gene said a prayer over the deceased, then left, closing the door behind him. He had not the strength, nor the ability to dig graves in the still-frozen earth. Their souls were now beyond the need for earthly care, so Gene moved on to a nearby barn for night shelter. Later in the dwelling, he located one of those military survival knives of quality. He took it with the sheath and a leather belt he found on a tie rack. There were some cartilages for his .22 and a .38 caliber hand gun with a box and a half of ammo. He was thrilled at having found a fishing tackle box with hooks and line.

Another three days up hills and down the valleys, through snowdrifts and fording icy-cold runoff streams, Gene's resolve to get back to Jessie and home hadn't been daunted. Catching a couple snowshoe hares and a grouse supplemented his supply of smoked fish. It amazed him how a little salt and pepper could change the complexion of a bland meal.

The last night before he would arrive in his home watershed, Gene couldn't sleep from excitement. It would be a very long day to just make home. Finally, before sunup, Gene broke camp and moved out. He could see far in the distance the ridges above his home. By midday, Gene was all in.

"You old fool," he muttered to himself, "you need to use your head. It'll still be there day after tomorrow. If you screw up, break a leg or whatnot, you may not get there a' tall. Pace yourself. Don't let haste make you careless."

"Ya," he replied.

After this stern self-talk, Gene started the steady and sure walk to the house. Nightfall came and Gene still was some five miles away. Funny, he hadn't seen a living soul in places where there should have been people. There were sporadic dwellings, cabins in the high country that usually had residents occupying them this time of year. Further, many of them were burned to the ground, leaving nothing but warped metal remnants of furniture and the remains of building footprints.

Making camp the final night, Gene pondered the meaning of so many destroyed buildings. "Deliberate, that's what it seemed to be. Deliberate razing of anything useful for people to survive with. This must have been a scorched earth action by someone."

At one of the burned-out cabins, a root cellar lay hidden by scorched brush some thirty feet to the side. Gene slipped to a vantage point and saw nothing indicating the presence of people. The root cellar had been well constructed with proper venting and the customary double door forming an airlock between outside and inside. Gene pulled the first, the outside door, open. The second door he swung to the interior. There stood shelves of home canned food in jars looking fresh as the day they were placed there. Dates indicated two to ten years old. Some of the older fruits were a little discolored at the tops of the jars, but Gene knew they would prove edible.

There were beans, some kind of red meat—presumably venison—peaches, applesauce, apricots, cherries, and a vegetable stew with cabbage, squash, potatoes, peppers, and a garlic clove for flavoring, canned whole corn, creamed corn, and two varieties of pickles.

"I have found the mother lode!" exclaimed Gene aloud.

He checked the dates on the meat and vegetable stew and liberated two of each. Closing the doors behind him securely, Gene proceeded to fix what he considered the first real meal he had had within the year in a shell of a misshapen pot that had protruded from the ashes of the burned cabin. He would have another tomorrow if this one didn't kill him from food poisoning. He believed he was safe, however. All his life he had eaten from these types of supplies, first from his mom's cellar, then from the preparations Jessie and he had put together.

He became over stuffed and lethargic from his protruding belly. How different that condition was and how miserable his gluttony had made him.

"Lord, I thank you for these meals I ate all at once," he prayed. "I ask you to bless the hands who prepared them."

Gene made an early camp near a stream, where he could drink fresh water to help flush the excess food from his system. Usually, he didn't like streamside camping because the noise of the water covered other sounds around the camp. This night he made an exception. Here he had encountered no recent sign of another man, woman, or child anywhere. That fact nagged him at the back of his mind.

By eleven the next morning, Gene reached his own home. The house, like the others, had been burned to the foundation, and the shops and other buildings were ransacked. His treasures had been strewn aimlessly about with good stuff being broken and destroyed. Gene's heart sank to a point of despair.

"I know, Lord, we are not to set our hope on things where rust will wear away, or stores that can be stolen, and items fires will consume, but why this senseless destruction?" he queried.

He turned and walked away to find Jessie at Jake's farm. That distance he covered in the longer part of a day. Nearing the farmstead, he could see things weren't right. It was too quiet. The dogs were silent, the shop door was open, and there seemed to be no livestock about. His heart sank again when he saw the ruins of the barn near the house. It had been partially burned, but not all the way down. A coyote darted out of the remains of the chicken house. Gene knew at that moment the property had been abandoned and left empty.

Poking about for a sign, he ran across the carcass remains of two of Jake's dogs. He could see the bullet holes in the chest on one and in the skull on the other. That only meant one thing. Jake and family had been under attack. Gene knew Jake and the signs of the battle which were evident. Gene found no sign of trails leading away from the ranch. He saw a few footprints in dried mud that were small for a man and large for a child. Bonnie had big feet. Jessie had long feet, which matched her long, slender hands. Jake's wife had small feet, but one was somewhat clubbed. These weren't her tracks, of that Gene was sure.

After scouring about, finding no discernible or useful information, Gene was almost beside himself. Jake's barns and shop looked similar the Gene's own in total disarray. He was now at a loss as to what to do next. He moved out to make camp to an obscure location where he could ponder the situation.

Morning arrived with Gene as tired from worry and concern as he'd ever been. Sleep evaded him nearly all night and when light came, he was groggy and not rested. He found himself melancholy and just plain blue in spirit.

"Lord, you know," petitioned Gene, "show me where Jessie and Bonnie are. I should have never left them. I didn't intend to be a fool, Lord. I thought I was doing the right thing. Seth wasn't there and the events of the last year except for at the Sullivans' have been in my way of thinking of little value."

With that, he fell into a deeply depressed frame of mind. Packing his camp, he decided to see if the Smith ranch was still there. By late afternoon, he could see from his vantage point on the ridge above the Smith ranch that the ranch house had been burned. Gene turned away, not wanting to see close at hand any further destruction. By dark, he worked his way up to a small cone-shaped peak called the Squaw's Tit from where he could see the entire valley below to all sides.

Here was where he remembered all that had gone before this past year.

"Lord, what has happened to the world I used to live in?" he muttered under his breath, "Was it time to wake up or was it time to make another diary entry?" He hadn't completed the last.

The two long trips to retrieve family members and the events from those trips had taken their toll on him and changed his physical condition and his confidence. He had his faith in God above but now was some fifty pounds lighter in weight to one hundred ten. His mindset was that his time on this wretched pitiful earth was getting short and it neared time to go home. The scripture plainly said he was but just a sojourner in this worldly place, the earth, that earth isn't his real home. Heaven is. He now wondered if he had missed the rapture and was in the tribulation. Times had been and were so hard now, but God had and continued sustaining him.

Lord, if I missed it, I pray Jessie and the family were caught up and out of this world of hard times. Maybe that's why I can't seem to find them, he thought. He knew he had a strong faith in God and Christ as savior. He couldn't imagine the others being raptured for anything less than the faith he believed.

The rare news which filtered through the national grape vine had been the Middle East was in full war, but the good old USA was now so crippled by events one year ago it had been deleted from the action as any viable credible power.

So here it is about to be, his last will and testament.

Continued journal entry:

"In the year of my Lord 2018, I, Gene Tucker, known as Shaky, bequeath all my possessions, what's left of them, which I now carry to Jessie, my wife, and then to my kids after her. Most of all, I bequeath any excess portion of my faith in God above to the one who finds this last will and testament. As for the memories of what the world was like before this total catastrophe came upon our land, I leave those to the public so they can understand and hopefully learn from mankind's mistakes. My hole-riddled moccasins and my hide coat are to be used to. . ."

When Gene came back to the present from remembering the past events, he sat a long time, disabled from depression and grief. He felt

314

the chill of the encroaching night and pulled his bedroll near him to stay warm. Eating that night never entered his mind. He fell asleep half covered, not caring, and despondent to the core of his soul.

This night was a cold one. This mid-spring morning produced frost and upon awaking, Gene chilled enough that he shivered. Startled to his senses from the cold, he set about kindling a small fire with dry brush. From where he sat, he could see the world. As small as it was, the world could see his campfire smoke as well. In his frame of mind, what did he care? There wasn't anybody left to see it anyway.

Making a hot tea of withered rose hips and eating the last of the heated vegetable stew from a Mason jar, Gene sat, hoping to see sign of human life deep in the valley. He could see smoke from the vicinity of the settlements. It resembled that of structure fires or industrial fire with chemicals billowing black followed by a lighter color of grayish yellow smoke plumes. Once he thought he heard a heavy boom like an explosion, but listening hard, he heard no others. He knew he would find people there but couldn't think of any reason Jessie, Jake and Meg would be in the middle of a population center. It just wasn't in their nature.

Reminiscing back to times when Jake and he were kids, Gene remembered the good times at cow camp. Grandma always had hot biscuits, bacon, eggs, and pancakes for breakfast. Those were the days before Granddad sold the property. The parcel of land was seven hundred sixty acres in an isolated plateau basin called Alkali Basin. There was one way in and one way out. It was as close to being an inverted box canyon as anything. The sides were protected by ramparts leading up to the basin from three sides. *Boy*, thought Gene, *I would like to see the Alkali Basin cow camp again, but if it's been burned, I just might die from grief.*

Just then, the light dawned. If Jake and the others had fled for safety, it might just be to the Alkali. He packed his camp, put out the fire, and started. The Alkali was some sixty miles as the crow flies to the southeast and there was a major canyon and two rivers to cross between him and the "Alkali."

Cutting again across what was considered US Forest Service lands, Gene set up camp some ten miles away at nightfall. Funny how before the EMP, the Forest Service seemed to be running these public lands like their own private holdings. They had been closing historical trails and roads. They required permits for access to in-holdings which had existed long before the Forest Service establishment date. They had withheld permission for water rights owners to maintain watershed structures that had been established long before the Forest Service came into being.

He thought about the "Sagebrush Rebellion" in Nevada some years before and wondered why it hadn't taken hold. Instantly, he knew the answer. Most cluster dwellers, city folk, had little idea of events outside the city cluster. Gene had come to think of city folk as cluster dwellers all dependent upon the presence of the cluster social, spiritual, and physical existence.

His depression seemed to have lifted at prospects of getting to the Alkali cow camp. It seemed all he needed to lift his spirits was a quest and a goal. Well, now he had one. Two more days found him nearly a quarter of the way, but the deep canyon deterred his path by at least three days. The trail he took was the one he believed his great-granddad had taken by covered wagon coming into the region so many years ago. Gene never was quite sure of its exact location but felt it was near, if not the one he was on now.

Still he saw no sign of other people. Many he feared had perished during the long, cold winter. People these days had been simply unprepared for the closing of power plants and grocery stores. They starved and died from lack of medications and many killed others out of desperation and or due to lack of respect for civil law.

The trail Gene followed was an ancient Indian trail depicted on the sandstone cliffs at the base of a shallow canyon near the entry of Alkali Basin access. The cliff writing depicted spirals indicating water, stick-figure deer and mountain sheep. One fattened figure, being misshapen, looked much like the talus slide on the side of a mountain across from the Alkali. Gene believed he was near the northern end of the depicted trail. The trail etched into the sand rock cliff went past the big canyon, showing a trail up and out the side Alkali Basin was located. Then, showing the high mountain parks, the trail turned toward the south. This was Gene's intended path.

Reaching the north rim of the deep canyon, Gene chose a spot farther down on the canyon side where a bench provided ample space to bed down. He reached it just before dark.

The morning sun warmed him as he consumed his meager breakfast. The trail, steep and treacherous, had loose rock underfoot. Sliding as much as climbing down, Gene reached the bottom exhausted by the effort. Now he faced the river. Gene believed this to be the location represented by the spiral in the pictograph. It wasn't a large river by world standards, but there was enough cold swift water to drown any man.

Working his way up, then down, the near riverbank, Gene located a ford where he could cross. Being spring time, the water was high. If later in the year, the crossing would have been much safer. Finding large forked driftwood of cottonwood origin upstream, Gene worked it loose and decided it would be better to attempt crossing above the ford, pushing across as far and as fast as he could before getting to the ford. The water was slow there before reaching the shallows of the ford where the velocity increased.

Pushing off, setting straddle of the fork in the floating log, Gene used a split driftwood branch as a makeshift paddle. His legs and butt felt like he was sitting in ice water and soon numbed. Paddling as fast as he possibly could, Gene started toward the far bank. He neared three quarters of the way to the far side and closed on the ford when his driftwood raft grounded on the sandbar underneath. Standing on numb feet and legs, he stumbled his way in knee-deep ice water to the bank. Throwing his gear on the bank, he climbed and scrambled his way up the bank out of the water.

Resting only shortly to catch his breath, Gene set about making a fire. He shivered violently. Having a steady enough hand to light the fire was only when he placed his elbow on the ground for stability. Soon his fire warmed his legs and numb toes. The sun was straight overhead and warmed the canyon floor with only three hours of sunshine. The sun was Gene's friend this day. He heated water and consumed it as hot as he could stand to drink. The shaking gradually ebbed, but his energy nearly was sapped. Studying the canyon wall, Gene located the trail leading out at the top of the rim. It wasn't so apparent from his location where the trail started from at the bottom.

Resting for an hour, Gene had an uneasy feeling about camping on the riverbank in this canyon. He didn't understand why, but the feeling motivated him to push on. The first two attempts at locating the trail out came to non-passable rock faces. Simple dead ends up the hillside forced him to retrace his steps back to the bottom. Gene lost time and all the direct sunlight. His third attempt to locate the way out appeared promising, but to stumble around in the dark on those steep loose rock trails would be foolhardy. Finding a slightly level bench above and below two cliff faces, Gene made camp well before dark. He might not find any better suitable campsite before the light faded. Setting up camp was simple and took little time, allowing Gene to study his surroundings from a different point of view.

Located some thirty-five feet from his own fire was a very old fire pit most likely used by an ancient Indian. On the ground further around the bench where the river and ford could be watched from above, Gene found flint chippings, partial arrowheads, and several skinning knives. As he studied a trail branching from the one he traveled, Gene saw a cave. Edging around the hillside, the cave opening in the basalt face was just tall enough for a small man to stand in and was some fifteen feet deep. With the ebbing light on the wall, Gene saw a drawing of elephants, or mastodons, with hunters carrying spears in pursuit. If this had been the days before the EMP, Gene would have contacted an acquaintance who knew about such things. In the present state of the world, nobody would care other than finding this curious. Gene made a mental note of what he saw and then returned to his own camp for the night.

He arose and ate before the sun peeked over the rim. It struck there much earlier than in the canyon bottom. Packed, he started up the obscure ancient trail. Remembering in his mind about the cliff writings near the Alkali, Gene seemed to recall a strange symbol near the spiral symbol for water. If he got the opportunity some-time, he would see if that strange symbol was a symbol for the cave and shelter.

Gene's climb took the better part of five hours, delivering him near the top of the canyon rim just a bit before noon. Resting, Gene ate a bit of smoked fish, drank a mouthful of water, and chewed on the tender stem of several buckwheat grasses which grew there. There was still a good rise above the canyon rim Gene would have to ascend before he could be sure of his location. Gene hadn't been to the Alkali many times in the last forty-five years and wasn't sure of the bearing from his location. He had taken the family there several times for outings, but the property was now owned by some outsiders, out-of-staters he thought, with access and use being restricted.

Upon ascending the nearest ridge, Gene was in awe of the vastness of this country and the remoteness land beyond. He could clearly see the distant mountain range where the Alkali was located. After locating Morgan Peak, a known landmark with a distinct skyline silhouette, he plotted his intended path. Being a semi-wilderness with miles of aspen and evergreen forests, this land was quiet and distant. There were few locations, however, that didn't have at least primitive roadways or trails where Gene would be traveling. None, however, took a direct route to the Alkali. There simply wasn't a direct route.

Interspersed throughout this land were pockets of private land holdings. Many had summer cabin sites. Some were ranch land holdings for pasturing livestock. Some of these in-holdings included patented mining claims. The boundaries of many of these were marked plainly with "NO TRESPASSING" signs, but other boundaries were not so clearly defined. By cutting across the landscape, Gene was sure to trespass some property owner's rights inadvertently. He would not do so intentionally, but these days it didn't seem to matter. There seemed to be no clear-cut rules these days. Then the thought came to him. What was so different now? Nothing had changed. The rules hadn't changed. Whether one chose to abide by the customary rules lay in the character of the man. All of a sudden, Gene realized he had been gradually modifying the rules to meet his very needs.

Did it matter that he had taken what he needed from the dead man's cabin after Gene had been robbed? Did it matter that he had taken the sheets from the remote ranch house for camouflage? Did it matter that he carried articles from the homestead for his survival? Did it matter that he had removed canned goods from someone's root cellar? Gene believed it did matter. He didn't consider himself a thief. He was in need at the time. It was simply a matter of survival. As near as he knew, no person was harmed by his actions. Did they really matter?

Chapter 30

Union and Division

C onsideration as to where the newlyweds would spend their honeymoon was given. Reality dictated the Marshals be back in the mix soon. Occasional gunfire drifted the miles up from the valleys below. The cabin where Laurie found Chuck and Bonnie was considered an option but quickly dismissed. Travel there would necessitate horseback travel, which at best could be risky. The Marshals all traveled most safely on foot using their strategic separation. The final decision came after Oliver made a suggestion. He knew of a line shack which was not far, was isolated, and had facilities for basic living. The water came from a cold spring and there was ample wood for the stove stored in the woodshed. Using the horses to get there would present little risk, as horse tracks were common in the area from the wandering cayuses. So it was settled; Chuck and Bonnie would be gone for two weeks.

The girls had laughed and giggled their way through the night. This relief was as much a release of the stress from the last winter months as from the celebration of the impending nuptials. Molly stood the night watch and was relieved by Gretchen for swing shift. The party was going strong when Molly entered the front door. They crashed before daybreak and got up with little rest preparing for the day's events.

Wednesday morning arrived with the women all excited about the expected ceremony. It would be a simple event. Minnie had modified a white denim skirt to fit Bonnie and also supplied a white blouse to accompany the skirt. Minnie retrieved her own bridal veil for Bonnie to use. Bonnie was taller than Minnie by some 14 inches, so Minnie's wedding dress was just the wrong size. Now, if Sammy were getting married, the fit would be near perfect.

Chuck was shorter than Oliver and stockier. Oliver offered his best dress coat for the affair, but Chuck just washed his clothes and himself, making the best effort to present himself as honest and clean. Bonnie had set the time to be ten o'clock sharp. Chuck, on the other hand, had said "about ten" and promptly was chastised by Minnie and Gretchen. They all laughed more. Chuck now had been banished from the dwelling. He went to take the watch until the time. Sammy offered to relieve Chuck of his watch when the time approached for him to make his appearance.

Sammy showed up about fifteen minutes early. "Hey dude, your destiny awaits you!" She announced her presence tauntingly.

Chuck smiled at her arrival, said nothing, and tapped her nose with his index finger, warning her she tred on the unknown.

Sammy said, "She looks real pretty. I haven't known her a long time, Chuck. She has always been pure business, but today Bonnie looks as happy as I have ever seen her. Instead of looking like a hardened old hide, she looks more like she's at her Quinceañera. I didn't know she had the girl in her."

Chuck looked at her, not knowing exactly what Sammy meant. He simply took it as some form of Mexican compliment. Walking crisply up the trail to the farmstead, he paused a moment at the edge, taking in the scene. Now wasn't a time to be careless. It was a time to enjoy, but to be vigilant.

The living room had been decorated with bows and ribbons. A few wild flowers in bouquets were set around. These were made of early violets, grape hyacinth, lupine, and crocuses from Minnie's flower garden and added natural beauty to an otherwise bland ranch house interior.

Ascending the three porch steps and crossing the porch to the front door, Chuck hesitated long enough to knock gently with his middle finger knuckle. Oliver opened the door, greeting him with a handshake and a grin.

"Come in young man!" stated Oliver. "You're just in time to meet your bride and lifelong partner. Come stand right here. Bonnie will be along momentarily."

Laurie stepped out of the hallway and proceeded in that hesitatingly long stepping wedding gate until she reached a predetermined spot near Oliver and Chuck. Next Bonnie in her white long-sleeved blouse, white denim skirt and veil-covered face took the same steps as had Laurie to the spot next to where Chuck stood.

Oliver proceeded with a scripted wedding ceremony, including the usual, "If anybody present has reason to object to this union, let him or her speak now or forever hold his or her peace" statement. "Do you, Bonnie. . . and do you, Charles. . .? Laurie, may I have the ring? I pronounce you husband and wife. You may kiss your bride."

Rice being in short supply was replaced by well wishes. A simple scratch cake from corn meal, three-tiered, covered with a honey glaze icing had been constructed by Minnie during the girls' celebration the night before. Minnie slipped out right after the short reception and led the horses packed with the supplies Bonnie and Chuck had assembled. Minnie, in true after wedding fashion, tied colored survey tape to the saddle horns and horsetails. There were orange, florescent green and blue ribbons without the presence of tin cans. She knew those ribbons would disappear as soon as the two were out of sight as much for safety's sake and from the custom of removing the tin can string from the bumper when away from the wedding revelers. She did manage to put some corn kernels in the bedrolls as a finishing touch. This was the most daring fun Minnie had partaken in since she poured dish soap in the fountain at the student union some fifty years past.

The two weeks passed rapidly for all. Spring activities commenced at the ranch. The new shiny wax green leaves of the Gambel oaks were popping and the bright green of spring grass inched skyward. The air warmed considerably in the day and the nights cooled as only spring nights can at that eight-thousand-foot altitude. The valley sounds carried to the ranch on the cold night air. Those sounds were sounds of war. It wasn't an occasional skirmish, but that of full blown firefight for the best part of two days. The marshals could only speculate about the meaning of the activities. The consensus was Colonel Whitmore's vets had engaged the MLS or visa-versa.

After a powwow, contacting the Judge was considered the best course of action. The problem was, where was he? They would wait for Bonnie and Chuck to return, lay out the plan they had contrived, and obtain Bonnie's input. She, of course, would have input. Bonnie and Chuck didn't return until a full day after the planed arrival. A gentle scolding was leveled.

Greetings all around were abundant while the atmosphere was lighthearted, if not celebratory. Chuck's face flushed as he perceived a subtle chiding from the women about the clipping of or at least the tethering of his wings. He, in his good-natured way, took it like the self-assured man he was.

When all had settled, dinner was served while Sam took her allotted turn at the watch. The conversation around the table centered around the rumbling sounds of war floating from the distant valley below. All assumed Colonel Whitmore's forces had engaged with the MLS. The assumption, however, was just that, an unsubstantiated assumption. Who else would have the ability and interest to challenge the MLS? All during the conversation, Bonnie listened and remained ever-so-quiet.

The following day, Bonnie and Chuck settled in the first-floor bedroom while Sammy moved upstairs. The conversation generally now centered around expectations for reactivation of law enforcement activities. All seemed apprehensive. Living in comfort during this winter at the ranch had softened each one's attitude and resolve about their mission. Samantha seemed the exception. She had stewed over the killing of her dad and siblings and now was full of revenge. Laurie spent time with her, explaining revenge was not a reason to stop the MLS, even though they all realized it had an influence on their motivation.

"Sam," Laurie said, "if Oliver has taught us anything this winter, it's that we aren't to act out of revenge. You know that. Remember the Bible says in Romans 12:19 that we are not to take revenge. God says 'It is mine to avenge. I will repay.' He also says He will heap burning coals upon the heads of our enemies. We have a job to do because it is right, not because we want to get even. I know it's a hard thing to remember with our passion and in the heat of battle, but we wouldn't be any better than them if we didn't. Doing it for the right reason is what justifies us. That is what makes it right, what we do. If we're acting out of revenge, we lose prospective about our mandate. We just can't let that happen."

Samantha's response was measured. "I understand all that, but I can't get the ire, the *almacenar odio*, out of me for what those men did."

Laurie and Bonnie walked together down the trail to the lookout talking girl talk as the best of friends do after recent events. Bonnie was indefinite about details of the honeymoon. She even blushed at Laurie's inquiry. Feigning shock when Laurie asked, Bonnie lightheartedly scolded her for being so inquisitive. They walked and talked for the better part of an hour.

"Laurie," said Bonnie, "don't you ever want to quit this business, I mean hunting men? I don't feel the same as I did when we started. Chuck has made me realize that there are more important things in life. I've never been happier than I am right now. I hope it lasts forever."

"Bonnie, we, the Marshals, think it is time to be active again," said Laurie. "We wanted to wait until you came back. We have a meeting planned for tomorrow. You're the leader and we need you to direct us."

Bonnie stopped dead still and looked at Laurie as if she'd said a foul word. She said nothing, then turned and they walked back to the farmstead, not saying a word. Laurie sensed she had struck a nerve much deeper than she might have realized.

Morning came with the happy little band and their hosts all pitching in to complete the chores. Minnie watched Bonnie with some interest but said nothing until alone in the kitchen with each other washing the breakfast dishes.

"Dearie, are you okay?" asked Minnie. "There seems to be a change in you this morning." Minnie had started calling Bonnie "dearie" as of late.

"It's nothing," said Bonnie. "I just am having some anxiety about going back to work. I really like my life right now. I only wish I knew where Daddy, Mama, and the others were. I pray every day that they are okay. That would be my primary focus now if anything. Minnie, you have been the best of friends. You've treated me like a daughter and always give good advice. What should I do now? Do you think I should go back to tracking down bad guys?"

"Dearie, you started a job with a purpose," answered Minnie in her usual meandering way. "If that purpose has been accomplished, then it may be time to find a new purpose, like say, your husband. Maybe together you could find your folks. I hope you can. As for me, dearie, you are the daughter I never had. Oliver and I have never been any happier than we have been since you and the others came. You see, and don't you let him know I told you, but he came here to withdraw from people after several disappointing pastoral appointments. He wanted to get away to think, meditate and pray for God's will. He believes it was in God's will you all came and I see a renewed faith and confidence in him. He has even talked about going to the valley to minster to the remaining survivors there."

Dishes complete, they entered the dining room. Everybody sat around the room waiting for Bonnie's arrival.

"What is this, an inquisition, or what?" Bonnie quipped.

"No," said Laurie, "we need to make plans."

Gretchen jumped in with, "It's nice here, but there are people down there who need our help. We took a pledge to uphold the law and we can't do it staying here in our own private paradise. We need to be about the business we started until it's done"

"Me too," said Molly. "I'm feeling like I bailed on the people who need our help. It's time for me to make a move."

"Bonnie, we have decided the time has come to act. We want your input," urged Laurie.

At that comment, Bonnie looked at each of them and as tears started welling in her eyes, she hurried out the door and ran down to the barn. She thought, *They were all there, even Chuck.* She didn't want to hunt men anymore! She was tired of the killing and the violence, and she had her doubts about how much good they had been really doing. They were all there, so who was on watch? With that, she went to the lookout point, where she could see the approaches to the ranch both upland and down.

Chuck offered, "Bonnie has lost the heart for the marshaling business. She told me so last week. She wants out. She feels Laurie should be the director with help from Molly on tactical stuff."

"Well, then, if that is how it is to be, I propose we, Gretchen, Molly, Sam, and I go to the Judge for his instruction. If Chuck and Bonnie want to stay or go, they should," said Laurie. "We need to start soon at any rate. Get your gear in shape and be ready to move out in the morning. We'll head down country, then back to the Judge's as quickly as we can."

"May I make a suggestion?" Oliver inquired.

He had their full attention, as he usually did when he spoke. He explained about the existence of an old logging road not far from the ranch called the Mindonhall Sawmill Road. He explained few people except for some old timers knew of its existence. It had mostly overgrown and seldom was used anymore. The US Forest Service had closed it to common vehicle use by the public like they did so many of the old trails and landmark roads. A few seasonal hunters were about the only ones who frequented it these days.

"The Mindonhall Sawmill road comes out of the foothills near Lumberton, about three or four miles from Judge Milliner's farm," said Oliver. "If he's there, this will save you a lot of travel time. I haven't been over it all the way, but it should serve you well and make for easier travel."

They asked a few questions and then agreed the Mindonhall Sawmill Road was the route they would take. They would go on foot, leaving the horses at the ranch for now. This was a good headquarters, as long as Oliver and Minnie didn't mind. The next morning, the four set out to find the Judge and seek further instruction.

Chapter 31

High-country Grandeur
and the Alkali

G ene worked his way through the valleys and hills. This high
country was cold at night and cool even in the summer. He
crossed swollen streams and caught fish by hand in the smaller
streams. He had taken to eating them raw on occasion when a small
fire wasn't convenient.

*Oh well, the kids ate sushi at those fancy city restaurants, didn't
they, and raw fish hadn't kilt them.* he thought. He really disliked
sushi but this was a necessity now.

As Gene walked, he thought about the events during the last
year. Some he chose not to dwell on. Some he enjoyed over and over
like Christmas with the Sullivans. He thought about his own family
and prayed they might be at the Alkali. Throughout all the pain and
hardships, the one event that struck him most was the dead family
he'd found frozen to death in the house. That image didn't leave him
even when he slept.

Gene estimated he'd covered some forty or forty-five miles as
the crow flies. He must have walked twice that just to cover the
same distance in the past seven or eight days. Funny thing, Gene
wasn't keeping track of time anymore.

"Why? What's the use?" he muttered to himself.

He realized he now was thinking the questions and muttering
the answers back. Sometimes he'd mutter the questions and then

mutter the answers back to himself. There was no one around to hear or to talk to and he hadn't seen anybody to talk to for a month. He justified too, he didn't want to lose his communication ability, and so he would practice when he could and practice would help occupy his time.

Morgan Peak now was within half a day's travel time. He could be at the Alkali in about two days, he estimated. He stopped and caught a dozen brookies by hand from a small stream. The small fire served to smoke them as they hung from a tripod made of willow stems. He had some trouble with the wind dissipating his smoke before it could envelop the fish to cure them. He made a wind barrier of woven willow stems and evergreen boughs. That helped. Above the tripod, the breeze dispersed the smoke, making his fire undetectable to casual observers except for the smoke smell downwind from his location. When the fish cured by day's end, he moved his location to camp for the night.

It was good he made the move. Being half a mile away, Gene saw a bear nosing around the smoke site. He had found the entrails and hardily sniffed at tripod frame that Gene had discarded to the side. Gene had neither the desire nor the equipment to take on a bear and so was glad to be out of the way when the bruin or boar arrived.

Early the next morning, Gene moved out, anxious to see the Alkali. He wondered if it had changed much. He wondered if Jake and the family would be there. With each thought, he muttered an answer to himself. If Jessie had been with him, she would have asked in a scolding way if his response was a positive affirmation. "What you speak is what you shall reap," she would say. He missed the lighthearted bantering with her.

"I wish I had an orange," he muttered to himself. "You old fool, you won't see another orange as long as you live."

"Well, I might if they get things fixed," he argued.

"Naw, things are too bad. Even the nearest citrus groves in Arizona would be overrun with starvin' people. There won't be enough to ship to these mountains for years."

"Ya, and no way to transport them either," he continued.

Then silence, he had won the argument. He liked when he won these arguments. He didn't like so much when he lost them.

Another thought came to his mind as he traversed a hillside. He didn't dare speak this question or even mutter it for fear someone might hear.

Why would anybody think I, Shaky of all people, was so important as to put out a wanted poster on me? he thought. The idea was beyond his comprehension. He contemplated a while longer until he came upon a not-so-well-traveled narrow gravel road. This was it! He was sure. This road led to the Alkali. He was some five miles from the property now but wasn't about to walk the road. He turned up the hillside above the road and paralleled it for a distance. Nearing the bottom of the Alkali Basin, the road continued on to other remote locations. The Alkali access road was not much more than a two-track dirt pathway. Gene couldn't see sign of activity on the road but held off to the side as he progressed.

He recalled a rise on the northwest side of the property where he could observe the cabin and entry access all at the same time. As children, they had played all about and knew when Mom was after them for not doing the chores or could watch the trail coming in when the cowboys returned from gathering cattle. No better vantage point than that spot existed from which to look the place over. Gene made his way through the trees and circled around out of sight until he could reach his vantage point. He slipped low Indian style up to a large rock that stuck up about four feet. If careful, Gene could become part of the rock and see clearly all the surroundings.

As he leaned on the rock, he could see people moving about in the cabin through the window. Several of which, two, he thought, had to be women. Details escaped his eye. He studied intently for half an hour in hopes of seeing more detail. All of a sudden the hair on the back of his neck stood just before the cold steel of a gun barrel touched it.

"Move slowly, friend," the familiar voice commanded. Gene did just as instructed. He turned slowly as he said, "Jake, I would have never thought you coulda sneaked in on me like that. How're doin', anyway?

Jake took one step back, studied the stranger a bit and said, "Shaky, is that you? We'd given ya up for long since dead. Lord-o-Friday, ya lost some weight, man. Come to the house and I'll feed ya myself."

Gene stood and offered his hand, which Jake readily took and shook and shook and shook. The cabin was just over a hundred yards away and Gene for the life of him didn't know how Jake knew him to be there. He asked Jake how he did it. Jake reminded him that Gene and Jake's great-grandpa had been an old Indian fighter. He'd passed some of that knowledge along.

"If you're protecting your homestead from marauders, you learn the shapes and sizes of all your surroundings. That rock up there where you sat seemed to have gained some weight. From the looks of it now, it didn't gain much weight."

"Have you seen Jessie and Bonnie?" Gene asked.

"Jess is inside," said Jake. "Bonnie, the last I heard tell, is heading up a Marshals' contingent appointed by that old US District Judge Millner from down Lumberton way. Never had much use for him. Anyway she's doing a bang-up job. She warned us before that MLS bunch raided the ranch. We got out, but none too soon. When I say bang-up, I mean literately and figuratively. That bunch killed Mike and Cindy. Those Marshals of Bonnie's tore that MLS bunch up. They jes keep sendin' more to replace the ones that get taken out. The last we heard was about early winter."

When they approached the door, Jake called out, "Look what I found sneakin' about lookin' for a meal."

Meg came to the door, thinking Jake had brought another mongrel dog home to feed. In a way, he had.

"Jessie, come here! It's Shaky. He's here at the door!" Meg exclaimed.

Jessie pushed through the door and stared at Gene.

"What on earth has happened to you? You're just skin and bones—and that hair. You've not had a haircut in months. Oh, come in and sit by the stove, you must be starved." Jessie mothered him. True, Gene hadn't had a haircut since he left for the other side of the mountains. He hadn't shaved for longer than that too. He didn't grow a thick beard and so even with a full beard, looked scruffy, fully unpresentable. The nearest thing to a bath he'd taken was when the work camp forced them all into the cold river. Now he thought he must be not fit to be in polite company.

I was once a respectable, well-dressed business man. Now look at what I am, he thought to himself.

He answered himself aloud, "I need a haircut and shave."

It bothered Gene some that he'd neglected his own hygiene so severely. He guessed he'd been too long in the hills. He'd longed for their company and now that he had it, there would have to be some adjusting in his ways. He wasn't going to be able to argue with himself anymore either, not aloud anyway, and he would have to bathe more regular. At least with a good haircut, the sores and scabs on his head might go away. Now he realized he probably would never win another argument. Jessie always won and she would stop the self-answering he'd been doing.

Fleas, well, they would go away with a close haircut and a good bath.

He didn't get a word in for twenty minutes as Jessie and Meg fussed over him. Jake, on the other hand, just sat in the corner where he usually sat, watching the commotion, the hill with the rock, and the property entryway with a monkey-faced grin on his mug.

In the ensuing days, Gene told of his adventures crossing the mountains. He told of the sites he had seen. He told of the time with Sullivans and their salvation commitments. He made light of some of the more serious events. He was almost beside himself with glee when he told of his treachery and the sugar cubes. He told of how God had protected him with a timely avalanche taking out his pursuer. It took him a lot of time and days to recount of his adventures. He literally lost track of time while being there. It was so, so good having Jessie close by and Jake's dry humor was a lift.

All these old cow-camps and line shacks had a cribbage board and at least one dog-eared deck of cards. Cribbage board and cards were more important in this part of the world than a good coffee pot, although not much more important.

In the days spent recuperating, Gene and Jake spent much evening time playing Cribbage. "Fifteen two, fifteen four and a pair is six and one for his nibs makes seven" was repeated innumerable times. Out of some hundred eighty games over five weeks, neither could best the other more than two or three games before the other would catch up and maybe pass as the overall winner. It was a good time, although the effort to stay alive had become a major chore. Gene's mind kept wondering about the children; grown as they were, he just couldn't push the thoughts aside. The thought of Bonnie being in danger bothered him.

Journal entry:

"This will be my last journal entry. I believe if I experience another alter-world, I will just stay in it. This real-life experience has been one beyond anything I could dream up. It has been a real nightmare. I don't need to refer to any journal to know now what is real and what is not. All I have to do is look at my reflection in a pool or a mirror."

Over the next few weeks, he gained strength and weight, even with as little as there was to eat. The cabin was small, so he continued to sleep outside. The nights became warmer than any he could recently remember. The one night he tried to sleep inside gave him claustrophobia so bad he didn't sleep. Restlessness had set in and he was in need to be out and about.

Gene had quit conversing with himself, at least outwardly. Jessie, on the other hand, could see when he did talk to himself inwardly and admonished him. "Stop that right now. Do you want people to think ya daft?"

Well, maybe a little, he'd think, *but I'm not totally crazy. Well, maybe just a little.*

Gene made up his mind to find Bonnie, wherever she was. He decided domestic life had become cushy and so made the announcement at supper. He was going to strike out the next day for Lumberton, some thirty miles away. He planned to find the Honorable Judge Alford C. Millner for information as to location of his baby daughter. Strange, Gene hadn't thought about Bonnie in that way since she was a preteen. Maybe he had gone a little daft.

Better keep quiet, he thought to himself. *You don't want to let on that you might be losing it. Am I losing it?*

The thought dogged him for the next few weeks.

Gene set off just a bit after day break. Jake had tried to dissuade him, telling him Jessie didn't want to lose him again like she thought she had before. Gene assured Jake as he had Jessie before, he would be okay. He'd done this before, and he'd return if he knew where to return to. If they moved, they were to leave a note or clue so he could find them. They had agreed, and he left not by the road, but by a back forest path where other people weren't likely to be traveling.

Lumberton wasn't so far away by direct line. It was, however, fifty miles by foot. He spent the first three days moving rapidly, then, as he closed on the remains of civilization, he became ever-so-cautious as to his movements. These were perilous times. This late spring time was a time when people would starve if they had survived the winter. Now, before growing season could produce sustenance, more would starve or in desperation rob, kill, and steal anything that would keep them alive. Many had already eaten the seed which could have multiplied one hundred fold when planted.

Gene saw few and they hid in fear and mistrust of any stranger. Those Gene had little concern about. The ones he did not see were of greater concern. He made a point not to go where he could be ambushed. Blind corners, hidden trail passages, and confining corridors like streets with rows of abandoned dwellings he avoided. If these homes were away from water, they most likely had been abandoned. He would detour a mile off his path, two if need be, to avoid such places of possible ambush. He had learned that particular lesson already.

At this point, he needed directions to the Judge's headquarters. He watched for an opportunity to ask questions of anyone who would be of little threat to himself. Two days after he started seeking information, a skinny child of about ten or twelve years approached him in the open, begging for food. Gene produced a handful of jerked meat as an inducement for information. The child took the food eagerly and directed Gene down the road about two miles.

Gene quickly moved out and away for fear of being mobbed by others for the food he carried. Upon reaching the indicated destination, Gene saw two heavily armed men. He watched some time and they seemed to be guarding the approach to the Judge's ranch. Gene decided to approach. The first demanded his purpose for being there.

"I've come looking for the Honorable Judge Millner," Gene stated.

"And what business would you have with him?" demanded the shorter of the two.

"My name is Shaky. I understand my daughter works for him as a Marshal. I need to see her. If he can help me, I'd be obliged.".

"I'll convey your message. What did you say your daughter's name is?" the guard asked.

"Her name is Bonnie Tucker." Gene noticed the look of interest from the second guard.

They disarmed Gene and set him where one could watch while the other disappeared down the access road to the ranch site. Sometime later he returned and stood talking to the other guard and then he turned to Gene and stared. Gene said nothing for a long time. After a time, he asked if he could talk with the Judge. The response was, the Judge was occupied and would let them know when he was ready.

Waiting another half an hour, Gene stood and was about to inquire further when a stout gentleman came walking down the road from Gene's right. Gene stepped back so as not to impede the man's progress. He drew closer, then stopped near Gene. The guards weren't disturbed by his presence.

"Well, they got you waiting I see," the man commented. "Been waiting long?"

"A while," replied Gene.

"You here to see the Judge?" the man asked, as if making casual conversation.

Gene sensed something about the conversation was not what it seemed to be on the surface. How did this guy know he was waiting? Why didn't the guards make a challenge of this guy like they had Gene? Gene decided to say nothing voluntary until this strange situation righted itself. The guards had his guns and pack, and yet this man walked around seemingly unarmed.

"You Judge Millner?" Gene asked.

"Why are you asking?" the man said, not answering Gene's question.

"Because I want to know and it's none of your business unless you're the Judge."

"You're kind of an insolent fella, aren't you old timer?" the man retorted.

Gene could see this was going nowhere. If this was the Judge, as Gene suspected, there would be nothing to gain by building animosity between them.

"I apologize if I insulted you. I'm just here to obtain some personal information, then I'll be on my way," Gene replied.

They stood looking at each other, each sizing the other up. Gene tried to not show his irritation with the situation. He was being made to wait a very long time at best, or there was some deception occurring, which wasn't a thing Gene appreciated.

Finally, the man made a comment which was as much a question as a comment. "So you're looking for one of my most valued officers, is that it?"

So this is the Judge, thought Gene. *Why is he being so evasive in answering a simple question?*

"If you're talking about my daughter Bonnie, yes I am. What can you tell me?" Gene was getting impatient now.

"Who are you, what's your name, and can you prove it?" the Judge asked. "We're not in a habit of giving information to anyone about our officers."

Gene hadn't thought about or even considered protocol that must be followed by these agencies. Gene hadn't possessed, nor had he carried, an ID for half a year now. How was he going to convince the Judge he was who he said he was? He explained his predicament, trying all the while to think of a way to convince the Judge he was Bonnie's dad.

"My name is Gene Tucker," Gene replied in near desperation. "Most people don't know that is my name. In fact, no one would know who I am if you called me Gene Tucker. Everybody simply calls me 'Shaky.' That is how I am known."

"Mister, you are going to have to prove you are who you say you are before I will give you one shred of information about my officer,"

Judge Millner flatly stated. "Bring me something, preferably a photo ID, or an unaltered photo of you both that establishes your identity, and I will be pleased to help you. If she is your daughter, you should appreciate the level of protection I keep around her. There are many who would like her demise. I don't believe you are one, but I'm not willing to take the slightest chance. I hope you understand. Will you tell me where I can reach you if Bonnie wants to find you?"

"Ah. . . I'm not sure. I've been traveling this last year looking for her brother across the mountains," Gene replied.

"Did you have success in finding him?" inquired Millner.

"No. . ." replied Gene, wondering how much he should reveal. "He was traveling out of state on business when the lights went out. I don't think he'd had a chance to return home yet. If that's all then, I'll try to find some form of ID and be back. If you see her, tell her I'm going home by way of my office. Maybe I can locate something that hasn't been burned or destroyed. I'll be back."

Gene mumbled, "Lord, I thought red tape was bad before the EMP; now it is worse. Obtaining documentation is going to be rough." Gene hadn't realized he'd reverted to mumbling to himself.

Millner must have heard part of Gene's thoughts because he responded, "I agree and I am ever-so-sorry things have to be this way. If you are who you say, be very careful. There's a sizable bounty out for your hide by one Sergio Campella."

Gene stopped momentarily, looked at the Judge, then started away. The Judge turned and walked past the guards on his way to the ranch stead. Passing the guards, he gave instructions for the return of Gene's pack and arms. The guns were returned, unloaded of course, and not given until the Judge was well out of sight.

Gene started much the way the Marshals had gone when returning to the settlements. He as a habit started looking for shelter early. This trek would take him close to Jake's ranch. He might stay there the day after tomorrow night.

336

Chapter 32

Tobias

A week had passed since the girls left the ranch. After Bonnie's drastic turn to domestic ways, she and Chuck decided to stay at the ranch with Oliver and Minnie. The warming spring sun made the days pleasant and each day was greeted by the four with anticipation of the next. These were good times and the past memories possessed by Bonnie and Chuck had become distanced from today;s life.

Bonnie took all the fencing material she could carry while Chuck carried several steel T-posts, a post driver, a claw hammer, and fencing pliers around the trail west that lead to the back pasture. The cow would be pastured there this spring. They worked until noon splicing fence wire the weight of snow had broken and set steel posts to reinforce weakened wood post sections. They worked well together, although Chuck had no idea how to splice barbed wire or how to stretch it. Bonnie showed him how to splice and stretch a wire tight as a fiddle string with nothing more than the claw hammer. This was a skill passed down to her by ancestors and which only a few knew unless they had been doing generations of fence mending. Most in these modern times used cumbersome rope wire stretchers or the ratchet style jack and ladder stretchers to tighten strands of barbed wire.

Meanwhile, Oliver and Minnie busied themselves about the house exterior cleaning, yard cleaning, and ordering the winter's general disarray. Oliver said, "God is not a God of disorder. We should strive to be beings of order, not disorder." Oliver raked the yard and cleaned the barn thoroughly before he started preparing the garden for early spring crop planting. Minnie had taken inventory of the seed saved from the previous year and the excess kept from years before. It was critical now to be a good steward of the seed. It wasn't like one could go to the seed store in town these days.

As busy and focused as he was, he suddenly saw a man walking up the entry road nearing the farmstead. He watched as he called out, "Greetings, stranger," all the while hoping to alert Minnie of the presence of the stranger. His greeting was of no avail. Minnie was in the depths of the pantry, moving and cleaning the contents therein. Evidence of unwanted residents the feline guard had let slip by lay on the floor and shelving.

The stranger appeared large-boned, thin, and a bit shorter than six foot tall. He was shabbily dressed and carried what Oliver guessed to be an old 8mm Mouser with the barrel sawed off. The stock was skinned up and scarred. The metal bluing had long since given away to rust in non-caressed places. The bayonet holder and a portion of the forearm went the way of the original barrel length. Oliver thought as the man approached, *What a shame to disfigure such a fine rifle.*

"Hello there, mister," the man greeted Oliver in an easy flowing statement. "Would you have food for a traveler? We're about as hungry as any person can be. I got some friends who need food too."

"Well, we don't have much, but we wouldn't think of turning a stranger away to starve. If you'll wait here, I'll fetch some food and fresh water," Oliver said as he tried to think how to warn Minnie about the new arrivals.

Rather than propping the rake against the side of the house as he usually would have done, he retained the rake up to the front porch and door. While he approached the door, he called out to Minnie. The man motioned to somebody down the road to come ahead.

"How many of you are there?" Oliver asked in louder than usual voice, feigning a touch of deafness in hopes Minnie would be forewarned.

As he stepped through the door, the stranger shoved through right behind Oliver, pushing Oliver ahead.

"I'm sorry, mister. I stumbled," The man exclaimed.

Oliver turned to him and said, "We don't allow guns in this house. Please, if you would, take it outside and wait. I'll bring some food to you and your friend there."

"No, mister. I believe I'll stay right here. Me and Pauli a comin' there. The other two can wait outside."

Oliver said nothing and in a moment Minnie came through the kitchen door.

"Oliver, who are you tal—" she stopped her question in mid-sentence.

"These men are looking for food. Can we rustle up something for them to eat?" Oliver asked.

"I can find something. Give me a moment and I will put it on. How many are there?" she asked.

"Well, Grandma, there are four of us, but we can eat like a dozen. Grandma, we haven't been introduced. My name is Tobias. The other there in the door, he's Pauli."

"Tobias," said Oliver, "a Greek name meaning, 'the goodness of God.'"

"Well, old man, I don't know anything about 'the goodness of God,'" Tobias sneered. "He hain't been so good to me, as near as I know."

Minnie set about fixing a meal of eggs, canned venison, and canned beans with onion stirred in, smothered in home-churned butter. She set a chilled pitcher of milk out. She set the plates and eating utensils out. Tobias stood where he could watch her and Oliver as they prepared the meal.

"You have kids living here?" he questioned.

Oliver quickly replied before Minnie could say anything. "We have no children."

"Uh huh," Tobias said with doubt in his voice. "You, for their sakes, better not be storing me, old man."

Oliver let that slide. He picked up two plates, filled them with food, and carried them to the door. Pauli confiscated one before the one youth outside could take hold. Tobias didn't wait to be served. He filled a plate to the brim afterward, allowing Minnie to fill a fourth for the other young man outside. As she started to the door, Pauli blocked her way, forcing her to hand the full plate to the young man by reaching under Pauli's arm. She turned back to the kitchen, contemplating what her next action should be. She settled on heating a pot of water to boil. When quizzed about her actions, she explained the dishes would need to be washed when the meal was done. All the while, she watched Oliver for any signal he might send.

Tobias's table habits put pigs to shame. He slurped and chewed with his mouth open all the time, allowing dribble to run down his chin, then wiped his mouth and face with his dirty shirtsleeve. He belched loudly, laughing and extolling how the belch was a sign of how good the food was.

Oliver watched for an opening, but Pauli was equally watchful of Oliver himself. The two outside were oblivious of the tensions inside. They ate as if they had not eaten in weeks. *They probably haven't*, thought Oliver. *Maybe they would eat, get sleepy, and doze for a moment. Too bad Minnie couldn't have slipped a sleeping pill in the beans*. Well, he would wait and Minnie would be ever watchful. Over the years, they had started to think alike and so they would wait for an opportunity. When it came, action would be sudden.

Tobias, however, didn't seem affected by a full belly. He just kept belching, laughing, and in general being obnoxious, seemingly trying to shock the residents to see their reaction. They didn't react. All of a sudden, Tobias got up and started looking into empty jars, pots, and containers, shaking them, turning some upside down and spilling the contents throughout Minnie's tidy kitchen.

She finally couldn't stand the intrusion any longer and demanded, "What are you looking for?"

"The egg money, Grandma. All you old farmer women have money in a jar, so where do you keep it?" he demanded.

"There isn't any. Where do you think I would get money? There isn't anybody around to buy eggs and if there were they wouldn't have money anyway. We would share," she replied with a little edge of spite in her voice.

Tobias grabbed her by the hair and pulled her around, showing her his ugliest threatening face. Oliver must have reacted, he didn't remember, because Pauli had stepped to him and shoved a ten-inch dagger into Oliver's stomach. Oliver struck him with a daunting backhand to the bridge of the nose, knocking Pauli against the wall.

Withdrawing the knife directly out the way it had gone in, he made an arching horizontal slash as Pauli came back off the wall toward him. Oliver could see Pauli's esophagus opened for a split second just before the carotid artery spurted blood all over the wall, window, and floor.

Tobias, seeing the commotion, turned to see Pauli grasping his throat. He started to raise his sawed-off rifle at Oliver when Minnie hit him with the scalding water followed by a glancing sharp blow with the pot to his head. He turned, striking Minnie on the head with the butt end of the rifle. Turning in time, Oliver slammed the rifle out of Tobias's hand. The gun hit the floor, discharging the bullet and sending it through the wall between the kitchen and Bonnie's bedroom, then out the window, shattering the glass as it went. Oliver reached for Tobias and in a desperate attempt to escape, Tobias turned to retrieve the gun. Oliver locked his left arm around the man's neck and shoved the knife as deep into his back as it would go. The entry point was between the ribs just below the shoulder blade on the right side. Oliver twisted the blade for maximum effect, grabbed the waist band on Tobias's pants, and hurled him out the open door into the dirt walkway beyond the porch edge. Tobias writhed for a short time, tried to arise, and then went limp in the dust. The two young men just stood with mouths agape as events unfolded.

Oliver turned toward Minnie, but halfway across the dining area, collapsed facedown on the dining table, scattering plates, glasses, uneaten food, spilled milk, and silverware. He held there for a moment, then slipped off the table crossways onto a chair, causing it to upset and bouncing a second backward as he thudded to the floor motionless.

Bonnie and Chuck had finished their task and frolicked, flirting, and generally playing with each other's affections as they returned toward the buildings. Chuck had caught Bonnie around a tree and gently set her to the ground before he planted a series of kisses on her. She giggled and relaxed at his advances.

A shot with the sound of glass breaking from a window shattering followed. They both sat up in wonder, then broke into a dead run to where they could see the house. Coming from behind the house, they could see nothing except the broken window in their bedroom.

For one of the few times in the past year, Bonnie was unarmed. Chuck likewise had put the idea of war behind himself forever. He planned to live a peaceful family life forever more.

Bonnie grabbed up a round rock just the size of a small grapefruit, although she hadn't seen a grapefruit lately. She found a 3/8s re-bar used in the past for electric fencing barrier and started toward the house. When she looked through the broken window, she could see Minnie's leg and foot on the floor through the open door. Chuck held the fencing pliers like a tomahawk as he went to the other corner of the house to peek around.

Together they moved as a team, two parts of a well-oiled machine. As Chuck came to the next corner at the front of the house, a young man with a rifle stepped face-to-face with him. Startled, he stepped back to raise his gun in defense just as Chuck slapped him alongside the head with the flat of the fencing pliers. He went down, dropping his rifle to the ground.

Bonnie, having emerged on the other side of the house, saw a man down in the walkway and another man, a youth, turned to run away from the house. She let fly with the rock, intending to hit him in the head. Her aim was errant and the rock struck him in the thigh, causing him to fall like a running horse with a broken leg. His gun went skittering across the driveway gravel far out of his reach as he reached to catch himself in the ensuing fall.

Having secured the outside, Chuck went in the house ready for combat. Bonnie was about to follow after rendering her captive immobile. She helped a little with a swift strike to the other leg using the re-bar and retrieved his unpossessed gun. As quickly as Chuck had entered, he came right back out the door. He had seen carnage in his life, in combat, and in medical emergencies, but nothing affected him like what he saw inside this dwelling. He ejected all he had eaten for the last day over the porch railing.

"Bon, don't go in there," he croaked. "Don't go in there. You can't do any good! Don't!" He heaved nothing for the second time. He regained his physical countenance and returned inside. Bonnie just stood, fearing the worst.

When he came back out he croaked, "Dead. They're all dead."

"Oliver, Minnie, and who else?" she asked.

"One other, I don't know who he is. It appears Oliver put up a good fight, but I don't know these people," he said.

"Oh God, why Oliver and Minnie?" she pleaded as realization set upon her. "God, please not Oliver and Minnie." She pleaded as she staggered to the porch rail, then sank to the ground in despair. Her realization had now become full-blown.

"We should have been here with them," she sobbed.

Chuck went to her and knelt with her. Then he heard something from her of which he hadn't been previously aware.

"God, what have you done with my daddy? Where is he? Where is Mama?" she blurted.

They spent many minutes there before Bonnie succumbed to exhaustion. Her emotion was so intense, both forgot about the two that they had disabled. The first Chuck had knocked senseless had regained his consciousness and now was trying to help the other escape the area. Chuck threw up the rifle and ordered them to stop. They, seeing the hopelessness of their effort, stopped their futile flight.

Settling Bonnie in the barn on the last of the remaining hay, Chuck secured the captives to a support post with discarded bailing twine left over from years past. He screwed up enough courage to reenter the house. Oliver and Minnie shouldn't be left that way. He went in and moved Oliver covered with a bedsheet to the porch. He gathered Minnie to place her with Oliver when he noticed an ever-so-slight pulse and nearly nonexistent breath. Lifting her gently, he placed her on her and Oliver's bed. He wet a rag with cold water and wiped the mess from the kitchen off her face. She had a large lump on the left side of her head. Chuck could see the swelling and the large hematoma under her hair. Her shallow breathing concerned him greatly.

Going back to the barn, Bonnie now sat staring into space. Her demeanor didn't indicate she was aware of the two tied to the post and they weren't drawing any of her attention.

"Bonnie, Minnie is still alive," Chuck gently said. "I didn't feel a pulse at first."

She turned her head toward him. He could see the tears, the anger, the frustration, and the resolve. That look nearly terrified him as he observed his love's pain.

"Bonnie, Minnie needs our help. I put her in their bed, but she's in bad shape. She needs our help. Bonnie, are you with me?" he calmly said again. Bonnie's red-rimmed eyes wonderingly looked up and found Chuck's as she slowly came around to reality from the shock she had been overcome by. Bonnie all of a sudden was up and ran toward the house. Chuck able to catch her before she reached the porch and directed her to the back door entry, shielding her from the carnage inside. When Bonnie had settled at Minnie's side, Chuck returned to the barn.

"Mister," one of the captives said meekly, "is there anything we can do? We didn't know Tobias and Pauli were going to do that. He, Tobias, was our leader and threatened to shoot us as deserters if we didn't stay with him. He was a rotten dude. Can I help you?"

Chuck weighed the circumstances and asked them a number of questions. Obviously, the older of the two was in a great deal of pain. As near as Chuck could tell, Bonnie's rock had cracked the bone in his leg. Chuck untied them and tended to the elder's leg. Chuck asked the younger of the men his name.

He replied, "My name is Chuck, short for my given name."

"And your given name would be?" queried Chuck.

The reply was slow in coming, "Well, it's Chucaro. It's a Mexican name. I'm named after my grandfather."

"Well, Chuck, my name is Chuck too," replied Chuck. "And what's his name?"

The younger Chuck said, "He's Bob. He's my older brother. We came to Riverton from Texas to work on a ranch just before the electricity went off. We were drafted by that MLS and assigned to Tobias as aids. He was a mean SOB to work for. He beat Bob twice and threatened to shoot us if we tried to leave."

Chuck had given Bob some of the last painkiller he had for the leg. Chuck believed the leg to be fractured but had no way to tell for sure. The other leg had been bruised and was very painful as well.

"And what is Bob short for—Robert?" Chuck asked as he tended to the older youth.

344

"Well, my formal name is Roberto, the same as my father," Bob replied.

"Do either of you know how to milk a cow?" Chuck asked.

"Of course," said Bob with some indignation. "We both do."

"The cow needs milking in a while. You can do that while I tend to your boss and clean up the house," Chuck flatly said.

Young Chuck offered his help. Chuck turned his offer down, fearing what the carnage would do to his mind.

"I'll tell you what, Chuck. We're going to need graves dug. The tools are in the shed. I'll show you where. We'll need three, but the other two are to be away from Oliver's. If you can start, it would be of help. In the meantime, I'll start on the preparations."

After checking in on Bonnie, who was reading scripture from Oliver's Bible and holding Minnie's hand, Chuck took young Chuck to the purposed grave sites. Leaving young Chuck to dig, he returned to the house and started removing Pauli to the porch, wrapping him in a sheet like Oliver had been. Next he did Tobias. When laid out the way they would remain for eternity, he started cleaning the gore from the interior. Occasionally he would look in on Bonnie. Nothing changed. Bonnie would wet a cloth and touch it to Minnie's lips. With another damp cloth, she would wipe Minnie's face and forehead. Minnie never so much as fluttered an eyelash or twitched a finger the whole time.

As much as he'd wanted to prevent it, it occurred to Chuck that Bonnie must have seen the living and dining room areas in all their carnage. She had to have seen the gore to retrieve Oliver's Bible.

After removing the blood-stained curtains and soiled throw rugs, Chuck started with a bucket of cold water and a mop, rendering the mop water crimson red. Now nearly dark, he dumped the last slightly pink mop bucket of water. Chuck cleaned and reordered the kitchen and set to preparing a simple meal. He was so occupied with the tasks he had been doing, he didn't hear or see young Chuck enter the back door with the pail of fresh milk.

"What'd ya want me to do with this?" young Chuck queried.

Startled, Chuck stepped back in surprise. "Oh, I guess we'll skim the cream, pour the milk into the jars, and cool them in the cellar out there," he replied. "If you want to bring Bob, we'll eat directly."

Young Chuck followed his instructions and disappeared outside with the jars of milk and cream. Moments brought him back with Bob in tow, his arm over his shoulder for support. Bob was pale from discomfort. When Chuck called Bonnie, she emerged from the bedroom looking more haggard than Chuck had ever seen her. Both boys stayed steady and wearily watched. No mistaking it, they were afraid of her. Bonnie had an abandoned look, that look of one who is in deep mourning. Her eyes looked hollowed, with dark puffy circles bordering each. She said nothing but sat with a bowl of home-canned venison stew and a glass of cool milk.

The young men took theirs, quietly sat, and started eating before Chuck joined them.

Bonnie exploded in a tirade about who and what they were. "Are you heathens? Haven't you learned to be thankful for the provisions, and yes, for life itself, which has been spared you each today?"

Startled, they both pushed back from the table as she lambasted them for their insensitivity. When she was done, Bonnie returned thanks for the meal, then demanded they commence to eat. They did watchfully and gingerly with the best manners their Mama had taught them. That also included Chuck, who wasn't very hungry after the day's events. He ate anyway, not wanting to draw Bonnie's ire further. Bonnie, on the other hand, ate little while slowly stirring the stew round and round and back and forth in the bowl. Finally, contents half-eaten, Bonnie returned to the bedroom and then came out and refreshed the water she had been tending to Minnie with.

"Bonnie, I'll sit with her a while. You need to get some sleep," Chuck offered.

She shook her head over and over slowly and with a tear running down her cheek. "There's nothing I know to do for her. I just don't know what to do," she croaked.

"I know," said Chuck. "I don't, either, except to pray and I know you've been praying. You know better than I about that."

They stood for a long time saying nothing, his arm around her shoulders and her hand gently holding Minnie's. He finally guided her to the soft chair at the end of the bed and provided a pillow for her to rest her head on. He sat in a straight chair for much of the night while both the others rested.

The youths retired to the barn where their bedrolls were located. The cow had been milked, the chickens penned up for the night. Bob had taken some Tylenol for the painful leg. Young Chuck's hands were sore from digging, but he was youthful strong and physically farm tough. This day and the week would leave a tattoo on his mind that would never go away.

Bob didn't sleep until nearly morning so wasn't awake when young Chuck had risen and started milking. Bonnie had stirred and built a fire in the stove before daylight crested the ridge in the east. A very warm morning it was for this early in the year, especially at this altitude. She poached eggs in milk and opened a jar of canned venison, which she fried in the heavy iron skillet Minnie always used for breakfast. She sautéed an onion and served it all on the plate when everyone had come in.

The Chucks spent the morning digging the graves to completion. The bodies of Tobias and Pauli were hauled up the hill and unceremoniously interned six feet under. The time would come later for formal services. Bonnie insisted in helping Chuck move Oliver's body to the grave site. They built a crude pine coffin in which he could rest. During that time Bonnie said nothing.

When time came for the graveside service, Bonnie read aloud from the NIV Bible:

Psalm 23 and Ecclesiastes 3 *1 There is a time for everything, and a season for every activity under the heavens:2 a time to be born and a time to die, a time to plant and a time to uproot,*

3 a time to kill and a time to heal, a time to tear down and a time to build,

4 a time to weep and a time to laugh, a time to mourn and a time to dance,

5 a time to scatter stones and a time to gather them, a time to embrace and a time to refrain from embracing,

6 a time to search and a time to give up, a time to keep and a time to throw away,

7 a time to tear and a time to mend, a time to be silent and a time to speak,

8 a time to love and a time to hate, a time for war and a time for peace.

9 What do workers gain from their toil?

10 I have seen the burden God has laid on the human race.

11 He has made everything beautiful in its time. He has also set eternity in the human heart; yet no one can fathom what God has done from beginning to end.

12 I know that there is nothing better for people than to be happy and to do good while they live.

At that point, Bonnie broke, sobbing as she had before. Chuck embraced her, consoling her and offering comfort. These were hard moments for all. Even young Chuck wiped tears from his face as he watched the agony in front of him. Finally, Bonnie placed an early spring flower on the pine board casket and turned to attend Minnie in the house. Chuck and Bonnie walked toward the house with his arm around her shoulders. He sent a silent signal for Bob and young Chuck to fill the grave over Oliver's remains. They waited until Chuck and Bonnie were beyond the range of the hollow sound of the dirt hitting the casket before they started shoveling.

In the days following, Minnie showed no improvement. Bonnie became quiet, contemplating. Chuck and the youth went about with daily chores. Chuck repaired the window with a new wood shutter. There wasn't glass to replace the broken one with. Winter fences were repaired, the garden was soundly tilled, and Chuck located a flat piece of sandstone on which he carved the headstone information for Oliver Saughterhill, Born 1931, Died 2019. Saughterhill was a long name to carve on the stone, but it was completed and done with great care. Chuck found Oliver's birth date in his Bible. He made two grave makers more out of slab wood for Tobias and Pauli.

Bonnie accompanied him when he hauled the stone to Oliver's resting place. The stone was a fitting addition at the head of the grave mound. They stood for a time paying respects, then walked hand in hand to the house.

Bonnie hadn't left Minnie's side for more than half an hour since the day of the event. She was realizing recovery for Minnie wouldn't happen. She said so to Chuck and he agreed. There just wasn't any response from Minnie to any stimulus they had tried. Her body was failing fast. She hadn't eaten and the only water she'd taken came from what Bonnie could get in her mouth with a damp rag slowly dripped so as not to choke her.

The next day, Chuck took young Chuck up to the graveyard and they started a new grave next to Oliver. They gathered wood for a new coffin and located another sandstone slab similar to Oliver's headstone to place on Minnie's grave when the time came. Two days later, Minnie expired. She never awoke from the coma. The following day, services were held and Bonnie again read over her friend and lately her mentor. She wept the same as before, then left the graveyard and went to the house. The boys completed the burying.

In the evening, Bonnie looked at Chuck with a direct firm stare. "I'm so sorry, Chuck. I truly am."

"What have you to be apologizing to me for?" he asked.

"I just can't sit by and let no-goods, marauders, and thugs do this to people. I took an oath to arrest and deliver perpetrators to trial and that's what I'm going to do," she said with firmness. "And I'm starting with these two!"

"Bonnie, these boys aren't criminals. You've talked with them, ate with them, and watched them work. They aren't bad guys," Chuck exclaimed.

"Honest, Miss Bonnie, Chuck and I never hurt nobody," said Bob. "We just fetched and carried for the others. We weren't mean like them, honest. Please, can't you let us go? We won't do anything bad to anybody ever."

Chuck and Bonnie were about to have their first fight, an argument that could affect their relationship forever. Chuck was at his wit's end trying to figure a way through Bonnie's resolve.

"I leave in the morning with these two. You can come along if you want," she said.

They all just sat speechless as Bonnie collected her weapons and travel equipment. There was no persuading her otherwise. She took the boys to the barn and tied them to the post they'd been first tied to, returned to the house and went to sleep without a word to Chuck. Chuck laid awake most the night, thinking through several possible resolutions, none of which seemed satisfactory. He thought about releasing the boys so they could escape.

That wasn't a solution, either. He decided he would vouch for the boys if and when they stood before the Judge. Hopefully after some sleep, Bonnie would come to her senses.

First thing in the morning, Chuck requested they talk. She agreed to listen only. He started with how important their relationship was to him. He followed with understanding how important her sense of duty was to her and how he wanted to encourage it. He needed her company and. . .

"Oh, Chuck, I love you so much, but please understand." Bonnie turned with tears streaming down her face and walked out the door. Going to the barn, she stopped, looked and then turned away toward the trail which led to the Mindonhall Sawmill Road over the plateau leading some thirty miles to the Judge's headquarters at Lumberton. Chuck in preparation for the trip had packed his gear as well. Grabbing it up, he ran to the barn, untied the ropes, and gave hasty instructions to Bob and young Chuck to stay with the place, take care of it, and be watchful of strangers.

"Trust no one. There will be more coming to the hills now that spring has broken. They'll be foraging for supplies. Stay vigilant always, always and be armed," he said over his shoulder as he followed his bride away from the closest thing to Shangri-La he had ever experienced.

Chapter 33

The Marshals Four

The Mindonhall Sawmill Road wound high in the spruce and aspen forests for the first twenty miles. Piles of slash lumber and sawdust mounds still existed after eighty years at the sites where milling had taken place. Millions of board feet of lumber had been harvested there and shipped out prior to the great depression. In the old days, logs were milled on the mountain, producing the lumber sold in the valley. Delivering lumber to the rail head at Lumberton became a daily event. The narrow gauge rail hauled the product to Riverton and points beyond. Many brave men hauled the loads of newly-sawn lumber down the Mindonhall Road to Lumberton on lumber wagons and later on lumber trucks. Many loads had been lost, as evidenced by the skeletal remains of wagons and trucks lying at inaccessible bottoms of ravines and hillsides.

The road started dropping into the valley with the meandering slope designed to control grade. This road hadn't been used for some eighty years. It was overgrown in many places and nearly not distinguishable had there not been travel ruts scarred in the forest floor. Several places the hard sand rock capstone had ruts worn into it. The trip was an easy walk, but long. There were places where the sand rock cliff had been carved out deep in the cliff to accommodate the large lumber wagons.

The four Marshals traveled Marshal-style, apart, where they could see signals from their partner. They had become rusty during the winter's stay at the Saughterhill Ranch. They all were tired after the first two nights' rest. Laurie showed the others how to make a bed in the old sawdust piles. The sawdust piles were considerably more comfortable than sleeping on the cold frozen ground. She exhorted them not to build a fire in the sawdust, as the fire would smolder for months or even years. The slash piles would do the same after the initial gigantic bonfire.

The third night there weren't sawdust piles to bundle in. Under a few pine trees where pine needles had collected from decades of shedding became the best option.

During the day, staying spread apart while descending the cliffside road was impossible. As an exercise, the first would lead to the far side of the cliffside trail and keep watch while the next moved across, and so forth. They had the opportunity to do this five times in two miles. The last would watch the rear while others proceeded ahead until the last followed past the exposure. The exposure to surrounding viewpoints dictated where the watches located themselves on either end. Molly was critical of the movements, making suggestions on how improvements could be made.

The next exercise was leapfrogging each other for the next five miles down the steepest of the decline where there was room to spread on either side of the road. At all times, line of sight visuals were maintained so hand signals could be sent. Those too had become rusty and Molly insisted on no vocal signals so the physical signals would be practiced.

Nearing Lumberton, they slowed their approach. Knowing the location of Judge Milliner's ranch compound, they planned the approach so as to conceal their presence until they arrived. Laurie and Gretchen advanced first, as they were best known by the residents. They could see one guard near the property boundary behind the buildings. Gretchen spied another in the barn loft overlooking the rear of the property. He had binoculars with which to watch. *This is too easy. There should be more.* She thought. Working their way past the outer perimeter guard, each would move while the other signaled the "all clear." Much to their surprise, they penetrated through to the barn. On the house side of the barn, Laurie started rapping lightly on the outside barn wall while Gretchen stayed concealed on the reverse side of the door where the guard should exit. When he did, Gretchen gently laid her gun barrel on the guard's neck, warning him to freeze.

"Is the boss home?" Laurie asked as she stepped out where the guard could see her.

He nodded affirmatively.

Gretchen said, "Well, go get him. We're here for further instructions."

Gretchen watched as Laurie accompanied the guard to the Judge's front door.

The guard rapped a coded signal, then abruptly stepped back. Laurie moved just as rapidly to the side before the door exploded in splinters from a shotgun blast. Gretchen, sensing something was wrong before the guard knocked, started moving to the back of the house. When she heard the shot and saw Laurie was all right, she moved like a cat to cover the back door. It cracked slightly, then the Judge emerged armed and wrapped in bandoleers.

"Judge, don't shoot! It's Marshal Gretchen," Gretchen shouted from a point of concealment. "Marshal Laurie is out front."

The Judge was ready for war. He demanded she show herself with his sawed-off 12 gauge Winchester pump ready on a split-second notice. Gretchen raised her hands high, holding nothing but air.

"What the h. . . . do you think you're doing?" he demanded. "Where's the rest? Who'd I shoot in the front?"

"Your Honor, everything's all right. We tested your security. It ain't so good if Laurie and I could get in this far. Please calm down. We are here to report for orders." Gretchen rapid-fired the comments.

The Judge studied her for a time and called out to the guard with Laurie to report on the double. He and Laurie came around the house. When he saw them, Judge Millner let loose with a string of cuss words that would embarrass a mule.

"What the ****** ** ****** do you two think you're doing, pulling a crazy stunt like this?" raved Judge Millner. "You should have been killed at the very least. I have a notion to fire you, then execute you for contempt of court. You made me blast my front door to pieces and scared the living daylights out of me. The only thing that went right was Murphy's signal on the front door. Laurie

Smith, how'd I miss shooting you? I won't miss again, you can be assured of that."

"We're awfully sorry, Judge," stammered Laurie, who was shaking from the intensity of the confrontation.

"How do you want your execution?" Judge Millner declared.

By this time, his beet-red face had paled and he had lowered his shotgun.

Molly's voice came from around the corner, "With all due respect, sir, you can execute us all, but you won't have much left in the way of marshals if you do."

"D****," he said. "D****. You all got in here without a whimper from my dogs. Murphy, where the h**** is Jones?"

"Right here, Judge," Jones said. "They got the jump on me."

"Who's left?" fired Millner.

"The guys up to the highway. I can see them coming," said Jones.

"Ya better stop them before someone gets killed, which they should for pulling a bone-headed stunt like this," Millner fired.

Jones moved without delay. The Judge commanded Murphy to get back on duty.

"Where are the others?" he demanded.

Molly responded, "Sam is waiting by the barn. She's some green, so I held her back. Bonnie and Chuck, well, they decided to get married and are retired, I guess."

She hadn't got the word "retired" out of her mouth before the Judge blew up and his face turned as red as it had in the height of their confrontation.

"Who the h*** said she could get married? It d*** sure wasn't me and it wasn't her daddy, and they will retire when I say and not before. We need them now more than ever, and that don't mean I won't hang you all for this little incident later!"

He turned and stomped back into the back door, motioning them to follow. Samantha was hand-signaled to come. She did. She now was introduced to the Honorable Judge Millner. He looked her up and down, offered a welcome, then turned, put some coffee on and set cups out all around.

"So, where is Bonnie?" Millner asked.

"Last week, we left her and Chuck at Oliver and Minnie Saughterhill's ranch over on Smaltz Mesa," said Laurie. "So why such an interest in Bonnie?"

Millner said, "I need her. She's a good Marshal and her life is in danger. The MLS put out a bounty on her this winter and on you too." He looked at Laurie. "They know who she is. They aren't sure about you. I want her safe. They want anybody who's associated with either of you, your family members, and any of your friends."

He continued, "The Vets Home Militia put a real hurt on the MLS. Those patriots, God bless them every one, two weeks ago took heavy casualties under the direction of Colonel Whitmore. The remnants from the MLS scattered throughout three counties. They're renegades and scoundrels. It's now time to go after them and we need every Marshal working hard to clean up this rabble. There are small bunches of the MLS, two to five men in a bunch wandering all over. They ran like rabbits when Whitmore hit them."

"Squirters," said Molly. It was the term they used in Afghanistan when one or more of the fighting force would break and run from the action.

Millner expounded. "Sixty-three of the MLS were killed and we lost twenty vets. The vets were outnumbered five-to-one, but training and fortitude prevailed. Three of our vets didn't die from gunshots. They had heart attacks. Whitmore captured about forty-some MLS and extracted the names of the others from them. I have a complete list here and he has a second. There is a third where only he and I know. Important you should know: Sergio Campella escaped. Word has it he is out for revenge on Bonnie and her father. He has some kind of vendetta, a fixation on destroying them each for separate reasons."

After a re-visitation of and a dressing down of the Marshals about the days "stunt," as he put it, the Judge demanded a written report on how the Marshals achieved penetration of his security. He expected it before they retired.

The day guard squad slept in the barn and the Marshals billeted in the bunkhouse. Breakfast came at seven a.m. sharp. A simple fare of one egg, fresh milk, and gravy with no toast was served.

"We keep only what we need and the rest goes to the area residents. It isn't enough, but we give what we can," the Judge said. "Laurie, I need to talk with you in private."

When apart, the Judge told of the visit from a man whom claimed to be Bonnie's dad.

"Do you know him?" he asked.

"I do, very well," she replied.

"Tell me about him: his description, his name, his mannerisms, and such," he said.

"Well, we call him Shaky. Shaky isn't his real name. I think it's Gene. Nobody knows him by Gene, though. He isn't big, maybe five-foot-six or seven tall. He kinda disappeared last year. He intended to go over the mountains to find Bonnie's brother Seth. That's the last we saw him."

"OK, that's good enough for me," said the Judge. "After we get caught up tomorrow, I want two of you to track him down and update him on all matters that concern him. Make sure he's not followed. We don't want him leading anybody to Bonnie. By the way, who officiated her wedding?"

Laurie answered, "Oliver did—he is ordained, you know. They rescued us all this winter—fed us, housed us, and ministered to us. We consider them as family, our uncle and aunt, you know. Oh, he said he sent his greetings to you. Oliver speaks highly of you, you know."

"I like Oliver and Minnie a great deal. I went to school with him and once later he was my pastor. I was displeased when he went," replied Judge Millner with some affection in his voice.

They returned to the Judge's study, where the others were waiting. Laurie took a seat near the bookcase. The Judge went through the rules as a review. He emphasized none of them could take vengeance and exact their own brand of justice, and each was expected to return any prisoner to stand trial along with evidence that supported the reason for their detainment. He went over the list of MLS names.

"You will copy these, memorize the names, and seek out each on the list. There's a second list of felons who have been found in violation of their heretofore awarded parole. These are to be considered under death sentence as pronounced at their trial when the parole was awarded. They are to be returned here dead or alive. If alive they will stand immediate summary execution.

"Miss Samantha, you're squirming. Do you have a problem with these orders? No, then listen up. In the absence of Marshal Tucker, Marshal Smith is in command. You will follow her command. If you screw up, it falls on her head, do you understand? Now I'm sending Smith and Deputy Ochoa on a special mission. Conroy and Brown, you are to proceed to the settlements and start tracking and apprehending bad guys. Listen to the residents for their opinion. You know what to do. I expect to see you all back here in one month or before.

"Do not break in again. I will shoot your pretty little butts as trespassers. In the cabinet over there you will find a set of handcuffs, each with keys. Don't lose the keys. These should be better than those ropes you use to tie your prisoners. Now I have court to hold. You're dismissed!" He walked out. They all sat silent for moments.

"Short, sweet, and to the point," said Gretchen at last.

"Well, get those names down and let's get outta here," barked Laurie, without meaning to sound like a sergeant. She was anxious to find Shaky ASAP.

They copied the names and then packed their equipment and left.

In leaving by the highway side driveway, Laurie stopped to talk to the guards. They were cordial but miffed a bit about the Marshals penetrating through security to the house on their watch.

"Don't do that again," said the taller of the two guards. "You caused us some grief and he'll not forget. We'll all be pulling double duty for the next two months."

"We apologize for that," said Laurie.

"The Judge said you stopped an older man the other day. He claimed to be the dad of one of the Marshals. Can you tell me if he indicated where he was going?" Laurie asked.

"No, ma'am. He said 'going home,' then headed off in that'a way. He didn't go the highway. He cut cross country out over them hills there. Didn't waste no time, neither," the guard replied.

"Thank you," Laurie replied. Then as an afterthought, she added, "We didn't intend to cause problems here, but if what the Judge says is correct, there are some badder dudes than us who would like to eliminate him. If we can get past you, well, those others who are far better than us with more experience could do better. Stay on your toes for all our sakes."

Laurie turned and left as Sam moved in parallel to her movements some forty yards off.

Sam first found decipherable tracks, which they believed to be those of Shaky. They coyote-trailed the tracks for some three miles losing them, then finding them several times. Then they vanished. Laurie was convinced these tracks belonged to Shaky because the style in which they had been hidden was a style which Shaky himself had taught her, Bonnie, and her sisters in outings a few short years earlier.

They located a camp for the night and spread out away from the central site to sleep. They started after Shaky again early the next day but realized he had widened the distance between them. Tracking him was taking a lot of time. Laurie made a calculated decision to head directly for Shaky's home in hopes to overtake him. The guard had indicated the general direction of Shaky's travel.

Twice they saw wondering groups of men seemingly scavenging and one group ransacking an abandoned dwelling. Sam wanted to take them full on, but Laurie reminded her their primary mission was to find Shaky. They skirted the groups and moved on while making mental notes of who and where they seemed to be headed. After two days' travel, they neared Jake and Meg's farm. The last time they had been here, it had been overrun by the MLS renegades, the dogs shot, with Jake and company missing. As they approached, they could see the premises occupied as new occupants had moved in. These occupants seemed to be a rough bunch, with one man in total command. This group numbered larger than the others. It numbered a dozen to fifteen altogether.

The Judge had said Sergio Campella had escaped with a contingent of men. Could this be them? Watching from a distance atop the rise on the west side of the farmstead, Laurie was sure she saw Campella twice. This must be them. They eased back behind the crest of the hill, being careful not to expose themselves to some unexpected lookout. Staying in the draws and using them for cover, they worked their way toward the Smith ranch some twelve miles upland.

Upon approaching the Smith homestead they eased to a vantage point that overlooked the property. This was homeland where the girls had played many hours and grown up knowing each nook and pothole. As Laurie watched, things didn't seem right. When she left, Sally, Josh, Sonja and her dad were living in the woods east of the burned-out farmstead. Easing along a little-known trail that cut around the buildings on the north, Laurie and Sam soon came to the grove where her family had been dwelling. The first person they saw was Josh. Laurie stopped and watched Josh. He seemed oblivious to her presence, she thought. About ready to call out to him, he spoke first.

"Laurie, how have you been?" he asked.

"Okay, Josh. Where is everybody?" she asked.

"Sally and your dad are on the ridge behind you. We spotted you a while ago and they went to cover the high ground. We didn't know who you were. Laurie, there's been trouble." Josh eased into the news.

"What trouble, where's Sonja?" she asked apprehensively.

"That's just it, Laurie. She's dead. They killed her, caught her by herself down at the creek packing water with her hands full and defenseless. She shouldn't have been by herself, but you know her, she was always one to just 'do it' without care. She was still alive when we found her, but, Laurie, it was bad, terrible bad. She told Zack who had done it and what they said their plans were. We buried her day before yesterday. Zack is tryin' to forgive, but he's devastated and deep angry inside. He's been prayin' a lot and we can see he's been crying. Sally too. Sally said she's never seen him so sullen and somber. We're trying to stay by him, but we can't go where he is. Laurie, they both need you." Josh spoke purposefully.

Before anything else was said, Sam, who was off to the side, indicated with a signal someone was coming. Laurie turned to see Zack and Sally descending from the hill behind, spread some hundred feet apart. Apparently they knew now who had entered their domain.

Zack said nothing. He engulfed Laurie with an all-encompassing hug. He just clung to Laurie as if he were afraid to release her. Sally hung back, edging around to Josh and watched like Sam did. Nobody noticed the tear tracing its way down Sam's cheek. When Zack finally released Laurie, he said, "You know?"

Laurie nodded her head.

Zack continued, "I thought I'd lost you both. Thank God you're okay."

"I'm fine, Daddy," Laurie squeaked. "Are you going to be okay?" She put hand on his cheek and the other reached out toward Sally.

"Well, I don't know, baby. I am better now you are here. I was afraid I lost you both and it was breaking my heart. I'm so glad you're here. Thank God, thank God," he said with his grateful raspy voice.

He grabbed her with another long embrace before turning to Sam with an inquisitive eye.

"Pardon me for my rudeness," he said quietly.

"I'm Zack Smith, Laurie's dad. This is my daughter Sally and her husband Josh. What might your name be?"

"It's nice to meet you, Mr. Smith. I'm Samantha Ochoa. I'm Laurie's friend and a Deputy US Marshal under her command." She spit it out in one long sentence. As soon as she said it, she wished she'd answered a simple answer instead.

"I'm pleased to know any friend of Laurie's, Miss," Zack replied, gaining some of his composure. Unfamiliarity tended to stiffen his composure. He turned to Sally and Josh, introducing them again. They each greeted her cordially. Sam's attention briefly focused on them and then as quickly refocused on the surroundings, being watchful for any sign of danger.

Being grouped like this in such emotional circumstances created a vulnerability Sam was not willing to allow and so she moved off to a vantage point some distance to the side where she could best observe the surroundings. Laurie made a mental note of the move and reacted to balance Sam's move. There was no appropriate time to be careless, not even now. She expressed her thought to the others and they moved accordingly. There would be time to console and comfort later.

Chapter 34

Homeward

A full year plus had passed since Gene had been to his office. He supposed it would be like all the other buildings he had seen on his forays. Most buildings that didn't have a readily accessible water source or some form of serviceable heat had been ransacked and pillaged for any useful item to aid in survival. All Gene could hope for was to find one of his desk pictures somewhat intact showing himself, Jessie, Seth, Bonnie, and Samuel standing before a backdrop of autumn Quaking Aspen trees. He would use it to identify himself to the Judge. He desperately needed to know about Bonnie.

Gene wasted no time after leaving the Judge's heading toward Pinedale where he once ran his successful business. Being careful to cover his trail, Gene moved as swiftly as he could toward Jake's ranch. He'd covered the best part of a three-day trip in a span of only two days. Crossing the river in the dark of night in order to approach Jake's ranch unseen, Gene was hidden clocked in the darkness. When the ranch house appeared through the darkness, Gene could see there were occupants. As he watched longer, there appeared to be at least half a dozen, maybe more.

Edging closer, Gene could make out characteristics of individuals. One in particular seemed familiar. It was, sure. Only one man kept his demeanor starched and pressed as his clothing. Gene had encountered him before in an alley of downtown Riverton. He had humiliated him beyond count and would pay the price if Campella caught him. If Sergio Campella knew he was watching right now, he would likely move heaven and earth to catch him.

Being ever-so careful, Gene changed his course of travel, skirting one of the low hills to the west of the ranch, then followed a steep ravine to near the top of the adjoining mesa. There he stopped. Traveling in this country after dark was not wise. He could from his stopping point observe any night campfires burning that would indicate the location of possible unwanted company like MLS members. When morning came, he could observe smoke to both the downwind and upwind directions and smell smoke from the upwind direction. He knew this vicinity well and there existed only a few likely sites where campers might be located. Sure enough, Gene could see the flicker of firelight on cottonwood trees near a small drainage with year-around water.

Resting under a large fallen cottonwood, Gene laid for a while just listening to the sounds of the country night. He took a great deal of pleasure in night sounds. There were few he didn't know. The sound of the Nighthawk swooping and circling vertical loops over and over again was one of his favorites. The shrill *peegnk peegnk* chirp was unmistakable to anyone who had ever heard it.

As he lay quiet, he sensed the sniffing and slow approach of a dog or coyote. It was unusual for a coyote to get this close to a man, especially at night. He was sure the animal wasn't a dog. As gamey as he must smell, the canine must have believed he'd discovered the feast of the week lying in wait. Knowing the animal would startle when he moved, Gene decided to wait until the canine came close. He could just make out shapes and movements by the sparse starlight. The light even faded as clouds moved from the southwest to the northeast, engulfing the celestial sparkles. Gene could see the beast with its outreached neck sniffing in his direction. No doubt this scavenger had dined on the remains of human carcasses before.

Gene stayed very still for a long time while the animal sniffed and sniffed and tested the air. Gene could smell the coyote, which meant the canine was upwind, otherwise he should have known Gene was still alive. Gene had never known a coyote to attack a large living being, but of course there could be exceptions. All of a sudden with the head thrown back a *yip yip yowl* came out of the skyward-pointed snout. Gene guessed he had just been invited as guest of honor to the family dinner. This dinner was going to be like the Thanksgiving turkey coming alive on the dining room table with a flurry of wings. Gene was nearly beside himself with glee at the surprise this feast was going to spring on his diners.

They scattered like someone had exploded a bomb among them. They didn't go far in any direction after the initial surprise. Gene could hear them stirring about in the dark. They were too cowardly to come in on him even in a group, Gene hoped. If they had eaten human food before, then all bets might be off now. Very possibly they had, in this day and age of unfettered death and mayhem, dined upon more than one human body after his or her demise. He should have spooked the first one right from the start. Bonnie had her mule, Gene had his curious imp. He liked a harmless prank and thought scattering the family pack would be amusing. It was, until they persisted. Now the joke was on him. The remainder of the night was a sleepless night. As daybreak came, the pack finally melted away to wherever coyotes spend their days after realizing Gene wasn't the next meal.

Carefully surveying the route ahead of him, Gene picked his way past several encampments of people, none of whom he knew or was familiar with. They seemed to be staying near the water where they could cook, wash, and retrieve drink. Funny somehow, these folks seemed not attuned to their environment. If it were Gene, he would have camped and defecated away from the fresh water sources. Being right on the water discouraged any remaining food game from approaching those sources. Gene saw two camps with men only having the appearance of military-type squads or more like banditos. He carefully maneuvered around those locations and moved on.

Being only half a day's distance from his old office, Gene pushed on. Now he started seeing ghostly representations of his once-known acquaintances. Many of these folks had aged decades in only the last year. Well, they might say the same about him. They appeared to be skin and bones, sickly, and mostly downcast. Gene saw Tom Summers for one. The last time Gene had seen him, Tom was a rotund five-foot-six inches tall, two-hundred-eighty-pound man. Gene didn't recognize him at first as he watched Tom shuffle past, not knowing Gene was close by. Tom now at most weighed one hundred pounds, including his clothing and the homemade bow with arrows he carried. Gene surmised the diabetes Tom suffered from for so long must have gone away. He looked gaunt but otherwise seemed to be unafflicted.

Gene saw a young woman who he believed to be only sixteen or seventeen with a newborn baby suffering a distended belly from starvation. This baby resembled the picture of those starving children seen on the TV ads for "Feed the Children," but much, much worse in real life. Gene himself was hit as if a bolt of lightning had struck him. He had not been around people, families, and even children for over a year. They were starving. How many? There was no way for him to know. He had isolated and insulated himself from such things and the shock now struck him with a blow that would have dropped an ox.

He always made a habit of staying away from the populace and off the common transportation routes during the past year. Now he had to be on the main road to Pinedale just to get to his old office. When he came to the slight bend in the highway, he could see part of the town, the older part, had burned to the ground. Well, no wonder. Even if there had been a fire department, there wouldn't be any water to fight a fire with. Public domestic water depended entirely upon electricity for delivery. Even with gravity flow systems, the electronic controls used these days became useless without electricity to manage valves and regulators.

Gene could see the brick structure where his office had been located. He could see the old Baptist Church on Main Street half a block away. There seemed to be people thereabout. He wished to avoid talking to anyone until he could get into his office.

People remaining in this location made since. Gene remembered the original Pinedale City water well was just across the street and easy to access. Gene wondered why, with all the ingenuity people had, they hadn't changed out those water control valves for manual controls. The water wouldn't be treated, but at least it could fill the pipelines from natural gravity flow.

When he approached, the front door of the building stood open. Watching, Gene saw no activity in or around the building. He approached the door and quickly stepped in. The foyer was dark. As he worked along the east wall toward the stairwell, he tripped and nearly fell over debris, likely the non-burnable parts of an old desk. Finding the opening to the stairwell, he pulled the metal door open wider and squeezed through. The stairs were built of metal framing filled with concrete used in commercial structures built in the mid-fifties. They were noisy to walk quickly on, so he carefully slipped up to the second floor where his office and a dental office had been located. Pushing open the second-floor stairwell door, he could see the place had indeed been ransacked. His office door hung on one hinge.

Past it, he could see the wood furniture and bookcases were gone. Splinters of wood from the furniture gave evidence that the furniture had been broken up—likely used for fuel. Scattered about the floor were the desk trinkets. His alabaster business card holder was in the corner. The metal remains of his wooden file cabinets with the remains strewn about the room presumably indicated the wood had been used. The wall plaques and his production awards were scattered about the floor. All were attached with hundreds of cobwebs, an indication no one had disturbed these rooms for some time. A broken award dish, his decorative pen holder minus the wooden base, and the facedown picture frame of his family were on the floor.

Gene quickly picked up the metal picture frame and turned it over to see his beloved family looking back at him through a dusty and dirt-stained glass.

Gene poked about more, then exited to the stairwell. He eased his way down to the first-floor exit. As he stepped out, he came face-to-face with half a dozen armed men. Three he recognized and for a moment he wasn't sure they knew him.

"Shaky, is that you?" the tall, gaunt Reverend Jones asked.

"It is, Reverend," Gene replied. "I needed this picture of my family."

"Well, don't stay around here," said Reverend Jones curtly. "They're looking for you and for Bonnie. She's become quite a problem for the people here. They've put out a big bounty for her and you. The word is there is a vendetta to be settled. If they catch you, they will make sure she hears and try to trap her using you as bait. There are ears and eyes everywhere looking to collect the bounty. You'd be advised to hightail it out of sight right now. We'll make sure no one follows. Do you understand?"

"Thanks for the information and thanks for the help. I'm on my way," Gene said. He then added, "I never been invited out of town before. At least there isn't tar and feathers involved."

He turned and exited east past the edge of town. The men followed at a distance. Gene saw them spread out left and right, perpendicular to his obvious direction of travel. When out of sight of any he saw, Gene made several backtracking and trail-covering maneuvers. Satisfied, he turned north a couple miles, then turned west past Pinedale a couple miles, then began to look for a campsite for the night.

Now he was near a location he had spent time in growing up as a youth. Some four hundred yards to the north was an abandoned coal mine. He made way for the mine. The dark had overtaken the evening. Gene's memory of the mine location was somewhat sketchy. He hoped nobody was using the mine now. Thinking over his plan, he abandoned the idea and found shelter near the Stevens Creek irrigation outtake. There was a nice spot sheltered by large pine trees and a thick grove of brush. Gene bedded down for the night.

Gene was determined to see the Judge in three days. That meant traveling in the barren, exposed adobe badlands to the south and west. There was little cover, except for the many adobe hills and ravines. In the summer the temperatures could reach one hundred twenty during the day. Gene always felt the heat was the reason why nothing grew there. There was no water, except for a couple small brackish streams. These would give a bellyache to any animal that drank from them. Gene filled his canteen and drank his fill from Stevens Creek before he dropped in to the "dobe" hills below.

He'd been careful to cover his tracks and cover his trail. He always made a practice of watching his back trail and traveling intentionally where he could observe his back trail. To do this took time and thought. He didn't want to take the time, but after the warning from the good Reverend Jones, Gene decided he didn't have a choice but to take extra care of his trail.

It proved to be a good decision because two hours after leaving his night camp, Gene spotted a man some half mile back on the trail where he had been. Gene set up a diversion to distract the man if he were tracking him. Gene changed direction several times. Finding hard-pan soil to backtrack on but hiding his tracks was next to impossible here. Gene thought about b-lining to the high country, where better cover existed. But the high country lay in the wrong direction for his purposes. After the first day, his tracker was still there. Gene now knew the man was tracking him. What Gene didn't understand was why he kept his distance. Could he be driving Gene toward a trap or was he waiting for others join up to take Gene captive?

Now the time had come for Gene to make a decision. He made a U-turn and made tracks right back past his tracker. During his change in direction, Gene had been within a couple hundred feet of the man on the other side of a small hill. Gene didn't want to dry gulch him. He wearied of the blood and violence. He'd experienced more than enough to last a lifetime. After Gene knew he was well past the tracker, he headed up the mountain. He'd picked a spot that set above Pinedale on the Battlement Cliffs. These rimmed the large mesa above. He wasn't taking time now, just making tracks as fast as he could. When he finally did stop, he could see part of his back trail for about a mile distant. Sure enough, the tracker hadn't stopped. He was still on his trail but seemed to be keeping his distance. Gene had widened the gap by a mile. When Gene arrived at a slide rock field, he became careful to leave evidence at the spot where he started crossing. Near the middle, Gene turned up the slide, being careful not to leave sign of that turn. He advanced two hundred feet to the top edge of the slide area and went out the direction he came in. He now was ever-so-careful not to leave a track there upon his exit.

Traveling two more miles below the battlement rim on a very plain and well-traveled game trail, Gene turned east back in the direction of his own home. The day was spent now and he found a camp in a natural cave at the base of the battlement. A bear had lived there and was not at home; it was likely foraging for food to fatten for the upcoming winter. Tomorrow would be the time to make the tracker believe he had ascended up over the battlements to the top of the mountain. The only trail to the top where one could climb up over the edge was close. Gene was near it now. The trail was a steep narrow break in the battlement rim where all kinds of wildlife traveled up and down. Gene would simply leave a discrete track here and there to point his trail up and over the top, but as for now he needed rest.

Even in the summertime, night temperatures here were cold. Gene slept well and yet just before sunrise the cool of the air at the nine-thousand-feet altitude woke him with a slight chill. He moved at first light to set his deception. Being careful not leave the slightest evidence of his retreat back down the passage, Gene was careful to not to leave evidence of his passage along the game trail, moving away eastward toward his own home. He broke off from the common trail and worked his way along pathways where deer and elk had recently traveled. He felt confident he would not be followed by anyone but a bloodhound.

Gene, now some five miles to the north of Pinedale, cut cross country toward the ridges that lead toward his home. Rather than going home, he would skirt the property and drop over the hills to the Smith ranch. He was easily two full days' hike from there. Still watching his trail from as far away as a mile, Gene saw no sign of any followers. Changing direction two more times so as to confuse his course of travel to any would-be unseen follower, Gene started down the hills back in the general direction of the Judge's headquarters.

Sitting atop the hill above the Smiths', where he and Jessie had first sat a year ago, Gene could see the burned ranch house and buildings. From this vantage point the balance of the farm wasn't viable. If the Smiths were there, they weren't at the burned-out farmstead. Gene decided to bypass the Smiths' and proceed directly to Lumberton. He watched the property for an hour, then started moving on a contour around the south face of the hillside he was on. He moved carefully, staying undercover from the sight of any who might be following his track.

Nearing a clump of juniper cedar, Gene rested on a stump created some hundred years prior by a fence post gather. The tree had been cut with a saw, leaving a blunt end stump unlike so many of those left by axe-sharpened cuttings.

"Mister, if you move, I'll blow your guts out. Do you understand?" the youngish female flatly stated with determination. She was behind him to his right and out of reach, but too close to miss if she had a weapon. Gene did as instructed. He lay facedown as instructed and placed his hands behind his waist. Quick as a cat, this little Mexican girl had the gun barrel at the base of his neck. Then she cuffed his hands. He started to try to talk his way out of this mess, but she was having nothing to do with it. His pack was abandoned and she had his rifle. That rifle wasn't much, but it would shoot. On the other hand, she carried a twenty-two over twenty gauge Savage combination rifle shotgun that had been cut down to make a combat weapon.

This brown-eyed girl moved him toward the Smith ranch. He hadn't seen anybody around or even sign of any presence there. So where had she come from? He tried again to make small talk, but she said nothing except "Move!" There was that distinctive Mexican lilt to her speech. Had the place been taken over by strangers? Nothing more was said as they walked toward the farmstead and then in turn past to a wooded area some three hundred feet to the east and behind the burnt out dwelling.

"I caught theese doode looking down on the place from up there. I brought heem to see what he knew. You want I should skeen heem or you want to do it?" she asked in an exaggerated Mexican accent to an unseen person.

Sally started to giggle, then bit her lip. "I'll skin him after we eat. Turn him loose, Sam. He's an old friend."

Gene had been captured three times, but this humiliated him more than either of the other two, yet the end results of this third capture was beyond measurable better than the other two. Sally gave him a big hug and introduced the little Mexican girl as US Deputy Marshal Samantha Ochoa. The thought of being captured by a little girl was barely dulled by the fact that the slight wisp of a girl was a US Marshal. Either way, he had been captured again.

Zack greeted him as if he were his long-lost brother returned home. Josh shook hands and Laurie, when she came in from her watch on the outskirts, gave him the hug a daughter would give a dad. They ate while Sam and Sally retrieved Gene's pack and belongings. The conversation was of good news. Included among the subjects of conversation were: Sally and Josh's marriage and Jake, Meg, and Jessie's being found safe. The conversation had avoided Sonja's misfortune but eventually came around to that news. Zack was visibly disturbed and turned away at its mention. Gene's heart simply ached from empathy for Zack, Sally, and Laurie. He needed to ask Laurie about news of Bonnie. But now wasn't the time. Their heavy hearts had overtaken the mood. Gene just sat, feeling the pain of his friends.

The following day, Gene prepared early to resume his journey. Laurie stopped him and took him aside. "Bonnie's okay. She met a great guy and they were married about a month ago. They're up—"

Gene stopped her before she could say where. "Laurie, it's enough I know she's safe for now. If they catch me, and I seem to be getting caught a lot lately, I can't tell them where she is, now can I?"

"No, I guess not," she replied.

"She's been concerned about you, though," said Laurie. "The Judge sent Sam and me to find you. He realized from what you said and what I confirmed you actually were Bonnie's dad. He's protective of his enforcement staff."

"Laurie, if you would take me toward where Bonnie is, then you can tell me where. I would like to see her. . . and her man. He must be somethin'." He paused a moment. "Laurie, if you would, what happened to Sonja?" Gene inquired.

Laurie turned away a bit, then elaborated through controlled emotions about Sonja's death and the brutality of the abuse she had received. After they had done, they tied her and beat her unmercifully, just enough to leave her alive. When Josh found her, she had been only partially clothed and he covered her with his coat and shirt. She had blood and skin under her broken nails and blood in her teeth, which Sally thought belonged to someone else. She lived long enough to tell Zack about the men and how many there were. Zack was tormented between wanting to let the Lord have vengeance and declaring all-out war on those "brutes," as he termed it. "Torment" wasn't a strong enough description for what he had been going through and the mix of emotions he felt.

Laurie explained the Judge sent her to find him with the news of Bonnie. Now that was done, she and Sam would join forces with Molly and Gretchen after they tracked and arrested the Sonja's killers.

"I'll take you to Bonnie if you like," she told Gene, "but I'll catch those dogs first."

"I would be grateful if you'd direct me toward Bonnie," Gene responded. "Maybe I can help you. I'd like to see them caught too."

They walked back toward the camp. Zack, Josh, and Sally were working on building a modest dwelling to meet the next winter's cold. They had gathered rock for the fireplace, half the logs needed for the exterior walls, and set a solid foundation for those walls. This home would have a dirt floor and two rooms. The second room would contain the old kitchen stove Zack had on the back porch at the burned-down house.

Gene's urgency to find Bonnie had been quenched some, but he still wanted to see her. Laurie and Sam were ready to move out the next morning. Gene was ready too. If Zack decided to go, he hadn't said so. Josh and Sally would stick to him like glue, whatever he decided to do. Zack tried to dissuade Laurie from leaving, but she explained she had a job to do. She would catch and arrest Sonja's attackers. Adieus being said, the three departed. Out of sight, Sam broke to one side, Laurie to the other. Gene stayed on the trail that led away from the site of the brutal attack.

Trailing was easy for several miles. They hadn't tried to cover their trail. Their direction being constant pointed the way. When they came to a paved road, their track angled onto the pavement and the accumulated dust and dirt on the seldom-traveled road pointed the way without doubt.

The Marshals found a camp that had been used for several nights. There was sign of blood and healing from wounds dished out by Sonja. Only one Marshal would confer with Gene at a time. The other always stayed vigilant. Gene showed both in turn what he could see and they did the same. Gene in turn passed the information on to the other when she came into the campsite. Gene studied the signals the Marshals used to communicate. He recognized some of the sign language that he and his kids had used when they were growing up.

About midday the fourth day, Gene stopped short, signing Sam to be alert of the hazard ahead. In turn Sam signaled Laurie. Gene couldn't see Laurie but believed neither could see the gathering in front of them. Working his way closer, Gene counted five. That would confirm what they'd found in the abandoned camp earlier and what Sonja's last words to Zack had been. Gene could see scratches on the face of one big man and another had a bloody, half-missing ear. He knew the marshals had orders to arrest if possible. He didn't understand how, being outnumbered in physical size and arms, the Marshals were going to pull this off.

He was intent on watching this crowd when he looked up, seeing Sam signal a retreat. Carefully moving back, he saw Laurie had pulled back some distance. Gathering in a discrete location, the powwow commenced. They determined to take the outlaws one by one as they ventured away or straggled behind. The plan was set. These men had no modesty. They stayed at the edge of camp to defecate and urinate. They stuck together in a bunch day and night for the next two days. Their comments were crude and their manners nonexistent. One time Gene heard a crude comment about Sonja from one that boiled his blood. These Marshals were a patient crew. They resembled Indians in their patience, in their precision and in how they planned every move. These two were cunning and Gene knew they would succeed.

A slight-built man just bigger than Gene left the group as if on a mission. He came out on Sam's side. Marshal Samantha Ochoa disappeared. Gene caught a glimpse of Laurie as she moved around the camp and paralleled Sam's direction. Gene heard nothing for hours. He so wanted to follow but feared messing up the plan of attack. All of a sudden, Sam appeared where Gene had last seen her. She carried an additional pistol strapped over her shoulder and under her arm. Laurie subsequently showed up in her regular position, where she had been before.

As evening came, another wandered from the camp with his rifle. He walked about two hundred yards from the camp where he shot a rarely-seen rabbit. Dressing it and skinning it, he forgot to tend to his surroundings. He never saw or heard the rock coming. Laurie was getting good at the "rocking," as the girls called it. A skull cracked with one of those lemon-sized rocks she liked to sling. He dropped without a sound. This man had a week-old bruise on his left cheek. Sam tied him, out cold as he was. They gagged and latched him to a nearby Russian Olive tree, not paying mind to the thorns that might be pricking the man. Frankly, Laurie couldn't have cared less. He was lucky to be alive if he did wake.

From Gene's new vantage point, he could hear the earless man and the scratched man grumbling about where the second man had gone. Finally, a third ventured to where the rabbit shot had come from. When he reached the area, he found the rabbit fur and entrails and began to swear. He mumbled about the need to share. Hunting about, he stopped instantly, seeing Sam squatted on her haunches tracing a pattern in the dirt with a stick.

"Well, little girl, whatcha doin' out here all alone?" he asked.

Sam replied, "Oh, I'm a US Marshal and I'm looking for someone to arrest, like you. You are under arrest for the rape and murder of one Sonja Smith. Drop your gun and lace your fingers behind your head now!"

Sam hadn't moved. His attention was riveted on such an innocuous being making such a bold statement. Looking about with suspension, he saw his compadres bound and gagged. Whirling about to run, he turned right into the business end of Laurie's gun.

"Whoa, now lady," he exclaimed. "Whatcha you doin'?"

"The girl you killed back there was my sister," she snarled.

"I didn't have nothin' ta do with. . ." he trailed off.

Too late, he was there and as far as Laurie was concerned, guilty. He made a lunge for her gun. Sam had slipped up on him from behind and smacked him a bruising blow over the head with a dead Cedar limb club. The weight of Juniper Cedar worked as well as Laurie's rock had on the other. Bound and tied to a tree before he awoke, they left him to gather a fresher and newer harvest. There were two left.

Three of their company having left and not having returned was making Scratch and Earless nervous. Both showed signs of anxiety now sensing something not quite right but not knowing what. Gene hadn't seen but knew the answer. These two wouldn't split apart, especially since the others had disappeared. Surely these Marshals wouldn't try to take these men one on one. Scratch's stature was as large as Sam, Laurie, and Gene all rolled into one. When Gene next saw Laurie, she motioned for another powwow. They decided Gene would approach the camp in a casual way as a sojourner might. The Marshals would approach from two other sides.

Gene downed his pack and after allotting time for the girls to attain their positions, moved toward the camp. A hundred feet or so out, he called, "Hello in the camp."

Both heads jerked around as if attached to the same string.

"Hi, gents. Do you have any spare food? I ain't eaten in three days," Gene continued.

"Who the . . . . are you?" Earless demanded.

"Oh, I'm just traveling to the place called the settlements. Do ya know how far they might be?" Gene continued, building up the distraction.

Both men were touchy and showing nervousness. The trick was to keep their attention without getting shot. Gene lifted his hands and stepped back, drawing their attention further. Then Laurie quietly commanded they freeze, as did Sam. Earless froze, but Sam had slipped in too close to Scratch and as he lunged, jerking her gun forward and to the side, and it went off. The twenty-gauge shot hit Earless high in the torso, causing him to slam sideways and down to the ground. Gene leaped to Sam's rescue, as did Laurie, after smashing Earless on the head with her rifle butt. Scratch had smacked Sam with his big fist, knocking her ten feet backwards. He was about to drop the hammer on her limp body when Gene fired. Laurie fired a split second later. The big man jerked, turned, and charged Gene from fifteen feet away. Laurie hit him with another shot to the head, which dropped Scratch at Gene's feet. Standing, shaking, Gene turned to see Earless down and moaning in his condition.

Sam, on the other hand, lay limp like a rag doll that had been tossed in a corner. Both went to Sam's side; she was out cold. Scratch had hit her on the forehead with his big fist and a lump was developing. Checking her eyes, Gene could see one pupil dilated.

This isn't good, thought Gene.

They would need ice but none was available. The river lay about a mile away and the water would be the coldest thing around. Gene's concern was that Sam might have a concussion bad enough her brain would swell. If they could keep her head cool with the water, they might stem some of the swelling. He didn't know for sure but wasn't willing to do nothing. He said so and they picked Sam up on a quickly-made makeshift litter and carried her as fast as they could to the river.

Nearly there, Sam started coming around. She showed confusion. She didn't know Gene and didn't know where she was. Laurie quizzed her about how she felt. Sam complained her head hurt terribly. She wanted to get off the makeshift stretcher, but Laurie convinced her to stay quiet. Upon reaching the water, Gene took an old bandana and wet it. He placed it on the girl's forehead for a moment. Sam winced at the touch. Gene gently encouraged her to lie quietly while he tended her wound.

"I need to check our captivities," said Laurie. She left Gene tending to Sam, who was unsure of the circumstances and why she had such a headache. She had no memory about anything for the last couple of days. So, there it was. They had three prisoners, maybe a wounded fourth, a disabled marshal who shouldn't be moved for at least a week, and an old man with one young woman remaining to carry the load. Gene knew Laurie to be capable with just a little assistance. He intended to provide that.

'Old man,' he wondered. *Where had that thought come from? Was it that I'm beginning to recognize my longevity? Yes. I feel ancient these days.*

Sam stirred, wanting to move around. Gene encouraged her to remain quiet for a long time. Sam rested with the wet rag on her head and over her eyes, which now were starting to turn black. Gene wished he had a cold steak for her to use.

Time passed, then Gene heard footsteps and quickly went to cover. One was bound, two were cuffed, and ropes were around all of their necks while Laurie walked off to the side and behind commanding the parade. Interestingly enough, the rope around their necks connected the three with a special twist. Laurie had tied a hangman's noose in the middle of the thirty-foot quarter-inch rope, placed it around the middle man's neck—not tight but snug. On each end, she had also tied a hangman's noose which then had been placed around each of the remaining necks, not tight but snug. In this way, making a break with their hands cuffed and bound would strangle the one making a break and his neighbor too.

She commanded a stop and allowed them to drink from the river. Was it sanitary? Not likely, but it was wet and these were condemned men at any rate. The old days of Miranda rights and prisoner rights went the way of electricity. They were allowed to rest and were warned to stay separated the length of their tether from each other. Gene caught a sucker fish and proceeded to dress and cook. It was a bony fish but edible for a poor man. Two of the prisoners scoffed at the fare while the third was happy to partake. Gene fed them one at a time, taking care not to be compromised as he did so. There wasn't much to eat, but it was something. Laurie and Sam watched from a distance while consuming their own food, although Sam didn't have much of an appetite.

Day dwindled into evening, then came the night. Complaining of a headache, Rockhead asked for painkiller. There was none for him or for Sam. Laurie continued to apply cool wet cloth to Sam's head. Gene stood the first watch after Laurie added a securing line to the neck tethers and tied the other end to a stout Tamarisk brush. The brush clump was small enough to make noise if the prisoners tried to work the rope loose and large enough to hold if put under great tension and strain. Sometime early in the morning Laurie relieved Gene at the watch. Sam rested, but Gene and Laurie were reluctant to let her sleep, so Gene and Sam talked until the wee hours of the morning.

The band of captors and prisoners lingered there on the bank of the river, allowing those with head injuries some recuperating rest. Gene harvested several more sucker fish, which they ate. The captured men stopped grumbling now as the morsels of roasted fish had taken on the taste of a delicacy. "Most foods taste good to a hungry man," Gene's mom used to comment.

After the third day, Laurie was anxious to start moving toward Lumberton. The biggest obstacle facing them monetarily was the crossing of the river. This river wasn't large, but cold and one would have to guard the captives while the other assisted Sam. Sam, however, was still a little confused, forgetful, and cranky, snapping at the slightest comment. During one such outburst, she threatened to "gut that pig" in Mexican if he didn't keep his eyes looking somewhere else.

Despite their objection, Laurie started the three into the water. Gene stood on the bank, overseeing the crossing with strict instructions should any one of the three try a break, he would shoot first, no questions asked. Laurie stayed up stream some thirty feet as they waded hip- then belly-deep in the frigid water. When across where Laurie could watch, Gene and Sam waded in. *By golly!* Gene thought. *This is cold like the river crossing on the log I made earlier. This crossing is wider and not as deep, but the sun hasn't pulled the chill off this water even at this time of year.*

Safely crossed and prisoners intact, they started toward Lumberton.

Chapter 35

Delivery

B onnie struck out from the ranch like a person possessed by an impending mission. Chuck was able to keep up but stayed back and to the side some distance, allowing Bonnie to be alone with her mind and thoughts. By staying apart, their travel resembled the buddy system that the Marshals had developed. Chuck knew Bonnie was aware of his presence. When ready, she would acknowledge him being there. In the balance of the day, they covered some ten miles toward Lumberton.

Their camps were separate from the other. Chuck ate cold fare, as did Bonnie. They kept within sight of each other, but Chuck stayed apart, waiting. Bonnie would join him when she had worked through her anger. At least Chuck hoped she would work through her frustration.

Chuck had become used to a bed. This sleeping on the ground wasn't his cup of tea anymore. The bed at the ranch was wonderful with Bonnie nestled beside him. Those had been the most pleasant times of his life. He longed for them now, but he supposed the honeymoon had ended.

Bonnie in her grieving was aware of Chuck's presence. She knew he was there, but somehow her "mule" had come alive and all she could think about between throbbing twangs of pain in her heart was cleaning up these bands of renegades, the remainder of the disjointed MLS.

Bob and young Chuck had described the running battles with the makeshift army that had attacked. They thought it to be a group of local resident vets who tired of the MLS confiscating goods and supplies and of their abuses. This bunch seemed to be organized. Bob didn't think they were a regular military organization. Bob said Tobias was one of the first to break and run, commanding Pauli, Bob, and young Chuck to follow. Several bunches scatted, running out before the end of the fighting. One group numbered a dozen or more men who included the boss, Sergio Campella. He, being an arrogant kind of guy, took the best with him. He was always well-dressed even in the conditions at the settlements camp. He was a no-nonsense and ruthless dictator.

Thinking back on her and Gene's leaving of Riverton, Bonnie thought this to be the same guy her dad had disarmed in the alley one day. At any rate, she made up her mind to check in with the Judge and then if allowed, she would go after Sergio Campella to arrest him alive and deliver him for trial, or kill him in the attempt. The thought never crossed her mind that she might be killed. Apprehending Campella for now was her goal. This man had been a scourge to the people and now he had placed a bounty on her head as well as her daddy's, and it wouldn't do. She had been fooling herself in her blissful relaxation with Chuck and the others these past weeks.

Chuck contemplated all angles having to do with Bonnie's personality. He had learned she was volatile and strong-willed, and when her mind was made up or set on something, there was no changing it. She had told him her daddy called that trait "her mule." It was simply in her makeup. He thought that in part must be why he had been attracted to her. She didn't quit. Now he wished she would. She had other attributes he loved as well. She was kind, very considerate of others, and willing to show anybody how to do what she knew. He would stick with her whether she wanted it or not. He had some mule too. Lord, help any of their offspring. Yes, he planned to have a family with Bonnie. He couldn't think of anyone better to raise his kids with.

The hint of daylight came after the resumption of their travel had started. Bonnie arose and was out much before dawn. Chuck, on the other hand, hadn't slept well and so heard the slightest sound from her camp. He thought he detected her moving off, so he packed quickly, following quietly at a distance. Now and again she would break a twig or trip over a small stone in the dark, which allowed a telltale sound to sneak through the air. These sounds to Chuck were no more than those a deer would make while walking in the forest.

Bonnie had located the Mindonhall Sawmill road and started moving fast, too fast for Chuck's comfort. She was good, but carelessness from speed could get her into trouble. Midday the second day, he could see her moving rapidly through the trees, pausing occasionally to look and listen. Chuck knew these pauses weren't often enough. On one occasion when she paused, Chuck maneuvered to get in plain sight, where he could signal her when she saw him. He wanted a powwow. She affirmed with her own signal. She had cooled her temper enough to stop long enough for a short talk with Chuck. They met under cover of a small grove of spruce and pine trees.

"Bonnie, please let me be your partner again," pleaded Chuck. "You know you're moving too fast for safety and if you get killed, you won't be able help anybody. We've worked out a system that has been very successful. Let's not discard it now."

"I know, Chuck, but I need to be back in action. It's been too long and I've taken way too much time off. I let my personal feelings detour me from my real obligation. If I don't get back to work, another Oliver and Minnie are likely to be killed or worse and I can't let that happen to anybody else if I can help it. Chuck, don't you see, it's important to not just me, but more importantly to some other Oliver and Minnie out there. I have to try to stop them before they hurt somebody else."

"Bon honey, I understand," Chuck replied, "but if you get careless and you get yourself taken out of action, you'll help nobody. Come on, girl, think about the best way to complete your job, not your anger at the bad guys. You and Laurie both told me you wanted to do the job right and not out of vengeance. Bon honey, I'll support you whatever you decide to do, but please think hard about your style and method."

Bonnie looked at him, said nothing, turned, and started down the trail toward Lumberton. Chuck did the same, spread out in typical travel fashion. He could tell she was considering what he said. She had slowed and now was being more cautious like she had been in the old times. Occasionally, she would signal him to take the advance, then retake the lead herself after a time, leapfrogging a distance around his location. When they reached the cliffside trails, Bonnie crossed first, descending to the cover at the far ends. Chuck followed rapidly where he passed her, then they spread out in normal fashion. Being late in the day, they stopped for the night. This was unfamiliar land and they wouldn't risk a fall or injury in the darkened terrain. They hadn't seen fresh signs of other people, but Chuck believed he cut the tracks of the other Marshals several times as they progressed along the trail.

Finding a sheltered site where a small fire might be concealed, they came together for a quick meal of hard-boiled eggs and heated water gathered from a cool high mountain stream. Tomorrow, time allowing, they would eat canned fish from a mason jar "put up" by Minnie some three months earlier. One pint would feed them both for several meals, but once opened, the contents would have to be heated each time before consuming to prevent possible poisoning. The canned sucker fish caught from the stock pond fed by a cool clear stream was an excellent good food. The many fine bones in the fish were dissolved during the canning process. The contents of the pint jar made the best fish patties. There wasn't a tuna or salmon patty in the world that could rival the taste of this delicacy. Funny, most people would discard this fish as trash on the shoreline after having caught one instead of a trout. Most had no clue.

They both had in their packs other jars of home-canned food. Bonnie had taken venison, as had Chuck. Included was a quart of vegetable stew in Chuck's pack which contained cabbage, carrots, turnips, onions, and tomatoes. These would need to be heated before consumption. They ate the eggs and the other spoilables first.

Having finished a short supper, they moved away from the small campfire some hundred yards perpendicular to the windward direction. They separated, then bedded down where they could see the other and could be seen by the other. Chuck was grateful Bonnie had seemed to come to her senses. She still was saying nothing except for the trail sign language, but he could see her mind working by her actions.

The Mindonhall Logging Road came out some distance from Judge Milliner's ranch and headquarters. Bonnie worked her way to the entry, being careful to not telegraph her presence unnecessarily to casual observers. Chuck moved parallel to her, being vigilant about everything and everybody they came near. Those who did see her stopped their activity and stared at her as she neared the guard post. Chuck joined her, watching their back trail as they approached.

"Well, Marshal, we heard you were retired," said the first guard as they approached. "I'll go tell the Judge you're here. He'll be pleased to see you. Mind you, he's going to chew your butt for not asking permission to get married. He's been mad about that for two weeks since he heard and you didn't let him know. He says so on a regular basis." He left the second guard with Bonnie and Chuck while he proceeded to notify the Judge of their arrival.

Judge Millner came out of the dwelling and up the hill with the first guard while two others followed. It took him some two minutes to cover the distance to their position.

"Who the h. . . . . is this?" he fired at Bonnie.

"Judge, this is Deputy US Marshal Chuck Overton. He is also my husband," said Bonnie with confidence while under the Judge's direct scowl.

"So you say," the judge fired back. "Who gave you permission to marry one of your subordinates? He *is* a subordinate, isn't he? You did appoint him to his post, didn't you? And who gave you permission to get married while on duty as one of my Marshals?"

The Judge turned and waved them to follow while the two guards stayed at their post. The second set of guards spread to either side and watched the surroundings with great care. Entering the dwelling, the Judge invited them to his study. There he proceeded to continue demonstrating his displeasure about thinking he had lost Bonnie's services.

"I understood you had retired to bliss and family life. Why would you come here now?" he queried.

"Your Honor, I came to get orders and find out where the others are," Bonnie replied.

"OK." He paused. "What changed your mind? Marriage not exciting enough for you? Surly you aren't bored with each other already."

"No, Judge," Bonnie replied. "Some men killed our friends Oliver and Minnie Saughterhill, with whom we were staying. Chuck and I were out repairing fence when they came. When we returned to the house, Oliver was dead and Minnie was gravely injured. Oliver killed both his attackers but not before they fatally wounded him and Minnie. They were the best people on earth. If someone would have arrested those thugs and brought them to justice, Oliver and Minnie might still be alive. I. . .We don't want that to happen to anybody else, so we're here to get your orders."

Much to Chuck's relief, she didn't mention Bob and young Chuck in her statement. Chuck wondered about it. She must have thought long and hard about the situation and decided the boys were not culpable for the murders.

"I see," the Judge said. "Tell me the details."

Bonnie started and after the first few sentences, teared up, then blubbered an unintelligible comment. Then she turned away. The Judge watched, not indicating a reaction. He knew this was difficult for her. He looked at Chuck, who continued the description of the murders. Chuck described what he found, the positions of the victims, and the wounds. He conveniently didn't mention the boys, hoping to keep them out of the picture.

"We left ranch in care of some friends. They are a couple of young men who came after the Marshals left to come here. We took them in and fed them in exchange for chores," Chuck said.

"Where were these two when Oliver and Minnie were being killed?" the Judge asked.

"They were outside the house not knowing what was going on," Chuck elaborated. "Oliver had dispatched the two before the boys could lend a hand. By the time they knew what was going on, Oliver and Minnie were both down. Bonnie and I arrived only seconds after the battle ended."

"I am so sorry to hear about Oliver and Minnie," the judge said. "We had been good friends and they were fine people. I too am now suffering another loss. Marshal, you are going to have to set aside your obvious personal feelings to do your job properly. We need you now more than ever. Factions of the MLS have been scattered over the country. They are a loathsome bunch and I want every last one of them brought to trial for their crimes against the people. Those who you catch who have been previously found guilty are to be brought here also for violation of their parole."

"I have a task for you," the Judge said, commanding Bonnie's attention. But before I give you your assignment, I also am going to require you to do something that may be very difficult. You will need to complete your assignment before you take off on me again. I just received word by courier that the National Guard under direction of the Governor arrived in Riverton. At my continued urging the Governor has finally sent a contingent to disband the MLS. You may or may not know, we had a pitch battle with them here. Colonel Whitmore, whom you have met, led a force of local veterans against the MLS headquarters in the settlements. We weren't quite so successful here, as the National Guard was in Riverton. The settlements' MLS fought back hard and everybody had casualties. That ringleader Campella escaped with a squad of men. Our troops were spent by the end of the battle, so made no effort to follow them.

"We believe we know Campella's general location, but we need scouts to find him and his men. I will send the other Marshals to do that after they report back. I need you to make a fast break for Riverton to contact the National Guard who will be coming. We need their manpower and equipment to take out these larger scattered bands of roving men, those MLS refugees from the defeat. It is imperative we get connected with the Guard right away. All my men here have their hands full guarding and caring for the forty prisoners we hold captive now. I want to send these back to Riverton with the army."

"Judge, I don't understand what you are concerned with. Why would I take off like you said?" Bonnie queried.

Judge Millner continued. "I met a man they call Shaky two weeks ago. He came here looking for you."

Bonnie gasped, then exclaimed, "Was he okay? Where was he? Where is he? I need to find him!"

The Judge held up his hand, arresting Bonnie's outburst, then added, "He is well. As I said, he was here looking for you. I wouldn't tell him anything because you are a hunted woman with a bounty on your head. The bounty is a big one and there are people who would turn in their own mother for that kind of money. He didn't have any identification and I turned him away with no information. I told him when he could provide identification, a photo, or a witness who I trust who would vouch for him, then I would help.

He continued, thinking back to the marshals' arrival. "Then, two days later your marshals showed up. They pulled that boneheaded stunt that nearly got Smith killed."

"Is everybody okay, and what about my dad?" Bonnie interrupted all in one breath.

"I'm getting to it. Everybody is okay, but I told your Marshals if they pulled a stunt like that again, I'd shoot them myself," he continued. "Smith described your father to a tee. It was almost like he was her father too. I sent Smith and Ochoa to retrieve him partially so I could speak with him and partially so he would be with some protection. Remember, they have a bounty on him as well. In the meantime until he is back here, I need you to contact the National Guard. After you've made contact and delivered my dispatch, you are to return here to see if Smith and Ochoa have brought 'Shaky' to us. I don't want you gallivanting off on your own trying to find him. That's Smith's job, not yours. I need you to do yours, do you understand?"

Bonnie, starting to fidget, waited for the Judge to get to the point. She started twice to interrupt him and he quelled her with the lifting of his hand. Bonnie indicated her understanding but was uneasy with the circumstances.

"How long will I be?" she finally asked.

"Not long, I think," said the judge. "According to the dispatch I received, the Guard is slated to leave Riverton the day after tomorrow. You don't have a lot of time to intercept them. They are mechanized and have transportation. They can cover the distance between Riverton and the settlements in a couple hours. You will need to be waiting for them before they get to the settlements. You need to be focused on your assignment and not on your dad. He was very okay when I saw him last. Now let us go eat supper. You both will need to get an early start in the morning."

Sitting down to supper, the Judge returned thanks, then they started on a rabbit stew with cornbread on the side. Plenty of butter and honey for the cornbread was provided and milk or water was plentiful for the beverage. *Whoever the cook is, they know their craft*, thought Chuck.

A rap at the door brought the Judge around with a snub-nosed 38 in his hand. The guard opened the door and stepped through, shutting it behind him.

"Boss, Marshal Smith has some prisoners out here," he stated.

Bonnie rose to her feet and stepped nearly to the door when the Judge called her back and ordered her to sit and stay. He went out the back door opposite the one the guard had come in through. The guard stayed with Bonnie and Chuck. He said nothing when quizzed by Bonnie. She now had narrowed eyelids and Chuck could see the resolve building in her. Within five minutes the door opened and Laurie with the Judge close behind entered the door the guard had come through. The guard exited.

"Bonnie, Chuck, what are you doing here?" Laurie exclaimed.

"It's a long story, Laurie. Oliver and Minnie are dead. We were out fixing fence. They were killed by some renegades. Oliver returned the favor before he died. We found them and that was all. We left some youngsters taking care of the place "till we get back.' Have you found Daddy?" Bonnie said and asked all in one statement.

"Yes, he's with us, or at least he and Sam are coming," Laurie spit out. "Sam's hurt and he's caring for her. They're moving much slower than I did with these prisoners. Bonnie, they killed Sonja."

She explained the circumstances and how Zack and Josh were set to track the murderers down when she and Sam arrived. Sam caught Shaky overlooking the place, captured him, and brought him in. Laurie convinced Zack and Josh the Marshals would take care of the attackers. Shaky was now a Deputy Marshal. She unfolded the complete story while the Judge stood back and listened.

"No, not Sonja," moaned Bonnie. "First Oliver and Minnie and now Sonja. No, no, no!" She sat back on the dinner chair. The spike had just been fully driven. Her resolve to eliminate the bad guys now was set in stone.

Not eating the balance of the supper set before them, Bonnie, Chuck, and a guard followed Laurie to Gene and Sam's location about three miles out. Sam sat resting while Gene stood watch within sight of Sam but from a distance. Bonnie saw Gene first and slipped up quietly when Gene said, "That's far enough, girl. Think you can slip in on your old man?"

"Daddy!" Bonnie cried as they embraced.

"I have never been so glad to see you as I am now," Gene said to his daughter, looking her over with an appraising eye.

"Daddy, you're all skin and bones. You're starving to death," she exclaimed.

"Nah, I am simply more fit than you've ever seen me," Gene claimed. "It's been a hard year, but I'm well and I'm as fit as I have ever been in my life."

"Daddy, I've lost Mama, Uncle Jake, and Aunt Meg," said Bonnie. "I don't know where they are or if they're even alive. We went to the ranch to help and they had left. There had been a battle and the dogs had been shot. Did you find Seth?"

"I didn't find Seth, but your mama, Jake, and Meg are all okay. I was with them for about six weeks. They were all fine when I left," he assured her.

"Well, where are they?" she asked.

"The Alkali," Gene answered.

Nothing more was needed; she understood. Then he added, "Sonja's dead. That bunch we brought in and two others killed her. Laurie, Sam, and I tracked them to their camp. Two put up a fight and they lost. We also almost lost Samantha for a while in the bargain. I have to appreciate Laurie's self-control. I'm not sure any person on earth would have blamed her if she'd have wasted them in the desert for what they did to Sonja. But she didn't; she brought them in the same condition she captured them. If they don't hang, they will go to hell when they do die. If they don't hang, they will die quicker than normal, I think. Zack was struggling with letting God take vengeance. He was struggling with forgiveness for what they had done. He wanted vengeance himself so badly. He has a strong faith to forgo his desire and to let God do it."

"Daddy, I'm married. I am now Bonnie Overton. Chuck's a wonderful guy. I know you'll like him. He's kind and thoughtful, and he's right over there." It dribbled out all at once.

"I know. Laurie told me all about it and him. It sounds as if you have a gem in him. I have been looking forward to meeting him," Gene replied.

Returning back to the Judge's with Sam in tow, they settled in the Judge's living room. Sam was placed in an upstairs bedroom for recuperation. She was still confused and subject to headaches. The consensus was she needed a lot of rest to recuperate.

"Shaky, is it?" The Judge said as he looked directly at Gene. "I do apologize for turning you away. You understand how careful we need to be?".

"Judge, your caution is appreciated," Gene replied.

"I assume you have been deputized," the Judge said as he turned to the gathering. He mumbled, "Getting awfully close to nepotism around here. Husband, father, and daughter under employ."

Having received a dispatch from the National Guard in Riverton, that information coupled with information Laurie and Gene had about Campella's location now changed previous plans. With the arrival of Laurie and Shaky, the Judge gave new instruction for the upcoming activities. Bonnie, Laurie, Gretchen, and Molly with four of the Judge's guards were instructed to surround Campella's camp and hold them there. They weren't in any way to attempt to take them head on. Chuck and Gene were instructed to intercept the Guard with dispatch from the Judge to assist in enforcing the warrants carried by the Marshals.

The Marshals were to have full jurisdiction and were to bring Campella to Lumberton for trial. The Judge wrote a new specific warrant for Sergio Campella's apprehension and a duplicate for Chuck to carry. He gave orders all others with Campella were to be arrested as well under new John Doe warrants and returned for trial. He then instructed Gene and Chuck to be on the move before daylight.

Chapter 36

A Son's Return

C huck and Gene covered two miles before the sun peeked over the eastern ridges. By noon they had covered some fifteen miles, nearly halfway to the settlements. They moved fast, almost at a dog trot. A year and a half earlier, Gene wouldn't have been able to cover such distance in so short a time. Now he was tired but not exhausted. He and Chuck traveled in the usual marshal fashion, spread apart some hundred feet, always keeping each other in sight when possible. They each carried minimal supplies except for their weapons. The Judge supplied each with a brand new pair of handcuffs for use. He had more faith in handcuffs than the ropes and twine the Marshals had been using.

Twice, Chuck signaled a stop. Both times he had seen people they wanted to avoid. They circled the first bunch and waited for the second to trudge past them. Neither group had a clue of their presence. Gene was grateful for the respite. *This Chuck seems a capable man*, Gene thought as he worked in tandem with him. He was suitable for Bonnie. While they waited for the people to pass, Gene snacked for energy on dried fish and drank from his water bottle to rehydrate. They moved on.

By four o'clock, they neared the settlements but had cut across out skirting farmlands and wasteland for a shortcut to the highway where the Guard would be coming. Approaching the dry canyon country, Gene saw evidence of groups of men who had traveled fast as if fleeing. They ignored those tracks except to make note of how many and their direction of travel for future reference. When they stopped, dark had overtaken the day. They now were on the south side of the river opposite the highway where the Guard should come. They were not over two miles from where Poole had met his demise. Tomorrow, they would ford the river, climb the far hillside to the top of the hill and wait for the army to show up.

Gene now hurt from the some twenty-five miles he had half walked, half run. His age was telling on him. His lungs ached from the constant excessive breathing. His bones and feet ached. His feet had become sore with blisters. Surprisingly, Chuck wasn't feeling a lot better. They both hurt too much to sleep well, but they would be on time. At dawn, they were on the move again.

Slower-moving at first, both stiffly worked their way with some pain to start the day. The river was wide where they chose to cross. It wasn't over two feet deep at any spot at this ford but was two hundred feet wide. The pioneers of old used this crossing on a regular basis. Easier access to the top of the mesa on the far side was up an intersecting dry drainage with an old wagon road at the bottom. It led to the flat bench above the river where the four-lane highway was located.

Reaching the mesa top above some miles away from the river, Gene realized how much damage wet feet can sustain when under constant pressure. He had known this before and now was reminded. The covering skin on his blisters had softened from the soaking and the sustained wetness of his moccasins caused them to rupture. Now he would need to be ever-so-careful to heal these blisters without infection setting in. With no medicine these days to treat infection, the risk from an infected blister could be death. Gene believed he wasn't ready to go yet.

The sun, now up, had reached mid-morning with Chuck on a knob overlooking the highway. He signaled the approach of the column. They weren't moving fast. They were being watchful so as not to fall into an ambush or an IED—lessons learned from Iraq and Afghanistan. Gene limped to the south side pavement shoulder and waited. Chuck watched a while longer awaiting their approach.

On the Mancos Shale knob watching some hundred feet in altitude above the surrounding land, Chuck could see for a long distance. Indians of old often built rock cairns as blinds to hide from wandering game. He now used one of those to hide his presence on this lookout. As Gene stood by, Chuck signaled an impending hazard in the distance in the path where the army column would be traveling. He then came on a run to the north side of the pavement shoulder and then along the road to Gene's location.

"I see people setting up what looks like an ambush about a mile from here. Thank goodness we got here first," said Chuck in a whisper.

Both he and Gene located themselves where they would be camouflaged from the would-be attackers, yet still in sight of the National Guard. Now the column, being three quarters of a mile away, approached at a faster rate than either Gene or Chuck would have liked. Now would be the time to show themselves and they did so, standing one on either side of the highway where the convoy was traveling. Waving his arm as they approached, Chuck used some universal signal he had used in the military. They seemed to understand and slowed haltingly to a stop.

"I have a dispatch for the column commander," Chuck said.

"Major!" one of the men in the front vehicle called out.

A slender man about six feet tall with very correct posture emerged from the Bradley second in line. The accompanying personnel were at ready on alert.

"Major, sir, I am Deputy US Marshal Charles Overton with a dispatch from the Honorable United States District Judge Alford C. Millner. Sir, he has sent this dispatch for you," stated Chuck in formal military style. "Sir, there is what appears to be an ambush being set up about a mile down the road near that grove of trees. I could see the activity from the hill up yonder while watching for you." Chuck pointed to the hill whence he had come. The Major didn't say a word. A Sergeant ordered two soldiers to the top, where they could scout and observe.

A young man stepped out of the Humvee from the passenger side saying, "Dad, what are you doing here?" It was Seth. Gene nearly dropped his weapon in surprise. The major turned as Seth walked to Gene, studying him for a moment. Gene and he grabbed each other as if each thought the other had been lost forever.

"Dad, I didn't recognize you. I was watching the Deputy here, not you. You're skin and bones. What have you been doing?" Seth fired statements and questions much the same as his sister might have.

"I'm fine, Seth. By the way, say hi to the Deputy here, he's your brother-in-law. He and Bonnie were married a couple months ago. What are you doing with the National Guard?" Gene stated and asked, not realizing he was exhibiting a family characteristic.

"I'll tell you later, Dad. It sounds like we have business to tend to right now," Seth replied. Seth introduced Gene to the major. "Major, this is my father. They call him Shaky. He'll know these parts better than I."

"Major, I am pleased to make your acquaintance. I am Deputy US Marshal Gene Tucker. If you will, just call me Shaky. I'm more like an old company scout rather than a regular."

One of the soldiers had indeed reported the movement ahead seemed to be the setting up an ambush. The Major ordered out an old USGS map to look at the terrain. After discussion with a Lieutenant, the Sergeant, and the returned scout from the hilltop, he studied the lay of the land from the contour lines on the map.

"Major, what are you planning to do?" Gene asked. "May I suggest, if you're planning on a flanking action, there is an old wagon trail that drops into the river bottom the way we came out. You could get men behind them going that way, then along the river bank without them knowing you're there. There's a small valley on the others side of the knob that will lead to high ground above their position on the other side. Four or five men could pin them down while four or five others could stop their retreat. They would be sur-rounded on all sides and the back, hopefully leading to surrender."

Looking at Seth, the Major turned to study the map. The scouts indicated the location of the ambushers on the TOPO. Then ten of his fifty men studied it and departed in two groups. Time synchronized for them to be in place, then the Major spread out another fifteen others to approach the ambushers. The fifteen carefully kept cover. When within a hundred yards of the ambush sight, the Sergeant called out to the ambushers to surrender their arms. He called out a second time. All of a sudden, there came shot sounds from near the river, then none. The soldiers on the hill fired several rounds, then all became quiet.

A dozen men emerged from the trees with their hands skyward. Close behind, three soldiers drove them at gunpoint toward the caravan. Two of the soldiers from the uphill side were also near with their weapons at the ready.

"Sir, all is all clear now," one returning soldier reported. "There are two bad guys down. The others are tending to their wounds. We have no casualties."

"Secure these men, then let's move out," said the Major. He turned to Chuck and Gene. "Are these the men the Judge is looking for?"

"No, sir," Chuck replied. "These may be part of the group, but the real bad guys are some fifteen miles ahead on the hardball. Judge Millner has a contingent of Marshals dispatched to pin them down until the calvary can get there."

Gene in his mind, somehow, had always wanted to say that, but he bit his tongue.

The major smirked with a slightly crooked smile and said, "Show me on the map."

Gene pointed the exact location on a second TOPO. It was Jake's ranch where they would be headed. Gene explained the lay of the land and where the marshal contingent was likely to be. The major questioned him closely about why he knew so much. Gene explained the ranch belonged to one of his relatives and he had been there a countless number of times. He also explained he had trained at least a third of the marshals, including their commander, from their childhood. He was certain what they would do. They wouldn't start an action unless they felt the target was about to leave. If so, they had orders to pin them down until literately "the calvary" came. And that is just what they would do.

The Major looked at him appraisingly, then indicated everybody should mount up and move out. They did and Gene rode, saving his battered feet from more anguish, sitting now facing Seth in the troop carrier.

"Seth, how did you get with the army? The last I heard from Barbara Plaster, you were out of town on some trip when the lights went out," said Gene.

"I was, but I'd just landed in Metropolis International when the lights went out," Seth explained. "I was seated beside and had been talking to the Governor's secretary on the plane. After we landed, I accompanied him to the Governor's mansion. I was there for six months helping run logistics. We started getting messengers from over here by courier and later ham. After we stabilized most of the chaos there, the Governor issued orders for the National Guard to start stabilization of the rest of the state. He knows Judge Millner and so when he started getting requests for assistance from him, he sent this unit to assist. He sent me with them as a civilian liaison and scout as I grew up here in an advisory capacity. Maybe he just wanted me out of his way. Anyway, here I am. Just a warning, Dad, the Major isn't excited about answering to some Federal Judge, but he has orders from the Governor to answer to this Judge." He paused. "When and where did you see Barbara Plaster?

"At your house," said Gene. "She was kinda watchin' the place when I got there. We talked some and she said she thought you were out of town. I came home."

"How did you get there?" Seth inquired.

"I walked," Gene said.

"All the way?" Seth replied.

"Yes. It took a while, but I made it," Gene replied.

"Dad, you said Bonnie is married to that Chuck fella?" Seth asked.

"Yes, Seth," said Gene. "He seems to be a fine fella. He and I both work for your sister. She's the head US marshal hereabouts. Can you believe it—she's the boss? She's good, too, and has surrounded herself with a capable tough staff including Laurie Smith among others. Did you see Samuel in Riverton when you were there?"

"Yes, he's okay," said Seth. "They had been pushed around by this MLS bunch, but God delivered them from any serious problems. We took over that gutless bunch, most of which folded up and many ran like rabbits. The rest surrendered without so much as a whimper when they saw the army come to town."

Gene was relieved at the good news. He told Seth of his Mom, Jake, and Meg and how he had found them almost by chance. He elaborated about Cindy and Mike's demise from battling with the renegades. Sally Smith was married to Josh Gilder and Sonja had been killed at the hands of some of those MLS who ran from Whitmore's militia earlier.

They talked the whole time while the others listened in silence. Traveling in this mechanized caravan covered territory amazingly fast. Gene had nearly forgotten how many miles could be covered by wheels.

Halting, Seth, Gene, the Sergeant, the Major, Chuck and others dismounted for a conference. They were some miles from the ridge on the west side of the ranch. They were reviewing the maps when one of the outposts ordered someone to halt. Marshal Molly Brown identified herself. Gene had no clue who she was, but Chuck stepped forward to vouch for her.

Molly reported Campella had started to move out, but some well-placed shots made them take cover. When they started out the back way, the others peppered their retreat with more shots. There was a group who had tried to sneak out to flank the snipers. They were captured by Molly and two of the Judge's guards, rendering them helpless. All was quiet momentarily. Molly laid out the Marshal positions and the positions of the bad guys.

"Is there an approach to the holdouts we can use to get close without exposing my troops?" the Major inquired.

"Yes, Sir," replied Molly. "You can move up the creek bottom to the pond. It will put you within a couple hundred feet of the dwelling. We can provide cover for you from the ridge to the east across the draw and from the hilltop to the west of their position. But please don't shoot our marshals by mistake."

"Just you make sure they don't shoot us," replied the Major.

"I'll need some time to spread the word. In the meantime, Campella and his bunch aren't going anywhere. They can't see the creek bottom from the dwelling and we'll keep them pinned down all week if need be," replied Molly.

"What makes you such an expert on this?" prompted the Major.

"Major, I did two tours of duty in Afghanistan as a forward logistics specialist. I know what I am doing. I did then and I do now!" Molly stated flatly.

The Major looked up, then asked, "Are you subject to reserve duty now?"

"No, Sir, I cleared twenty-two months ago. Besides, I am under orders from a Federal Judge at present. Thank you for asking," Molly firmly stated. "With all due respect, sir, if you will sync time and make a plan, I'll get to delivering orders."

They laid down the strategy and Molly left. A squad would approach the dwelling from the base of the pond dam with the Sergeant in command. From there, he would command a surrender of those held up in the dwelling. They would be covered from the hills above by the Marshal sharpshooters: Bonnie, Laurie, and Gretchen.

Gene thought there might be enough food supplies for the hold-outs to last six months or so. There wasn't, however, a ready supply of water, as the domestic water systems had long since ceased to function. The only water available now was in the creek and access to that was being denied by the sharpshooters. Any liquid and moisture would come from the ample stored goods in Jake's bunker.

The soldiers moved out on foot and a quarter mile from the ranch stead, the detail split off with the balance holding in reserve. The plan was when the detail attained the position, the equipment would move to within earshot of the dwelling. The speculation was Campella's group would understand the gravity of the forces they faced, making a fight a non-option. After that took place, the Sergeant would demand full and complete surrender. There would be no other option for the renegades.

Being mid-afternoon, the outlaws stalled for time, clearly wanting darkness to come. They would make a break to escape after darkness fell. The Marshals' plan, however, was if the outlaws didn't surrender within the hour, an assault would be launched. The major broke out mortars. The 120mm was held in reserve. The killing power of the 120mm would destroy the dwelling, machine shop, garage, and anything within one hundred feet radius.

Gene drew on the back of a TOPO the layout of the dwelling, machine shop, and garage as near as he could remember. Jake had built an underground survival shelter from an old transportation container, a bunker with food stock enough to last a year. It was impregnable from the outside, as near as Gene knew.

These fugitives were to be taken alive and returned for trial if at all possible. If they didn't fire on the army or Marshals, initial assaulting fire wouldn't be initiated by the guard. No fire came from the ranch stead. The army threat was simply ignored. A mortar setup was in place and a round dropped a hundred feet to the northeast of the dwelling. The Sergeant again demanded surrender from cover. He again was ignored totally.

The sunset showed gorgeous oranges, grays, and light blues fading into the low light of evening. Another mortar was set up to drop rounds at irregular intervals around the buildings intending on not hitting them. If the outlaws thought they could make a break under cover of darkness, they might run into an unexpected mortar explosion.

The major had sent two squads, one guided by Gene and the other by Seth to reinforce the Marshals' positions. This thickening of the surrounding lines was to prevent any sneaky Pete from trying to slip out. Set to drop rounds on the closest creek water hole, one of the mortars made it muddier and deeper. Again these defining explosions were at irregular intervals. No man in his right mind would risk a drink of that brackish muddy water at the risk of being blown up by mortar fire.

No one slept during the night. The explosions would come just before sleep might take over or just after it had. The flashes were bright and instant and if one watched, one could momentary see the surrounding land characteristics. It wasn't unlike seeing a close lightning strike and every bit as noisy.

Just after twilight, a white flag waved out the side door. Surrender was coming. The sergeant commanded instructions. Observing the commotion, the marshal sharpshooters were ready with the cover fire if needed. Walking out the door one by one, the fugitives filed down the driveway single file until out of sight from the dwelling around the blind drive lane corner. They were commanded to lie facedown, at which time the soldiers bound their hands with plastic ties. One man's wrists were so large, the ties linked together double to fit around his wrists.

Fourteen in all surrendered to captivity. Campella wasn't among them. When interrogated, nobody would or could tell where he was. Bonnie, having descended to the point of action, was livid. She was about to skin somebody at any moment. She picked a grizzled man whom she had captured before. He would know her resolve. Gretchen was there and between them he divulged Campella had escaped during the night with two others. Gretchen kept talking to him kindly as Bonnie after attacking the man was held back. She had to be restrained and was about to be turned loose by Chuck and a guard who had been restraining her. Gene and the major watched with interest while the honed good cop/bad cop act played out with expertise.

With the prisoners under safe custody, Bonnie served the arrest warrants, completing the full arrest. Molly would take over the marshals' duties with help from the guards and the army.

"Major, Marshal Molly Brown will assume the marshal command with your assistance from here to the Judge's headquarters. Marshal Smith and I are going after Campella and the others," Bonnie resolutely said.

She and Laurie turned and started. Gene and Chuck, glanced at each, turned and followed. Fifty feet out, Bonnie turned as if to confront her dad and husband to send them back. She stood, then as if changing her mind, returned to her direction of travel with Gene and Chuck spreading to the sides as Laurie had already done.

Having spread to the far outside track, Chuck was the first to find trail signs of the men they were tracking. Signaling to Laurie, who was the one in his line of sight, she in turn signed to the others. Now that they had the trail that had been left carelessly during the dark of night, following was easy. Chuck advanced ahead of the others on the trail. Gene and Laurie proceeded on the outside other end of the line. Nearing noon the sky became overcast. As Gene scanned the terrain ahead, it so happened he was looking in the direction to the right when he saw the muzzle flash. He heard the sound as he saw Laurie reeled and go down. The others must have heard the rifle report. Gene threw up his own Savage model 99E and scoped the spot. Instantly he saw the movement and the glint of reflection. He placed the crosshairs on the glint location and fired. The reflection disappeared. Chuck, on the other hand, was up and running toward Laurie at full speed. When he got there he went down and out of sight.

Laurie grimaced with pain. The bullet had grazed her upper arm, tearing a gash in the skin on the outside just above her elbow. She held a bandana covering the wound. Chuck was relieved at of the lack of severity when he cut her sleeve away. He bandaged and treated the wound. Then, after seeing Gene's signal of the source of the shot, he advanced carefully up the hill.

Arriving at the clump of scrub oak where the sniper had been, he found Gene's target. The rifle stock had been shattered by the .243 Winchester bullet. The gun remained there, but the man was gone. The evidence of a wound was indicated by blood on the leaves, leading away from the sight. Tracking in oak brush generally is more difficult, but now there was a slight blood trail to follow. A man could hide indefinitely in this thick brush and never be found without the assistance of heat indicating equipment or dogs. They had neither. By watching the wildlife, Gene might perceive an indication of foreign human movement or presence. Deer will move out. Squirrels will chirp and chatter. Birds will startle and fly.

Collecting in a protected location, Chuck and Laurie told Bonnie and Gene of Laurie's condition. Plans were made to watch far hillsides and wildlife movement. Chuck would stay on the blood trail, watching out for booby traps. Any indication of directional change or hillside contouring would be signaled. Off they went again.

The trail direction changed twice, once to the left and then to the right. These men were following a general heading that lead to a high-mountain pass seldom used by a casual traveler. There was purpose in the movements and someone knew the country well enough to target this route.

Gene signaled Bonnie and they met yet again. They planned to swing wide and travel hard to get in front of the fugitives before they reached the pass. Chuck and Laurie would follow slowly and carefully, not pushing the runners. Laurie had been sickened by the wound and it slowed her. When all understood, Gene and Bonnie took off on a fast dogtrot to go around the three fugitives. Oh, how Gene's dogs hurt from the blisters. If they could get to the pass before the others, they would have a chance at a surprise capture.

Near evening, it was clear the pass destination was unattainable before dark. They stopped for a bite and hydration. Pushing on, they found a likely sight for the night's respite. Dawn came early and the morning was cool at this elevation. Cold as it was, they dared not to light a fire.

Taking off just before sunup, they reached the crest of the pass. This pass was a tree-covered dip arching low between two mountain peaks. There was a distinct game trail that led over and disappeared down the other side into the foliage beyond. The forest floor was covered with years of accumulation, the discarded pine, and spruce needles that fell from the trees all during the year. This allowed for silent movement. Studying the game trail, Gene could see no evidence any person had passed here recently. Bonnie took the far side of the trail, where she found cover behind a fallen spruce tree, and Gene took cover behind two fallen logs crossed like the legs of a sleeping man. Now they would wait.

Mid-morning had arrived when a buck deer came bounding over the trail near Bonnie fleeing away from something or better yet maybe someone. Twenty minutes hadn't passed when the first of two men came ascending hurriedly along the pass trail. Gene wished he'd had set a trap, maybe a deadfall or a snare or a taught line, to trip them if they ran. Too late. They were now here.

Sergio came second in line behind a burly bewhiskered mountain of a man, some six—foot-six-inches tall and husky at that. Gene threw a rock as far behind the men as he could, cracking branches when it landed in the brush. Both whirled with their guns at the ready, looking for something to shoot at.

Bonnie with resolve and behind cover quietly said, "Gentlemen, don't twitch a muscle. Drop 'em. You are under arrest."

The burly man froze and then gently laid his rifle on the ground. He didn't seem concerned he was being taken captive. Sergio, on the other hand, broke into a dead run back down the trail from whence he had come. Bonnie ordered the big man to the ground with his hands stretched behind his back. With Gene's gun to his head, Bonnie cuffed him tightly. Gene made a set of rope hobbles like he would use on a horse, which limited the man's foot movement.

Watching carefully down the trail in case Sergio returned, Gene set off trailing the disturbed foliage where Sergio had stepped and tromped. Bonnie tied the man mountain to a larger live aspen sapling with the top bent down that acted as a spring keeping the tether tight on the captive. She joined Gene in hot pursuit of Sergio.

"Lady, you can't leave me here like this. If he kills you, I'll be a dead man before I get out of this," the man shouted as she disappeared behind Gene.

Sergio acted like a panicked wild animal. He came to the wounded man who had been following. The wounded man hadn't been able to keep up, so they had left him to fend for himself. In Sergio's mind, he would serve as a distraction if the Marshals caught up. He also thought the same about the big man when he broke and ran away. The big man's name was Frances Daisy. Sergio hadn't counted on the efficiency of Gene and Bonnie in securing Mr. Daisy.

Gene came to the wounded man first. He was just barely functional. Gene secured him with cuffs, wrapping his arms around a six-inch aspen. Bonnie caught up and they spread out to follow Sergio. Some ten minutes later, a shot rang out, muffled by the evergreens. By Gene's estimate, he and Bonnie were a quarter mile away. Moving rapidly in a leapfrog fashion, with Gene on the right and Bonnie on the left, they covered the distance in about five minutes. By leapfrogging spread apart, one could always be quiet listening while the other moved along some distance away.

Another shot sounded and Gene knew they now had gotten close. Watching, Gene could see Chuck sneaking to his right. Gene made a turkey call. Chuck froze in his tracks. He turned to see Gene's signal. Chuck indicated Sergio's location to be someplace to the right of Gene. Gene signaled Bonnie.

"Where's Laurie?" Gene signed to Chuck.

She was down the hill covering his back. So they had Sergio cornered at the base of a rockslide field. Gene, Bonnie, and Chuck circled in a semicircle, advancing on Sergio. He wasn't going to be taken easily.

Sergio wasn't in sight. Gene had hunted this area many times for elk and deer. He stopped both Bonnie and Chuck. Setting them in place, he went back around the rockslide and circled to the top edge. He spotted Sergio hiding among some large rocks below Gene's vantage point. Gene wanted to shoot the scoundrel right where he hid but decided he had to try for the capture. Out of sight, Gene made another call, this time a calf elk bleat sounding a lot like *she-it* in a high pitch tone.

Sergio looked around and saw nothing as Gene remained out of sight behind his own rock. Gene made the sound twice more, hoping to cause Sergio to give away his position. It worked. He had been concentrating, studying Gene's location, forgetting to watch behind him. Bonnie, however, slipped in on him with the skill of an Indian brave. She didn't say a word. She hit him with the butt of her rifle just about ear level. He went out like a burnt-out 60-watt bulb. His rifle clattered among the rocks and he slipped partially into a crevice. It took all three to extract his dead weight out of the hole before he came to.

Epilogue

S pring of the following year was in full swing. The Marshals had captured many of the MLS and returned them for trial. The Judge summarily pronounced death sentences on those found guilty using proof, corroborating evidence, testimony about marauding, robbery, and killing, then executed them after trial. Others, like Bob and young Chuck, who had been pressed into service by the MLS were sentenced, then paroled in order to lead a productive life in society. The army stayed a couple months, then left to enforce national security. They left for a more urgent task of protecting the country from a large influx of illegal Middle Eastern immigrants crossing the Texan, Arizonan, Canadian, and Mexican borders.

Many more American citizens had starved over the second long winter. The old and infirm had mostly become the now "dearly departed." Judge Millner had declared new governments to be established through the democratic fashion. There would be a counsel for the humanitarian good and welfare of the populace, not unlike the former county commissioners. They were to be elected, as was the new sheriff. Molly had determined to run for the new counsel. Gretchen campaigned for the sheriff's position. Gene and Jessie started setting up home life back on the mountain where their home had once been. Jake and Meg returned to the ranch but soon discovered the task too much to handle at their age and asked Gene and Jessie to share the burden with them. Gene felt older and didn't feel the need to fight the cold and snowy winters of the higher elevation at their former home any longer. Chuck and Bonnie returned back to Oliver and Minnie's ranch some thirty miles south of the settlements. Laurie and Seth had rekindled an earlier relationship from years before. Cindy and Mike's place was empty and with Zack's blessing, Sally and Josh moved in and took over that farm. Laurie and Seth joined Zack at the ranch to raise calves. Samantha met Roberto and young Chuck. They all decided to stay on at the ranch with Bonnie and Chuck.

Sergio cussed Gene all the way to Lumberton between spasms of headache. He, like others, was sentenced after trial and hung by the Judge for his deeds. Gretchen, on the trail of one fugitive or another, returned many for justice. She was wily and never killed one of her captives. That didn't mean to say she hadn't whipped some soundly. Gene never heard again from the Sullivans. He thought often of them and prayed for them on a regular basis. Samuel and family continued to work in the ministry realm, helping others gain a better understanding of eternity after life here on earth.

The cost of the EMP had been devastating, but out of the ashes arose a semblance of the old society. More people were turning to local area community churches, thankful for the sustenance that had been provided them. Eighty percent of the population had succumbed. All remaining had come to near starvation. Overweight people were nonexistent. In the third year, an assemblage of twenty-first century life started to once again emerge in a recognizable pattern.

A man from Arizona came through the area peddling form one of the rare small loads of citrus fruit. A friend of Shaky's from the settlements traded for a small bag of oranges. He sent word to Gene that he was in possession of them and if Shaky would come to get a couple, he could have them. Gene immediately responded by going there to get one. He obtained two, one for now and one for later. On his return home Gene encountered a young boy of about seven or eight years of age.

"Mister," said the child, "do you have anything to eat? I sure am hungry."

Gene being a person with fondness for kids hesitated a moment, then said, "Would you like to share an orange?"

Setting leaning against an old cottonwood tree the two talked. The boy was alone as his family had all died. His name was Daymon

Chilsy. After they finished the last of the orange, Gene inquired of the child, "Would you know my friend Jesus?"

"No Sir, I don't think I know Him."

"Well, Daymon, it goes like this, 'In the beginning. . . . .'"

CPSIA information can be obtained
at www.ICGtesting.com
Printed in the USA
LVHW051543110419
613829LV00018B/995